Swiss Annuities and Life Insurance

Secure Returns, Asset Protection, and Privacy

MARCO GANTENBEIN, TEP

MARIO A. MATA, TEP

John Wiley & Sons, Inc.

Published by John Wiley & Sons, Inc., Hoboken, New Jersey.
Published simultaneously in Canada.

For general information on our other products and services or for technical support, please contact our Customer Care Department within the United States at (800) 762-2974, outside the United States at (317) 572-3993 or fax (317) 572-4002.

Wiley also publishes its books in a variety of electronic formats. Some content that appears in print may not be available in electronic books. For more information about Wiley products, visit our web site at www.wiley.com.

Library of Congress Cataloging-in-Publication Data:

Swiss annuities and life insurance : secure returns, asset protection, and privacy / Marco Gantenbein, Mario A. Mata [editors].
    p. cm.
Includes bibliographical references and index.
ISBN 978-0-470-11811-5 (cloth)
  1. Insurance, Life–Switzerland.   2. Annuities–Switzerland.   3. Investments, Foreign–Switzerland.   4. Investments, American–Switzerland.   5. Commercial law–Switzerland.   I. Gantenbein, Marco, 1975–   II. Mata, Mario A., 1954–
  HG9148.S95 2008
  368.32009494–dc22   2007043563

Printed in the United States of America.

10 9 8 7 6 5 4 3 2 1

Contents

Foreword

A nnuities and life insurance play an increasingly important role in international trust and estate planning. Wealth management professionals will therefore find this new book a useful source of information and reference. In many circumstances, annuities and life insurance can offer an alternative, or complementary, solution to more traditional structures used for asset protection or estate planning, such as trusts or foundations.

In many countries, life insurance and annuities are becoming widely used for estate planning for individuals, both from a tax standpoint and for long-term wealth structuring. Often the receipt of life insurance proceeds by the policy beneficiary is not taxable as income. Properly structured, life insurance and annuities allow an individual to pass significant wealth to a subsequent generation without any tax consequences.

Switzerland has an outstanding position as a platform for financial services, and its insurance products enjoy the same high reputation. Swiss insurance law contains a number of unique features that are described in this book, and traditional Swiss annuities can provide an attractive low-risk component in a diversified portfolio.

I have therefore no doubt that this book—the first of its kind—will be a valuable resource both for individual investors as well as for estate planners and wealth management advisors.

Richard Pease
Chairman Worldwide
Society of Trust and Estate Practitioners (STEP)

About STEP

The Society of Trust and Estate Practitioners (STEP) is the leading professional body for the trust and estate profession worldwide.

STEP members come from the legal, accountancy, trust and corporate administration, banking, financial planning, insurance, and related professions and are involved at a senior level in the planning, creation, management of and accounting for trusts and estates, executorships administration, and related taxes.

Members of STEP include the most experienced and senior practitioners in the fields of trusts and estates.

STEP was founded in 1991 with the aim of bringing together all the senior practitioners in the various fields and cutting across professional boundaries. Through meetings, seminars, lectures, and the exchange of technical papers and reports, members share information, knowledge, and experience, and benefit from the network of contacts that membership provides.

www.step.org

About This Book

This book presents in-depth yet practical information on the most important issues concerning Swiss annuities and life insurance. It is designed as a guide for asset protection lawyers, tax lawyers, estate planners, financial advisors, other private client advisory firms, and family offices, as well as private investors who are interested in diversifying investments outside their home country and who are particularly interested in Switzerland as a place to invest. The use of concise and precise language reflects its character as a handbook and reference source. In particular, the authors have endeavored to express the terms and concepts involved as transparently as possible in order to make them easily accessible even to those without a legal or financial background. In most chapters, footnotes are largely avoided for the sake of clarity.

The address section has been carefully researched and lists important, relevant contact information. However, the publisher, editors, and authors cannot guarantee that the addresses listed in this publication are all correct, even though they have been selected with great care.

This book can in no way substitute for legal, investment, or other advice. The editor, publisher, and authors therefore unreservedly exclude any liability for losses or damages of any kind—be these direct, indirect, or consequential—that may result from the use of this book or the information it contains. Although all the authors have undertaken their research with great care, they obviously cannot guarantee completeness and correctness, and neither can the editors or publisher.

Any comments and suggestions, praise or criticism will be gratefully received. If you as the reader feel that a particular topic or address should be removed from or added to this volume, please let us know.

By all means write to Marco Gantenbein via e-mail at marco .gantenbein@sacg.ch or by conventional mail to: Marco Gantenbein, Swiss Annuity Consulting Group, Schifflände 26, 8001 Zurich, Switzerland. We will be happy to compensate readers who supply useful information with an appropriate gift.

Acknowledgments

This publication arose from the idea and need for a first-rate, up-to-date, and useful handbook about Swiss and Liechtenstein annuities and life insurance. While there have been many different publications in the past, mainly information brochures, nothing of this kind had been attempted before. The publisher, John Wiley & Sons, Inc., concurred with this idea. Together with the editors, they are now pleased to present the result to interested readers.

A great deal of specialist knowledge, work, and effort has gone into this project, and it has certainly proved worthwhile. As an expression of its overall concept, this volume can unquestionably be seen as a pioneering achievement. The authors, editors, and publisher hope that our readers share this viewpoint as well as our enthusiasm for the project.

At this point, we would like to express our sincere thanks to all those who have contributed to and supported this book. Special thanks are due to our colleagues at Swiss Annuity Consulting Group and Henley & Partners, in particular Matthias Kümin and Christian H. Kälin, as both of them made a tremendous effort to produce this book. Furthermore, we also thank all the coauthors and the publisher, as well as the Society of Trust and Estate Practitioners. Thanks to their valuable support, they have also contributed significantly to the successful publication of this book.

Marco Gantenbein
Mario A. Mata

Introduction

Swiss retirement provisions and life insurance enjoy an equally good reputation at international level. The country's social security provision is complemented by a broad offering from private life insurers. It rests on three pillars: the first, Federal Old-Age and Survivors' Insurance (AHV), is financed on a pay-as-you-go basis; the second one, Occupational Insurance (BVG) for gainfully employed persons in Switzerland, operates by the formation of coverage capital; and the third pillar represents voluntary assurance designed to meet individual needs. This modular system contributes to assuring an adequate income in old age.

A total of 600 billion Swiss francs covers the claims of Swiss policy holders in the second sector. For many Swiss citizens, their pension funds are also their most important asset and illustrate the vital importance of this sector.

The Swiss state recognizes this through different supervisory activities. Thus the Federal Social Insurance Office (FSIO) monitors the relevant social insurance systems while the Federal Office of Private Insurance (FOPI) supervises the life insurance companies. Private life insurers provide cover for about a fifth of the funds invested in the second sector.

FOPI monitors the solvency of the life insurers. The new supervisory law that came into force on January 1, 2006, has significantly improved this supervision. The instruments of the risk-based supervision are of particular note: the Swiss Solvency Test (SST) adequately maps the economic situation of insurers, and the qualitative supervisory instruments focus on aspects such as corporate governance and risk management. These supervisory activities are designed to assure the security of the industry as well as social security in a fast-changing insurance market.

This book aims to promote a better understanding of the Swiss insurance market and its interaction with social security. A group of leading experts from Switzerland and abroad illuminate diverse aspects of this topic from various angles. I am convinced that this book will provide interested readers with all relevant and key facts concerning Swiss annuities and life insurance while at the same time documenting the various checks and balances now in place between the domains of insurance and supervision.

Monica Mächler
Director
Federal Office of Private Insurance

List of Abbreviations

1984 act	U.S. Tax Reform Act of 1984, Public Law 98-369
403(b)	U.S. retirement plan for employees of educational institutions
408(n)	Specific IRS code authorizing IRA custodians
457	U.S. retirement plans for government employees
AGI	Adjusted gross income
AHV	Alters-und Hinterbliebenenversicherung (Swiss old-age and survivors' insurance)
AI	Swiss Accident Insurance Act
Art.	Article
AS	Amtliche Sammlung des Bundesrechts Official Collection of Federal Laws
AVO	Versicherungsaufsichtsverordnung (Liechtenstein Insurance Supervision Ordinance)
BGBl	Österreichisches Bundesgesetzblatt (*Austrian Federal Law Gazette*)
Bn	billion
C.B.	Cumulative Bulletin
CHF	Swiss franc
Cir.	Circuit (referring to U.S. Courts of Appeals)
Code	U.S. Internal Revenue Code of 1986, as amended
COLI	Corporate-owned life insurance
COLI Best Practices Act	Part of the Pension Best Practices Act, Public Law No. 109-280
Comm'r	Commissioner of Internal Revenue
CPA	Certified Public Accountant
CSCE	Conference on Security and Cooperation in Europe
CVAT	Cash value accumulation test
CVP	Christlichdemokratische Volkspartei (Christian Democratic Party)
DVA	Deferred variable annuity
e.g.	exempli gratia (for example)
EC	Execution Code
EEA	European Economic Area

EFTA	European Free Trade Association
Est. Plan. J.	*Estate Planning Journal*
Est.	Estate
EU	European Union
EUR	Euro
EVSG	Austrian Law on International Insurance Contracts in the European Economic Area (Österreichisches Bundesgesetz über internationales Versicherungsrecht für den europäischen Wirtschaftsraum)
EWG	Europäische Wirtschaftsgemeinschaft European Economic Community
EWR	Europäischer Wirtschaftsraum (European Economic Area)
Ex.	Example
F.2d	*Federal Reporter*, 2d series
FATF	Financial Action Task Force
FDIC	Federal Deposit Insurance Corporation
FDP	Freisinnig-Demokratische Partei (Free Democratic Party)
Fed. Reg.	U.S. *Federal Register*
FMA	Financial Market Authority (Liechtenstein)
FOPI	Swiss Federal Office for Private Insurance
Form 1040	U.S. Resident tax filing form
FOSI	Swiss Federal Office for Social Insurance
GDP	Gross domestic product
GMO	Génetically Modified Organism
GPS	Grüne Partei der Schweiz (Swiss Green Party)
GST	Generation-skipping transfer
HAVE	Haftung und Versicherung Liability and Insurance
ICA	Liechtenstein Insurance Contract Act
IICA	Liechtenstein International Insurance Contract Act
ILIT	Irrevocable life insurance trust
Internal Revenue Code	U.S. Internal Revenue Code of 1986, as amended
IRA	U.S. Individual Retirement Account
IRC	U.S. Internal Revenue Code of 1986, as amended
IRS or Service	U.S. Internal Revenue Service
ISA	Liechtenstein Insurance Supervision Act
ISO	Liechtenstein Insurance Supervision Ordinance
IV	Invalidenversicherung (Swiss disability insurance scheme)
LES	Liechtensteinische Entscheidungssammlung
LGBl	Liechtensteiner Landesgesetzblatt

Lit.	Littera
LJZ	Liechtensteinische Juristen-Zeitung
LOB	Swiss Federal Law on the Occupational Old-age, Survivors' and Disability Benefit Plans Act
LTR	Private letter ruling
M&A	Mergers and Acquisitions
MAGI	Modified adjusted gross income
MEC	Modified endowment contract
MGC	Modified guaranteed contract
N.Y. Est. Powers & Trusts Law	New York Estates, Powers and Trusts Law
N.Y. Ins. Law	New York Insurance Law
NAIC	U.S. National Association of Insurance Commissioners
NCCT	Noncooperative countries and territories
Nr./N	Number
OASI	Swiss Old Age and Survivors' Insurance
OECD	Organization for Economic Cooperation and Development
p.	Page
para.	Paragraph
PPLI	Private Placement Life Insurance
PR	Public Relations
Priv. Ltr. Rul.	Private Letter Ruling
Prop. Treas. Reg.	Proposed regulations promulgated by the U.S. Secretary of the Treasury under authority granted by the U.S. Internal Revenue Code
QTIP	Qualified terminable interest property as defined under U.S. Internal Revenue Code § 2056(b)(7)(B).
Regulation section	Reference to U.S. federal Treasury regulations
Rev. Rul.	Revenue Ruling
Rev'd	Reversed
SchKG	Schweizer Bundesgesetz vom 11. April 1889 über Schuldbetreibung und Konkurs (Swiss Federal Act on Debt Enforcement and Bankruptcy of April 11, 1889)
section	Reference to U.S. Internal Revenue Code sections, unless otherwise indicated
SEP	Simplified Employee Pension
Seq./Seqq.	Following
SIA	Swiss Insurance Association
SIBA	Swiss Insurance Brokers Association

SIMPLE	Simple Savings Incentive Match Plan (for employees)
SIPC	Securities Investor Protection Corporation
SME	Small and medium-size enterprises
Solo 401(k)	U.S. Individual 401(k) Retirement Account, strictly for sole proprietors
SPS	Sozialdemokratische Partei der Schweiz (Swiss Social Democratic Party)
SR	Systematische Sammlung des Bundesrechts Systematic Collection of Federal Laws
SST	Swiss Solvency Test
State of N.Y. Ins. Dep't	State of New York Insurance Department
STEP	Society of Trust and Estate Practitioners
SVP	Schweizerische Volkspartei (Swiss People's Party)
T.C.M.	U.S. Tax Court memorandum decision
T.M.	Tax Management Portfolio Series
TAMRA	U.S. Technical and Miscellaneous Revenue Act, Public Law 100-647
Tech. Adv. Mem.	Technical Advice Memorandum
Treas. Reg.	Regulations promulgated by the U.S. Secretary of the Treasury under authority granted by the U.S. Internal Revenue Code, as such regulations may be amended
U.S.	United States
UBIT	U.S. Unrelated Business Income Tax
UN	United Nations Organization
USD	U.S. Dollar
VAG	Versicherungsaufsichtsgesetz (Liechtenstein Insurance Supervision Act)
VR	Liechtensteinisches Versicherungsrecht (Liechtenstein Insurance Law)
VVG	Bundesgesetz vom 2. April 1908 über den Versicherungsvertrag, Versicherungsvertragsgesetz (Swiss Federal Act on Insurance Contracts of April 2, 1908)
W-2	Form used to report taxable income to the IRS
WTO	World Trade Organization
ZPO	Liechtensteinische Zivilprozessordnung (Liechtenstein Civil Procedure Act)

CHAPTER 1

Why Switzerland?

Christian H. Kälin

Partner, Henley & Partners, Zurich

Switzerland is a federal republic rooted in a long tradition. It is arguably the only country in the world where people with different languages, religions, and cultures have formed one nation that has successfully evolved over centuries and become one of the world's most stable and secure democracies. Indeed, regardless of the various myths about Swiss history, and despite the fact that it has—like every other country—also known some darker chapters in the past, Switzerland is a success story. Its success was made possible by accidents of history, political foresight and necessities in the past, and luck, as well as the hard work and diligence of many generations.

Switzerland is a modern country with a strong identity, made up of more than two dozen different cantons, each having its own traditions and peculiarities. It is a country that has been held together for centuries, and still is, by common objectives and ideals rather than by a common language, culture, or religion. Its cantons are considered to be sovereign, that is, autonomous, politically independent entities within the framework of a federal constitution. Each of the Swiss communes (municipalities) also enjoys broad autonomy. Although many things now are treated more uniformly throughout the country—including the laws and regulations concerning the annuity and life insurance sector—in many important areas, regulations differ between the cantons and even between communes.

Switzerland has attracted foreign investors for decades. It is certainly one of the most attractive countries in the world in which to invest and do business. The country has outstanding political, social, and economic stability. This, combined with an excellent communications and transport infrastructure, efficient public services, comparatively low taxation, as well as a beautiful, clean, and safe environment, make it the ultimate choice for investment and business.

The financial services sector and particularly private banking and insurance have built a unique international reputation that attracts clients from all over the world. World-class banks and insurance companies, well-functioning capital and stock markets, and highly sophisticated financial services play a central role in Switzerland's economic prosperity. Investors who choose to invest with Swiss insurance companies benefit from this financial expertise.

Overall, Switzerland has probably the soundest finances of all the countries in the world; accordingly, it enjoys the highest ranking in creditworthiness, as shown in Figure 1.1.

AN OPEN, MULTILINGUAL SOCIETY

Switzerland has four national languages: German, French, Italian, and Romansh. Romansh was made an official national language only a few years ago, testifying to Switzerland's clear and continuing commitment to a multicultural and multilingual society.

Most Swiss speak at least one foreign language. Pupils start learning languages in elementary school, where English is increasingly being introduced into the curriculum. Today, from the secondary school level on, English is the most favored second language throughout Switzerland.

In businesses with international scopes of operations (and there are many in this country), English is the universal language of communication along with the various national languages. This is particularly so in Zurich, Switzerland's economic and financial capital, but also in Geneva and other cities. In fact, English is so widely spoken in the country that it is sometimes called the fifth national language, or the lingua franca of modern Switzerland.

Thanks to the country's openness, which—contrary to popular belief—includes its attitude toward immigrants, an enormous diversity of languages is actually spoken there.

Switzerland is home to a large number of international organizations. Most of the United Nations organizations, such as the United Nations Educational, Scientific and Cultural Organization, the International Labour Organization, and the World Health Organization are located in Geneva. The World Trade Organization, the International Red Cross, the World Intellectual Property Organization, the Universal Postal Union, and many others are also located in Switzerland.

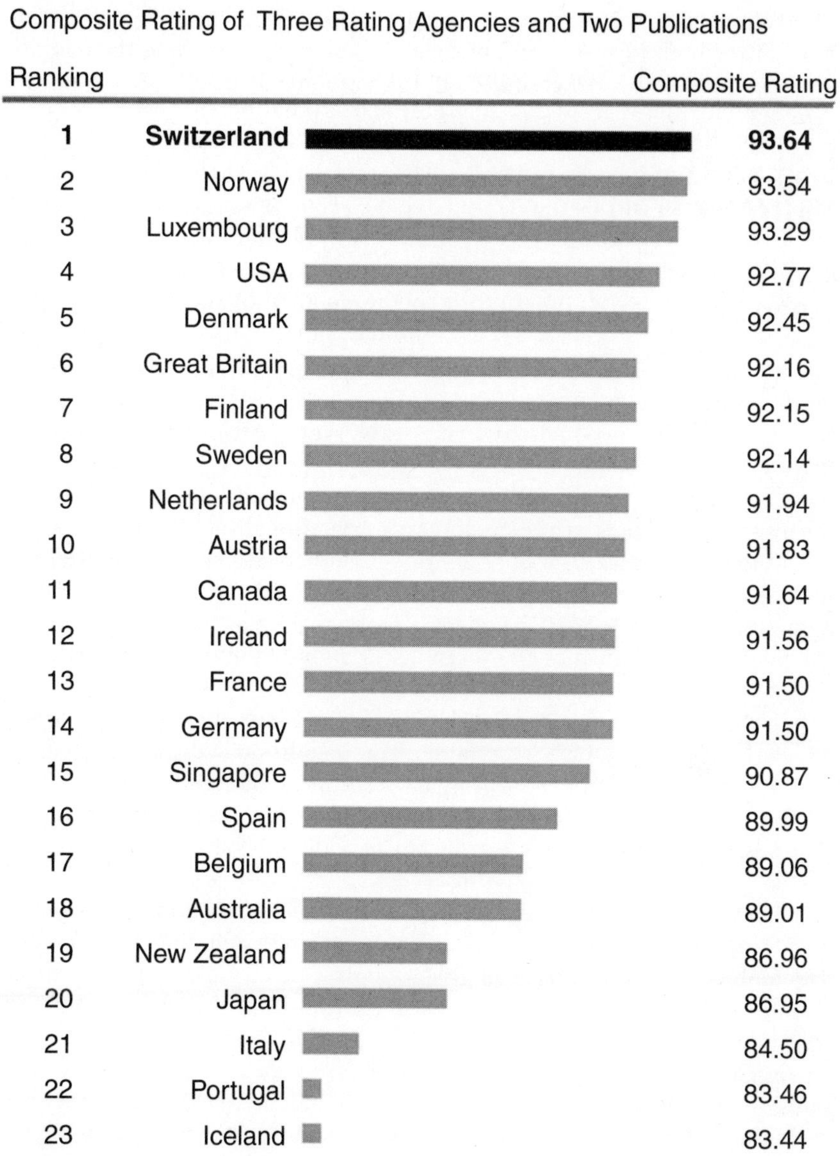

Composite Rating of Three Rating Agencies and Two Publications

Ranking		Composite Rating
1	**Switzerland**	**93.64**
2	Norway	93.54
3	Luxembourg	93.29
4	USA	92.77
5	Denmark	92.45
6	Great Britain	92.16
7	Finland	92.15
8	Sweden	92.14
9	Netherlands	91.94
10	Austria	91.83
11	Canada	91.64
12	Ireland	91.56
13	France	91.50
14	Germany	91.50
15	Singapore	90.87
16	Spain	89.99
17	Belgium	89.06
18	Australia	89.01
19	New Zealand	86.96
20	Japan	86.95
21	Italy	84.50
22	Portugal	83.46
23	Iceland	83.44

FIGURE 1.1   Creditworthiness of Nations

The widespread language skills and multicultural environment are important for both investors and businesses based here, enabling the banking and insurance sector to serve a very international clientele.

HIGHLY QUALIFIED, RELIABLE, AND MOTIVATED PEOPLE

When you invest or do business in Switzerland, you will notice immediately that you are mostly dealing with highly qualified, reliable, and motivated people.

Besides the language diversity, Switzerland is well known for its strong work ethic and the high productivity of its workforce. Indeed, it has one of the world's highest productivity levels per worker. Individualized agreements between employers and employees have forged peaceful labor relations that have held for more than 60 years. There are virtually no strikes, and the unemployment rate is extremely low by international standards.

Managers here are not only multilingual, they also have more extensive international business experience than in any other country. A multicultural approach and the foreign language capabilities of a large proportion of the population mean that the Swiss labor pool is highly skilled and thus productive.

In the financial services sector, including and in particular in insurance, Switzerland's skill pool is very large. The breadth and depth of expertise and experience of employees in Swiss insurance companies, brokers, and advisors—at any level, from office clerks to the top management—is such that customers can not just expect but actually receive competent service that is second to none in the world.

Switzerland also has an excellent education system and scores highly in international comparisons of education and research and development. The high concentration of reputable schools, universities, and research institutions, set in a multicultural environment, attracts bright students and researchers from all over the world.

Regardless of which survey or research results you consider, Switzerland ranks among the top in overall quality of life on an international scale. For years the survey from Mercer Human Resources Consulting[1], probably the most comprehensive report on the subject, has ranked Swiss cities at the very top in the world for quality of life. Clearly this quality of life factor contributes significantly and translates directly to the quality of work, services, and excellent products for which Switzerland is famous. The legendary Swiss quality is strongly linked with the excellent physical environment that Switzerland offers and that makes the country one of the best places in the world to live, as shown in Figure 1.2.

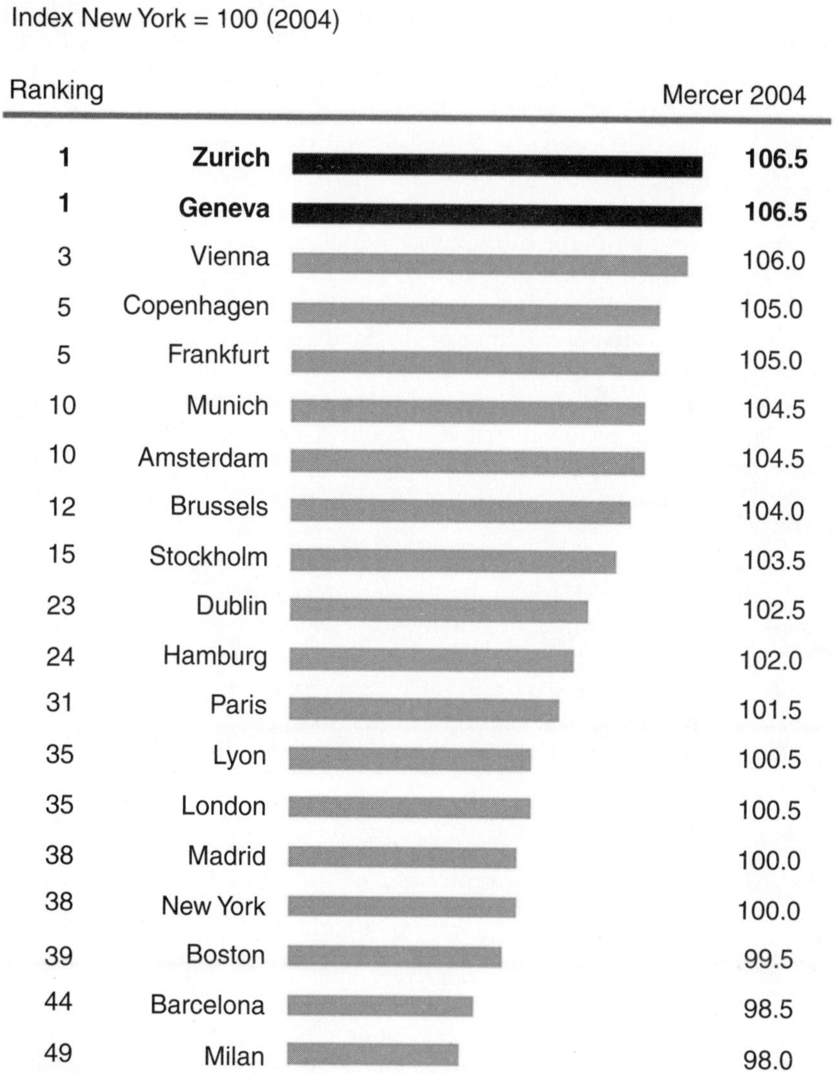

Index New York = 100 (2004)

Ranking		Mercer 2004
1	**Zurich**	**106.5**
1	**Geneva**	**106.5**
3	Vienna	106.0
5	Copenhagen	105.0
5	Frankfurt	105.0
10	Munich	104.5
10	Amsterdam	104.5
12	Brussels	104.0
15	Stockholm	103.5
23	Dublin	102.5
24	Hamburg	102.0
31	Paris	101.5
35	Lyon	100.5
35	London	100.5
38	Madrid	100.0
38	New York	100.0
39	Boston	99.5
44	Barcelona	98.5
49	Milan	98.0

FIGURE 1.2 Quality of Life

STABLE ECONOMY AND RELIABLE LEGAL SYSTEM

Switzerland has a long tradition of liberal trade and investment policies. The Swiss legal system is strong and sophisticated, investment and business law is highly developed and well defined, and solid laws, regulations, and policies protect investment. The Fraser Institute[2] ranks Switzerland third internationally in terms of economic freedom, and according to the Heritage Foundation[3], Switzerland ranks among the world's most liberal countries. An independent monetary policy, the strong protection of property rights and individual freedoms, and the sophistication and quality of the financial sector are viewed as particular strengths of the Swiss economy.

More than two-thirds of the Swiss population is employed in the services sector, which generates about 70 percent of the country's gross domestic product (GDP), a rate comparable to that of other highly developed countries. The distinctive feature of the Swiss services sector, however, is the unique position of financial services, which is a major pillar of the Swiss economy. Banks alone contribute more than 11 percent of the GDP, and the insurance sector contributes about 3 percent of the GDP of the entire country. The share of total value added by the financial services sector in Switzerland is about twice as high as in the United States or in Germany.

Nearly a third of the world's offshore wealth is managed from Switzerland, which therefore clearly ranks number one worldwide in this area. Over a very long period of time, foreign investors who have placed their assets in Switzerland have never been affected by war, economic crises, or unstable governments. Switzerland is the ultimate "safe haven" with a uniquely stable and predictable investment environment, thanks in part to a strong, reliable legal system, which provides real protection of privacy and strict regulation against abuses.

For many, Switzerland's respect for personal and financial privacy is one of the important pillars on which the financial services rest. The value of personal privacy and the protection of the private sphere are deeply rooted in the Swiss tradition and are reflected in the legal system. It is therefore no surprise that Switzerland ranks at the top worldwide with regard to the protection of the private sphere. (See Figure 1.3.) More than elsewhere, in this country both the government and the people are aware of the importance of privacy not only in client relationships in the financial services sector but throughout life, especially regarding strict control and regulation of information collected and held by government authorities.

The country's own stable currency, the Swiss franc (CHF), is another reason why Switzerland stands out internationally. Viewed over the long term, the Swiss franc is arguably the world's strongest currency. It is overseen by a truly independent national bank that carefully controls the money supply and other monetary indicators. Switzerland has never imposed exchange controls on the outflow of funds.

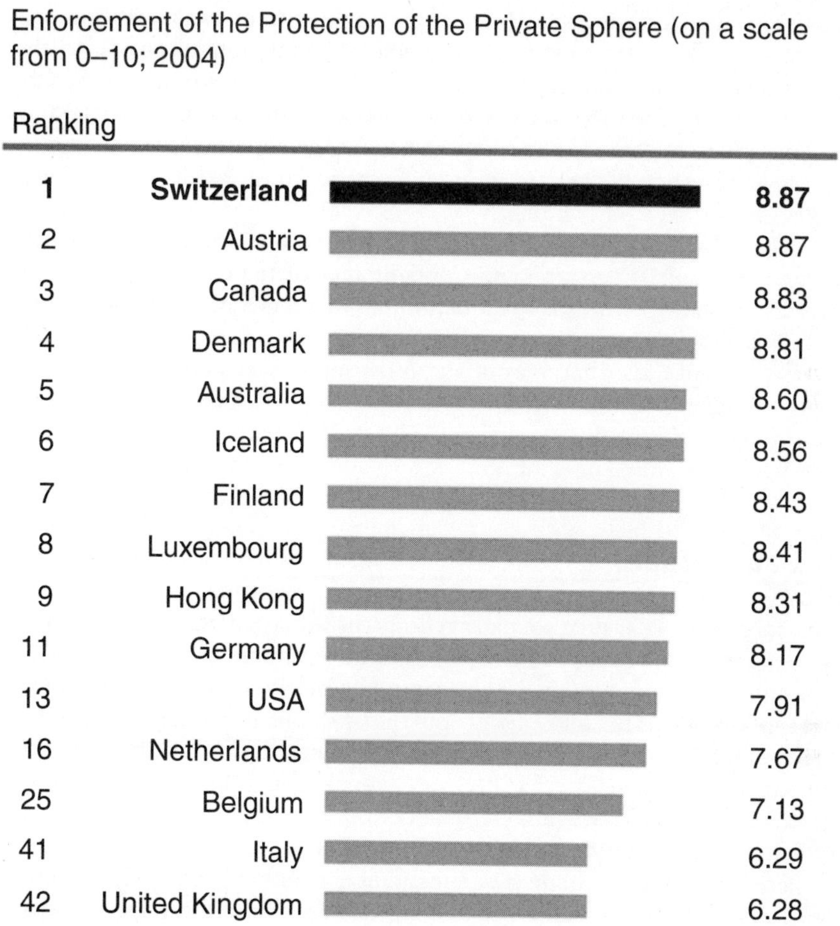

Enforcement of the Protection of the Private Sphere (on a scale from 0–10; 2004)

Ranking

Ranking	Country		Score
1	**Switzerland**		**8.87**
2	Austria		8.87
3	Canada		8.83
4	Denmark		8.81
5	Australia		8.60
6	Iceland		8.56
7	Finland		8.43
8	Luxembourg		8.41
9	Hong Kong		8.31
11	Germany		8.17
13	USA		7.91
16	Netherlands		7.67
25	Belgium		7.13
41	Italy		6.29
42	United Kingdom		6.28

FIGURE 1.3 Protection of the Private Sphere

A STRONG INSURANCE SECTOR

As readers will learn in this book, the Swiss insurance sector is unique in many ways. Although it is not the oldest, it has a long tradition and it is fair to say that it is certainly the safest in the world. Not one insurance company has ever gone bankrupt or failed to meet its obligations, and strict supervision of the insurance business ensures this track record will remain. Switzerland is one of the most important insurance centers in the world, if not the most important center, and the insurance industry is an important part of the Swiss economy. The sector benefits from a very sophisticated legal and regulatory framework that is geared toward protecting the interests of insured clients and beneficiaries. Holders of policies issued by Swiss insurance companies enjoy a degree of security and protection that is maintained more strictly than in any other country. The sector also benefits from certain tax advantages but perhaps above all from the wealth of experience and know-how nurtured in this sector over generations.

The Swiss themselves are known to be very well insured: Switzerland has the world's highest per capita spending on insurance premiums overall and also the highest per capita spending on life insurance premiums, as Figure 1.4 illustrates.

Switzerland also has one of the most highly developed occupational pension systems in the world. As Swiss pension funds are obliged to fully fund their liabilities, by 2004 they had accumulated assets of about CHF 500 billion.

TAX ADVANTAGES

The country's tax system strongly reflects the Swiss federal structure. Fiscal sovereignty is an entitlement of the federal government as well as of the cantons and their communes. Each canton has its own tax laws with its own tax rates, different tax allowances, and the like. The relative independence of the cantons in the sphere of taxation ensures healthy competition, making the tax burden moderate for both individuals and companies when compared with countries worldwide. The tax burden may vary greatly between individual cantons and even between communes.

For foreign investors in Swiss insurance, taxation is generally minimal or nonexistent; investments can be made, can grow, and can be taken out of Switzerland largely free of tax.

Interest and dividends that accrue in Swiss insurance policies are also exempt from withholding tax. This tax, which otherwise generally applies at a rather high rate of 35 percent, makes investments through Swiss insurance significantly more attractive than comparative investments in Swiss bank deposits or Swiss government bonds.

Swiss insurance companies do not have to give any information about their policy holders to the Swiss tax authorities. In fact, revealing any information related to clients of Swiss insurance companies and Swiss banks is strictly protected by law. Information can be given only in strictly defined circumstances, mainly in case of criminal offenses, money laundering, terrorism financing, and the like. If a foreign government or tax authority requests information, the rules are even stricter; the foreign authority must

Amount Spent on Insurance Premiums per Capita and Country
(without social security; in US$; 2004)

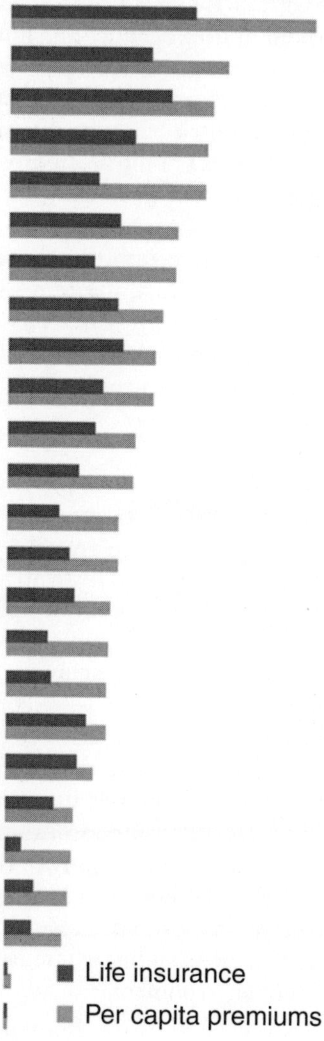

		Pre Capita Premiums	Life Insurance
Switzerland		**5,660**	**3,431**
United Kingdom		4,059	2,617
Japan		3,771	3,003
Ireland		3,670	2,313
USA		3,638	1,658
Denmark		3,116	2,038
Netherlands		3,094	1,562
Belgium		2,876	2,005
Finland		2,714	2,127
France		2,698	1,768
Sweden		2,358	1,602
Norway		2,321	1,323
Germany		2,051	930
Australia		2,041	1,129
Italy		1,913	1,238
Canada		1,872	723
Austria		1,847	811
Hong Kong		1,833	1,484
Singapore		1,621	1,300
South Korea		1,243	874
New Zealand		1,215	272
Spain		1,146	489
Israel		1,041	461
Russia	■ Life insurance	98	34
China	■ Per capita premiums	36	25

FIGURE 1.4 International Insurance Ratios

essentially go through the Swiss legal system, which safeguards the rights of all parties involved.

Reporting on assets held at Swiss financial institutions, including insurance companies, is the sole obligation of the investor. More in the past than today, this fact has led to certain abuses. Often foreign investors would deposit their assets in Switzerland and not report this information in their home country, where they have their tax residence and possibly should make appropriate declarations. Switzerland's position has never been to encourage the evasion of taxes in foreign countries; however, it also does not want to be involved in the collection of taxes for foreign governments and, as mentioned earlier, has a strong tradition of protecting individuals' rights to financial privacy.

Switzerland does offer many genuine tax advantages for foreign investors, and more so today than ever before. Certain insurance products available in Switzerland and Liechtenstein now offer very attractive tax advantages that are legal, sound, and compliant with tax systems in investors' home countries. Accordingly, specific insurance products offer tax deferral or other tax advantages for citizens worldwide.

COMPETENT AND FRIENDLY GOVERNMENT AUTHORITIES

In Switzerland, the government administration works efficiently on all levels. Whether a request is made at the local communal office, questions arise about a tax return, or an inquiry is sent to a department of the federal government in Berne, the Swiss public administration is well organized, efficient, and run by friendly and helpful civil servants. It has been said that the Swiss public administration is both the friendliest and the most competent in the world. This is certainly very pleasant for everyone living in the country, but it is a crucial advantage for investors and businesses: Administrative matters are efficiently and speedily expedited; key government officials, such as tax commissioners, are easily and directly accessible; and issues of any kind are normally resolved in a constructive atmosphere. Indeed, very few nations can match the positive impact the Swiss public administration has on the country's business and investment environment.

CHAPTER 2

Switzerland: The Basics

Clive H. Church

*Emeritus Jean Monnet Professor of
European Studies, Centre for Swiss Politics,
University of Kent, Canterbury*

Understanding Swiss annuities and life insurance is likely to be helped by knowing a little about the bases of contemporary Switzerland. Swiss financial services operate not in a vacuum but against a wider and unusual sociopolitical background. Even though the country is not free of the problems that afflict all western societies today, it remains a very attractive place in which to holiday, live, and do business, thanks to its efficiency, prosperity, and stability. In turn, these benefits are largely due to Switzerland's very distinctive political arrangements.

Understanding what Switzerland is like today, and what it may be like tomorrow—for it changes more than is often thought—demands two things. One is looking back, not so much into the distant past but into the period around World War II, which was when the main outlines of contemporary Switzerland emerged. This *Sonderfall,* or special case, has had a major impact on the way both Swiss and outsiders think about the country. More recently, however, some of the foundations of Swiss achievement have shifted, internationally, economically, and politically, putting the traditional model and its supporters under some pressure, since external change has called prevailing Swiss practices into question.

The other need is to consider the structures under which Switzerland currently operates, economically and, especially, politically. Economic activity is now improving though there are still some problems of growth and liberalization. There is also considerable argument about tax competition. Social services are, moreover, an increasing concern for the Swiss. Politically, while the parliament, government, and the key processes of consultation, federalism, and direct democracy still apply, the country is becoming increasingly polarized, a situation that has implications for the working of government and the forthcoming elections. Externally, relations with the European Union (EU) remain the main, and somewhat difficult, problem facing the country.

LONG-TERM ORIGINS

In many ways Switzerland is a modern construct. In the Middle Ages, there was no state as such, merely a set of alliances between the communities around the northern end of the St. Gotthard Pass. These liaisons go back beyond Switzerland's conventional foundation date of 1291. The profits from transit traffic between Italy and Germany over the St. Gotthard helped the original allies to resist outside pressures and brought new communities into their leagues or alliances. The allies also consolidated the legal arrangements by which their relations were managed. By the fifteenth century, the leagues were able both to ride out internal social conflict and, collectively, to become a major military power.

However, the leagues' expansion was checked, first by their own divisions over mercenary service and then, especially, by religious conflict. The conflict led to the emergence of what were virtually two states. To avoid foreign affairs pulling the two sides totally apart, a policy of neutrality was adopted. Thanks to this, as well as to a tradition of mercenary service, banking, and watchmaking, the Swiss developed prosperous but oligarchic societies. The old order was overthrown by the French invasion of 1798, which turned the loose confederacy that had grown out of the leagues into a single state. However, neither acceptance nor stability ensued. So, with the Mediation of 1803 and, especially, with the collapse of the Napoleonic Empire between 1813 and 1815, there were moves back toward the old order. However, economic change and political radicalization undermined the social and political settlement of 1815. Conflict between Protestant-based radicalism and conservative Catholic forces ultimately erupted in a short civil war out of which emerged, in 1848, the first proper Swiss Federation.

The new republic acquired more powers through the constitutional revision of 1874. Thereafter, it rapidly achieved stability, thanks to the way the expansion of federalism and direct democracy allowed the defeated Catholic conservatives to take a full part in politics. The country was thus able to ride out both World War I, which greatly divided the Germanic and Latin communities, and the acute social conflict produced by industrialization, including a general strike in 1918. After the war, in a search for security, Switzerland briefly set its neutrality aside to become a member of the League of Nations. At this time, moreover, Switzerland was not yet an extremely rich country. Indeed, it suffered surprisingly badly during the depression of the 1930s.

SONDERFALL YEARS

From the unpropitious circumstances of the 1930s, the country first overcame enormous external challenges and then achieved unparalleled prosperity and stability, leading many people to talk of the *Sonderfall Schweiz*. This change occurred in stages, and did not mean there were no changes or problems. However, the idea that Switzerland was a special case or exception was to be very influential in shaping the contemporary Swiss sense of identity.

The first stage of the Sonderfall came in the late 1930s when, alarmed by the rise of Italian fascism and German Nazism, Switzerland decided to leave the League of Nations and revert to absolute neutrality. Internally it developed its own socioeconomic resources by agreeing to the Labor Peace (banning strikes and lockouts), planning for meeting the economic stresses of war, and bringing socialists and business into government. At the same time it began to distinguish itself from Nazi Germany by making a greater use of German Schweizerdütsch dialects.

This change, supported by the maintenance of armed neutrality and firm government policy, provided a basis for the second phase of the Sonderfall: resisting pressures during the war from both Nazis and the Allies. Switzerland's position was strengthened by its economic value to both sides. As a result, threatened invasions never took place and the country emerged from the war largely unscathed physically. Most Swiss put this down to their own political skills and institutions, notably armed neutrality. However, not everyone then, or since, accepted that Switzerland had treated both sides equally or had fulfilled all its humanitarian commitments. Many felt Switzerland had leaned too far toward the Nazi regime in its treatment of Jews, its acceptance of gold sales, and its slowness to recognize the turning of the tide of war. So, in 1945, the country decided not to apply for United Nations entry, fearing that to do so would invite a humiliating rebuff from the Allies.

Nonetheless, the country, having been spared the rigors of war, was able to take part in the great postwar European boom. So, in a third stage of the Sonderfall, the country was transformed by an almost uninterrupted pattern of growth (averaging 5 percent per year) through expansion in manufacturing and, especially, services. This economic boom helped social promotion at home, making the country more middle-class, as well as attracting inward labor migration. Labor relations remained good, encouraged by new constitutional recognition of the policy-making rights of capital and labour. Social welfare also developed on a generous scale. The country was then able to ride out the depressions of the 1970s by switching more deeply into the service sector and by not renewing foreign workers' contracts.

Politically there was equal achievement, as the country became increasingly tranquil and moderate as the Social Democrats (Sozialdemokratische Partei/Parti socialiste Suisse [SPS]) dropped their Marxism and became full partners in government. From 1959, thanks to what became known as "the Magic Formula," all parties were represented equitably and proportionately in government. Women were finally given the vote in 1971. Internationally, the country also improved its standing: helping to set up the European Free Trade Association, joining the Council of Europe in 1963, signing free trade and technical agreements with the European Community after 1972, and playing a more active humanitarian and peace making role, including through the Red Cross.

All this was seen domestically as making the country very much a special case. Swiss skills had not merely resisted the Nazis but had turned the country into one of the richest, freest, and most democratic societies in the world. It also avoided the tensions of the Cold War. All this produced stability and local self- government, resulting in a well-ordered society. Everything, including the trains, ran on time. The Sonderfall also meant a high, not to say paradigmatic, level of internal unity, untroubled by religious or social conflict. Strikes were thus virtually unknown and crime was relatively rare. Economically, thanks to its competitiveness and its quality output, Switzerland enjoyed a very high standard of living coupled with low inflation and virtually no unemployment. All this gave most Swiss increasing self-confidence even if there were some concerns about suffocating conformity.

CHANGE AND ITS EFFECTS

This situation lasted into the 1980s, after which the foundations of the Sonderfall began to weaken. Internationally, the circumstances that had allowed Switzerland to stand aloof from the Cold War and the European Union ended. Economically, with the country enduring first a long period of sluggish growth and then a major depression, economic and social realities began to change. And the balance of politics began to alter, calling the old basic stability into question. Whether, and if so, how, to adapt to these changes became a key dividing issue in Swiss politics.

International Dimension

After an active and successful role as a neutral mediator, notably in the Helsinki process, Switzerland found its position called into question by glasnost, the revolutions of 1989, and the collapse of the Soviet Union. With the end to the Cold War, the country hardly needed an army, especially one that was nominally the biggest in Europe even if it was a militia and not a professional force. Nor was there so much call for Swiss good offices. Neutrality was also coming under attack because of what were seen as shortcomings in the Swiss role during World War II and the way heirs of bank accounts lost by victims of the Holocaust had been treated.

The country was forced to adapt this element of the Sonderfall by, first, redefining neutrality in a more flexible way. Second, after a referendum in 1989 in which a third of voters called for the abolition of the army, reform programs were instituted to slim it down and enable it to play new roles at home and abroad. Third, the government commissioned detailed research into Swiss behavior during the war. These reports showed that, while many of the charges leveled against the country were unfounded, it had not always lived up to its humanitarian responsibilities. The government therefore apologized for this and proposed a Solidarity Fund by way of reparation. The banks were also forced to search for dormant accounts—5,570 of which were eventually found—and to agree to a global compensation deal. Such accommodation was resisted by traditionalists who later helped to block the funds.

At the same time, the way that the European Community enlarged, completed the Single Market, and deepened its integration in the run-up to Maastricht threatened Switzerland's cozy relations with Europe. Because the consultation promised by the 1984 Luxembourg Process had not materialized, the Swiss welcomed the 1990 talks, which eventually led to the October 1991 European Economic Area (EEA) Agreement. Unfortunately, this agreement also failed to offer the country sufficient influence in decision making, and hence provided insufficient respect for its independence. So it was only accepted on sufferance, with an application for entry to the Community being tabled in May 1992. This move complicated things where the EEA was concerned. And so, with declining trust in government, a divide between inward-looking rural regions and more outward-looking urban ones (notably in French-speaking areas), a vote for EEA entry was defeated on December 6, 1992.

The country was left very divided and was forced back to bilateral deals with the EU. Switzerland also lost the competitive stimulus that countries like Austria gained from joining the EU's Single Market. Negotiations, moreover, were slow, painful, and drawn out. In fact, they were completed only in 1998. Then, despite fierce internal opposition, public consent to the deals was given in May 2000 and the bilateral agreements began to come into effect in June 2002 and after, in a staged process. The likelihood of EU membership was further reduced by the ill-judged refusal of pro-Europeans to withdraw a demand for immediate entry talks. Their initiative was crushed in March 2001, leaving the authorities to negotiate a second set of bilateral talks, which they successfully did in 2004. Most of these were unchallenged, but entry to the Schengen and Dublin conventions was bitterly resisted, as was extension of free movement rights to the new eastern members of the EU and the solidarity payments for them. Popular approval for these further agreements was only narrowly achieved in 2005–6. All this meant that foreign policy, instead of being a support for the Sonderfall, became not merely problematic but a cause of economic uncertainties and deep political divisions.

Economic Downturn

At the same time, world and local factors began to take some of the gloss off Swiss economic performance. Enhanced global competition, the general malaise of the 1990s, and the effects of outside crises all had severe effects. Domestically the hard franc policy and the parlous state of government finances depressed the economic basis of the Sonderfall. There was also a lack of liberalization, leading to high costs and the toleration of cartels.

The result was very slow and limited growth leading to the first real recession since the 1940s. Growth averaged only 1.25 percent compared to the Organisation for Economic Co-operation and Development (OECD) average of 2.75 percent. In the 1990s exports fell off and domestic demand dropped. Hence downsizing became common, some banks faltered and bankruptcies multiplied. The emblematic case was that of the national airline, Swissair, which in 2001 was grounded and forced into liquidation and merger. Such closures and restructuring meant that unemployment became a real problem, reaching as much as 6 percent at times and averaging an unprecedented 4 percent. This had a deleterious effect on the social climate, increasing societal insecurity and making relative poverty a problem. Health and social welfare budgets consequently became major issues. The Sonderfall was also threatened by the resurgence of the language divide and a series of disasters, such as the 2002 Uberlingen air crash, which called Swiss quality into question, at least where its air traffic control service was concerned.

Political Realignments

Although the much-praised political structure did not really alter after 1980, it was used in more partisan and destabilizing ways, due to changes in the party system. The calm and consensus of the Sonderfall gave way to more contentious, European-style politics. The party system also began to change in the 1980s with the rise first of new far-right movements, responding to a new wave of immigration, and then of the Greens. At the same time the center right, and notably the Christian Democrats (Christlichdemokratische Volkspartei [CVP]), began to falter.

Even more significant was the dramatic reorientation of the Swiss People's Party (Schweizerische Volkspartei [SVP]). From being the third of the four main parties, drawing essentially on agrarian support, it developed a new center of gravity, pulling in lower-middle-class and blue-collar voters. It also began to establish itself in previously untouched cantons, including French-speaking Switzerland, first by absorbing smaller right-wing parties and then by eating into the mainstream center right electorate of the Radical Democrats (Freisinnig-Demokratische Partei [FDP]). It owed its success to its new organization, dominated by its urban Zurich wing under Christoph Blocher, its controversial public relations style, and its clear focus on a few key identity-related issues: opposition to asylum seekers and other migrants, defense of Swiss political traditions against the establishment, and fierce resistance to European and international entanglements. By the early years of the new century it became the country's largest party. And, in 2003, it seized a second seat on the Federal Council from the Christian Democrats. This went to Blocher, who became Minister of Justice. Since then the party has used its position inside and outside of government to challenge both convention and policy, notably on Europe.

With smaller parties imploding, the other mainstream parties of the center right failing to rebuild, and the Social Democrats and the Greens holding their own (and sometimes outpolling the SVP), politics became increasingly polarized and confrontational. Hence reform became harder to achieve as traditionalists clung to the old ways even though these had been rendered questionable by external developments. With trust in government and system also continuing to decline, political stability was affected by conflict and change.

PRESENT-DAY SOCIOECONOMIC STRUCTURES

Despite the difficulties experienced in the 1990s, the inheritance from the past means that Switzerland remains one of the strongest and most diverse economies in the world. In fact, it is now enjoying a healthy upward cycle. Socially it is also more populous and urban than before. It is highly educated as well as having several languages and religions. Yet there are problems in both economy and society.

Economically Switzerland is less agricultural than myth suggests, although farming is relatively productive and also highly protected. It accounts for 3.6 percent of the workforce and 1.5 percent of gross domestic product (GDP). Manufacturing, which rests on innovative research, labor flexibility, and high skill levels, specializes in chemicals, machine tools, and watches. It employs 23.7 percent of the workforce and produces 34 percent of GDP. This is dwarfed by the contribution of the service sector, which makes up 72.7 percent of the workforce and 64.5 percent of GDP. Retailing, financial services, and hospitality are among leading sectors, along with government, which is bigger than often assumed. Large firms tend to be more outward looking than most and also account for a disproportionate amount of GDP. The small and medium-size enterprises that dominate all three sectors, notably in agriculture, are sometimes more inward looking. Despite being trade dependent, the national market is somewhat fragmented and overregulated. This limits competitiveness, dynamism, and growth. Nonetheless, the country still enjoys remarkably high per capita GDP while profitability and growth seem to be rising dramatically (reaching 2.7 percent in 2006), as is the country's trade surplus. Inflation and interest rates are now very low, and the budget is now in surplus.

Demographically the country is growing. It has 7.5 million residents, over a fifth of whom are foreign in origin. Despite this, the population is aging. The number of families is increasing and their size is decreasing due to rising divorce rates and a later age of marriage. However, while there are problems with drugs and AIDS, the Swiss have low levels of out-of-wedlock births.

The population is increasingly urban and educated. Two-thirds of the resident population live in the 10 largest conurbations while rural areas continue to lose people. The country has good apprenticeship and secondary educational systems; the latter, like the universities, are run by the cantons. However, there is a relatively low university population. The federal polytechnics in Lausanne and Zurich are the peaks of the system.

The Swiss are also divided by language and religion. Sixty-four percent are German speaking, which means they speak in one of the Schweizerdütsch dialects and write in standard German. Of the others, 20 percent speak French, 6.5 percent Italian, and 0.5 percent Romansh. In terms of religion, 41.8 percent of the resident population is Catholic, 35.3 percent is Protestant, and 4.3 percent is Muslim while 11 percent admit to no creed. Figures for Catholics and Protestants are higher among native Swiss.

Swiss society is still clearly stratified by capital, income, and education. Capital is very unequally shared. Moreover, the wealthiest fifth of the population enjoy 45 percent of total incomes and the poorest fifth only 7 percent.

Hence relative poverty is rising. Unemployment, now running at 3.3 percent, and health care and pensions are placing an increasing strain on the social welfare budget, which now equates to 30 percent of GDP. The fact that 120,000 people cannot afford health insurance premiums has not helped the social climate, even though, overall, Switzerland remains a very calm and secure environment.

TODAY'S POLITICAL STRUCTURES

Dealing with these problems falls to a political structure that, although changing, remains significantly different from those of the West. While it works through normal constitutional channels, such as parties and parliaments, not to mention structured consultation procedures, it differs in its decentralized federalism and, especially, in its intensive use of direct democracy. This makes Swiss politics extremely people oriented. However, as mentioned, recently the political climate has become more confrontational and polarized. So the system is under pressure and faces difficulties in trying to resolve emerging problems.

Constitution

The ultimate political framework for Switzerland is provided by its new constitution. The original draft, produced in 1848 and considerably revised in 1874, was replaced in 1999 after much discussion and consultation. The changes were made because the old version had become very long and cumbersome, thanks to the many additions produced by direct democracy. Although new laws can be introduced at cantonal level by referendum, this cannot be done nationally. Hence people who want policy change have to seek a constitutional amendment. Although relatively few initiatives succeeded, large chunks of policy detail were written into the constitution over the years. Moreover, some of its older elements were no longer wholly relevant or comprehensible.

The new version has simplified the text stylistically and generally reordered it and, to a lesser extent, reoriented it. The new draft highlights popular sovereignty and human rights. It also gives the communes a new status and encourages decentralization. At the same time it opened the way to changes in the country's judicial structure that are now coming into effect. Moreover it laid down some new principles for political life.

The state structure that emerges from this new constitution remains both largely unchanged and relatively limited. The country still observes a strict separation of powers, with small collegiate executives and powerful parliaments. The structures of federalism also remain, as do the now-extended mechanisms of direct democracy. The constitution continues to be policed by the Federal Tribunal (Schweizerisches Bundesgericht/Tribunal Fédéral), although this cannot quash laws as can the U.S. Supreme Court. The Federal Tribunal has absorbed the old insurance court and been joined by new penal and administrative courts.

Parties and Parliament

The Swiss parliament has often been regarded as weak because it is a militia parliament composed of nonprofessionals and meeting for relatively short sessions. In fact, the parliament, as a body, is surprisingly important and is becoming more so because of the changes in the party system. The parliament represents the confederation, electing and controlling the government. It also has the ultimate say on legislation. Equally, most of its members are quasi-full-time politicians, often with several directorships and public posts.

The parliament is a perfect bicameral structure. The upper house—the Council of States (Ständerat/Conseil des Etats)—is made up of 46 members, 2 from each full canton. The lower house—the National Council (Nationalrat/Conseil National)—has a fixed complement of 200 allocated among the cantons in proportion to population. Both houses have exactly the same powers. Bills are considered first in committee and then in plenary sittings. Where the two houses fail to agree, there are reconciliation exchanges until agreement is reached.

However, the parliament is driven by political parties and their changing balance has made them more significant. Swiss parties are essentially cantonal formations, with often differing views, relatively loosely coordinated nationally. The SVP is an exception, being increasingly disciplined, focused, and perpetually campaigning. The SVP insistence on party rights dominated the 2003 governmental elections. The other main center right parties, the Radicals and the Christian Democrats, are looking to new programs and leaders to curb their electoral losses. The Social Democrats, who work closely with the Greens, are moving to the left though they ally with the center on some issues. However, with even the biggest parties well short of a majority, cooperation is essential, so that the will of parliament as a whole still counts. Hence, even though the SVP won more Lower House seats in the 2007 elections, it still needs allies, especially in the Upper House. There the various Green forces made a significant breakthrough, as they did in the National Councils. The mixed performance of the other parties suggests they have yet to devise effective new strategies.

Government and Governance

Comparatively speaking, Switzerland has a small as well as a fairly limited state apparatus. The central government employs some 35,000 national civil servants who remain important in policy development. At the top of the governmental system is the Federal Council (Bundesrat/Conseil fédéral), a college of seven departmental heads, elected by Parliament for four-year terms depending on the electoral strength of the parties. Hence, at present there are two each from the People's Party, the Radicals, and the Social Democrats and one Christian Democrat. The council is chaired by the ministers in rotation, thus giving the country an unusual form of annual presidency.

The college is also assisted by a chancellery (Bundeskanzlei/Chancellerie fédérale), which equates to the British cabinet. The ministries are defense, civil protection and sport, economic affairs, energy and environment, finance, foreign affairs, and home affairs. All parts of the administration are subject to them. At present, the convention that the council works as a team, separate from the nominating parties, is under pressure.

The federal government has a wide range of duties including budgeting, defense, external relations, legislating, and supervising. However, many of its powers are shared with the cantons, and most of its decisions are implemented by the latter rather than directly. Likewise, many state activities are carried out by voluntary and private bodies so that Switzerland is thought of more as a governance system than a top-down governed country. The confederation is financed partly by time-limited powers to levy direct taxes and partly by various minor sources including service charges. It has struggled to avoid deficit in recent years, but the year 2006 ended comfortably in the black.

Consultation and Policy Making

Policy is not made purely by parliament and government. It emerges in part from a wide, and often overlooked, system of consultation of social interests. Thus employers and unions are fully involved in the preparation of legislation. This is a legacy of World War II and the state's move into economic management, which, as already noted, led to consultative rights for employers and unions being written into the constitution. Cantons, experts, and social movements are also involved. The process is not free of challenges and difficulties, yet it symbolizes the Swiss desire to base politics on the popular consensus.

When legislation is felt necessary, the relevant administration informally tests the waters before producing a draft bill. The draft is then sent out for formal consultation, which is usually publicly recorded. Next the bill is revised in light of comments received and, if approved by the Federal Council, submitted to parliament. The latter can also engage in further consultation while coming to its own decision. Once approved, the law is normally open to a referendum challenge within 100 days. If this does not happen, the act then goes into effect.

Federalism

Another area where Switzerland diverges from the norm is in its robust federal structure. The cantons are basic components of Switzerland and retain something of their sovereign status, being self-contained political entities with their own governments, parliaments, and judiciaries. They, and their component communes, enjoy large resources and have wide responsibilities. Cantons and communes in fact raise and spend more of the national income than the Federal Council. And they are subject to only limited political and judicial control from the center. This situation has enabled the country to cope with linguistic differences. The cantons can also compete in matters of taxation and inward investment although they also often cooperate through a dense network of treaties, or "concordats." The center is dependent on the cantons for implementation of virtually all its legislation and policies.

They are also major players in national politics, being statutorily built in to national decision making. Moreover, they have large political rights and, in May 2004, were able to resist Federal Council financial reforms, which they believed would deprive them of much-needed funds. In fact, the cantons constitute a major pressure group through a series of conferences that bring together cantonal ministers. Finally, they provide the basic constitutive structures for parties, pressure groups, and other forms of political activity. The experience people gain at cantonal level is often used nationally thereafter.

Nonetheless, the system has problems. Some cantons are too small to cope with their responsibilities or with the special needs of big cities. Their finances have also been under strain until recently. And the division of duties with the central government has been unsatisfactory, requiring a new apportionment of duties and costs to reduce disparities and help cantons with structural problems. Approved in November 2004, this is only now coming into effect.

Direct Democracy

Even more distinctive is the Swiss use of direct democracy, which goes well beyond the rather restrictive meaning normally conveyed by the English term "referendum." It is a much more widespread process of allowing the people to decide policy and other matters. It is particularly prominent at the local level and especially in German-speaking areas. Besides making legislative decisions, this direct democracy can involve administrative rulings, financial allocations and treaties, or even whether to recall governments. Hence the Swiss have to vote several times every year at varying levels.

There are two main classes of direct democratic votes. Some are mandatory and have to be held on certain "urgent" government acts, such as many treaties and all constitutional amendments. Propositions by the authorities and those resulting from initiatives, when 100,000 signatures (collected over 18 months) can propose changes to the constitution, are voted on. These propositions usually require a double majority of people and cantons, which means that the small German-speaking cantons have a considerable weight.

Other votes are optional. The government can choose to submit certain acts to a vote. And most legislation can be subjected to what the Swiss call a referendum if 50,000 citizens challenge a bill within 100 days of its completing its passage through parliament. The whole process has been speeded up of late and government has lost some of its ability to delay votes. Normally both challenges and initiatives are organized by cross-party committees of enthusiasts, though increasingly parties use them for their own purposes.

Direct democracy has had a huge impact on Swiss politics. However, very often its effects have been conservative with most initiatives being rejected, at least the first time round (as female suffrage was). For this reason, direct democracy has been seen as a barrier to necessary reforms. Yet it can also spring unpleasant surprises on the authorities, as with the recent imposition of mandatory full life sentences for sex offenders and the rejection of easier naturalization.

With the people as the ultimate sovereign, politics are normally conducted consensually, pacifically, and tolerantly. However, this is changing somewhat with increasing media influence and more aggressive party styles. Equally, because some people still feel excluded, unconventional political action is not unknown. Nonetheless, the Swiss are very proud of their ultra-democratic system, and support for it is a basic element of political culture. Swiss political culture is, in fact, much more nationally minded than is often appreciated. There is a strong sense of nationhood based on its unusual political institutions. Acceptance of the political system is the thing that holds the diverse population together.

ISSUES AND PROSPECTS

In the last year or so there has been less concern over the economy than was previously the case. Profitability and confidence have been restored and the economy is powering along, with prospects for 2008 looking good.

Nonetheless, both the government and the OECD continue to urge the need for structural reform, including in the welfare system. The government has indeed been seeking to implement a growth-oriented policy. However, popular resistance to liberalization, notably in electricity and postal supply, has made this a slow process.

Transport, energy, and environmental issues can also cause concern. Thus the new Alpine base rail lines are proving very expensive. Flight patterns into Kloten airport near Zurich have also caused much dissent. Similarly, nuclear power and genetically modified foods are proving controversial and unpopular.

Social services remain a major headache. Proposals to divert national bank profits to the pension system were defeated in September 2006. Government changes to the system and its financing have also fallen at referendum. Standardization of family allowances has, however, been agreed upon. There is also much controversy over possible changes in the retirement age. Legislation on sickness and accident insurance and an increasingly costly health system has proved problematic. However, renewed proposals to replace a plethora of health insurance funds with a single national system were roundly defeated in March 2007. Partly for these reasons, there is a growing gap between rich and poor, and a surprising number of people are now below the poverty line.

Politics have become increasingly polarized in recent years, between the radical right wing People's Party on one hand and the Social Democrats and the Greens on the other. Both the SVP and the Greens made new gains in cantonal elections over the winter of 2006–7. Hence the 2007 election campaign started early and was fiercely fought. The SVP is targeting antiracism policy, asylum, minarets, naturalization, and, above all, the EU. The SPS is seeking to regain its status as the biggest party and to defend both the welfare state and international openness, but its position is complicated by the Green surge. The centrist parties are hoping to reverse recent electoral declines, but early evidence shows the FDP still losing ground to the SVP. The outcome of the next election, while hard to predict, may be more significant than is often assumed.

Relations with the EU remain very controversial. The government wishes to build on its existing bilateral relations with the EU so as to make them closer and more coordinated. However, the SVP and its allies are bitterly opposed to such a move. And while an accommodation is possible, things currently are complicated by the question of tax competition since the EU believes that very low cantonal taxes for business and rich foreign celebrities are contrary to the 1972 Free Trade Agreement. Berne rejects this accusation, even though some on the left are opposed to internal tax competition, and the problem has somewhat soured relations with the Union.

Even if the SVP finds current foreign policy too activist, it has generally been popular with the public at large, partly because it has been hostile to Israeli activities in Lebanon and in favor of United Nations reform. Army reform also continues to be contested. Despite its economic and other achievements, the country will have to find solutions to a number of problems in the coming years. However, the basic strength of the system suggests that it will be able to do this.

USEFUL ADDRESSES

Christian Democratic Party
Secretariat General
Klaraweg 6
Case postale 5835
3001 Berne
Tel. (+41) 031 357 33 33
Fax (+41) 031 352 24 30
http://www.cvp.ch
E-mail: info@cvp.ch

Department of Foreign Affairs: Press and Information Service
Palais Fédéral Ouest
CH-3003 Berne
Tel.: (+41) 031 322 31 53
Fax: (+41) 031 324 90 47 / 48
E-mail: info@eda.admin.ch

Federal Chancellery, Information Service
Palais Fédéral Ouest, 3003 Berne
Tel. (+41) 031 322 21 11
Fax (+41) 031 322 37 06
http://www.admin.ch/ch/f/autorita.html
E-mail: webmaster@admin.ch

Federal Parliament: Information Service
CH-3003 Berne
Tel. (+41) 031 322 87 90
Fax (+41) 031 322 53 74
http://www.parlament.ch
E-mail: information@pd.admin.ch

Radical Democratic Party

Secretariat General
FDP Schweiz
Neuengasse 20
Postfach 6136
CH-3001 Bern
Tel. (+41) 031 320 35 35
Fax (+41) 031 320 35 00
http://www.fdp.ch
E-mail: info@fdp.ch

Social Democratic Party

Spitalgasse 34
Postfach 7876
3001 Bern
Tel. (+41) 031 329 69 69
Fax (+41) 031 329 69 70
http://www.spschweiz.ch/
E-mail: info@spschweiz.ch

Swiss People's Party

General Secretariat, Bruckfeldstrasse 18
Case postale, 3000 Berne 26
Tel. (+41) 031 300 58 58
Fax (+41) 031 300 58 59
http://www.svp.ch
E-mail: info@udc.ch

CHAPTER 3

The Life Insurance Industry in Switzerland

Peter Lüssi

*Swiss Industry Leader Insurance,
PricewaterhouseCoopers, Zurich*

Peter Fierz

*Swiss Knowledge Manager Financial
Services, PricewaterhouseCoopers, Zurich*

The life insurance industry in Switzerland caters to the needs of various parties (individual life or group life) with different types of products. This chapter highlights the most important stakeholders and products. In the second part, we name the "top 13" players in the market and analyze their market shares and specialties. In the last part of the chapter, we list some of the most current market trends and market drivers, such as distribution channels and client and employee-focused strategies. That part also talks about "exotic" products in Switzerland, such as products targeting the 50-plus demographic.

SWISS RETIREMENT BENEFIT PLANS

Life insurance is available in two forms: as individual or as group life insurance. These policies offered by Swiss private insurance companies offer protection against life's risks—old age, death, and disability—and form an integral part of the three-pillar concept established in the Swiss constitution (article 111) of retirement, survivors', and disability schemes based on compulsory as well as voluntary benefit plans. (See Table 3.1.)

TABLE 3.1 Retirement Benefit Plans

Pillar 1	Pillar 2	Pillar 3
Governmental Benefit Plan	Occupational Benefit Plan	Private Benefit Plans
Securing a person's livelihood	Preservation of accustomed living standard	Savings/investments and private insurnace/ annuities
Old-Age and Survivors' Insurance (OASI)	Accident Insurance Act (AI)	Linked private plan 3a
Disability Insurance Scheme (IV)	Federal Law on the Occupational Old-Age, Survivors', and Disability Benefit plan (LOB)	Voluntary private plan 3b
Supplementary benefits	Benefits beyond legal requirements	

Compulsory Insurance

Any person living or working in Switzerland falls under the mandatory coverage provided by the Old-Age and Survivors' Insurance (OASI) and Disability Insurance Scheme (IV), or "pillar 1" of the Swiss social safety net. In addition, from a certain minimum salary level onward, all employees in Switzerland are covered by the social insurance/employee benefit schemes pursuant to the Federal Law on the Occupational Old-Age, Survivors' and Disability Benefit Plans Act (LOB) and by coverage pursuant to the Accident Insurance Act (AI), both together forming "pillar 2" of the safety net.

Voluntary Insurance

Individuals can obtain supplementary, nonmandatory coverage by taking out a linked life insurance policy (paying into linked bank savings plans) or by taking advantage of pillar 3 coverage and savings offerings (life insurance, bank savings plans, etc.).

The term "linked" refers to the fact that those products offer tax advantages but are also subject to federal restrictions and provisions. Hence, this type of insurance serves the sole purpose of a benefit plan.

In pillar 2 (i.e., the occupational retirement benefit schemes), businesses can provide for their employees by taking out voluntary coverage that exceeds the compulsory LOB minimum coverage in the form of supplementary insurance and executive retirement plans. The self-employed have the option of contributing to their own voluntary pillar 2 savings.

Private Life Insurance

Private life insurance enables people to cover economic risks of life according to individual requirements. These requirements, along with a person's specific personal wishes, are decisive in obtaining coverage for benefits and protection, whether in connection with linked plans (pillar 3a) or with voluntary (nonlinked) plans (pillar 3b).

Life insurers are institutions offering persons insurance against risks. They essentially cover three risk categories:

1. Death of policyholder resulting from illness or accident; benefits in the form of a capital payment or survivor pensions
2. Disability of policyholder resulting from illness or accident; benefits usually in the form of daily allowances or pension payments, seldom also in the form of capital payments
3. Age of policyholder; benefits in the form of lump-sum payments in case of inheritance or in the form of temporary or lifelong pension payments

Most of the items listed under "Main Private Insurance Types Offered" (available in connection with life insurance policies for providing pillar 3b, or voluntary, nonlinked coverage) are also available in pillar 3a plans, or linked coverage, assuming that certain tax criteria are satisfied.

Main Private Insurance Types Offered

Mixed Insurance (Combined Endowment and Straight Life Insurance)

Mixed insurance, the most frequent type of cash-value insurance, offers combined coverage for old-age and surviving dependents (i.e., insurance providing for cash value buildup and a death benefit). A policy is concluded for an endowment or face value of CHF 80,000, which is paid out along with the accumulated bonuses or participating policy dividends at the age of 65. Should the insured person die before this time, the insured capital including the accumulated bonuses is paid out immediately to the designated beneficiaries.

Straight Life Insurance (Insurance Providing for a Death Benefit)

Straight life insurance provides for insurance benefits (lump-sum cash settlement or income payments) that are paid out to the beneficiary if the insured dies within the guarantee period (i.e., before the insurance term expires).

There are numerous options, depending on the needs and wishes of the insured (e.g., term life insurance with increasing or decreasing face values). In addition, fixed (constant) premiums or rolling premiums (recalculated every year on the basis of the increasing death risk associated with advancing age) are also available.

Retirement Annuities   Instead of a lump-sum cash benefit, regular retirement payments can be arranged that provide lifelong income in a specified amount for the life of the insured. Retirement annuities can generally be combined with protection for surviving dependents by taking out a policy on two lives, that is, a policy payable to two insured persons (e.g., continued payment of the full retirement benefit to the surviving widow), or a provision is made that all the remaining premiums that have been paid in but which were not drawn out as income payments be reimbursed to the beneficiaries (survivors) with no interest (annuity policy with a money-back guarantee).

It is never too late to arrange for annuities. The amount of retirement income payments financed by paying in a certain amount of capital is higher the older the insured person is when starting to draw the annuity payments. Furthermore, income tax is payable on only 40 percent of self-financed retirement income.

Disability Income Insurance   Whereas daily sickness and accident allowances are paid only during extended temporary disability or for a specified limited period (the disability impairing an individual's ability to earn a living, thus resulting in lost earned income), disability income insurance generally provides benefits for permanent disability to the age of 65 or 63/64 (i.e. until benefits can be collected under the OASI).

Other Insurance Types   Apart from the range of key offerings of private insurance companies, there is a wide variety of other life insurance policies. These include:

- Insurance policies providing for several scheduled payouts to the insured (cash-value life insurance plans with a graded endowment)
- Juvenile insurance (education endowment insurance)
- Unit- or index-linked policies (cash-value life insurance of which the benefits are dependent on the performance of unit shares or are linked to a stock index)
- Convertible insurance policies enabling the policyholder to change currencies during the term of the insurance

Unit-Linked Life Insurance   Under the header of unit-linked or nontraditional life insurance products, a clear trend has formed in recent years toward a group of products that allows insured persons to participate more actively in the developments on the financial markets. In most companies, the proportion of this type of insurance policy is still below 10 percent of total individual premiums. However, driven by the above-average performance of capital markets, the strong increase in the demand for such products will no doubt also increase their popularity with insurers.

Linked Private Plans (Pillar 3a)

By taking out a linked insurance policy, resident employed persons subject to Swiss tax liability have the option of acquiring extra protection for themselves while enjoying a number of tax reductions at the same time.

- Up to a certain amount, the premiums paid for linked coverage (exclusively and irrevocably used for providing for one's old age, premature death, or disability) can be deducted from the direct taxes payable at the federal, cantonal, and municipal level.
- The surrender value of a linked policy is not subject to net worth tax.
- The benefits are taxed as income when disbursed, but at a reduced rate and separately from a person's other income.

As of 2007, the amounts paid for retirement benefit plans can be deducted from occupational income in this way:

- Employees and self-employed persons who are already insured in pillar 2 (LOB): Maximum deduction: CHF 6,365.
- Employees and self-employed persons who are not insured in pillar 2 (LOB): Maximum deduction: CHF 31,824.

Contrary to the voluntary benefit plan, the linked benefit plan is subject to a one-time tax charge upon payment of the capital.

The deduction of annual premiums has more of an impact on reducing one's tax burden than the burden posed by taxes payable on benefits when disbursed.

However, such special tax treatment is subject to these funds being exclusively and irrevocably used to provide for one's old age, premature death, or disability. What does that mean for the insured?

- The benefits paid through the policy cannot be assigned nor can they be pledged or seized. Consequently, the group of beneficiaries who can be designated is limited.
- Advance payout of benefits is precluded.

■ Terminating provident schemes via advance drawings of the retirement benefits or surrendering the insurance policy is possible only as an exception (e.g., for contracting into a pension fund, going into self-employed business, leaving Switzerland for good).

■ Exceptions are also made when the funds are drawn for financing the purchase or construction of owner-occupied residential property or obtaining shares in same.

MARKET OVERVIEW AND DEVELOPMENT

In order to gain an overview of the Swiss life insurance market, we rely on the statistics published by the Federal Office for Private Insurance (FOPI) in 2005 and on the figures published by the companies themselves in their annual reports.

Twenty-seven insurance companies are subject to direct supervision by the "Life Insurance" division of the FOPI (as per 31 December 2005).

Another 10 life insurers from the Principality of Liechtenstein offering policies in Switzerland are supervised by the Financial Market Authority of the Principality of Liechtenstein. The insurance supervision activities of the Principality of Liechtenstein and Switzerland are mutually recognized and coordinated by means of an international treaty.

According to the Federal Office for Social Insurance (FOSI), life insurance companies in Switzerland insure a total of 1.83 million persons.[1]

Market Volume According to Gross Premiums

The figures published by the FOPI (see Figure 3.1) show that the direct Swiss insurance business amounts to a premium volume of approximately CHF 30 billion. Premiums recorded are at a level comparable to that of 1996/7. From 1998 to 2002, total premiums oscillated on a relatively high level, between CHF 31.3 and 34.7 billion, only to slump by 6 to 7 percent in 2003. Compared with the previous year, total premiums decreased again in 2005, by 1.5 percent.

The FOPI's "official figures" for 2006 were not available at the time of this writing. However, the individual company figures suggest that total gross premiums will again be slightly below those of the previous year. Otherwise, only minor changes are expected. In the individual insurance business, particularly products with lump-sum premiums are losing popularity, whereas annuity insurances with recurring premiums have improved. Unit-linked insurances maintained a continuous growth of approximately 5 percent, but the collective insurance business stagnated or decreased slightly.

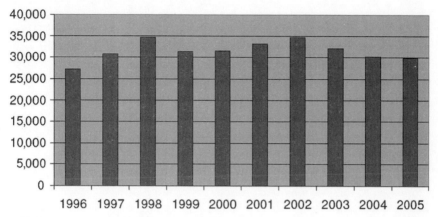

FIGURE 3.1   Life Insurance Market in Switzerland, 1996–2005 (in million CHF)

After the introduction of the 2.5 percent stamp duty in 1998, the volume of premiums for individual insurances experienced a sharp decline. In times of low interest, such additional burdens hold little attraction for clients.

The life insurance business makes up 59 percent of the premium volume of the entire Swiss insurance industry and is thus clearly its most important domain. Whereas most categories of indemnity insurance experienced an increase in premium volume in 2005, the life insurance sector dragged the Swiss total insurance volume down, which resulted in a combined decrease of 0.2 percent compared to the previous year.

Collective insurance schemes make up more than two-thirds of the entire premium volume of Swiss life insurers. This corresponds to a premium income of CHF 20 billion.[2]

When singling out the individual insurance business, 2005 was a year of growth at the favorable amount of 14.6 percent. However, the CHF 10.1 billion of recorded premiums represents a level that is still 38 percent below the all-time high of 1998 (CHF 16.4 billion). Both the capital insurance and annuity insurance branches are following the general shrinking trend. Capital insurance records at 54 percent below the 1998 high, annuity insurance at 46 percent. The apparent decline in the individual insurance business is countered with the increasing popularity of unit-linked life insurance. This product group also experienced a slump after 1998, but recorded an increase in premiums of 83 percent compared to the previous year (57 percent above the volume of 1998).

The importance of lump-sum premium insurances can be clearly determined: Lump sums in capital insurances are close to extinction (in 2005, they were already 87% below the level of 1998); lump sums in annuity insurances remained practically the same at a premium volume of 46 percent below that of 1998; and the same trend toward stability is observed with the growing unit-linked life insurances (i.e., lump sums increase at the same rate as the premiums).

In their annual reports, insurers themselves keep stating that the low interest level in Switzerland is the reason for the low demand for lump-sum contributions in individual life insurance policies (besides the stamp-duty issue mentioned earlier).

The collective life insurance business saw a slightly different development. Premiums from retirement benefit plans decreased by 8.2 percent compared to the previous year. Among other things, this decrease is the result of a number of insurance companies abandoning the collective insurance segment. However, this trend is also influenced by another aspect: There has been a strong trend in retirement benefits (pillar 2) toward independent collective insurance funds in recent years, to the debit of life insurers. In 2005 alone, approximately 200,000 insured persons followed that new trend.

Until 2004, the so-called interest risk deduction was considered to be "golden handcuffs" and deterred many companies. Due to the fact that life insurers were entitled to make hefty cuts in the policy reserve of companies that turned their backs to them in times of rising interest, it made little sense or was impossible for many employers to transfer their retirement benefit plans from one life insurer to another. The policy reserve reductions were usually substantiated with losses in the bond portfolio typical for rising interest rates. The life insurers charged the resulting book loss to departing clients. This interest risk deduction was a massive competitive obstacle, and the parliament, at its first revision of the LOB, decided that insurers may reduce policy reserve only if clients intend to bail out in the first five years of their contract.

This rule is to be reversed again in 2007. The Federal Council proposes to permit interest risk deduction for "extraordinary" interest circumstances, as otherwise the survival of life insurers might be at risk.[3]

The Swiss Insurance Association publishes annual statistics on the international density of insurance policies. Switzerland, with premiums of approximately US $5,600 per capita (excluding social security), is clearly top of the list. More than US $3,000 of this amount is spent for life insurance every year.

Market Shares and Participants

The Swiss life insurance market is dominated by large Swiss companies, despite the fact that two subsidiaries of foreign insurance groups, Allianz

TABLE 3.2   Life Insurance Market in Switzerland, Gross Premiums, 2005 (million CHF)

Company	Gross Premiums 2005
Swiss Life	7,949
AXA/Winterthur Leben	7,027
Basler Leben	2,655
Zürich Leben	2,200
Helvetia[1]	2,179
UBS Life	1,601
Allianz Suisse Leben	1,587
Generali Personenversicherungen	1,100
Pax	870
Genevoise Vie	696
Mobiliar Leben	654
Schweizerische National Leben	430
Vaudoise Vie	218
Others (14 companies)	607
TOTAL	29,773

[1]The FOPI's statistics for 2005 list its former name, "Patria." In our overview of market players, we are using the current name, "Helvetia."

Suisse Leben and Generali Personenversicherungen, hold substantial market shares. (See Table 3.2.) Since Winterthur Group was sold to AXA, this market participant is to be considered a mixture between the two types (both a traditional Swiss brand and under foreign control).

Together, Swiss Life and Winterthur Leben hold more than 50 percent of the market share and are thus clear market leaders. (See Figure 3.2.)

Overall, 27 life insurance companies are subject to supervision by the FOPI in Switzerland. Of them, 13 are considered "major" life insurers (more than CHF 200 million gross premiums per year). The negative growth of total gross premiums observed since the end of the 1990s is now accompanied by a concentration of market participants. In 1996, as many as 31 life insurance companies were active in the market.

Next we highlight some characteristics of the 13 most important life insurers. The information was compiled from the companies' annual reports.

Swiss Life   Together with AXA/Winterthur, Swiss Life is the market leader in the life business. Swiss Life Holding is domiciled in Zurich and emerged from Schweizerische Rentenanstalt, which was incorporated in 1857. Schweizerische Rentenanstalt was the first national company offering life insurance under Swiss law. The "Swiss Life" brand was introduced in

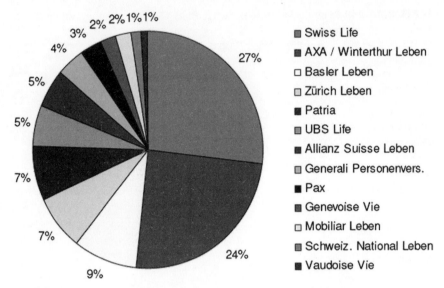

FIGURE 3.2   Life Insurance Market Shares in Switzerland, 2005

2004 and is intended to emphasize the company's positioning as a specialist in the financial retirement benefit business.

Upon incorporating La Suisse's life business, the group sold all other business areas of its former subsidiary.

In its 2006 annual report, the group considers itself to be a "focused European life insurer."

The collective insurance business accounts for 77 percent of approximately. CHF 8 billion gross life premiums. These CHF 8 billion correspond to 40 percent of the overall group premium volume. The remaining 60 percent are generated abroad.

As with most market participants, a clear increase in nontraditional (e.g.. fund-unit-linked) products characterized the past few years. For the time being, such nontraditional products make up no more than 3 percent of all individual insurance types (similar to direct competitors at the top of the major life insurers in Switzerland).

The group proceeds from the fact that in the years to come, market growth in private and occupational benefit plans will be much stronger than general market growth in Europe.

Swiss Life pursues a consistent multichannel strategy and has been relying increasingly on strategic cooperations in Switzerland (e.g., with Helsana, the leading health insurer, and Mobiliar, the leading property insurer). Such a strategy facilitates access to new client groups. With its subsidiary, Banca del Gottardo, the Swiss Life group is also active in private banking.

AXA/Winterthur Leben   Winterthur was a part of Credit Suisse Group until 2006, when it was sold to AXA. In terms of size (gross premiums in 2005: CHF 7.0 billion), it is Swiss Life's direct competitor at the top of the market. Third-ranked Basel Leben is about two-thirds smaller.

Since we used the FOPI's official figures of 2005 for our market overview, AXA Vie must be mentioned at this point. In the 2005 statistics, it is still listed as an independent company with gross premiums of CHF 179 million The largest part of AXA Vie's income (74 percent) was generated in the individual capital insurance business.

Winterthur's gross premiums are mostly made up by proceeds from the collective insurance business (83 percent). With CHF 6 million premiums from the collective insurance business, Winterthur is almost at the same level (in absolute CHF amounts) as the industry leader, Swiss Life, although the latter's portion from the collective business is slightly smaller (77 percent). Hence, the two control more than 60 percent of the collective insurance business in Switzerland.

Basler Leben   In 2005, Baloîse generated 70 percent (CHF 2.7 billion) of the group's life business in Switzerland. In principle, its activities abroad are limited to Germany and Belgium. Sixty-eight percent of the Swiss business consists of collective insurance schemes.

Like Zürich Leben, which is comparable in both size and positioning, Basler is faced with the problem of being in the third or fourth rank, respectively, without being able to focus on special market niches. The company performs below average in all segments (collective, capital, annuity or fund-unit-linked life insurance). According to its self-portrayal, Basler Leben is mainly a driving force in the full-value insurance segment (collective insurance).

Basler Leben's banking partner for the distribution and investment of assets is Bank SoBa.

Zürich Leben   According to FOPI's statistics for 2005, Zürich Leben is number four in the Swiss market (gross premiums at CHF 2.2 billion). However, its annual report ranks the company as the "third-largest life insurer in Switzerland" and discloses an amount of CHF 2.8 billion. This statistic is an anticipation of the full absorption of Genevoise in the next year, while the FOPI statistic separates the two companies and lists Genevoise with a premium volume of approximately CHF 700 million.

Similar to its direct competitor, approximately 70 percent of its premium volume is generated in the collective insurance business. Another similar feature is that despite the growing importance of unit-linked policies, the volume of these nontraditional products is still relatively modest. At Zürich

Leben, unit-linked products make up a mere 5 percent of all individual insurance policies.

For its distribution, Zürich Leben relies heavily on a mix of all distribution channels to which the group has access, such as brokers, independent financial consultants, and banks.

Helvetia The group has been appearing on the market under the uniform name of *Helvetia* and a standard Europe-wide logo since September 2006. Its previous name, *Helvetia Patria,* has been abandoned. On a group-wide level, 54 percent of gross premiums are generated with the life business, of which 78 percent is in Switzerland.

In this group, too, 70 percent (CHF 2.2 billion) of its overall premiums in the Swiss life business are generated with the collective insurance business. Hence, in 2005, the collective life insurance segment was one of the driving elements at Helvetia.

Compared to other (larger) peers, unit-linked products make up a more substantial part of its individual insurance policies: 14 percent. However, according to figures already available for 2006, this trend has weakened again (13 percent).

Helvetia, too, benefits from a number of strategic cooperations in Switzerland. For the individual life insurance segment, this is primarily the Swiss Association of Raiffeisen Banks (SVRB). For occupational retirement benefit plans, continued favorable growth rates in the collective funds of Swisscanto were achieved together with the Association of Swiss Cantonal Banks.

UBS Life UBS Life is an unusual market player insofar as its entire business of approximately CHF 1.6 billion is generated in the unit-linked life business (except for a relatively negligible volume of capital insurance policies with gross premiums of less than CHF 5 million); more than 99 percent of them are lump-sum premiums. UBS Life therefore has a business model that is fundamentally different from that of the other life insurers. It hardly depends on recurring annual premiums. The company's enormous growth in the past years can be explained by the access to various distribution channels within the UBS banking group.

Allianz Suisse Leben This large German insurance group with its Swiss subsidiary, Allianz Suisse, stated in its press release of March 14, 2007:

> *From this year onwards, the life insurance segment is Allianz Suisse's core business. This upgrade results in a number of initiatives that are in the process of being realised. Our focus is on new competitive*

products in the individual and collective life business. A new fund-unit-linked life insurance product will be launched in the next few days. The collective life insurance business (retirement benefit plans) will also soon feature new product lines; they are primarily tailored to the needs of small and micro-enterprises (e.g. start-ups) and to SMEs.

Overall, Allianz Suisse generates a volume of CHF 1.6 billion in its life business in Switzerland, of which 61 percent is in the collective insurance segment. In its individual insurance business, 35 percent stems from nontraditional products.

Similar to Basler Leben, Allianz relies heavily on full-value insurance in the collective insurance business.

The Allianz group in Switzerland also includes Phénix, Compagnie d'assurances sur vie in Lausanne. They earned approx. CHF 44 million in premiums in 2005.

Generali Personenversicherungen   Sixty-four percent of Generali's premiums in Switzerland is earned with the life insurance business: 96 percent in the individual and 3.5 percent in the discontinued collective life insurance business. In mid-2001, Generali decided to focus its energy on the individual life business and phase out the collective business, which had been showing poorer and poorer margins. Seventy-seven percent of the individual life premiums are earned with fund-unit-linked insurances.

Thus, holding a market share of over 50 percent, Generali is the market leader for its core product, the fund-unit-linked insurance. It has been a leading specialist since 1990. In the linked private plan (pillar 3a) sector, Generali has absorbed more than 60 percent of the total new business.

Generali, too, operates a consistent multichannel distribution strategy. Since there is no obvious strong banking partner within the Generali group, Generali started a cooperation with the Migros group for its distribution in Switzerland.

PAX   The life insurance business is the core activity of PAX. Compared to the CHF 871 million in gross life premiums, the group's income from health insurance amounts but to a fraction. With 59 percent of its premiums stemming from the collective insurance business, PAX is slightly below the market average.

Among Swiss life insurers, PAX is selling the largest portion of unit-linked products in individual insurances (37 percent of all individual insurance premiums).

The company operates with a mixed distribution that focuses on brokers but includes other partners, such as health insurance companies and other insurers.

Genevoise Vie   Since we rely primarily on FOPI figures from 2005, we still include Genevoise Vie as a separate insurance company. As a consequence of the reorganization of its global strategy in the life insurance business, Zurich Financial Services Group combined Genevoise's activities with those of Zürich Lebensversicherungsgesellschaft in 2006. Thus, Genevoise fully abandoned its former business activity. Genevoise also withdrew its brand from the market.

In 2005, Genevoise recorded gross premiums of CHF 696 million, of which 69 percent were generated with collective insurance policies. This is the reflection on a small scale of its parent, Zürich Leben.

Mobiliar Leben   For Mobiliar, the life insurance business is a much smaller area than the nonlife segment. Seventy-four percent of premiums earned were generated in the indemnity segment (CHF 2.0 billion), CHF 654 million in life. Within the life business, only 53 percent of gross premiums are related to collective insurance schemes. Mobiliar is a Swiss insurer that focuses exclusively on markets in Switzerland and Liechtenstein. Its special focus is on risk insurance.

In 2005, Mobiliar renamed the well-established brand of its life business, Providentia, to Mobiliar in order to be able to benefit further from this strong brand.

The company describes reinsuring personnel welfare institutions as its most important business area. In 2005, approximately 35 percent of all partially autonomous personnel welfare institutions were insured with Mobiliar. In the occupational retirement benefit segment, part of the business is shifting from insurance companies to independent collective foundations. Mobiliar considers this shift to be potential new business in the reinsurance business.

The portion of unit-linked products in individual life premiums amounts to 22 percent and is thus of essence for Mobiliar.

Schweizerische National Leben   Overall, Schweizerische National Leben recorded approximately CHF 430 million in gross premiums in 2005. National's collective insurance business is also below the average (54 percent) compared with its peers.

In the individual life insurance business, National is the bottom of its league with regard to unit-linked products. Such products generate merely slightly more than CHF 1 million.

Vaudoise Vie According to premiums earned, Vaudoise Vie is the smallest of the 13 life insurers presented in this market overview (gross premiums CHF 218 million), particularly since it focuses exclusively on the individual insurance business and no longer offers collective insurance products. However, considering the individual insurance business on a stand-alone basis, its premium volume would be larger than Genevoise's or National's. In 2005, Vaudoise transferred its entire collective insurance business to Swiss Life and absorbed Swiss Life's former individual insurance segment.

As the company's domicile is in Lausanne, it is hardly surprising that most of Vaudoise's clientele is in French-speaking Switzerland. It is interesting to know that Vaudoise's subsidiary in Liechtenstein, Valorlife, generated premiums of more than CHF 820 million—this is almost four times the volume in Vaudoise's home market, Switzerland.

Other Companies Skandia Leben did not make it to the list of the "big 13" since it sells exclusively nontraditional products. With a unit-linked premium volume of CHF 146 million, it is in the top 10 of this specific segment.

MARKET TRENDS AND MARKET DRIVERS

What is going to happen to the life insurance industry in Switzerland? There was a continuous decline in premiums in the past few years (2004–2006). However, this trend weakened with each year, and at the annual press conference on the 2006 financial year, the president of the Swiss Insurance Association expressed his hopes that this trend has reached its bottom and that a stabilization will take place.

Distribution Channels

According to a recently published survey[4], brokers see themselves as the big winners in distribution in the years to come. And indeed the insurance companies plan to rely mostly on brokers and independent distribution channels. Brokers expect their greatest challenge to come from financial planners, but not via direct distribution or the Internet. Hence, it is less surprising that the brokers themselves make relatively little use of the Internet for their activities, their knowledge transfer, or specific training. Instead, the traditional personal appointment is still their preferred method, closely followed by telephone calls. In the settlement of their transactions, too, new technologies and the Internet play only a small role.

In the brokerage business, a kind of subterranean, slow-moving consolidation is taking place. Most brokers state that they intend to grow in the near future. The ideal broker business size of six or more staff is usually strived for. A strong beneficial effect of combinations within broker networks and pools is also being mentioned.

Since the introduction of the Federal Law on the Supervision of Insurance Companies on January 1, 2006, acting as a broker is subject to minimum requirements. Brokers expect insurance companies to support them directly in the necessary basic and specific training. Here, too, traditional channels such as technical magazines and personal networks are used much more than the Internet.

Client-Focused strategy

In their annual reports, virtually all insurance companies make gearing their businesses toward their clients' needs one of their main concerns. Basler places particular emphasis on this aspect, having introduced its "client value model." This behavior marks a clear turning away from the traditional product orientation. According to Basler, it is not so much the product itself that has a profile on the market but much rather the quality of the services rendered by the individual employees of an insurance company. In addition, client satisfaction surveys such as Helvetia's are very popular with clients.

Literature uses the term "customisation," the tailoring of an offer to a certain client profile. By considering the needs of an individual client, companies are trying to play on the product's emotional appeal. However, this is successful only if the client is actively involved in its relationship with the insurer.

The crucial factor is to find out what exactly the client wants as an individual. Different types of insured persons have different needs, but these general trends should be considered:

- Most clients want to deal with the insurance company as little as possible.
- While clients' expectations rise, they are not prepared to pay more.

An ideal mix for the future must be found in this triangle of emotions, wanting to be left in peace, and costs without additional income.

Employees

In 2005, life insurance companies under FOPI supervision in Switzerland employed a total of 9,364 persons. Of these, 7,384 were office staff and 1,980 were field staff. As with premiums, the total staff number has experienced a decrease of 20 percent since its high of 12,341 employees in 2000. However, this statistic issued by the FOPI is not entirely representative, as it does not contain any data on AXA/Winterthur. Furthermore, it is extremely difficult to make a clear distinction between employees of the life and the nonlife segment in certain companies. We will not comment further on the FOPI's division into office and field staff, as such separation might not give full credit to the very diverse company models.

According to the Swiss Insurance Association (SIA), a total of 45,606 persons were employed in private insurance.

Comparing recorded premiums with reported numbers of personnel gives a very interesting perspective. Premiums per employee range from CHF 1.6 million (Zürich, Generali, National) to CHF 4.4 million (Allianz). Due to its business model, UBS Life is the big exception again with CHF 64 million per employee.

In the increasingly tight Swiss labor market, insurance companies place more and more importance on the quality of their employees. In this context, Zürich describes the current situation as being characterized by talent management.

Outsourcing and Shared Service Centers

As with all other financial services segments, outsourcing and shared service centers are late-breaking issues in the life insurance business. This trend is further supported by the fact that the players in the Swiss market are members of internationally active groups. However, nationally active companies such as PAX have also started outsourcing parts of their business divisions, such as information technology.

Many experts think that, to date, we have only seen the tip of the iceberg with regard to the offshoring trends in the financial industry. While the existing offshore centers have traditionally engaged in back-office functions that had set features, such as being standardizable and modular, the most recent trend takes this segment further, clearly heading toward active business-generating revenue.

Offshoring is often a hazardous undertaking: Differences between the mentality and culture of the home market and the offshore center can be real obstacles in the practical realization of individual projects. There are rather clear-cut limits to any activities beyond the back-office function in offshore life businesses.

Swiss Solvency Test/Solvency II

An insurance company requires capital in order to be able to bear risks for its clients, the people it insures. The Swiss solvency test (SST) is a principle-based system that was developed using market-consistent valuation methods. It is intended to determine the available capital and the capital required to cover the relevant risks.

The results of previous field testing (since 2004) show that the market risk is the prevailing risk and that, on average, the capital requirements assessed in the SST are double the amount of the previous Solvency I requirements. By 2008, all companies active in Switzerland will have to adhere to the SST.

The European Union is in the process of developing and implementing the new regulatory and principles-based solvency provisions under the name of Solvency II. The Solvency II framework was published in July 2007, with implementation planned in 2010.

Embedded Value

The embedded value concept was conceived from the demand for better valuation in the life business. However, no real standard has emerged from the competing models of the traditional or European embedded value, so that any embedded value figures published in the annual reports of the insurance companies still cannot be compared properly. Rather, the calculation bases and models have to be interpreted in detail, especially because they are subject to changes every year even within the same company, while the standard is still only being developed.

Most large insurance companies publish an embedded value in their annual reports, often accompanied by the assumptions used.

Process Optimization and Cost Management

In the annual reports of both 2005 and 2006, most companies rank process optimization and tight cost management as the top priority for the present and for the future.

For this, several approaches can be applied. For example, Swiss Life has reduced its administrative systems to one information technology platform in each of the collective and individual insurance segments. At Mobiliar, the various individual life insurance applications are consolidated.

Zürich, on the other hand, is benefiting from its introduction of best practices to its core processes. This and an international network of service partners in more than 120 countries has enabled the company to increase the productivity of its life agents active in Switzerland by 20 percent. The importance of international networks is also reflected in the way Zürich develops new products. Products with a possibly large impact on the risk situation are developed by local developing task forces but must be approved by a global committee.

By building a cross-border competence centered in its unit-linked life business and centralizing the investment management, Helvetia is following a similar path.

Allianz focuses more on strengthening the cooperation with its sister company in Austria.

Consolidation/Mergers and Acquisitions

When Credit Suisse sold its insurance division to French AXA, it substantiated this move by stating that Winterthur was too small to survive on its own.[5] But where does this leave all the other market players in Switzerland, which are even smaller or at least not substantially larger themselves?

Since the crisis in 2001, most insurance companies have gained enough earning power to grow by acquisition. According to Winterthur's chief executive officer, consolidation in Europe is being driven much more than in the United States. In the meantime, the same service guidelines apply throughout the continent.

It is a peculiarity of the Swiss market that some smaller companies are organized as cooperatives (e.g., Mobiliar, Vaudoise); this makes combinations and acquisitions more complex.

50-plus Target Group

Today's senior citizens are healthier, wealthier, and much more active than previous generations. This makes them a very attractive target group for insurance products. Although the market for insurance products for the elderly is as heterogenous as the present generation of 50-plus itself, more and more insurance companies have started developing new products specifically for this target group.

The main feature for 50-plus insurance schemes is less the provident nature of their products but a safeguarding or even improvement of the standard of living in the third chapter of life. Upon their retirement, insured persons often wish to be accompanied more closely as their need for security and protection against risks increases with age. They place high importance on maintaining personal contact with their insurance agents and appreciate unsolicited explanations and information on new risks and insurance products. This is a direct contradiction to the current trend of outsourcing insurance segments to client portals and the Internet, a trend that may be very much oriented toward the demands of young clients but misses the needs of the majority of the population who are over 50.

A survey reveals that only 36 percent of insurance companies have begun to develop products tailored to the needs of persons over 50 years. Only every third insurer offers financial consulting especially for older people. Seventy-eight percent of insurers have no facilities to support senior citizens in inheritance and testamentary questions, and only 21 percent offer advice on security and accident prevention.

In Germany, the "Ideal" insurance group has established itself as a market leader for insurance products for senior citizens. Items such as long-term care insurance for the elderly are a recognized standard product; to date, however, no equivalent product is offered in Switzerland. Ideal went even further in its specialization in the German market; it absorbed the largest German funeral service company and is planning to build its own nursing homes.

In Switzerland, the former Fortuna (now part of Generali) recognized the potential of a market for the elderly 30 years ago but was not able to turn this into significant benefits. The main difficulty at the time was that the elderly did want products and services that were tailored to their needs, and they had a serious problem with being called "elderly."

At present, Helvetia intends to become the undisputed number one expert for the "50-plus" segment in Switzerland. Its current difficulty lies in the fact that the majority of insurance agents have had no experience with long-term care insurance and the like and can therefore not supply adequate advice. According to Helvetia, already every second client is over 50 years old.

Demographic aging in Switzerland offers an enormous market potential for insurance products for the elderly. According to a scenario established by the Federal Statistics Office, the number of 65-year-olds and older will rise by 90 percent, to 2.2 million, by 2050. The number of people over 80 will increase in particular, with this group's share of the total population rising from 4 to 12 percent.

Compared with the average of all persons insured, the senior citizen target group offers a number of advantages:

- Older people are much more concerned about risks.
- Senior citizens often have a better payment behavior.
- They are clearly less price-sensitive.
- As retirees, they are available for consultations and meetings during the day.
- In addition to a low risk of cancellations, the elderly are often wealthy.

"Bancassurance" versus Cooperative Agreements

At the end of the 1990s, "bancassurance," or one-stop finance, was a buzzword. In Switzerland, Credit Suisse paid a fortune to incorporate Winterthur and thus have its share in the insurance market. Financial services and products needed to be as comprehensive as possible and available under the same roof. Today, upon the divestiture of Winterthur to AXA in 2006, these considerations seem to be a thing of the past—for good. However, a clear trend is now emerging of entering into cooperative agreeements with financial service providers. Almost no insurance company does not have close ties with an independent bank or other financial institute.

As the parent of Banca del Gottardo, Swiss Life even has a banking partner within its own group. It goes without saying that this bond is even closer with UBS Life. And Basler Leben cooperates closely with SoBa, while Allianz has entered an alliance with the various cantonal banks. Helvetia, too, has agreements with the cantonal banks (its collective insurance business, Swisscanto) and also works with the Swiss Association of Raiffeisenbanken.

There are also cooperative agreements outside the pure banking sector, such as Generali's with the Migros group. In this way, Generali benefits not only from Migrosbank's know-how but also from the latter's huge network of retail shops throughout Switzerland.

And finally, the insurance sector itself also offers opportunities for cooperation, as seen in Mobiliar's ties with PAX and Swiss Life.

CHAPTER 4

Insurance Regulation in Switzerland

Monica Mächler

Director, Swiss Federal Office
of Private Insurance, Bern

The Federal Office of Private Insurance (FOPI) is the regulatory authority for the business operations of private insurance companies and insurance intermediaries in Switzerland. The scope of supervision exercised by FOPI comprises the areas of life insurance, non-life insurance, and reinsurance including supplemental private health insurance.

As of January 1, 2006, a new, risk-based supervision regime is in force. It has been developed by FOPI and is enacted in a modern, totally revised Insurance Supervision Act (ISA) and the associated Supervision Ordinance (SO).

PRIVATE INSURANCE SUPERVISION IN SWITZERLAND

Insurance regulation applies to companies set up under private law that engage in the activity of insurance in Switzerland. Excluded are the pension and health schemes under social security law and certain other activities.

NEW SYSTEM OF INSURANCE REGULATION

New Orientation of Supervision

The focus of supervision continues to be the protection of insured parties, that is, the protection of the interests of clients of Swiss insurance companies against insurer insolvency and abusive practices. At the same time, the Swiss parliament has in recent years deliberately favored a liberalization of the insurance market, which allows insurance companies to maintain their comparative advantages in an increasingly competitive international environment and to promote their attractiveness in global markets. The ongoing convergence of insurance markets not only creates new challenges for insurers. It also prompts the development of international supervision. The new Insurance Supervision Act has paid particular attention to these challenges, focusing as it does on the supervision of the risks arising from these developments. As a consequence, FOPI has had to address the question of how to tackle new actuarial and financial risks proactively. The goal now is to develop a set of tools that pinpoint the risks relevant to the solvency of insurers early on.

Quantitative and Qualitative Examination of the Risks

Risk-based supervision takes these requirements into account. The Swiss Solvency Test (SST) constitutes its core element. The SST is a new approach to ascertaining the ability of insurers to manage risks. It provides for determining a target capital that is necessary for an insurer to survive the risks assumed with adequate probability. The SST primarily pursues two objectives:

1. Capital needs have to be established based on an assessment of all risks inherent in the total balance sheet of the company. Thus, risk management in insurance companies should be promoted intensively.
2. The target capital has to function as a warning signal. If the available risk-bearing capital is less than the necessary target capital, this does not mean that the enterprise is insolvent. Rather, either the necessary capital must be built up over a certain period of time or the risks are to be reduced correspondingly.

In addition to the central questions of reserves and solvency, the new regime establishes a further dimension of supervision: increased attention to the qualitative review of the various risks.

The models complementing the SST are therefore deliberately embedded in an overall, comprehensive assessment of the general risk of company management. Those tools are dedicated to the organizational processes and primarily supervise the qualitative aspects of the insurer's overall business organization. They are also intended to motivate the insurance companies to initiate ongoing internal improvement processes. The key idea behind this model is self-supervision and self-assessment based on relevant requirements of the supervisory authority. Nonetheless, the authorities will intervene if the self-assessment leads to unsatisfactory results. This form of qualitative supervision is especially suited to the processes of corporate governance, risk management, internal controls, and, at a later stage, business processes such as claims management

Revised Insurance Supervision Act

The new orientation of insurance supervision is at the core of the new Insurance Supervision Act. The main goals of the act are to secure the long-term stability of the insurance companies and to improve the protection of insured parties.

With the entry into force of the new ISA, the Swiss Solvency Test has been introduced as the fundamental model for assessing the ability of insurers to handle risks and corresponding capital needs. Transition periods are provided to adjust to the requirements under the SST.

The new ISA in general replaces preventive product checking with principle-based methods and monitoring to protect the insured. The monitoring includes, for example, inspections at the insurance companies and supplementary reporting. Furthermore, through the introduction of the SST stricter solvency monitoring has been introduced. In the socially sensitive areas of occupational pensions and supplemental health insurance, the preventive approval of products will, however, continue unchanged.

The new ISA makes insurance intermediaries (e.g. brokers and agents) subject to supervision. The main goal is to establish a public register of regulated insurance intermediaries. Inclusion in this register is mandatory for all intermediaries who are not bound to one particular insurer. The new regulations impose various requirements concerning expertise and personal qualifications. The main driver for this change has been customer protection.

The new ISA also creates the explicit legal foundation for the supervision of insurance groups and conglomerates, and it expands the supervisory responsibilities in the areas of corporate governance, transparency, and consumer protection. In particular, disclosure requirements on insurance companies have been increased considerably. In addition, all insurance companies are required to designate a responsible actuary. The responsible actuary ensures that there are sufficient technical provisions at all times, and according to Article 2 of the FOPI Ordinance is responsible for the technical part of the business, having to report at least once a year to the management of the company in this regard.

Reinsurers are now subject to almost the same solvency supervision as direct insurers.

Facts and Figures

With an annual premium volume of about CHF 7,100 per capita (direct insurances without social contributions), Switzerland has the highest insurance ratio in the world. The premium volume of Swiss private insurance in 2005 amounted to approximately CHF 187 billion worldwide, about 70 percent of which originated abroad. The sector employed about 135,000 people in 2005, of whom approximately 92,800 worked outside of Switzerland. As of December 31, 2006, 216 private insurance and reinsurance institutions were subject to the supervision by FOPI: 101 Swiss and 45 foreign direct insurers and 70 Swiss reinsurers. Of the direct insurance institutions, 27 were life insurers (4 of which were foreign) and 119 were non–life insurers. In addition, FOPI supervised the supplementary health insurance operations of a total of 48 health insurance plans.

SUPERVISION OF ANNUITY AND LIFE INSURANCE ACTIVITY IN PARTICULAR

The main responsibilities in the supervision of life insurers correspond to the responsibilities in all branches of supervision of private insurance:

- Licensing of insurance operations
- Review and approval of business plans
- Ongoing supervision of insurance operations
- Review of annual regulatory reports
- Review of solvency (Solvency I and SST)
- Review of reports on technical provisions and tied assets
- Withdrawal of license, termination of insurance operations

With the exception of coverage for occupational pension plans, the tariffs and general conditions of insurance (GCI) for life insurance policies no longer need to be approved in advance by FOPI. Even though there is no longer an approval requirement, FOPI is still authorized to conduct reviews and inspections to ensure that the GCI applied conform to the law and that the tariffs applied neither disadvantage the policy holders nor endanger the solvency of the insurance company.

In the area of coverage for occupational pension plans, however, the so-called preventive approval requirement still holds. This means that the rates and terms for occupational pension plans must be submitted to FOPI before they are offered on the market. FOPI verifies whether the terms conform to the law and whether the premiums fall within a range that protects policy holders from abuse, and that the solvency of the insurer is secured.

Important elements of life insurance supervision include the monitoring of technical reserves and reserves (Articles 16–20 of the Insurance Supervision Act and Articles 54–67 and 70–95 of the Supervision Ordinance) and of the solvency margin (Solvency I, SST). Articles 23 to 26 and 37 to 40 of the Supervision Ordinance describe how the solvency margin of life insurers is calculated.

The "Life Insurance" division supplements its supervisory function with the inspection of the supervised life insurers. It also responds to requests for information and complaints from policy holders. In the area of occupational pensions, special coordination and cooperation with other regulatory authorities of the federal government (e.g., Federal Social Insurance Office, FSIO) and the cantons is necessary. FSIO and the cantonal regulatory authorities supervise institutions offering occupational pension schemes.

OCCUPATIONAL PENSION SCHEMES

Social Insurance System in Switzerland

The Swiss social insurance system is essentially based on three pillars: the Old Age and Survivors' Insurance, which, together with the Disability Insurance, cover the basic needs of the insured persons and constitute the first pillar. Only with the Federal Law on Occupational Benefit Plans concerning Old-age, Survivors and Invalidity, which entered into force on 1 January 1985, did the parliament introduce a guaranteed minimum pension and mandatory coverage as a second pillar. Together with the first pillar, the performance target is to achieve a retirement income of about 60 percent of the last salary—a goal that is met in practice but not laid down precisely in the law. The third pillar consists of personal savings plans, aimed at increasing retirement income according to personal needs and desires. It is voluntary and enjoys tax advantages.

Second Pillar: Occupational Insurance and Pension Plans

Autonomous Pension Funds and Collective Institutions   Pension funds have existed in Switzerland for over 100 years. In particular, the machine industry instituted such schemes at an early stage. As long as occupational pensions were voluntary, only those employees whose employers had their own pension fund enjoyed protection. This changed in 1985: The mandatory coverage of the Pension Act covers all employees with an annual income of at least CHF 19,890 (as of 2007).

Employers without their own pension funds can affiliate their plans with collective occupational pension plans. These collective plans include backup plans, pension plan associations, and collective institutions. There are autonomous collective institutions and those covered by private life insurers. The collective plans are subject to the Federal Law on Occupational Benefit Plans concerning Old-age, Survivors and Invalidity and are under the supervision of the FSIO.

The collective institutions covered by the private life insurers have only limited assets of their own. Normally, the life insurers offer the pension systems full coverage of all savings and risk benefits. In particular, the life insurer guarantees payment of the minimum interest on the old age credit balance subject to mandatory Pension Act coverage. In addition, the life insurer converts this balance into guaranteed pensions according to the pension conversion rate specified by the Pension Act once retirement age is reached. The capital investments remain with the insurer and are invested in accordance with the requirements of the ISA.

Differences between Private Life Insurers and Pension Funds   Investments for occupational pensions total approximately CHF 600 billion in Switzerland. Of these, CHF 120 billion are covered by life insurers on behalf of the reinsured pension schemes. Private life insurers differ from pension funds in several essential points.

In addition to technical provisions, private life insurers must have their own funds in the form of equity capital and reserves, indexed to their business volume (Article 9 of the ISA) (Solvency I) and now also assessed according to their risk structure (SST). Such requirements do not apply to pension funds and collective institutions. By continuously monitoring the fulfilment of own funds requirements for private life insurers, timely measures can be taken in the event of undesired developments, so that insufficient coverage can be prevented in the case of life insurers, in contrast to pension schemes. This means that FOPI already takes corrective measures when the funds of a life insurer fall below a certain threshold. Currently, this threshold is calculated according to preestablished requirements. In the future, it will be estimated and determined even more precisely according to a risk-based approach. This ensures that strict protective measures benefiting the policy holders are initiated long before a life insurer's coverage becomes insufficient.

Transparency Requirements   As part of the first LPP revision, the parliament has adopted new transparency requirements for occupational pensions.

These requirements entered into force on April 1, 2004, and are now part of the new ISA, so they also affect life insurers. In addition, further transparency provisions expressly included in the Pension Law are aimed at private life insurers that conclude insurance contracts for occupational pensions:

The three main thrusts of the transparency requirements are:

1. A separate safety fund for occupational pensions
2. Since the 2005 fiscal year, requirement for a separate annual business accounting report for occupational pensions, containing in particular a compilation of administrative and sales costs; and also information on returns on capital investments, the calculation of the minimum conversion rate, and further important information
3. Rules to determine and distribute surplus sharing and introduction of a minimum payout rate for occupational pension insurance contracts subject to surplus sharing

CHAPTER 5

The Role and Supervision of Swiss Insurance Brokers

Moritz W. Kuhn

Partner, Meyer Müller Eckert, Zurich

The development of independent insurance brokers is closely linked to the recent history of the insurance business. In 1990, the then antitrust commission (now known as the competition commission) ordered the commercial insurance cartels to be dissolved. Only a short time later, the tariff agreements in the life insurance business were wound up. This laid the cornerstone for an open and competitive insurance market in Switzerland. From 1993, the relevant Swiss supervisory law was adapted in stages to European Union (EU) law. At the same time, efforts were made to completely revise the Swiss supervisory law. This was particularly necessary because the law was made up of numerous individual regulations and was thus far from transparent. A number of laws came into force on January 1, 2006: not only the new federal law on the supervision of insurance companies of December 17, 2004[1] but also the order on the supervision (AVO) of private insurance companies of November 9, 2005,[2] and the order of the Federal Office of Private Insurance (FOPI) of November 9, 2005.[3] The AVO-FOPI imposed supervision on independent insurance brokers by the FOPI for the first time. The partial amendment of December 17, 2004, of the federal law on insurance contracts dating from April 2, 1908 (VVG), also came into force on January 1, 2006.[4]

The amended Article 3 and 3a revised VVG, which impose the obligation on insurers to provide pre-contractual information, came into force on January 1, 2007.

The preliminary draft for a total amendment of the VVG (VE-VVG) of July 31, 2006 was prepared by an expert commission of the Federal Council. The VE-VVG also stipulates changes in various provisions of the Insurance Control Act VAG (VE-VAG); it was published in autumn 2006.[5]

DEREGULATION IN EUROPE AND SWITZERLAND

European Developments

Abolition of Preventive GTCI and Tariff Checks   The liberalization and deregulation of the European insurance supervision law that began in Europe at the end of the 1980s led to an integrated European insurance market. A key factor was the coming into force of the third coordination directives for life and non-life business (3. KoRL L and NL) in the EU on July 1, 1994. According to the directives, insurers in the retail and consumer sector no longer had to submit their general terms and conditions of insurance (GTCI), tariffs, and underlying technical procedures to the responsible supervisory authorities for authorization before applying them.

The earlier type of insurance supervision involving the government's preventive authorization of conditions and control of premiums prevented, to a certain extent, genuine price competition while favoring the cartel formation typical of the insurance business and leading to an oligo-political market structure (few big insurance companies, few small, specialized, insurance companies). Experience has shown that competitive pressure is stronger in a less regulated market, as was the case in both England and the Netherlands from an earlier date. Additionally the framework conditions of the supervisory laws and the economy as a whole make it easier for interested parties to gain a foothold in these domestic markets. With the new laws, tougher price and premium competition is to be expected, a situation that often leads to insolvencies and insurance bankruptcies in countries with liberal insurance supervision. Therefore, considerable differences exist among the EU countries to the present regarding the extent of their insurance supervision and its application in practice.

The consistent elimination of the preliminary control of the underlying GTCI, tariff, and technical procedures has given insurers much greater scope in configuring their insurance portfolios.

Price Competition, Product Content, and a Higher Degree of Transparency
In the 1990s, the market was increasingly characterized by tougher, sometimes ruinous, price competition, numerous products, and less transparency for consumers.

Home-Country Control and Single License System   Analogously to bank supervision, the 3. KoRL L and NL implemented uniform home-country control across the EU combined with the single license system for all risks and products. Accordingly, now the supervisory authority of the home country completely supervises an insurance company's activities within the EU, whether these activities concern local insurance business carried out at the head office or at a branch office, or business conducted via the cross-border services traffic in the country where the activity takes place. A single license (approval) then also permits a life or non-life insurer to set up branches and agency networks in all other EU countries or to simultaneously offer products via the freedom of services (cross-border business) provision directly from the head office as well as from branches in the EU in the country where this activity takes place. The supervisory authorities of the country in which the head office is located (home-country control) may carry out on-the-spot tests within the scope of its financial or solvency supervision, either directly or via local agents in the country where the activity takes place.

Financial and Solvency Supervision   The EU has decided, on the basis of the liberal supervision system traditionally applied in Great Britain, the Netherlands, and Belgium, to introduce financial and solvency supervision at a pan-European level, thus abolishing the system of strict substantive insurance supervision found especially in Germany and Switzerland. As already mentioned, the introduction of the solvency system allowed the preventive GTCI and tariff checking, which represent a significant feature of substantive insurance supervision, to be abandoned.

This innovation means the introduction of a multistage continuous checking procedure oriented to the second bank coordination directive that comprises all insurance business within the scope of the establishment law and the free movement of services to the same extent.

The financial or solvency supervision of an insurance company includes in particular a determination of its solvency, actuarial reserves as well as representative assets in line with the regulations or practices found in the home country on the basis of specifications issued at EU level for the company's overall business activity.

The solvency range stipulates a minimum of own funds (equity capital; expected profits; hidden reserves on real estate and securities, etc.). Solvency must be guaranteed up to the amount of the minimum guarantee fund, or the authorization to operate will be revoked. The responsible authority of the home country may also insist that every insurance company has to have regular administration and accounting departments and to run appropriate internal checking procedures (controlling). Article 10 3. KoRL L and Article 11 3. KoRL NL stipulate the information that the individual insurance companies must make available to the responsible supervisory authorities. The focus is on accounting, financial, and statistical information.

Swiss Developments: Voluntary Adaptation to EU law

Insurers   Under the effect of deregulation in the EU, Switzerland has voluntarily adapted its insurance supervision acts to EU law or the relevant EU directives in stages since 1993. With the coming into force of the new Insurance Control Act (VAG) on January 1, 2006, the Federal Office for Private Insurance abolished the preventive checking of the premium tariffs and products (GTCI) hitherto applicable, with the exception of life, private health, and elementary damage insurance. However, nonnational insurers still are prohibited from operating in Switzerland without authorization from the FOPI. They may carry on their business only via branches or subsidiaries domiciled in Switzerland. Swiss insurers have no direct access to the EU insurance market unless they have a subsidiary based within the EU.

Independent Insurance Brokers   The same restrictions also apply to nonnational and independent insurance brokers. If they wish to operate in Switzerland, they must be registered with the FOPI. Without Swiss registration, however, nonnational independent insurance brokers may still handle risks in connection with ocean shipping, aviation and cross-border transportation, risks located abroad, and war risks.

Swiss independent insurance brokers are not permitted to pass on to a nonnational insurer either business concerning clients who are Swiss nationals/residents or risks located in Switzerland.[6] However, insurance brokers have enjoyed a boom in their activity as distribution channels, in part as a result of deregulation and its associated price competition.

BROKER REGULATIONS IN THE EU

Strengthening the Single Market

In view of the great importance of independent insurance brokers, the EU has issued a brokerage directive aimed at protecting clients[7] that the member states were obliged to implement by January 15, 2005. This directive will contribute to greater efficiency of the single market for insurance by broadening the types of insurance products available as well as ensuring appropriate protection of consumer interests.

Mandatory Registration in the Home Country

Every insurance broker must be entered in a professional register in his or her home country. This requires not only a good reputation and proof of the necessary commercial requirements but also professional liability insurance as well as sufficient funds. Registration gives the broker the right to operate in all EU countries either locally or in a cross-border context.

Comprehensive Information Obligation

Insurance brokers in the EU have an obligation to inform their clients of whether they work on behalf of one or several insurers (dependent insurance broker) or act as independent consultants who advise their clients on all products from all insurers available on the market.

DYNAMIC DEVELOPMENT OF INDEPENDENT INSURANCE BROKERS ON THE SWISS MARKET SINCE 1990

New Products

As a result of deregulation and the abolition of cartels, standard products have disappeared. Instead, clients are faced with a large number of products, a situation that automatically implies a great need for advice. Against this background, the market offers independent insurance brokers favorable conditions to thrive. The share of the entire insurance market (premium) generated by independent brokers in Switzerland is approximately 10 to 15 percent, and between 70 and 80 percent in the segments of major/industry risks. The insurers are increasingly moving to handle and build up this sales channel separately.

Increasing Market Shares

Brokers have gained in importance, particularly in the sector of large and midsize enterprises with between 50 and 100 employees. In addition, government and semigovernment institutions (power utilities, transport operators, hospitals, state-run care homes, etc.) and public corporate bodies (municipalities, cantons, etc.) have increasingly begun to make use of the services of independent insurance brokers.

Market opportunities for independent insurance brokers will improve significantly, especially at the expense of contracted field agents. Industry surveys show that company-own advisors or agents currently have an 80 percent share of the bulk business. By the year 2010, the market share for contracted agents will drop to 54 percent in the private client business; it will make up 50 percent in the small and midsize enterprise segment and a mere 15 to 20 percent in the industry business. This decline will be accented still further by the increasing influence of the brokers. Although independent insurance brokers are also exposed to a competitive shakeout, they are expected to be responsible for 90 percent of the insurance volume in the industry sector and 50 percent in the small and midsize enterprise segment in the future. These figures show that the Swiss brokerage market is still below the European average.

BROKER REGULATIONS IN SWITZERLAND ACCORDING TO THE NEW VAG

Contracted and Independent Insurance Brokers

The VAG and AVO, a relevant act and its associated order, came into force on January 1, 2006. Like the applicable law in the EU, VAG also makes independent and noncontracted insurance brokers subject to supervision by the FOPI. After January 1, 2006, as soon as an insurance broker makes contact with a client, the broker is subject to specific information and disclosure obligations in Switzerland. Insurance brokers must inform their clients whether they are independent or are under contractual obligation to one or several insurers. The type and degree of such an obligation must be completely disclosed.

Legal Duty to Register for Independent Insurance Brokers

Independent insurance brokers must be registered, whereas dependent and contracted brokers (field agents of an insurance company) may register on a voluntary basis. Registration requires brokers to pass a specific test, a condition that is waived in the case of successful professional activity as insurance broker for at least five years.

Preconditions for Registration

According to Articles 184 to 186 AVO, several conditions must be met in order to become a registered broker:

- The broker must demonstrate sufficient professional qualifications (successful completion of an examination or equivalent certificate).
- Insurance brokers cannot have been convicted of a crime due to actions incompatible with the activity of an insurance broker, and they cannot

have any outstanding judgments against them. They must also possess the capacity to act.

- In order to cover their liability from infringement of their professional obligation to exercise due care, insurance brokers must have taken out a professional liability insurance with an insured sum of at least CHF 2 million or equivalent financial security.

According to Article 183 Section 1 lit. c AVO, insurance brokers are no longer considered to be noncontracted or independent if they have concluded a cooperation or other agreement with an insurance company that infringes on their independence from the company. Most independent insurance brokers have concluded cooperation agreements with various insurers, which remunerate the brokers for services rendered to policy holders through commissions. The commission system is the dominant and most frequently occurring form of remuneration in Switzerland. Commission agreements do not infringe the independence of the insurance broker, as they have to be disclosed to the client in accordance with VAG. Up to now, very few Swiss brokers work on a client-fee basis; in those cases they are remunerated directly by the client whom they represent.

Professional Qualifications

According to Article 44, paragraph 1 lit. a VAG and Art. 184 Para. 1 AVO, the professional qualification is demonstrated by an "examination or other equivalent certification."

Examination Regulations of the FOPI   The qualifications for brokers are implemented on the basis of the examination regulations issued by the FOPI on September 19, 2005, as well as of the code of practice issued by the VBV examination commission on December 6, 2006. The FOPI commissioned the VBV to implement the broker qualifications on this basis. For this purpose, the VBV set up a training course; successful completion of the course enables the broker to receive the professional qualification of "Insurance Broker VBV," which entitles him or her to be entered in the professional register.

The purpose of the examination is to qualify persons active in insurance brokerage who have acquired the necessary theoretical and practical professional knowledge. Insurance brokers can then certify their status as fully qualified professionals vis-à-vis their clients. These regulations for examination are applicable throughout Switzerland. They apply to those independent insurance brokers who are subject to mandatory registration as well as to others who wish to be entered in the register.[8] The examination commission defines what is required to obtain the professional qualification as an insurance broker. The FOPI also must approve the curricula and objectives.

The content covers these fields:

- General knowledge of the insurance business
- Personal and social insurance for private households and businesses
- Non-life and liability insurance policies as well as other property insurance policies for private households and business
- Legal knowledge

It is up to the candidates to prepare themselves for the examination by means of suitable training. The organization set up by the FOPI ensures that a training course is available. Successful examination performance is a requirement for gaining the qualification certificate.

Transitional Provisions   Independent insurance brokers subject to registration who lack professional qualifications and wish to carry on their activity without interruption had to demonstrate that they satisfied the requirements by December 31, 2007.

After July 1, 2006, insurance brokers with more than five years professional experience also had to take the examination. The transitional provision requiring proof of five years of practice ran out on June 30, 2006.

Examinations   The examination designed to gain the title of an "Insurance Broker VBV" consists of a written and an oral part. The oral examination must take place within a month of the written one.

The written examination is carried out throughout Switzerland simultaneously at various regional locations in the approved examination centers. It is conducted online on the examination platform www.intermediary-at-insurance.ch.

The curricula for the written examination are organized in the four professional sectors outlined above.

The practical oral examination with a simulated client consulting session is also held in the regional examination centers on the basis of specific mock cases.

The curriculum for the oral examination is divided into two parts:

1. Private households: single persons, families, self-employed persons
2. Small businesses

In the oral examination, candidates tackle a practical case from their field of expertise, either by answering questions on the insurance needs of a private household (single persons, families, self-employed persons) or on the financial security of a small business. The candidate selects his/her option at registration.

Candidates initially have 30 minutes to prepare a rough solution based on a specific approach and the subsequent discussion with the client (the examiner). In a discussion with the "client," which also lasts 30 minutes, candidates have to propose a solution, briefly justify the solution, and answer any further questions.

The written and oral examinations form a unit, and candidates must pass both parts. Candidates who pass both parts of the examination with a mark of at least 4 obtain certification as an "Insurance Broker VBV."

The examination result is issued only after both parts of the examination have been taken. Candidates are notified by the VBV in writing.

Equivalent Training Courses/Examinations　　The insurance industry offers several Swiss and international qualifications, which are equivalent or at a higher level, such as a professional certificate or degree in the private insurance business. Those who are able to produce such a certificate are exempted from taking the examination.

These qualifications are currently recognized as equivalent:

- Swiss federal certificate as an actuary
- Swiss federal diploma as an insurance expert
- Swiss federal certificate as a financial accountant
- Swiss federal diploma as a financial accounting expert
- NDS Financial Consultant FH
- Dipl. Financial Advisor/in IAF/expert on property, assurance, insurance and financing (according to the 2006 regulations with the "insurance" module)
- Chartered Insurance Broker (CIB) of the Insurance Institute of Switzerland

Partial Equivalences for "Insurance Broker VBV"　　There are also two partial equivalences for Insurance Broker VBV:

1. *Five years of practice.* Those who have worked as insurance brokers in the preceding five years do not have to take the oral part of the examination for becoming an "Insurance Broker VBV."[9]
2. *Completed apprenticeship in the insurance industry.* Those who have completed a commercial apprenticeship in the insurance industry a maximum of five years ago can dispense with the written examination for becoming an "Insurance Broker VBV."

The FOPI decides on equivalences upon request of the examination commission. Applications for equivalences must be submitted to the VBV office.

Moreover, VAG and AVO stipulate that insurance brokers must hold professional liability insurance with a minimum coverage of CHF 2 million per year. This obligation is waived if a third party has concluded a professional liability insurance that includes coverage for the insurance broker. The insurance broker may also offer equivalent financial security instead of professional liability insurance. The supervisory authority shall decide in each individual case what other financial securities may be considered as equivalent.[10] Those wishing to be registered as both dependent and independent brokers must demonstrate the financial security required for both forms of brokerage.[11] The strict terms of admission to the Swiss Insurance Brokers Association (SIBA), the leading insurance brokers' organization in Switzerland, has stipulated this requirement since 2001 (although only with a coverage of CHF 1 million). AVO stipulates that those who work simultaneously or partially as dependent and independent brokers must demonstrate the required financial security for both forms of insurance activity.

OUTLOOK

After January 1, 2006 (when the revised VAG took effect), independent insurance brokers are subject to the same FOPI supervision as insurance companies. In this way, the legislation aims to protect current and potential policy holders more effectively from malicious or erroneous advice and its consequences (liability due to incorrect advice).

It is hoped that the quality of insurance brokerage will improve as a result of the newly introduced mandatory registration based on an examination.

CHAPTER 6

Asset Protection Through Swiss Annuities and Life Insurance

Joachim Frick

Partner, Baker & McKenzie, Zurich

In addition to profit, asset protection can be an important goal for investment planning. An investment is not only supposed to be profitable, but in the event of debt collection or bankruptcy proceedings the assets should be protected from seizure by the creditors. The discussion that follows shows that Swiss life insurance policies are suitable to protect the assets of Swiss or foreign investors from being seized by their creditors to a large extent. This discussion focuses on Swiss life insurance policies with a surrender value.

ASSET PROTECTION

In principle, Article 79 para. 1 of the Swiss Federal Law on Insurance Contracts (VVG) provides that the designation of beneficiaries expires when the life insurance policy is seized in a debt collection procedure or the policy holder is declared bankrupt. In general, the creditors' rights take precedence over the beneficiaries' rights.

However, under Swiss insurance law, there are two exceptions in which beneficiaries of a Swiss life insurance are protected against any debt collection and bankruptcy procedures and the policy cannot be seized by creditors: (i) if the policy holder irrevocably designates the beneficiaries or (ii) if the

The author thanks Muriel Pasche, MLAW, for her valuable contribution. This chapter is based on an article in German which the author has written and published with Dr. Alois Rimle, LL.M, in: *Der Schweizer Treuhänder* (December 2003).

policy holder designates his or her spouse and/or descendants as beneficiaries of the Swiss life insurance. In these two cases, the creditors' rights give way to the beneficiaries' rights, subject, however, to avoidance actions under applicable Swiss debt collection and bankruptcy law.

IRREVOCABLE DESIGNATION OF BENEFICIARIES

The policy holder can designate a third-party beneficiary in the event of survival, death, and/or disability without the insurer's consent (Article 76 para. 1 VVG). In the absence of individual designation of a beneficiary, most general life insurance policies provide a standard beneficiary clause including a cascade of subordinated beneficiaries. The designation of a beneficiary is a unilateral declaration of intent on the part of the policy holder. Both the designation itself and the revocation of such designation are not subject to specific formal requirements (Article 77 para. 1 VVG); the beneficiaries need not even be aware of the designation. However, it is important that the insurer knows who the designated beneficiaries are in order to be able to provide the insurance benefit or surrender the insurance value to them. The designation is recorded on the policy.

The policy holder holds the right to revoke the designation; after a bankruptcy, the policy in principle remains in the policy holder's estate and may become subject to enforcement proceedings. In the course of the enforcement proceedings, the said right may be executed in favor of the policy holder's creditors in order to realize the insurance claim to their benefit.

However, if the policy holder waives his or her right to revoke the designation, the insurance claim resulting from such designation may, pursuant to Article 79 para. 2 VVG, not be subject to enforcement measures in favor of the policy holder's creditors, as the irrevocable designation results in the exclusion of the insurance claim from the policy holder's estate. The beneficiary becomes entitled to the insurance claim (i.e. the insurance claim then belongs to the beneficiary's estate).

The irrevocable designation of beneficiaries is subject to strict formal requirements. Pursuant to Article 77 para. 2 VVG, the designation qualifies as irrevocable only if the policy holder signs a declaration on the insurance policy waiving his or her right to revoke the designation and then physically hands over the policy to the beneficiary. The nature of the irrevocable designation implies its finality, and the designation can no longer be unilaterally revoked by the policy holder. Thus, any subsequent change requires the approval of the beneficiary and the return of the policy to the policy holder. Economically speaking, the irrevocable designation is similar to an assignment or a security of the Swiss life insurance policy. The beneficiaries now benefit from the economic value of the insurance claim.

DESIGNATION OF SPOUSE AND/OR DESCENDANTS AS BENEFICIARIES

The basic principle, according to which in the event of a revocable designation the creditors' rights take precedence over the beneficiaries' rights, does not apply if the policy holder (here necessarily a natural person) designates his or her spouse and/or descendants as beneficiaries. Article 80 VVG provides that if the spouse and/or the descendants of the policy holder are the beneficiaries, neither the insurance claim of the beneficiaries nor the insurance claim of the policy holder can be included in enforcement proceedings initiated by the creditors of the policy holder. Insurance claims are treated like indispensable items (Kompetenzstücke) pursuant to Article 92 of the Federal Debt Collection and Bankruptcy Law (SchKG): They are unattachable and thus cannot be seized by creditors. The only exceptions are liens. If the policy holder has granted a lien on the insurance policy to one of his or her creditors and has physically handed over the policy to such creditor (Article 73 para. 1 VVG), pursuant to Article 80 VVG, the creditor's rights take precedence over the beneficiaries' rights.

If the realization of the insurance claim in the course of debt collection or bankruptcy proceedings is excluded according to Article 80 VVG, the beneficiaries automatically replace the policy holder as the insurer's contractual partners at at the time of issuance of the certificate of shortfall or the declaration of bankruptcy of the policy holder (Article 81 para. 1 VVG). Such assignment of the insurance claim takes place ex officio, and the beneficiaries become the new policy holders with all rights and obligations, unless they explicitly waive the subrogation. Where the beneficiaries waive the subrogation, the insurance claim becomes a seizable asset and therefore subject to the enforcement proceedings. The beneficiaries are obligated to notify the insurer of the assignment by providing a written confirmation from the enforcement authorities (Article 81 para. 2 VVG). However, the failure to notify the insurer in no way affects the assignment of the claim; the transfer of the rights takes place independently of such notification. One has to be aware that as long as the insurer is in good faith (i.e., has not been notified of the subrogation), the insurer may consider the original policy holder to be its contractual partner and may provide benefits and disburse the surrender value to the original policy holder.

If the beneficiary has been irrevocably designated, it is obvious that the insurance policy must be protected from seizure by creditors of the policy holder, as it is no longer the policy holder but the beneficiary who is entitled to the asset of the insurance claim and the surrender value. In the event of a revocable designation of the spouse and/or descendants of the policy holder as beneficiaries, however, the asset protection derives from a sociopolitical special rule and is not based on a disposition of the policy holder to irrevocably designate a beneficiary. Due to the socially protective function of life insurance, assets actually belonging to the policy holder are excluded from his or her estate in debt collection or bankruptcy proceedings and are assigned to the policy holder's closest relatives. The policy holder's creditors go empty-handed. The concept of family protection and support of Article 80 VVG requires that the policy holder must at the same time also be the insured person. The relatives are in need of financial protections only if the policy holder and the insured person who is the relatives' principal support are one and the same. Furthermore, the provision requires that the spouse and/or the descendants have to actually exist (a child may still be unborn) at the moment of the seizure of the assets or the declaration of the bankruptcy. That means that a mere standard clause in the life insurance policy containing a cascade of designations (e.g., that designates the spouse and in the absence of a spouse the descendants and in their absence designates other relatives) does not establish a designation according to Article 80 VVG and does not result in an enforcement privilege if the policy holder at the time of the beginning of the enforcement proceedings is for example divorced, widowed, and childless. Also, the spouse and/or the descendants have to be the primary beneficiaries. This means that if the prior-ranking beneficiary is someone else, the spouse and/or descendants do not benefit from the privilege according to Article 80 VVG even if they are mentioned as backup beneficiaries (cf. Küng, in: Honsell/Vogt/Schnyder (eds.), Kommentar VVG, Basel 2001, ad Art. 80).

RULES ON FRAUDULENT CONVEYANCE

Due to the above-mentioned far-reaching legal enforcement privileges of life insurance claims, there is an enhanced possibility of abuse in connection with the designation of beneficiaries of Swiss life insurances. Article 82 VVG therefore explicitly provides for the application of the rules on fraudulent conveyance of Article 285 et seqq. SchKG (avoidance actions) to life insurances in favor of third parties. Consequently, the irrevocable designation of beneficiaries and the designation of the spouse and/or descendants as beneficiaries may be challenged by avoidance actions in the course of enforcement proceedings against the policy holder. Both said designations are voidable in enforcement proceedings against the policy holder if the latter has damaged his or her creditors by such designation. As a result of a successful avoidance action, the designation becomes void and the respective assets are seized and included in the enforcement proceedings to the extent necessary to satisfy the creditors involved.

The SchKG provides for three different avoidance actions:

1. Actions to avoid a gift (Article 286 para. 1 SchKG)
2. Voidability for intent (Article 288 SchKG)
3. Voidability due to insolvency (Article 287 SchKG)

Article 286, para. 1 SchKG provides that with exception to the customary minor presents, all gifts or gratuitous settlements in favor of a third party made by the debtor during the last year before the commencement of enforcement proceedings are voidable. Pursuant to Article 286 para. 2 SchKG deemed equivalent to a gift are transactions through which the debtor obtained for himself or herself or a third party a life annuity, an endowment, or a usufruct. Thus, under Swiss debt collection and bankruptcy law, the gratuitous designation of a third party as beneficiary of a life insurance can be qualified as a gift or a gratuitous settlement. Pursuant to Article 286 para. 1 SchKG the designation is voidable if made within one year before the policy holder's assets are seized or before the policy holder is declared bankrupt. Whether the policy holder at the time of the designation was already insolvent or even overindebted is irrelevant. Consequently, the policy holder's subjective intent and the beneficiary's good faith are immaterial. Of relevance is merely the objective element of the "suspicious period" of one year. The one-year period begins with the execution of the irrevocable designation of the beneficiary and the handing over of the policy to the beneficiary (Article 72 para. 2 VVG). Regarding the designation of the spouse and/or the descendants of the policy holder, the one-year period starts with the designation. If the gift or a legal transaction deemed equal to a gift is made before the "suspicious period" of one year, the avoidance based on Article 286 SchKG is impossible. It must also be noted that the designation of the spouse and/or the descendants justified by legal financial support obligations for the family is not regarded as gratuitous and therefore is not voidable. The avoiding party has the burden of proof regarding the execution of a voidable transaction during the "suspicious period" as well as of the damage done to the creditors.

Moreover, where an avoidance according to Article 286 para. 1 SchKG fails, a privileged designation of the spouse and/or the descendants or an irrevocable designation of beneficiaries may, according to Article 288 SchKG, be deemed to have been made with the intention of putting creditors at a disadvantage or favoring certain creditors. According to this provision, all transactions carried out by the debtor within the five years preceding the seizure of the assets or the declaration of bankruptcy, with the intention recognizable by the other party, of damaging his or her creditors or treating certain of his or her creditors more favorably than others, are voidable. Hence, the designation of beneficiaries is voidable if the policy holder intended to damage his or her creditors and the beneficiaries were aware of such intention. On the beneficiary's part, no intention to damage the creditor is required; negligent ignorance is enough to fulfill the element of being aware of the policy holder's intention. In this case, the party bringing the avoidance action must prove all objective and subjective facts including, among others, that the debtor's transaction damaged the assets, that such transaction was carried out during the suspicious period, that the debtor intended to do harm, and that the contractual partners knew about this intention. No assumptions are to be made to the disadvantage of the counterparty.

In Article 287 the SchKG also provides for the so-called voidability due to insolvency, which in relation to life insurances hardly ever becomes relevant. The provision may apply only if an already insolvent policy holder has irrevocably designated a beneficiary during the year prior to the seizure of assets or the declaration of the bankruptcy in order to settle a debt. In addition, the beneficiary has to be aware of the policy holder's insolvency (cf. Küng, op. cit., ad Art. 83).

An avoidance action is forfeited two years after the notification of the certificate of shortfall or the commencement of the bankruptcy proceedings (Article 292 SchKG). Place of jurisdiction is the Swiss domicile of the debtor. If the debtor is domiciled abroad, the avoidance action can be brought to the courts at the (Swiss) place of the debt collection procedure of the bankruptcy (Article 289 SchKG).

It must be kept in mind that, despite the enforcement privileges, the insurance claim may be provisionally seized in order to give the creditors the possibility of an avoidance action (i.e., to argue that the designation was invalid or that the rules on fraudulent conveyance require an annulment). The rules of procedure regarding the treatment of insurance claims in enforcement proceedings are set forth in the Ordinance on the Seizure, Arrest and the Realization of Insurance Claims pursuant to the Federal Law on Insurance Contracts.

The possibility of enforcement proceedings and the exclusion of the seizure of the insurance claim in the course of the enforcement are generally of great importance concerning life insurance policies with a surrender value, but may also apply to other insurance of the persons (e.g., mere death risk insurance). In the event of an endowment insurance, the beneficiaries are fully protected if the irrevocable designation was made in relation to all kinds of benefits (i.e., names the same beneficiary in the event of survival and death). This way, the insurance claim is excluded from the enforcement procedure as a whole. Should the designation be irrevocable only in the event of death, the position of the beneficiary is not as strong, as the insurance claim in the event of survival may be seized by the creditors. Should the insurance claim in the event of survival, however, actually be realized by the creditors, the claim in the event of death of course expires (cf. Küng, op. cit., ad Art. 79).

Due to the legal assignment of the insurance claim to the spouse and/or descendants according to Article 81 VVG, all claims related to the insurance subrogate to the beneficiaries regardless of whether the designation (only) applies in the event of death. Article 81 VVG even applies to single-premium policies with an initial high surrender value where the spouse and/or descendants acquire all the rights connected with the policy but do not have any obligation to pay future premiums. Thus, the enforcement privileges in favor of close relatives are very far-reaching (cf. Küng, op. cit., ad Art. 81, 82).

FOREIGN ENFORCEMENT PROCEEDINGS

Where the policy holder resides abroad, Swiss life insurance policies may become subject to foreign enforcement proceedings. The question is whether a Swiss insurance policy of a foreign policy holder is protected if included in foreign debt collection or bankruptcy proceedings. In cross-border enforcement proceedings the territoriality principle—an immediate result of national sovereignty—applies. As a consequence, the enforcement authorities of a country have access to only those assets of a debtor located in their country. Hence, in order to determine whether enforcement authorities may seize the policy holder's assets in an international setting, the relevant question is where a certain asset is located, at home (i.e., on the territory of the policy holder's country of residence) or abroad.

Whether an asset is located at home or abroad depends on its actual location. According to Swiss doctrine, an insurance claim is generally a claim not embodied in an instrument (i.e., the insurance policy qualifies as an evidence certificate only). The location of a mere claim is based on fiction. In order to determine the local jurisdiction in Swiss enforcement and bankruptcy law, the location of a claim is identified by normative allocation. As a general rule, claims are deemed to be located at the creditor's domicile in Switzerland. If the creditor's domicile is abroad, the claim is assumed to be located at the domicile of the third-party debtor in Switzerland (e.g., the Swiss insurer), for practical reasons, as the jurisdiction at the place of the debtor's domicile is most likely to implement the enforcement measures. But it is of course also arguable to locate the claim at a foreign branch of the insurer or at the domicile of the foreign creditor. It is therefore possible that a foreign jurisdiction competes with the Swiss jurisdiction regarding the enforcement of the life insurance claim.

In certain cases, an insurance claim may be embodied in an instrument. With respect to their location, instruments are treated like "objects," and therefore the asset's location is determined according to its physical location. The insurance policy can be regarded as an instrument (Namenpapier) if it explicitly contains a so-called double-sided presentation clause (doppelseitige Präsentationsklausel) by which the insurer commits to pay out the insurance claim only upon presentation of the insurance policy. Such legal instruments are treated as assets and are deemed to be located at the place where they are physically kept. Despite being legally possible, such embodiment of the insurance policy is very rare in Switzerland.

Foreign enforcement proceedings are subject to foreign law. In foreign enforcement proceedings, the beneficiaries of a Swiss life insurance not embodied in an instrument have to claim their rights according to the foreign law. In doing so, they may first argue that the location of the life insurance claim must be deemed to lie in Switzerland and that thus the insurance claim cannot be included in the enforcement proceedings due to its local limitation. If foreign law should turn out to be applicable to the Swiss life insurance claim, the beneficiaries may further argue that pursuant to such law, their rights as beneficiaries precede the rights of the policy holder's creditors.

In the event of an irrevocable designation of beneficiaries (Article 79 para. 2 VVG), the insurance claim is excluded from the estate of the policy holder under Swiss law. This aspect, which derives from the Swiss VVG (i.e., Swiss insurance contract law) should usually also be respected in foreign enforcement proceedings, and the protection of the insurance claim should be ensured. In the event that the foreign conflict of laws provide for the application of a foreign substantive law instead, the outcome is the same if the foreign law recognizes that the value of the insurance claim is excluded from the estate of the policy holder on any legal grounds whatsoever.

In the event of a (revocable) designation of the spouse and/or the descendants, one may agree that the privilege—even though stated in the VVG—is part of public enforcement law, and therefore a foreign authority is not bound by the privilege unless the foreign conflict laws provides for the recognition. The claim could therefore be prosecuted in favor of the creditors regardless of the designation if the foreign law does not provide for a similar privilege in favor of the family of the policy holder.

If the insurance policy issued in Switzerland is embodied in an instrument, the situation is more straightforward. If the original policy (i.e., the instrument), is located in Switzerland, the location of the insurance claim would most likely be deemed to lie in Switzerland and therefore not be included in foreign enforcement proceedings.

Should the claim against a Swiss insurer be included in the foreign enforcement proceedings despite the enforcement privileges and be assigned to the policy holder's creditors, there is still the issue of the actual enforcement of the foreign enforcement judgment. If the Swiss insurer has a branch office or a subsidiary in the country of the policy holder's residence, the foreign subsidiary may be obliged to pay out the surrender value of the life insurance to the benefit of the policy holder's creditors.

If, however, the foreign bankruptcy decree actually has to be enforced in Switzerland, due to the lack of a foreign branch office or subsidiary of the Swiss insurer or because the foreign law does not allow for the enforcement of the assets of the foreign branch office or subsidiary, Swiss law applies. Article 166 of the Swiss Federal Code on Private International Law (CPIL) provides for the official recognition of foreign bankruptcy decrees in certain circumstances and subject to special conditions. According to Article 170 para. 1 CPIL, the recognition of a foreign bankruptcy decree has the same effect as set forth under Swiss law (i.e., Swiss enforcement and bankruptcy law are applicable). Consequently, the enforcement privileges according to the VVG as well as the exception of the above-mentioned rules on fraudulent conveyance (Article 171 CPIL) are to be respected. The competent Swiss court concerned with the recognition of the foreign decree would thus most likely deem the insurance claim to lie in Switzerland (at the domicile of the debtor) and grant the asset protection pursuant to the VVG, which has failed under foreign law. In consequence, the competent Swiss court would have to refuse the seizure of the life insurance claim.

It is possible that the foreign policy holder requests the payment of the surrender value of the life insurance in favor of his or her creditors either because the policy holder has changed his or her mind or because of pressure from the foreign enforcement authorities. This would of course impede the asset protection according to the VVG. It is self-evident that the irrevocable designation according to Article 79 para. 2 VVG inhibits such action, as the designation may be revoked only with the beneficiary's consent. Thus, the insurer will not pay out the surrender value as long as such irrevocable designation remains valid.

The situation is slightly different when it comes to the revocable designation of the spouse and/or the descendants according to Article 80 VVG. The policy holder may freely dispose of the insurance claim as long as no enforcement proceedings are initiated against the policy holder (Article 81 para. 1 VVG). At the moment of the seizure of the assets or the declaration of the bankruptcy, the life insurance policy is assigned to the spouse and/or the beneficiaries unless the latter explicitly decline such assignment. Thus, the policy holder can no longer dispose of the insurance claim, and the insurance claim is excluded from the enforcement proceedings. Furthermore, any instruction to the contrary received from the policy holder may be the result of duress exercised by the foreign bankruptcy administrator and therefore, invalid under Article 29 of the Swiss Code of Obligations. This means that a Swiss insurer aware of the ongoing enforcement proceedings has to deny the foreign policy holder's request to disburse the surrender value in the event of a designation of the spouse and/or the descendants as beneficiaries.

However, the Swiss insurer will regard the policy holder as the contractual partner as long as the insurer has no knowledge of the enforcement proceedings, and the insurer may validly disburse the surrender value, provide benefits to the policy holder, or amend the life insurance policy according to the wishes of the latter. It is therefore important that the policy holder immediately informs the insurer of any initiation of (foreign) bankruptcy proceedings.

POSSIBLE OPTIMIZATION OF ASSET PROTECTION IN FAVOR OF FOREIGN POLICY HOLDERS

Asset protection through Swiss life insurances under the Swiss VVG does not work in favor of Swiss policy holders only but, to a large extent, also in favor of foreign policy holders. However, a policy holder residing outside of Switzerland runs the risk that the Swiss insurance claim might be included in foreign enforcement proceedings in favor of his or her creditors. This might lead to the realization of the claim in a foreign enforcement proceeding, e.g. if a foreign branch or subsidiary of the Swiss insurer is made to pay out the surrender value of the life insurance pursuant to the foreign law.

When assessing the suitability of a Swiss life insurance as a possible investment for a customer residing abroad, it is essential to make legal inquiries regarding asset protection in the customer's country of residence. First of all, it should be determined whether a claim against a Swiss insurer would, pursuant to the foreign law, be considered an asset located in the policy holder's country of residence that could be included in foreign enforcement proceedings. In this respect, it could prove helpful if the original policy documents—especially if embodied in an instrument—are physically located in Switzerland. If they are, it should further be clarified whether Swiss asset protection under the Swiss VVG would be recognized in the customer's country of residence or whether other, comparable protection principles would apply. In the absence of adequate asset protection in the customer's country of residence, it should be determined whether it would be possible, pursuant to the foreign law, to seize assets of a foreign branch or subsidiary of the Swiss insurer in order to realize the insurance claim. A Swiss life insurance offers the same level of asset protection to customers residing abroad only if, based on these inquiries, the realization of the insurance claim in the customer's country of residence is legally not possible.

In addition, for foreign policy holders, there is a higher risk that a Swiss insurer would disburse the surrender value in good faith upon request of the policy holder after the latter has been declared bankrupt even if the spouse and/or descendants are the designated beneficiaries. In general, it cannot be expected that the insurer makes inquiries regarding possible ongoing foreign enforcement proceedings concerning the policy holder. In order to prevent the Swiss insurer from making a payment in good faith in such a case, the beneficiaries should obtain evidence from the foreign enforcement authorities and the policy holder should immediately inform the insurer of any foreign bankruptcy proceeding and of the assignment of the life insurance to the spouse and/or descendants.

CONCLUSION

The records show that the enforcement of life insurance claims is rare. The creditors of the policy holder cannot seize the insurance claim under Swiss enforcement and bankruptcy law if the policy holder has irrevocably designated a beneficiary or has designated his or her spouse and/or descendants as beneficiaries, subject to the rules on fraudulent conveyance. There is no limit regarding the privileged amount in the enforcement proceedings; this enables the policy holder to protect large amounts of funds from being seized by the creditors. If foreign law applies because the policy holder resides abroad, Swiss asset protection may fail. This risk may, however, be avoided by making inquiries regarding the laws of the the policy holder's country of residence before the life insurance is purchased, by keeping the policy documents in Switzerland, and by immediately informing the Swiss insurer of any foreign enforcement proceedings against the policy holder. Thus, by way of designation of beneficiaries in a Swiss life insurance policy, the policy holder may construct extensive financial provisions for family or other beneficiaries and simultaneously broadly protect assets from being seized by creditors.

RELEVANT VVG PROVISIONS

Article 73 VVG—Legal nature of the policy; assignment and pledge
[1] *A claim derived from a personal insurance contract cannot be assigned or pledged by endorsement or simple transfer of the policy. To be valid, the assignment and pledge must be in written form, the policy must be transferred, and the insurer must be notified in writing.*

[2] *[. . .]*

Article 76 VVG—Insurance for the benefit of a third party. a. Basic principle. Scope of benefit

[1] *The policy holder is entitled, without the insurer's consent, to designate a third party as beneficiary.*

[2] *The beneficiary clause may extend to the whole insurance claim or may be limited to a part of it.*

Article 77—b. The policy holder's power to dispose

[1] *Even if a third party is designated as beneficiary, the policy holder may freely dispose of the insurance claim, be it inter vivos or upon death.*

[2] *The right to withdraw from the benefit clause only terminates if the policy holder has waived the right of withdrawal in the policy by signature and has transferred the policy to the beneficiary.*

Article 79 VVG—d. Legal reasons for expiry

[1] *The beneficiary clause expires when the insurance claim is seized or the policy holder is declared bankrupt. It revives when the seizure or the declaration of bankruptcy is suspended.*

[2] *If the policy holder waived the right to withdraw from the beneficiary clause, the insurance claim established by the beneficiary clause shall not be subject to debt enforcement proceedings in favor of the policy holder's creditors.*

Article 80 VVG—e. Exclusion of compulsory execution of the insurance claim

Subject to existing pledges, neither the policy holder's nor the beneficiary's insurance claim are subject to debt enforcement proceedings in favor of the policy holder's creditors if the policy holder's spouse or descendants are benefited.

Article 81 VVG—f. The spouse's and descendants' right of subrogation

[1] *All rights and duties deriving from a life insurance contract shall be subrogated to the policy holder's spouse and descendants if they were named beneficiaries and if a loss certificate is issued in the name of the policy holder or the policy holder is declared bankrupt, unless the policy holder's spouse and descendants expressly refuse this subrogation.*

[2]*The beneficiaries are obliged to notify the insurer of the transfer of the insurance policy by presenting an attestation of the debt enforcement office or the bankruptcy administration. If there are several beneficiaries, they have to designate a representative who shall receive the communications due by the insurer.*

Article 82 VVG—g. Reservation of the avoidance action

With regard to the provisions of this Act concerning the insurance for the benefits of a third party, the provisions of article 285 et seqq. Of the Federal Act on Debt Enforcement and Bankruptcy of 11 April 1889 are reserved.

RELEVANT SCHKG PROVISIONS

Article 92 SchKG—4. Indispensable items
[1]*[. . .]*

[2]*[. . .]*

[3]*The special provisions regarding unseizability contained in the Federal Statute on the Insurance Contracts (articles 79 paragraph 2 and 80), [. . .] are reserved.*

Article 285 SchKG—A. Purpose. Entitlement
[1]*Actions to avoid transactions pursuant to articles 286 to 288 serve to enable the realization of the assets in question.*

[2]*Actions to avoid transactions may be brought by:*

1. *any creditor who holds a provisional or definitive certificate of shortfall;*
2. *the bankruptcy administration or, pursuant to articles 260 and 269 paragraph 3, each individual creditor.*

Article 286 SchKG—B. Types. 1. Actions to avoid a gift
[1]*With the exception of the customary occasional presents, all gifts and voluntary settlements which the debtor made during the year before the seizure of assets or the opening of bankruptcy proceedings are voidable.*

[2]*The following are deemed equivalent to a gift:*

1. *transactions in which the debtor accepted a counter-performance out of proportion to its own;*
2. *transactions through which the debtor obtained for himself or a third party a life annuity, and endowment, a usufruct or a right of habitation.*

Article 287 SchKG—2. Voidability due to insolvency

[1]*The following acts are voidable if the debtor carried them out during the year prior to the seizure of assets or the opening of bankruptcy and was at the time already insolvent:*

1. *the granting of a collateral for existing obligations which the debtor was hitherto not bound to secure;*
2. *the settlement of a debt of money by another manner than in cash or by other normal means of payment;*
3. *the payment of an unmatured debt.*

[2]*However, the transaction is not avoided if the recipient proves that he was unaware, and need not have been aware, of the debtor's insolvency.*

Article 288 SchKG—3. Voidability for intent

Finally, all transactions are voidable which the debtor carried out during the five years prior to the seizure of assets or the opening of the bankruptcy proceedings with the intention, apparent to the other party, of disadvantaging his creditors or of favoring certain of his creditors to the disadvantage of others.

Article 289—C. Avoidance Action. 1. Jurisdiction

The avoidance action is brought before the court at the respondent's place of domicile. If the respondent is not domiciled in Switzerland, the action may be brought before the court of the place of the seizure of assets or of the place of bankruptcy.

Article 292 SchKG—E. Forfeiture

An avoidance action is forfeited:

1. *with the elapse of two years after service of the certificate of shortfall (article 285 paragraph 2 number 1);*
2. *with the elapse of two years after the opening of the bankruptcy proceedings (article 285 paragraph 2 number 2).*

Asset Protection Through Swiss Annuities and Life Insurance: View from the United States

Mario A. Mata

Partner, Cantey Hanger LLP, Dallas

The uncertainties of the U.S. judicial system, coupled with increased exposure to seemingly uncontrollable jury awards, has resulted in U.S. citizens and their professional advisors reexamining the benefits associated with wealth preservation and transfer strategies other than those available in the United States. This chapter focuses primarily on the use of the Swiss annuities and Swiss life insurance products by U.S. citizens to achieve both asset protection and, in some cases, significant tax planning opportunities.

AMERICA'S ATTRACTION TO SWISS ANNUITIES AND LIFE INSURANCE PRODUCTS

Swiss annuities and life insurance products have recently enjoyed a significant increase in popularity with American citizens as a result of the increasingly litigious nature of the U.S. legal system. Historically, Americans have sought the benefits of annuity contracts to provide for their long-term retirement benefits. Life insurance has been used both to financially support an individual's family, in the event of the insured's premature death, and to integrate into a well-drafted wealth preservation strategy that minimizes estate taxes and maximizes the amount of wealth that could be transferred to subsequent generations.

The fact that minimal protection from outside creditor claims is available for annuities and life insurance policies in most states has exposed such policies to creditor claims that an insured is unable to protect against. In fact, even in those states where annuities and life insurance policies have enjoyed unlimited protection from creditor claims, courts have recently embarked on a trend that essentially denies the unlimited creditor protection to such policies that are deemed to be more of an "investment product" than a traditional annuity or life insurance policy. As a result, Americans have sought to identify annuity and life insurance products and strategies that will help protect these very significant parts of their overall wealth preservation planning.

For many Americans, one solution has been the Swiss annuity, which enjoys significant asset protection benefits as a result of Swiss insurance law. However, Swiss life insurance policies also have increased in use in recent years as high-net-worth individuals become familiar with the significant protection available to Swiss insurance products under Swiss law.

Variable life insurance policies issued by Swiss insurance carriers typically require a significant minimum premium investment—typically no less than $1 million to $2 million paid over a five- to seven-year period. Swiss annuities have been particularly popular with Americans of all income groups because of the minimal investment, often as low as $250,000, that is necessary to acquire a Swiss annuity and thus enjoy its numerous benefits.

LACK OF UNIFORM PROTECTION IN THE UNITED STATES FOR ANNUITIES AND LIFE INSURANCE

Employment-related retirement plans in the United States generally enjoy good protection from creditor claims under federal law and under most state laws. Any employment-related retirement plan that is covered under the U.S. Employment Retirement Income Security Act (ERISA) provides strong "anti-alienation" provisions to protect those plans against the claims of creditors of plan participants. Employment-related retirement plans that do not qualify for federal law protection typically are protected by state law in most states. However, these protections apply only to retirement and similar plans, whether in the form of annuities or otherwise, that are directly related to an individual's employment. Only a handful of states provide protection for annuities and life insurance policies that individuals purchase to supplement their income upon retirement or to provide for their families upon their premature death.

Annuity Protection under U.S. Law

As of the writing of this chapter, only 10 states provide for unlimited protection of annuities and the proceeds from those annuities against the creditor claims of the annuity owner.[1] A total of 16 states, including Colorado, Connecticut, Iowa, Massachusetts, Rhode Island, and Virginia, provide no protection whatsoever against creditor claims against an annuity or annuity payments received by an annuitant. The bulk of the remaining states provide for limited protection for annuity payments or policy proceeds. In some cases, the amount of annuity payment that is protected from creditor claims is a very small amount, typically varying from $350 to $500 per month; some states, such as Pennsylvania, limit to $100 the amount of the monthly annuity payments that are exempt from creditor claims. In other states, annuity payments of a limited amount enjoy similar protections but only if such payments are being made to the dependents of the annuity owner, such as a dependent's spouse and children. As will be discussed, that is similar to the protection afforded annuities in Switzerland, but without any limitation on the amount of the benefits protected from a creditor's claim.

Life Insurance Protection under U.S. Law

Like annuities, life insurance policies are fully protected in the hands of their owners in only 10 states. Many states provide limited or no protection whatsoever to the owner of a life insurance policy. However, unlike annuities, many states do provide that the proceeds of a life insurance policy (i.e., the insured individual has died) are fully protected from creditor claims if such proceeds are paid to, typically, family members and other dependents of the insured. However, even in most of those states, should the owner of the policy be subject to creditor claims that are reduced to judgment prior to the death of the policy owner, a judgment creditor could seize the policy while the owner-insured is still alive and, in most cases, redeem the policy for its cash surrender value. If an owner-insured's intent is to own a policy to provide for dependents upon his or her death, irrespective of potential financial misfortunes, that goal cannot be realized in the majority of states if the owner-insured owns that policy when claims against him or her are reduced to judgment.

Court Trend to Circumvent Exemption Statutes

Despite the fact that some states have provided generous and sometimes unlimited protection for annuities and life insurance policies, a disturbing trend in some states has resulted in courts adopting mandated exceptions to otherwise favorable state exemption laws. In other words, despite the protections provided by some state laws for annuities and life insurance policies, some courts have unilaterally decided that such protections should not be available in all cases, notwithstanding the clear language of state law providing for such unlimited protection. In most cases where courts have ignored the unlimited exemption available under state law, they have found that the annuity or life insurance policy that the debtor sought to protect had characteristics that made it look more like a sophisticated investment product than a traditional annuity or life insurance policy intended to provide a reasonable basis of support during retirement or provide proceeds for the individual's family upon his or her death.

In the case of *Dona Anna Savings & Loan Association, F.A. v. Dofflemeyer*,[2] the language of the New Mexico exemption statute at that time provided that "any interest in or proceeds from a pension or retirement fund of every person supporting only himself is exempt from . . . attachment, execution or foreclosure by a judgment creditor."[3] New Mexico law clearly provided for the unlimited protection of annuities and life insurance policies. In its analysis, the court took note of the accepted use and definition of an annuity when the exemption statute was first adopted in 1887 by the New Mexico legislature. The court reasoned that, in 1887, the exemption was ostensibly adopted to provide an exemption statute to "protect families from becoming destitute as a result of misfortunate through common debts which are generally unforeseen."[4] In the years since the exemption statute had been adopted, the legislature had never attempted to change the definition or the amount protected from creditor claims of the owner of the annuity. In fact, some annuities had essentially become sophisticated agreements that, in many cases, provided significant tax deferral to high-net-worth individuals. Thus, pursuant to the court's analysis, a high-net-worth individual purchasing a $5 million annuity in Texas, for example, where annuities are fully exempt from creditor claims, could, using the New Mexico court's rationale, find that a $5 million annuity was far in excess of what the legislature had in mind when it first adopted the unlimited exemption for annuities for the purpose of protecting an individual's retirement and enabling the person to provide for his or her family upon disability or retirement. In any event, the New Mexico court held that, despite the state's unlimited exemption of annuities, an annuity would not be entitled to the exemptions against creditor claims available under state law if it was nothing more than a tax-advantaged investment contract even though it was technically an annuity.

A similar situation occurred in the state of California, where a debtor attempted to claim an exemption of his annuity under state law while the bankruptcy trustee argued that the annuity was merely an investment vehicle and therefore did not qualify as an annuity or life insurance under relevant California exemption laws. At the time, California law provided that an annuity would be exempt from creditor claims only if it was qualified as a life insurance policy. After reviewing the history of the exemptions available under California law for annuities and life insurance, the court ruled that where the annuity contains some attributes of insurance and some of investment, the analysis must include a determination of the primary purpose of the annuity. If the primary purpose of the annuity was investment, then the annuity would not qualify as life insurance for purposes of the exemption statute. After reviewing the facts, the Ninth Circuit Court of Appeals held that the annuity contract was primarily an investment contract and, therefore, not entitled to exemption and protection from claims of creditors under California law.[5]

Concern over Continued Erosion of Existing U.S. Protections

While very few courts have addressed this issue in the United States, many professional advisors are concerned about the increasing trend to reclassify as an "investment contract" a policy, issued by an insurance company, that is structured either as an annuity or a life insurance policy. This chapter does not discuss the intricate Internal Revenue Service (IRS) rules governing the taxation of investments inside such products, but it is important to recognize that the IRS in its regulations and rulings has made it clear that, before a life insurance policy can enjoy the tax-free accumulation of investment income inside the policy, it must first qualify as a true life insurance policy. Among other factors, a true life insurance policy includes an element of risk that has been assumed by an insurance carrier in exchange for a premium paid. Thus, if a life insurance policy does not meet the necessary "risk" requirements of the Internal Revenue Code, the tax law will not consider it to be a life insurance policy entitled to tax benefits associated with the deferral of income from investments held by the policy itself.

Likewise, it is not difficult to see that insurance products, particularly annuities, that may enjoy protection from creditor claims by statutes adopted over 100 years ago bear little resemblance to tax-advantaged annuities and complex variable life insurance products available today. Thus, while annuities purchased by Americans from their earnings with the primary goal of supplementing their retirement income will likely continue to enjoy applicable state protections, if any, modern annuity and life insurance products offered to high-net-worth individuals are likely to run the risk that, in the event of creditor attack, a court may find that the contract is nothing more than an investment contract rather than a traditional annuity or life insurance policy entitled to whatever exemption or protections that might be available under state law. As will be discussed, this problem can be avoided through the use of Swiss annuities and Swiss life insurance products that benefit from significant protections against creditor claims pursuant to

Swiss law, in addition to any additional protections that might be available to such policies when integrated into an estate planning or similar wealth preservation structure such as an international trust or a self-settled state trust such as those now available in 13 states of the United States, including Delaware.

FORTRESS OF ASSET PROTECTION: SWISS INSURANCE PRODUCTS

Swiss annuities have enjoyed a significant boom in popularity among U.S. citizens for a variety of reasons. However, it is the greatly enhanced asset protection benefits that Swiss annuities provide that have made them so popular with U.S. citizens and their advisors. Curiously, most U.S. individuals and their financial and legal advisors are unaware that the safeguards built into Swiss law that make Swiss annuities so attractive are also available to protect life insurance policies issued in Switzerland. Moreover, many of the reasons why Swiss annuities are favored by U.S. persons likewise apply to life insurance policies.

Other advantages of Swiss insurance products are also popular with Americans. For example, Swiss annuities and life insurance products usually can be purchased with less acquisition cost than their U.S. counterparts. Swiss annuities, in particular, provide far more flexibility in terms of options available to the purchaser and to the beneficiaries of an annuity upon the death of the principal annuitant. Nevertheless, the asset protection benefits associated with the Swiss annuity and life insurance products are the primary attraction to U.S. purchasers, especially in light of the litigious environment that exists in the United States.

SWISS ASSET PROTECTION BENEFITS VERSUS VULNERABLE U.S. ANNUITIES

Most annuities available in the United States are issued by heavily regulated but well-capitalized domestic insurance companies. As a result, a U.S. person acquiring a policy issued by a major U.S. company can find peace of mind in knowing that the annuity will pay its benefits as provided for in the contract. However, the principal risk to the owner of a U.S. annuity comes not from the potential financial failure of the issuing company but from the threat of potential creditor claims, which, in most states, allow a successful claimant to reach most, if not all, of the intended benefits of the annuity policy. In the United States, the level of creditor protection afforded an annuity is governed by the law of 50 individual states. Swiss annuities, however, are governed by federal Swiss law. In Switzerland, the protection afforded to annuities and life insurance policies is found in the Swiss Insurance Act, which applies equally to annuities and life insurance policies issued in Switzerland. However, Swiss law does differentiate between situations where a third party has been named the beneficiary of the policy and those situations where a spouse and/or descendants of the insured have been named as beneficiaries.

If the policy holder has irrevocably designated a third party as a beneficiary of a policy, such policy may not be seized by the creditors of a policy owner. In interpreting Article 79, paragraph 2 of the Swiss Insurance Act, the Federal Supreme Court of Switzerland has held that in the case of enforcement measures against the policy owner, there is in the estate of the policy owner no insurance claim, and the policy owner has no right to revoke the beneficiary's rights as normally would be the case. Therefore, the creditors of the policy owner may not seize, have levied, or have otherwise seized the insurance policy. The Federal Supreme Court has also held that this principle was expressed in Article 79, paragraph 2 of the Swiss Insurance Act. According to that article, if a policy owner has waived his or her right to revoke the designation of beneficiaries of a policy, any rights emanating from such designation may not be seized by the policy owner's creditors.

If the owner of the policy, whether it is an annuity or a life insurance policy, has designated his or her spouse and/or descendants as beneficiaries of the policy, an even more protective rule applies. Articles 80 and 81 of the Swiss Insurance Act provide that where the spouse and the descendants of the policy owner are the named beneficiaries of an insurance policy, whether such designation is revocable or irrevocable, the policy may not be seized by the creditors of the policy owner. Moreover, even if the policy owner were to be declared bankrupt, the designation of the beneficiaries may no longer be revoked by the policy owner. Instead, pursuant to Article 81 of the Act, the spouse and/or descendants of the policy owner automatically become the owner of all rights and duties of the policy owner as provided for in the relevant insurance policy.

It is a foregoing provision that is well known within the United States as providing protection for annuities. If the annuity is subjected to a creditor's claim, or if the owner of the annuity is declared to be bankrupt, the designation of the spouse and/or dependents of the annuity owner essentially becomes irrevocable, thus insuring that the annuity will not become an asset that is subject to seizure by creditors or part of the policy owner's bankruptcy estate. Instead, the spouse and/or dependents of the policy owner automatically inherit any and all rights that the policy holder held in the annuity or life insurance policy, even if the owner of the policy still held the right to revoke the beneficiary designations.[6] Assuming that the acquisition of the annuity or insurance policy does not constitute a fraudulent conveyance, a subject discussed next, the provisions of Articles 79, 80, and 81 of the Swiss Insurance Act basically insure that, with proper planning, the owner of an annuity or life insurance policy will always be able to protect his or her interest in it even if he is the beneficiary of the policy, or the ownership and benefits of the policy will accrue to the policy owner's spouse and/or dependents, thereby protecting the policy from the claims of creditors. Nevertheless, as with any transaction in the United States and most jurisdictions of the world, the initial acquisition cannot be a fraudulent conveyance under Swiss law.

Consequences of Fraudulent Transfer

As in the United States, Swiss law provides that a transfer that is deemed to be fraudulent against creditors can be set aside or certain actions of the annuity or life insurance holder, such as beneficiary designations, will be ignored if they fall within the parameters stipulated by the Swiss Debt Collection and Bankruptcy Act. Article 82 of the Swiss Insurance Act specifically provides that the protections otherwise provided by the Act will not protect a policy holder against creditor claims if, for example, the irrevocable designation of a third party or the designation of a spouse and/or descendant of beneficiaries of a policy are in violation of the Swiss Debt Collection and Bankruptcy Act. Therefore, if the policy holder is declared to be bankrupt or the policy is seized by a creditor within one year of the designation in question, the purchase of such policy and/or the designation of beneficiaries would be considered to be a transaction voidable by creditors. As a result, creditors would be able to seize the policy or, in the event of bankruptcy, the policy itself would become part of the bankrupt estate.

Court-Ordered Revocation of Beneficiary Designation

Most professional advisors in the United States who are familiar with U.S. insurance products are also aware of the power of U.S. courts, particularly federal and bankruptcy courts and their judges. It is not unusual, given the appropriate fact pattern, for a U.S. judge to order a debtor or bankrupt to take certain actions to recover assets from a third party that is holding assets that a U.S. court might consider assets of the U.S. debtor. However, because of the way that Swiss insurance law is written, by the time that such orders are issued by a U.S. court, the debtor subject to creditor claims or the debtor in bankruptcy will have, under Swiss law, already irrevocably lost the power to request action regarding the Swiss insurance policy, even if ordered to take such action by a U.S. judge. No Swiss insurance company will comply with the request of such former policy owner since, under Swiss law, such owner automatically loses the right to own or control any rights he or she may have once held under the policy.

Assuming a fraudulent acquisition and/or designation has not occurred, Article 81 of the Swiss Insurance Act provides that the owner of an annuity that has designated a spouse or dependents as beneficiaries loses the right to change that beneficiary designation upon any attempted seizure of the policy by a creditor or the owner of the policy being declared a bankrupt. Thus, at the moment of such an occurrence, all rights formally held by the owner of the annuity or life insurance policy automatically pass to the spouse and/or dependents of the formal annuity owner under Swiss law. Thus, should an insurance company receive an order by a foreign court to change a beneficiary designation that the owner of the annuity or policy might have made prior to being declared a bankrupt or having the policy seized, the Swiss insurance company would not legally be able to abide by such foreign court orders since, under Swiss law, the former owner of the policy no longer has the right to exercise such powers. Instead, such powers have automatically passed to the spouse or dependent beneficiaries of the policy holder. Of course, if the annuity or policy holder has made an irrevocable designation of a third party as policy beneficiary, the Swiss insurance carrier must ignore a court order by a foreign court to disregard such designation, assuming the designation was not fraudulently made under Swiss law.

Thus, a Swiss annuity or life insurance company that has been properly structured and not purchased as part of an effort to evade creditor claims will essentially guarantee that the intended beneficiaries of the policy are able to benefit from the policy, notwithstanding creditor actions abroad. Moreover, as previously mentioned, additional insulation from creditor claims can be achieved if the annuity or life insurance policy is owned by an international trust that is established by the policy holder or intended policy holder well before any actual or potential client claims accrue.

Use of an International Trust to Own a Swiss Annuity or Life Insurance Policy

There are numerous benefits to using an international trust as part of a legitimate asset preservation plan for a client. This area of law is constantly changing as a result of modern and progressive asset protection trust legislation enacted by multiple offshore jurisdictions and constantly changing U.S.

laws and court decisions, which make it critical that any offshore planning be fully compliant with applicable U.S. tax law and a plethora of federal laws that might be applicable to any proposed transaction. Failure to take into account all possible issues could quickly result in the client not benefiting from the many advantages of an international wealth preservation trust.

A comprehensive discussion of the issues involved in the use of international trusts by U.S. persons is beyond the scope of this chapter. However, most of the advantages that a U.S. person can derive from using an international trust are applicable to any high-net-worth individual in the world. As a result, the readers should review Chapter 8 as well. It is important to note, for purposes of this chapter, that an international trust established by a U.S. person can be a tax-neutral "grantor" trust or a "non-grantor trust." If the U.S. person is interested primarily in asset protection, with potential estate planning benefits integrated into the structure, it is likely that he or she will want to establish an international trust that is considered a "grantor trust" for U.S. tax purposes. In a nutshell, a U.S. "grantor trust" is basically a tax-neutral trust for purposes of U.S. income, gift, and estate tax purposes. As a result, if the trust is properly structured as a U.S. grantor trust, the trust itself does not provide the settlor of the trust with any tax benefit, nor does the settlor of the trust incur any additional tax liabilities. Nevertheless, as discussed in Chapter 8, there are multiple benefits associated with the use of an international trust, even if it is considered a grantor trust for U.S. tax purposes. In fact, it is usually mandatory to have a foreign structure in place for a U.S. person to acquire a foreign insurance policy, since such foreign insurance company is, by definition, not licensed to do business in the United States. Thus, in virtually any case where a U.S. person seeks to purchase a life insurance policy from a foreign insurance carrier, including all major Swiss insurance companies, it will be necessary to establish a foreign structure, preferably a tax-neutral structure such as an international "tax-neutral" trust, in order to allow the foreign insurance company to sell the policy insuring the life of the U.S. person. In those circumstances, an international wealth preservation grantor trust that is tax neutral for U.S. tax purposes is the ideal vehicle for acquiring a Swiss life insurance policy or a Swiss annuity.

Tax Planning with Variable Offshore Life Insurance Policies

Possibly the hottest trend in wealth preservation planning for high-net-worth individuals in the United States is the use of Swiss life insurance products for both asset protection and income tax planning. The use of life insurance as an investment vehicle is not new. A typical whole life insurance policy has an investment element to it that grows with the policy. Although policies sold in the United States do not necessarily offer the greatest investment options available, income earned or generated by the investment element of a properly structured life insurance policy is tax-free. Thus, income earned by the life insurance policy is able to grow "tax-free" much the same as a 401(k) retirement plan. Investments held by the policy can also grow tax-free. Tax-free accumulation of income is best suited for those interested in building a retirement nest egg or simply accumulating assets that can be passed to the next generation. However, should the policy owner have an unexpected need for cash, he or she can simply borrow against the policy. Thus, the policy can earn income tax-free, then make the funds available to the insured through tax-free loans if necessary.

A life insurance policy sold by a Swiss insurance company can be structured similar to policies sold in the United States. As such, income earned by the Swiss life insurance policy is tax-free. However, unlike policies sold in the United States, policies sold offshore have very significant financial benefits and investment options that are not available in the United States. These advantages have resulted in offshore life insurance policies becoming very popular investment products in the United States as well as a source of tax-free income. Although not every Swiss insurance company offers a U.S.-tax-compliant life insurance policy, some of the larger Swiss insurance companies will do so through a privately placed Swiss life insurance policy.

Such policies must be structured properly to comply with U.S. income tax laws regarding insurance policies. Moreover, since these policies are not registered in the United States, typically they are not available to U.S. persons. However, as discussed, they can be sold to an international trust established by a U.S. citizen.

Other Advantages of Swiss Policies

Other significant advantages to the use of offshore life insurance policies make them significant planning opportunities for high-net-worth individuals and their advisors.

Cost   One of the principal advantages of offshore life insurance is its reduced cost compared to domestic policies. Policies sold in the United States typically are sold by commissioned agents who command significant upfront commissions that are paid out of the policy's premium dollars. In order to support such commission payments, domestic insurance companies must set premiums that are higher than those of insurance companies that do not need commissioned agents to sell their policies. Likewise, the heavy regulation associated with the U.S. insurance industry results in significantly higher overhead costs, which have a direct effect on the cost of policies. However, in jurisdictions that specialize in insurance products, such as Switzerland, overhead and administrative costs are significantly lower. The cost savings realized by Swiss insurance companies are reflected in their lower insurance premiums.

Private Placement   A typical life insurance policy placed with a Swiss insurance carrier is essentially a privately negotiated contract between the insured and the carrier. Because of the size of the policy and premiums involved, a Swiss life insurance carrier is willing to negotiate a policy that incorporates significant provisions that might be relevant or important to the insured individual. In other words, a life insurance policy—which is nothing more than a contract between the insurance company and the insured—can be negotiated much the same way as an arm's-length contract that is negotiated between two parties. This flexibility provides the insured the ability to address specific issues that might be important to him or her.

Asset Management   In addition to the tax benefits associated with such policies, Swiss life insurance products offer significant flexibility in the management of policy investments, much the same way as 401(k) retirement plans do. The insurance company can place the investment potion of an insurance policy with any qualified asset manager in the world, even one suggested by the insured. The Swiss insurance company will open an account with the investment manager in its own name. In this segregated account, the client's assets can be managed by the asset manager selected by the Swiss insurance company, even if such asset manager was originally suggested by the insured or the insured's financial advisors. Although the insured cannot have day-to-day control of the assets in the segregated account, he or she can approve a proposed asset manager before deciding to fund the international trust that will purchase the policy. Thus, the insured has the benefit of knowing that the assets are being managed by a money manager that he or she has approved of in advance. However, only the insurance company can actually select the asset manager or have any input into day-to-day investment decisions, although they can delegate that investment management authority to a qualified third party-asset manager.

Tax Treatment of Insurance Policy Income

As indicated, income earned by the investment portion of the life insurance policy, properly structured, is free from taxation in the United States. The laws governing these rules are quite complex. However, in order to enjoy tax-free status, it is critical that the policy have a life insurance element that is actuarially consistent with the amount of the premium paid and the insurability of the insured. In other words, the life insurance portion of the investment must be "true" life insurance; otherwise, its status as a life insurance policy will be totally ignored. The U.S. federal tax rules that govern the taxation of investments owned by any life insurance policy, domestic or foreign, are beyond the scope of this chapter. However, prospective purchasers of Swiss insurance policies must retain the services of a qualified U.S. tax advisor to insure that any life insurance policy issued by a Swiss insurance company is compliant with U.S. tax laws.

Ultimate Tax Deferral Using Foreign Non-Grantor Trusts

A significant exception to the "tax-neutral" treatment of an international trust is a foreign "non-grantor" trust. A foreign non-grantor trust is one that is established outside the United States by a U.S. resident or citizen. It is an irrevocable trust in which the grantor makes a "completed gift" for gift and estate tax purposes. However, in order to achieve the tax benefits associated with a foreign non-grantor trust for U.S. tax purposes, the trust must not have any U.S. beneficiaries during the life of the settlor and the settlor's spouse and for a period of one year thereafter. During this time period, the foreign non-grantor trust may have foreign beneficiaries and typically will have at least one foreign charitable organization as a beneficiary. However, during the life of the settlor and the settlor's spouse and for a period of one year after their death, a foreign non-grantor trust will almost always accumulate all income and capital gains from non-U.S. sources and not make any distributions until such time as U.S. beneficiaries are eligible to receive distributions, beginning one year after the last to die of the settlor and the settlor's spouse.

The income and estate tax advantages of a foreign non-grantor trust are significant. The foreign non-grantor trust is treated as a "nonresident alien" for U.S. income tax purposes. Therefore, as such, the foreign non-grantor trust will be taxed only on its U.S. source income. Moreover, if the non-grantor trust is not active in a U.S. trade or business, the capital gains generated within the United States will not be taxable to the trust. If the foreign non-grantor trust has no U.S. source income, it is possible to accumulate income and capital gains from foreign sources tax-free (assuming the income is earned in a tax-free jurisdiction).

Once the foreign non-grantor trust is eligible to have U.S. beneficiaries, distributions made to those beneficiaries are taxable in the same manner as distributions from a domestic non-grantor trust. However, any appreciation in the value of the foreign non-grantor trust will have been excluded from the settlor's estate for federal estate tax purposes. Possibly the most efficient use of a foreign non-grantor trust by a U.S. citizen is the establishment of a foreign irrevocable life insurance trust.

Foreign Irrevocable Life Insurance Trust

In Chapter 14, the authors describe the multiple benefits of an irrevocable life insurance trust, commonly referred to an ILIT. A properly structured ILIT will allow a U.S. citizen to establish a trust that will own life insurance upon the life of the insured who is usually the settlor of an ILIT trust. Assuming that the ILIT is properly structured and maintained, the death of the insured settlor will not have any tax consequences in the United States. Specifically, the proceeds from the life insurance policy will not be taxable to the owner of the policy, the ILIT, nor will the proceeds from the policy be includable in the taxable estate of the now-deceased insured settlor who formed the trust. The benefits of such a structure are obvious and extremely advantageous. However, significantly greater benefits can be achieved if the ILIT is established as a foreign non-grantor ILIT.

As discussed, a foreign non-grantor trust is an irrevocable foreign trust where the settlor has established a trust that, for U.S. income, gift, and estate tax purposes, the settlor has retained no rights whatsoever in the trust. As a result, the trust is treated as a nonresident alien for U.S. tax purposes and is taxable only on its U.S. source income. However, unless gifts to the trust are exempt from the generating-skipping tax (GST)[7], subsequent generations of beneficiaries would pay such tax, essentially a form of estate tax, upon the death of a beneficiary. However, with proper planning, even this tax can be avoided and significant tax benefits gained through the use of a properly structured foreign ILIT.

Under such a strategy, the settlor of the foreign ILIT typically will make gifts of cash to the foreign irrevocable life insurance trust much the same way as is done with a domestic insurance trust. The cash is used to pay policy premiums. The transfer of cash to the foreign ILIT will constitute a taxable gift. If the individual establishing the trust has not fully utilized his or her gift tax exemption, he or she will be able to transfer as much as $1 million in cash to the foreign ILIT without incurring any actual out-of-pocket gift tax expense. At the same time, the settlor would allocate the $2 million generation-skipping tax exemption to the insurance premiums.[8] Upon the death of the settlor, the entire insurance proceeds will be excluded from the settlor's estate for estate tax purposes. However, if the settlor allocated a portion of the GST exemption to all of the gifts made to the foreign ILIT, the life insurance proceeds themselves will also be free from GST tax in perpetuity. Thus, no tax would be payable upon the death of any beneficiaries and the trust would not be subject to taxation in the United States except for any of its U.S. source income.

SUMMARY

While annuities and life insurance policies are both good investments and crucial to part of any long-term financial planning strategy, the extent of protection available to an annuity or life insurance policy owner in the United States varies according to the state in which the policy holder resides. However, the overwhelming majority of states in the United States provide little or no protection to the owners of annuities and only slightly better protection for the proceeds from life insurance policies, although not to the actual policies themselves during the lifetime of the insured owner.

Conversely, Swiss federal law specifically incorporates protections into its law governing Swiss insurance products and life insurance policies. Under Swiss law, Swiss annuities and life insurance policies are expressly protected against creditor claims or bankruptcy proceedings, assuming the acquisition or other action taken by the owner of the policy does not constitute a fraudulent conveyance under Swiss law. As a result, any attempt by a creditor to seize the policy will, in many cases, automatically prevent the policy holder from making any beneficiary changes or, in those cases where the actual or contingent beneficiaries are the spouse and dependents of the policy owner, such policy automatically is converted into a policy for the benefit of such spouse and dependents.

In light of the lack of uniformity in U.S. state law regarding the extent to which annuities and life insurance policies are protected, depending on the size of the investment in the Swiss annuity or life insurance product, an increased level of protection against creditor claims can be achieved by having the Swiss annuity or Swiss life insurance policy owned by an international trust that has no ties to the United States. Such a trust would need to be irrevocable, and, except in rare circumstances where specific tax planning is contemplated, the trust would be established as a tax-neutral grantor trust. In any event, by having the Swiss annuity or Swiss life insurance policy owned by the international trust, a significant amount of additional insulation from potential creditor claims is achieved.

As with any type of investment, it is important that a U.S. citizen seek the advice of competent tax counsel before pursuing any type of investment, particularly one that has significant foreign elements associated with it, such as a Swiss insurance product or an international trust. Nevertheless, with proper planning, an individual can establish a wealth preservation structure that can provide maximum preservation of assets, including Swiss annuities and life insurance policies, which will withstand creditor challenges, thus allowing the structure ultimately to provide for the financial security of the individual and his or her heirs.

Global Wealth Preservation Planning Using Swiss Insurance Products and International Trusts

Mario A. Mata

Partner, Cantey Hanger LLP, Dallas

The modern international trust, particularly when used for sophisticated wealth preservation planning, bears little resemblance to trusts that originated in medieval England almost 1,000 years ago. Yet the international trust has become a crucial part of modern wealth preservation planning, particularly in light of the global nature of wealth in today's increasingly mobile society. Although the common law trust is a concept that has its origins in the United Kingdom, even some civil law jurisdictions, including Switzerland, have taken steps to recognize the concept. In fact, the very recent ratification by Switzerland of the Hague Convention on the Law Applicable to Trusts and on Their Recognition will have a very significant effect on the country as a financial center and will provide yet another significant option to those who are desirous of using a common law trust for purposes of long-term wealth preservation planning.

This chapter focuses on the multiple benefits that derive from the use of a common law trust, even in jurisdictions that are not accustomed to the trust concept, such as Switzerland and all of Latin America. Moreover, the decision by Switzerland to ratify the Hague Convention on Trusts will help solidify the country as the private wealth management capital of the world, particularly in light of its extensive experience in private banking and the vast array of financial products available, including Swiss annuities and life insurance.

This chapter focuses on the proper use of an international trust for the acquisition of Swiss annuities, Swiss life insurance policies, and other lawful wealth preservation and tax planning purposes. Individuals in different parts of the world may have different goals but, more important, different legal and tax issues applicable to them in their home jurisdiction. Any information provided herein, particularly tax planning strategies, must be read in conjunction with the law and taxation applicable to the reader. Accordingly, persons contemplating any of the planning strategies discussed in this chapter should consult with competent local legal and tax counsel.

INTERNATIONAL TRUST

The use of an international trust as part of a comprehensive wealth preservation strategy has gained new recognition and acceptance in today's volatile society. Any high-net-worth individual, or even those of modest worth, should consider the benefits, goals, issues, and risks involved in establishing an international wealth preservation trust as part of a comprehensive wealth management plan for anyone with significant business holdings or investments. The benefits of an international trust are all too obvious in those situations when a client without a well-drafted international trust, but with substantial assets at risk, becomes involved in a legal dispute that places his or her wealth at risk.

Unfortunately, often many high-net-worth individuals and their advisors do not consider the benefits of an international wealth preservation trust until it is too late. Advisors should be prepared to advise their clients adequately about the benefits of international trust planning. Businesspeople-turned-defendants by a major lawsuit are unlikely to question the merits or moral significance of protecting assets with a professionally established international trust. If such people have not protected their personal assets with an international trust prior to the threat of litigation, they are likely to ask why professional advisors did not counsel them to do so. In fact, it is this author's belief that failure to advise wealthy or at-risk clients of the benefits of international trusts may constitute malpractice if clients' assets are needlessly exposed to a subsequent judgment or other legal claim.

In today's global society, properly structured international trusts have become generally acceptable throughout the world as a legitimate means to deal with the many uncertainties that can threaten the wealth of any individual and his or her family and heirs. Moreover, international trusts have become a common tool for long-term tax and wealth transfer planning. They often involve the use of insurance products, such as Swiss annuities and Swiss life insurance.

BENEFITS OF A GLOBAL TRUST

There are numerous benefits to using an international trust as part of a legitimate wealth preservation plan for a client. This area of the law is constantly changing as a result of modern and progressive asset protection trust legislation enacted by multiple offshore jurisdictions and constantly changing laws and regulations. It is vital that any international wealth planning be fully compliant with applicable tax law and a plethora of local laws. Failure to take into account all possible issues could quickly result in clients not benefiting from the many advantages of an offshore wealth preservation trust. A brief summary of the advantages of using an offshore wealth preservation trust for the high-net-worth client or family follows.

Self-Settled Trust Permissible

Most offshore jurisdictions will permit a settlor to establish a self-settled trust wherein the settlor retains beneficial enjoyment or control over the trust assets and/or the administration of the trust, something that historically is not possible in many parts of the world, including the United States. Although it is typically a better planning strategy to avoid any unnecessary control on the part of a settlor, the fact that the settlor has retained a beneficial interest in the trust or has a right to exercise certain defined powers in the trust has, in many jurisdictions, been expressly permitted by statute.

Chilling Effect of an International Trust

Potential creditors and their attorneys will not welcome the news that an individual's assets have been sheltered in an international trust. An international trust constitutes an additional hurdle for creditors to overcome. The mere logistical obstacles presented by the distance of some of these offshore jurisdictions is enough to drive creditors to the settlement table.

Nonrecognition of Foreign Judgments

Even if a creditor were to obtain a judgment against an individual, most offshore jurisdictions will not recognize a foreign judgment. Under the law of most offshore jurisdictions, a creditor must file suit in the jurisdiction in which the trust is located if a creditor intends to enforce a judgment against assets of the trust. Plaintiffs and their attorneys are sometimes surprised to learn that contingency fee arrangements are unique to the United States and, in some offshore jurisdictions, outright illegal.

Confidentiality

A legitimate wealth preservation plan contemplates that a debtor will be prepared to make full and complete disclosure, if required to do so, regarding the transfers that were made into an international trust. Secrecy should never be a necessary element of a legitimate wealth preservation plan. Nevertheless, the strict laws that require maintaining client confidentiality that are found in most offshore jurisdictions are a benefit valued by many individuals who wish to keep a low profile for a variety of reasons. Typically, unless an individual has committed a crime that is also a crime in the jurisdiction in which the trust is located, an offshore jurisdiction will not provide confidential information about the debtor's affairs without that individual's consent. This is particularly important to clients in high-risk jurisdictions, such as much of Latin America where kidnapping is a thriving business and a constant concern to those with significant assets at their disposal.

Unambiguous Fraudulent Transfer Laws and Statute of Limitations

Few offshore jurisdictions condone a fraudulent conveyance. However, most offshore jurisdictions have attempted to clarify the issue of fraudulent conveyance by drafting clearly defined fraudulent conveyance legislation. This modern legislation has attempted to eliminate many of the ambiguities and unpredictable results that have caused uncertainty for both debtors and creditors alike, in both the United States and the United Kingdom. Likewise, most jurisdictions have acted to shorten the statute of limitation periods applicable to fraudulent conveyances. (Contrary to popular belief, the Cayman Islands, commonly considered a debtor haven, has a six-year statute of limitations!)

Alternative to Premarital Agreements

Regrettably, the sacrament of marriage is not as sacred as it once was. It is not uncommon to have as a client someone who is working on his or her third marriage. If the client has begun to accumulate wealth, notwithstanding prior divorces, future marriages can be problematic when the issue of prenuptial agreements is first discussed. The need for a premarital agreement can be avoided altogether through the establishment of an international trust prior to marriage. It not only avoids the unpleasant task of asking a future spouse to sign a premarital agreement, it also prevents the need to make the vast financial disclosure required under most applicable laws to make such agreements enforceable. In fact, the future spouse does not even need to know about the existence of the international trust. Upon divorce, the assets in the trust are safely and legally outside the jurisdiction of a divorce court.

Marital Property and Forced Heirship Laws Overridden

A settlor may be surprised to learn that in most states in the United States and in many foreign jurisdictions, an individual is not able to freely dispose of property as he or she desires at the time of death. Forced heirship laws throughout the United States and many foreign jurisdictions grant spouses and children of the decedent certain heirship rights in the decedent's estate. These types of problems can be addressed through the use of an international trust established in a jurisdiction that has adopted legislation to prevent the application of forced heirship laws and forced marital property laws in the debtor's home jurisdiction.

Ideal Alternative for Testamentary Wealth Transfer at Death

Individuals who have accumulated significant investments and modest to high net worth often live in countries where the testamentary disposition of an estate upon death is an extremely costly and time-consuming affair, often dependent on the filing of an inventory of assets with local officials. Such disclosure includes the type of information that one would not want to have made public in light of the risk that persons with even modest wealth face from kidnapping and extortion in Latin America and other parts of the world. On the contrary, it is not uncommon for high-net-worth individuals in Latin America to maintain a very modest lifestyle. Relying on local courts and government officials to administer the testamentary disposition of an individual's estate upon death can highlight the extent of an individual's wealth and potentially place family heirs at risk if information about their inheritance becomes public knowledge.

In the United States, individuals in certain states will use a "living trust" to transfer assets at death in lieu of costly probate proceedings. Similarly, use of an international trust is ideal for those individuals who desire to provide for the smooth transition of their wealth to their heirs and future generations without the need to deal with the administration of those assets as part of a decedent's estate. Instead, upon the decedent's estate, all that typically changes is the beneficiaries of the international trust. Typically no other administrative proceedings regarding assets held by the trust are required, particularly in Latin America and similar jurisdictions. The trust document itself includes the individual's testamentary intentions. As a result, individuals are able to pass their wealth from one generation to the next without any type of public disclosure. Moreover, the placement of a significant part of a client's wealth in an international trust, particularly investments held outside of their home jurisdiction, helps to safeguard such assets against political and other similar threats, such as government confiscation, currency controls, and other governmental action, that may interfere with an individual's ability to reap the benefits of his or her wealth. In fact, if a client who is a resident of Latin America or the Middle East has these kinds of concerns, he or she is an ideal candidate for an international trust. Such a trust should be established in a jurisdiction where the client's holdings are held in strict confidence except in those situations in which a serious crime is involved.

ADVANTAGES OF USING AN INTERNATIONAL TRUST TO OWN SWISS ANNUITIES AND LIFE INSURANCE

As discussed elsewhere in this book, Swiss annuities and Swiss life insurance policies are governed by federal Swiss law. In Switzerland, the protection afforded to annuities and life insurance policies is found in the Swiss Insurance Act, which applies equally to both annuities and life insurance policies issued in Switzerland. However, Swiss law does differentiate between situations where a third party has been named the beneficiary of the policy versus those situations where a spouse and/or descendants of the insured have been named as beneficiaries.

If the policy holder has irrevocably designated a third party as a beneficiary of a policy, such policy may not be seized by the creditors of a policy owner. In interpreting Article 79, paragraph 2 of the Swiss Insurance Act, the Federal Supreme Court of Switzerland has held that in the case of enforcement measures against the policy owner, there is in the estate of the policy owner no insurance claim and the policy owner has no right to revoke the beneficiary's rights, as normally would be the case. Therefore, the creditors of the policy owner may have levied or otherwise seized the insurance policy. The Federal Supreme Court has also held that this principle was expressed in Article 79, paragraph 2 of the Swiss Insurance Act, according to which, if a policy owner has waived his or her right to revoke the designation of beneficiaries of a policy, any rights emanating from such designation may not be seized by the policy owner's creditors.

If the owner of the policy, whether it is an annuity or a life insurance policy, has designated his or her spouse and/or descendants as beneficiaries of the policy, an even more protective rule applies. Articles 80 and 81 of the Swiss Insurance Act provide that where the spouse and the descendants of the policy owner are the named beneficiaries of an insurance policy, whether such designation is revocable or irrevocable, the policy may not be seized by the creditors of the policy owner. Moreover, even if the policy owner were to be declared bankrupt, the designation of the beneficiaries may no longer be revoked by the policy owner. Instead, pursuant to Article 81 of the Swiss Insurance Act, the spouse and/or descendants of the policy owner automatically become the owner of all rights and duties of the policy owner as provided for in the relevant insurance policy.

These provisions of Swiss insurance law are well known within the United States and around the world for providing protection for Swiss annuities and Swiss life insurance policies. If the annuity is subjected to a creditor's claim, or if the owner of the annuity is declared to be bankrupt, the designation of the spouse and/or dependents of the annuity owner essentially becomes irrevocable, thus insuring that the annuity will not become an asset subject to seizure by creditors or part of the policy owner's bankruptcy estate. Instead, the spouse and/or dependents of the policy owner automatically inherit any and all rights that the policy holder held in the annuity or life insurance policy, even if the owner of the policy still held the right to revoke the beneficiary designations.[1]

These provisions of Swiss law provide excellent protection to the owner of a Swiss annuity or Swiss life insurance policy, particularly where the owner's spouse and/or dependents are the named beneficiaries. However, such protection comes at a price. If the owner of the annuity or life insurance policy is not subjected to threats from third parties, then there are no adverse consequences to the direct ownership of such policies in an individual's name. However, they do have an adverse effect on the flexibility that the owner of an annuity or life insurance policy typically enjoys, primarily the right to modify the beneficiary designation of the annuity or life insurance policy.

While the tax consequences to different citizens of the world will differ, for U.S. citizens, the triggering of the protective provisions of Swiss law could have adverse tax consequences if the operation of such protections constitutes a taxable gift to the owner of the policy. From a personal and practical standpoint, the protections afforded Swiss annuities and life insurance policies, when triggered, forever prevent the owner of the policy from electing beneficiary revisions that might be desired in the future as a result of changed circumstances, such as the addition of additional beneficiaries, the omission of one or more beneficiaries, and, very importantly, the decision to add or drop a spouse, particularly if an individual was single when purchasing the policy or, if married, was subsequently divorced. However, many of these problems can be avoided by using an international trust to own the Swiss annuity or Swiss life insurance policy.[2] If the Swiss annuity or Swiss life insurance policy is owned by an international trust, particularly if the trust owns the policy since inception, the many potential legal claims against an individual, even if those claims are reduced to judgment, will not result in any changes to the annuity or insurance policy since it is the international trust, and not the individual personally, that owns the policies. Thus, assuming the international trust is not a party to whatever litigation or other claim has affected the insured individual, such claims will not affect the owner of the policies, as the owner is the trust. This fact enables the trustee of such trust to continue to enjoy the flexibility of making potential changes to the material terms of the Swiss annuity or Swiss life insurance policy, such as the right to change the ultimate beneficiaries of the policies, particularly in those situations where an individual's circumstances have changed.

COMING TO AMERICA: PRE-IMMIGRATION PLANNING

While U.S. tax laws governing the use of pre-immigration trusts have been tightened in recent years, with proper and timely planning, there still exist very significant tax planning opportunities available to a non-U.S. citizen contemplating becoming a resident or citizen of the United States. Such planning is crucial since U.S. citizens and non-U.S. citizens who are "residents" of the United States (commonly called "resident aliens") are subject to taxation on their worldwide income. In addition, all U.S. citizens and any resident alien who resides in the United States with the intent to remain in the United States are subject to estate taxation on their worldwide assets upon their death. However, with careful planning, particularly if the non-resident alien can avoid "resident" status in the United States for at least five years, it is possible to structure current foreign holdings in such a way as to minimize income tax liability in the United States and, in most cases, totally eliminate estate taxation of assets held outside the United States.

U.S. Residency Rules

In determining the status of a non-U.S. citizen for tax purposes, it is critical to determine the person's status as either a resident alien or a nonresident alien (NRA). As indicated, U.S. citizens and resident aliens are taxed on their worldwide income. A non-U.S. citizen can become a "resident" of the United

States by one of two means. One of them is by obtaining a "green card," an immigration permit that grants the non-U.S. citizen liberal rights to travel in and out of the United States for the purposes of employment. Non-U.S. citizens who obtain a green card are automatically considered residents of the United States for U.S. income tax purposes, provided they are present in the United States for at least one day in the year.

Non-U.S. citizens also are deemed to be residents of the United States for income tax purposes if they meet the "Substantial Presence Test." Under the Substantial Presence Test, a person is deemed to be a resident of the United States if, for a given calendar year, that person either (a) is present in the United States for 183 days in that year, or (b) is present in the United States for at least 31 days of that year and has present in the country for an average of more than 121 days per year over that year and the two prior years. Of course, there are exceptions to this general rule such as those for diplomats, full-time students, teachers, and employees of certain international organizations.

Taxation of Non-U.S. Persons

Generally speaking, persons who are not citizens or tax residents of the United States are nevertheless subject to U.S. taxation on certain types of income, such as:

- U.S. source "trade or business" income
- Dividends from U.S. corporations (but not the proceeds from the sale of U.S. securities)
- Rent from U.S. real state, including capital gains from the sale of real estate
- U.S. source royalties

Interest earned on U.S. bank accounts and time deposits is not considered to be U.S. source income and therefore is not subject to U.S. taxation.

Persons who are not U.S. citizens or resident aliens will, upon their death, nevertheless be subject to an estate tax and the generation-skipping tax on certain assets held within the United States upon their death. Examples of assets subject to such taxation are:

- Real estate located within the United States, including a residence
- Personal property located within the United States including jewelry, artwork, antiques, and similar items
- Shares of stock in U.S. corporations (the location of the stock certificates at the time of death is immaterial)

- Cash and cash equivalents on deposit in United States brokerage accounts (as opposed to those on deposit in U.S. banks, which are not considered U.S. situs property for estate tax purposes)
- Interest in partnerships that either do business in the United States or own assets in the United States.

If the person is not a U.S. citizen or resident alien upon his or her death, estate taxation on these assets typically can be avoided by holding the assets in a foreign corporation.

Use of Foreign Trust in Pre-Immigration Planning

A qualifying foreign trust established by a nonresident alien at least five years before becoming a U.S. citizen or resident alien is not subject to income taxation by the United States, except to the extent that the trust has "U.S. source income." Thus, by way of example, if a foreign trust holds no assets and has no income in the United States, the foreign trust would not be subject to taxation at all in the United States. However, if such foreign trust was established by a foreign person who, within five years of establishing the trust, becomes a U.S. citizen or resident alien, the foreign trust will be deemed to be a U.S. taxpayer for U.S. income and estate tax purposes. Nevertheless, income earned by the trust prior to the person becoming a U.S. citizen or resident will escape taxation in the United Sates.

Of course, without exception, any "U.S. source income" earned by the trust is subject to taxation in the United States. Generally speaking, that is a rule that applies to all foreign persons or entities. To put it another way, there is virtually no way to avoid paying income tax on earnings from most U.S. sources.

Foreign Corporations

If a non-U.S. person is able to establish a foreign trust five years prior to becoming a U.S. citizen or resident alien, that trust should include the client's ownership interest in foreign corporations. Foreign corporations owned by a U.S. citizen or resident alien will be subject to special tax rules in the United States if they are classified as foreign personal holding companies for U.S. tax purposes. Income earned by a foreign corporation classified as a "foreign personal holding company" will be taxable in the United States to the U.S. shareholders of the company. However, the status of a foreign corporation as a "foreign personal holding company" can be avoided if it is wholly owned by a pre-immigration foreign trust established five years prior to the client becoming a U.S. citizen or resident alien. This occurs because the trust is classified as a "nonresident alien" for U.S. tax purposes. In other words, it is a foreign nonresident for all U.S. tax purposes. As a result, the "controlled foreign corporation" tax rules of the United States, rules that govern the taxation of passive income earned by a foreign corporation that is predominantly owned by U.S. persons, are simply not applicable to the foreign corporation if owned by a properly structured pre-immigration trust.

Planning for U.S. Residency Prior to Five-Year Period

Even if a non-U.S. person intends to establish residency within five years, there are still significant benefits associated with transferring assets into a foreign trust prior to immigrating to the United States. Unless a non-U.S. person acquires a green card, a foreign person can typically defer becoming a U.S. tax resident for several years, even if not successful in reaching the preferred five-year benchmark. Thus, until the non-U.S. person becomes a U.S. citizen or resident alien, all income earned by the foreign trust will continue to remain free from taxation in the United States until such time as the client becomes a U.S. citizen or resident. In fact, in light of these facts, it is often advantageous for an individual to "accelerate" the recognition of income prior to becoming a U.S. citizen or resident alien, thereby avoiding U.S. taxation on that income after establishing his or her U.S. residency.

Likewise, even if the client intended to become a citizen or resident of the United States almost immediately upon arrival in the United States, significant planning opportunities still can be recognized by having the client make nontaxable gifts of assets to family members or trusts established for their benefit. Since the client would not be a citizen or resident of the United States at the time that the gifts are made, he or she can make unlimited gifts without incurring gift tax liability in the United States. Thus, to the extent possible, the client should consider gifts, either directly or in trust, to those persons that will be the ultimate beneficiaries of his or her estate. By doing so, those transferred assets completely escape gift and/or estate taxation in the United States upon the client's death, even if the client is a U.S. citizen or resident at the time of his or her death.

Funding a Swiss Life Insurance Policy Prior to Immigrating to the United States

One of the significant attractions of a U.S. tax-compliant variable offshore life insurance policy is the ability to defer taxation on the income earned by investments held inside the life insurance policy itself. If a life insurance policy is a U.S. tax-compliant policy, the bulk of premiums paid for the policy will constitute part of the value of the policy which can be used to make such investments. However, funding of such a policy can be problematic if an individual already has an investment portfolio that he or she desires to have transferred into the life insurance policy to benefit from such tax advantage. Specifically, if a U.S. citizen or U.S. resident alien pays the premium of such a policy with appreciated assets, typically appreciated marketable securities, the transfer of such assets to the insurance company for purposes of paying the premium constitutes a "sale or exchange" of the assets transferred. In other words, use of appreciated securities or other assets to pay the premiums on the policy will be treated, under U.S. tax law, as if the individual had first sold the assets, recognized the resulting gain for income tax purposes, and then transferred the sale proceeds to the insurance company in payment of the policy premiums. Typically the only way that a U.S. person or U.S. resident alien can avoid such a result is to use cash to pay the premiums for the life insurance policy. However, if an individual who is not a U.S. citizen or U.S. resident alien purchases an offshore variable life insurance policy, including any Swiss life insurance policy, with assets that have appreciated in value, such individual will not incur a taxable gain upon the transfer of his or her portfolio of marketable securities to the insurance company in payment of the premiums since such individual would not yet be subject to taxation in the United States. As a result, an individual who is not yet a U.S. citizen or resident alien but who is contemplating moving to the United States could benefit significantly by transferring his or her portfolio of marketable securities into a product like a Swiss life insurance policy prior to becoming a citizen or a resident alien in the United States. Such a transfer would not be taxable in the United States and would result in the client's portfolio of investments being owned by the life insurance policy, which, if structured as a U.S. tax-compliant insurance policy, will not be taxable to the individual upon becoming a U.S. citizen or resident alien. Moreover, while it is not necessary to utilize an international trust to achieve such tax benefits, it is the author's view that using an international trust to acquire a product such as a Swiss variable life insurance policy provides such individual with enhanced wealth protection benefits.

Clients with Existing Foreign Trusts

Often a foreign citizen contemplating redomiciling to the United States will not be concerned with the application of the "five-year test" before becoming a domiciliary of the United States for tax purposes. It is entirely possible that a non-U.S. person will have structured his or her assets, for asset protection or tax purposes, in such a way that he or she is able to establish U.S.

residency at any time without incurring otherwise avoidable adverse tax consequences. However, such circumstances are likely to exist only if the planning was undertaken by professional advisors who drafted the structure with a possible redomiciliation to the United States in mind.

Most foreign trusts drafted by non-U.S. attorneys grant the settlor of the trust significant power over the trust, the trustee, and the trust protector. In fact, foreign trusts are often drafted to be fully revocable by the settlor. Unfortunately, a revocable foreign trust, or a foreign trust where the settlor has retained significant controls over the trust, will not qualify as a true "foreign trust" for purposes of determining the ability of the foreign trust to avoid taxation in the United States. For example, a revocable trust is nothing more than a "grantor trust" for U.S. tax purposes and, as a result, is treated and taxed directly to the settlor of the trust. It is therefore extremely important to examine a client's existing structure carefully to determine whether that structure will qualify as a true foreign trust for income and estate tax purposes in the United States. If it does not, the existing structure will have to be modified or, in some cases, totally restructured or replaced, in order to implement a structure that will not be subject to U.S. taxation on anything other than its U.S. source income.

Tax Compliance

The tax planning discussed in this chapter addresses only taxation issues governed by United States law. Typically most foreign trusts are established in a jurisdiction that does not subject the trust to taxation provided (a) the income from the trust is from sources outside that jurisdiction and (b) the beneficiaries of the trust are all persons who reside outside that jurisdiction. However, even if income from a trust is tax-free in its country of organization, it is not necessarily tax-free in the country where the settlor of the trust resides. Therefore, any planning that is undertaken for a client considering redomiciling to the United States must be coordinated with applicable tax law in the client's primary home jurisdiction. This is particularly important for persons who reside in jurisdictions that tax the transfer of assets into any type of trust.

SELECTING A FAVORABLE JURISDICTION

Great care must be used in selecting the situs of an international trust. The availability of the characteristics that must be included in an international trust should be specifically identified in the governing legislation of any jurisdiction being considered for the situs of an international trust. Among the factors that should be used in evaluating a particular jurisdiction are:

- Nonrecognition of foreign judgments
- Recognition and protection of self-settled trusts
- Recognition and protection of trusts wherein the grantor has retained significant control over trust assets or administration
- Confidentiality
- Unambiguous fraudulent conveyance laws and favorable statute of limitation periods
- Recognition of trust provisions that override the forced heirship laws or marital property laws of the debtor's home jurisdiction
- Favorable tax law (almost all offshore jurisdictions exempt foreign trusts from taxation in their jurisdiction)
- Availability of competent and financially strong trustees
- Availability of local professional services, including legal counsel
- Compatibility of the offshore jurisdiction with the settlor's language and culture
- Existence of a modern and stable government

This list is by no means exclusive. Some issues will be more relevant to certain clients than others. No two clients are alike. And, more important, there are numerous offshore jurisdictions to choose from depending on the particulars of any one individual client or family. The discussion that follows is a summary of available options.

Overview of Principal Offshore Jurisdictions

All offshore jurisdictions that are active in seeking wealth preservation trusts have also been active in modernizing the law governing such trusts. However, there still exists a broad range of options and differences among the various jurisdictions.

Traditional offshore havens, such as the Isle of Man and the Cayman Islands, continue to offer a multitude of advantages. However, they are not necessarily the most advantageous jurisdictions from an asset protection standpoint. Some jurisdictions, such as Nevis and the Cook Islands, have adopted favorable legislation that was drafted with asset protection goals in mind. Jurisdictions such as New Zealand are not typically considered offshore havens; New Zealand does not even have a codified trust law. Instead it relies on the common law concepts of trust law, although the country does recognize a self-settled trust. Many individuals, especially foreign individuals, are attracted to New Zealand since the country is not on any type of watch or black list. As a result, it is a jurisdiction that has become popular in recent years with high-net-worth individuals.

Finally, although it is very new to the foreign trust jurisdiction competition, Switzerland has become a viable option for an international trust in light of its ratification of the Hague Convention on Trusts, which took effect on July 1, 2007. Switzerland is arguably the financial capital of the world, and despite what some would call its obsessive commitment to banking secrecy, it continues to enjoy an excellent reputation with the international financial community. Of course, because the law is extremely new and not very well understood by most practitioners, including Swiss professionals, it will be some time before viable trust structures are available in Switzerland.

A very brief outline of the various categories of jurisdictional options available to a typical planner is next, followed by a more detailed discussion of Nevis and New Zealand. Both continue to be popular with global professional advisors despite their different approaches to asset protection. Finally, due to its potential effect on the international trust community, the concept of trusts in Switzerland is discussed in a separate section.

Jurisdictions Commonly Used for International Trusts   As with any complex legal issue, the ideal jurisdiction for establishing an international trust for an individual or family is affected by issues too numerous to discuss in detail here. There is a wide range of jurisdictions from which to select a situs for the client's trust. The trust law in these jurisdictions can vary significantly.

In recent years, some jurisdictions have adopted very "specific" asset protection trust legislation expressly drafted to aggressively protect the assets transferred to a trust by a solvent debtor. Alternatively, other more "traditional" jurisdictions have intentionally decided to avoid such a strategy and instead rely on the common law that has developed over many years. Other jurisdictions, sometimes described as middle-of-the-road jurisdictions, have elected to adopt moderately debtor-friendly legislation to complement their existing common law, which has been extensively developed over many years.

The client's individual needs and realities may also affect the choice of jurisdiction. For example, individuals who are on the board of directors of a publicly held company that reports to the U.S. Securities and Exchange Commission may prefer to use a more traditional or contemporary jurisdiction rather than one with more aggressive legislation. However, most professionals and other individuals involved in high-risk endeavors usually prefer to use a jurisdiction that has very favorable asset protection legislation. In the end, the client's advisor must carefully evaluate the client's goals and needs when recommending an appropriate jurisdiction.

Jurisdictions with Specific Asset Protection Legislation A handful of jurisdictions have adopted legislation specifically designed to provide statutory clarity in the area of asset protection trusts. Jurisdictions with specific asset protection legislation have attempted to incorporate into their statutes very specific language regarding virtually every part of an international trust established for any reason but primarily if established for asset protection purposes. For example, while virtually all of these jurisdictions are traditionally common law jurisdictions, such as the United States, most, such as Nevis and the Cook Islands, have placed great emphasis on overruling certain common law concepts that are typically used to pierce a self-settled trust. Thus, although the concept of a sham trust is recognized in virtually all of these jurisdictions, specific asset protection legislation jurisdictions will, for example, address specific common law concepts that are expressly permitted under local law but might not otherwise be found in the traditional common law jurisdiction, such as the right to form a self-settled trust where the settlor of the trust can also be a beneficiary of the trust.

Likewise, these jurisdictions typically outline specific powers held by certain individuals, including the settlor/beneficiary of a trust, which are deemed by statute not considered to be a "badge of fraud" although, under common law, they typically would be. Last, while such jurisdictions incorporate the ability of a creditor to set aside a transfer to a trust that is considered to be a fraudulent transfer, strict statutes of limitations exist governing the ability of a creditor to challenge a transfer to an asset protection trust. Although such jurisdictions typically do have fraudulent transfer statutes, generally a creditor must prove, beyond a reasonable doubt, that a transfer to the trust was done with fraudulent intent.

Jurisdictions with specific asset protection legislation include the Cook Islands in the South Pacific, Nevis in the Caribbean, and St. Vincent and the Grenadines in the South Caribbean.

Traditional and Middle-of-the-Road Jurisdictions Several jurisdictions that have historically relied on traditional notions of trust law have, in recent years, modernized their trust law to incorporate the realities of self-settled wealth preservation trusts. However, these middle-of-the-road jurisdictions have adopted legislation that, while debtor-friendly, is not necessarily as protective as that found in Nevis and the Cook Islands. Thus, while these jurisdictions can be considered to have very good asset protection legislation, they have nevertheless retained, for the most part, fundamental common law trust concepts considered indispensable in many commonwealth jurisdictions, notwithstanding the modification of the common law by modern trust legislation. Jurisdictions that can be considered to fall into this category include Bermuda, the Bahamas, and the Cayman Islands.

The Channel Islands have historically been a favorite of individuals in Europe, particularly the United Kingdom. The Channel Islands include the Isle of Man, Jersey, and Guernsey. The trust law in the Channel Islands relies, to a large extent, on the common law adopted by those jurisdictions from the United Kingdom. Nevertheless, some of these jurisdictions have recently adopted legislation to modernize their existing trust law.

Certain jurisdictions have, in past, been criticized for literally accepting anyone as a client without too many questions asked. In fact, one could argue that the Isle of Man, for example, which was once the jurisdiction of choice for individuals in the United Kingdom, was built by funds siphoned out of the United Kingdom by individuals desiring to avoid the extremely high income tax rates in that country. Likewise, the Cayman Islands were well known at one time as the ideal jurisdiction for Latin American individuals and even many Americans desiring to establish trusts with funds from questionable sources. After all, it is not a coincidence that the Caymans, a small Caribbean island with a mere 31,000 residents, is the fifth largest financial center in the world and, at last count, has close to 700 banks or similar financial institutions.

In an effort to reflect their commitment to the strict demands of internationally accepted KYC ("know your customer") guidelines, both the Isle of Man and the Cayman Islands adopted very strict legislation well before most other jurisdictions. In retrospect, the legislation in the Cayman Islands was found to be overly burdensome and has now been slightly modified to prevent the choking effect that it had on business. The Isle of Man, which is heavily influenced by the United Kingdom and desirous of becoming a member of the European Union, continues to abide by a very strict code of conduct and KYC requirements that include concepts rejected by the United States. One specific KYC requirement adopted in the Isle of Man but not in the United States was a part of what is known as the Gatekeeper Initiative. That requirement would have essentially required attorneys and other professionals, including trustees, to disclose to tax and law enforcement officials information that might come to their attention regarding past or contemplated tax evasion schemes or intentions even before the professional advisor has had an opportunity to warn the client against such actions. Thus, many practitioners consider the Isle of Man's KYC requirements to be burdensome. Nevertheless, it continues to be popular with "traditionalist" professional advisors who prefer to use a foreign jurisdiction that has trust law based strictly on common law concepts and has a large array of professional trust companies to assist the client with such planning.

DETAILED DISCUSSION OF POPULAR JURISDICTIONS

As discussed, the jurisdiction best suited for a specific client's goals will vary based on circumstances, including the purpose of the trust, the domicile of the settlor, the expected duration of the trust, and the tax consequences, if any, of selecting a particular jurisdiction.

Nevis: Jewel of the Caribbean

The Caribbean island of Nevis has been described by one commentator as the jewel of the Caribbean. Many consider its trust legislation to be the best trust law available.

The island of Nevis is located in the Leeward Islands in the eastern Caribbean approximately 1,200 miles southeast of Miami and 225 miles southeast of Puerto Rico. The island has a current population of 9,500. English is the official and commercial language. The island, together with St. Kitts and Anguilla, formerly formed the West Indies Federation, a British colony until 1967. At that time, Anguilla seceded from the federation. In 1983, the Federation of St. Kitts and Nevis attained full political independence. Her Majesty Queen Elizabeth II is still considered the formal head of state of the Federation of St. Kitts and Nevis although the role is strictly symbolic in nature.

Nevis is an independent member of the British Commonwealth. It has its own political subdivision under the federation, with its own assembly. Under the constitution of the federation, Nevis may become an independent state by a two-thirds public referendum vote of its citizens. The legal system in Nevis is based on the English common law and is part of the West Indies court system. As a result, the court system in Nevis is very much like that found in virtually all former colonies of the British Commonwealth. The court of last resort, as in most Caribbean jurisdictions, is the Privy Council in the United Kingdom.

Nevis International Exempt Trust Act   The Nevis International Exempt Trust Ordinance of 1994, as amended in 2000, is modeled after the trust legislation of the Cook Islands. The ordinance is specifically tailored to make Nevis a preferred jurisdiction in the Caribbean for the establishment of asset protection trusts. Nevis does require the registration of an international trust, which is a very simple procedure that involves only the name of the trust, the name of the local registered agent, and the address of the registered office. The trust agreement itself is not filed with the government.

Under Nevis trust law, the same person can, but is not required to, be the settlor, the beneficiary, and the protector of the trust. Any of these persons can be residents or nonresidents of Nevis.

Controlling Law of Nevis International Trust   The trust law in Nevis provides the maximum amount of flexibility with respect to the law that shall control a Nevis trust. The trust agreement can provide that certain matters or provisions of the trust will be governed by a law other than the law of Nevis. Specifically, Section 4(1) of the Nevis Trust Ordinance provides that the proper law of a Nevis international trust shall be:

- The law expressed by the terms of the trust or intended by the settlor to be the proper law.
- If no such law is expressed or intended, the law with which the international trust has its closest connection at the time of its creation.
- If the law expressed by the terms of the trust or intended by the settlor to be the proper law, or the law with which the international trust has its closest connection at the time of its creation, does not provide for international trusts or the category of international trust involved, then the proper law of the international trust shall be the law of Nevis.

Exclusion of Foreign Laws   Section 29 of the Nevis Trust Ordinance clearly provides that no international trust governed by the ordinance and no disposition of property to be held by a Nevis trust shall be declared void, voidable, or subject to being set aside or defective, nor is the capacity of any settlor to be questioned by reason that:

- The laws of any foreign jurisdiction prohibit or do not recognize the concept of a trust either in whole or in part.
- The international trust or disposition avoids or defeats rights, claims, or interest conferred by the law of a foreign jurisdiction upon any person, or contravenes any rules, law, judicial, or administrative order or action intended to recognize, protect, enforce, or give effect to any such rights, claims or interest.
- The laws of St. Kitts and Nevis with the provisions of the Nevis Trust Ordinance are inconsistent with any foreign law.

In addition to the clear language of Section 29 of the ordinance, Section 48 provides that "forced heirship" rights—that is, foreign law that mandates the inheritance or the disposition of property upon death contrary to the settlor's wishes or contrary to the provisions of a Nevis trust—are not enforceable against a Nevis trust or the assets of the trust.

Protection Against Creditor Claims   A creditor seeking to set aside a transfer to a Nevis trust must establish beyond reasonable doubt that the transfer constituted a fraudulent disposition. The Nevis Trust Ordinance expressly states that a trust settled or established or a disposition to the trust shall not be fraudulent as against a creditor or a settlor:

- If settlement, establishment, or the disposition to the trust takes place more than two years from the date the creditor's cause of action accrued.
- If the settlement, establishment, or disposition takes place before the expiration of two years from the date that the settlor's cause of action accrued, the creditor fails to commence an action before the expiration of one year from the date of settlement, establishment, or disposition.

Any action to set aside a trust settlement or a disposition to a Nevis international trust must be commenced in the High Court of Nevis. Any creditor filing an action in Nevis against a Nevis trust must file a $25,000 bond to secure payment of costs with the ministry of finance.

Foreign judgments are not recognized in Nevis. Foreign laws have no application in Nevis. Therefore, in order to pursue a claim against assets in Nevis, whether held by a trust or otherwise, a claim must be tried in a Nevisian court, with Nevisian attorneys. As indicated, a creditor wishing to challenge a transfer to a trust in Nevis as being fraudulent must bring an action within one to two years, depending on the circumstances.

Trust Protector   Nevis law provides for the appointment of a trust "protector" who oversees the trustee's operation of the trust. The protector is not involved in active management of the trust but does have veto power over certain decisions of the trustee. The protector may also replace a trustee or relocate the situs of the trust if necessary. The role of a protector is extremely important in international trust law. The protector is basically the guardian angel of the trust and is charged with specific responsibility for approving the most significant activities of the trust by being granted the authority to consent to major decisions of the trustee. The extent to which the protector has veto power over trustee actions can be as limited or as broad as the settlor desires but must be stipulated in the trust agreement itself. The Nevis Trust Ordinance also makes clear that the protector has a fiduciary duty to the beneficiaries of the trust. Thus, the protector's role is one of loyalty to the beneficiaries of the trust and, in that capacity, must act to protect the best interests of the beneficiaries at all times.

The protector of an international trust may be the settlor, a trustee, or a beneficiary of the trust. If the trust is settled in Nevis by a resident of the United States, the better practice is for the protector to be an individual or entity located outside the settlor's home jurisdiction. In any event, there can be more than one trust protector. The Nevis trust laws specifically contemplate that more than one protector can serve in that capacity. Should that be the case, the vote of a majority of the protectors would control and decide any actions taken with regard to the trust.

Trustee and Private Trust Companies   Nevis is a jurisdiction that allows a settlor to establish a private trust company to act as the trustee of a Nevis trust. Specifically, under Section 2 of the Nevis Trust Ordinance, the trustee of an international trust may be a company formed under the Nevis Business Corporation Ordinance of 1984. Of course, a local registered resident and agent for the corporation must be appointed in Nevis. However, there are no restrictions on the ownership of the corporation that will act as the trustee of a Nevis trust. What these provisions do is to allow a settlor the flexibility of forming a private corporation in Nevis, to be owned by friends or family of the settlor, that will act as trustee of the Nevis trust established by the settlor. In this way, the decisions of the trustee are basically being made by individuals with whom the settlor is familiar and comfortable, particularly if the trust is to continue in existence well after the death of the settlor.

Confidentiality   Section 57(1) of the Nevis Trust Ordinance specifically provides that the Confidential Relationships Act of 1985 shall apply to every trust registered under the Nevis International Exempt Trust Ordinance. As a result, all judicial proceedings, other than criminal proceedings relating to international trusts in Nevis, shall be heard in the strictest confidence, and no details of the proceedings may be published by anyone without the express permission of the court. The Confidential Relationships Act was adopted by St. Kitts and Nevis in 1985 to sanction the duty of nondivulgence of information imparted under conditions of business or professional confidence. The act applies to all confidential information with respect to business of a professional nature that arises in or is brought into St. Kitts or Nevis and to all persons who came into possession of such information at any time thereafter, whether within or outside of St. Kitts or Nevis. The term "confidential information" is defined to include information concerning any property, or relating to any business of a professional nature or commercial transaction that has taken place, or that any party concerned contemplates may take place, which the recipient is not, other than in the normal course of business or professional practice, authorized by the principal to divulge. As a result, under law applicable in both St. Kitts and Nevis, any trustee, bank, or person in Nevis is obligated by law to maintain as confidential any information that is divulged to such person in connection with any business matter in Nevis, including any matter involving a Nevis trust. Nevis law provides for severe criminal penalties for violation of the Confidential Relationships Act.

New Zealand: A Viable Compromise

New Zealand is not typically considered an "offshore" jurisdiction by practitioners. It has neither asset protection legislation nor is it a tax haven. In fact, it is typically considered a high-tax jurisdiction, like Britain or France. However, New Zealand's close association with the Cook Islands, a progressive trust jurisdiction and former New Zealand protectorate, combined with favorable tax legislation for nonresident trust income offer some very unique planning opportunities for New Zealand trusts. Some of the principal benefits of a New Zealand trust are these:

- New Zealand is a well-known and well-respected member of the British Commonwealth. It has a modern economy, a democratically elected government, and all of the benefits usually associated with an English-speaking democracy. The legal system is based on the English common law model that also forms the basis of the U.S. legal system.
- Although New Zealand does not tax trust income earned outside of New Zealand, it is nevertheless not known as a tax haven. As a result, it has avoided the scrutiny usually reserved for offshore financial centers, some of which have not had the best of reputations. New Zealand has also avoided the money-laundering issues that have plagued many offshore jurisdictions. New Zealand has not been blacklisted by any of the major countries that have adopted anti–money-laundering or tax haven legislation. As a result, New Zealand has become very popular with many wealthy Latin American and European families.
- New Zealand has a modern infrastructure. It is accessible by most major airlines and has a communications network as modern as any in the world. Its major metropolitan centers have abundant professional talent available, many of whom have been educated in the United States, England, and Australia. Most of the major international banks of the world are represented in New Zealand.

New Zealand has a close economic and political association with the Cook Islands, a jurisdiction that arguably has the best asset protection legislation in the world. Should it become necessary, a New Zealand trust can easily be transferred to the Cook Islands, thus benefiting from the strong asset protection safeguards available in the Cook Islands.

SWITZERLAND FINALLY RECOGNIZES COMMON LAW TRUSTS

Switzerland is undoubtedly the international private banking capital of the world. Its strict banking privacy laws, ostensibly designed to protect individuals of different nationalities, are known throughout the world. Swiss banks are recognized for their stability, privacy, and protection of private client assets and information. What is commonly referred to as Swiss banking secrecy dates back to the Swiss Banking Act of 1934, although such secrecy laws have been updated to deal with the modern realities of money laundering and finances associated with terrorist activities. Thus, while Switzerland has modified its laws to allow its banks to cooperate with law enforcement agencies in regard to serious crimes, it nevertheless remains the favorite jurisdiction for the management and protection of investments of high-net-worth individuals throughout the world who seek banking privacy.

In light of Switzerland's reputation as the private banking capital of the world, most are surprised to learn that historically the concept of trusts has not been recognized by Swiss law. Switzerland is a civil law jurisdiction whereas trusts are based on the Anglo-Saxon common law typically found in jurisdictions with direct or indirect former ties to the United Kingdom. Since Switzerland is not a common law jurisdiction, it never legally recognized the trust as a separate and distinct legal institution. Thus, a trust operating in Switzerland typically deposits assets in the name of a corporate trustee for the benefit of the trust. Nevertheless, the Swiss would be the first to admit that the trust constitutes an important concept in international private banking, particularly when integrated with estate and testamentary planning common for high-net-worth individuals. Yet, since the concept of a trust was totally alien to the Swiss civil law, the common law trust has never been recognized legally by Switzerland.

Ratification of Hague Convention on Trusts

Over the years, Switzerland has dealt with the multiple legal and practical problems associated with the operation of trusts even though they are not legally recognized as such under Swiss law. Nevertheless, even court decisions in Switzerland generally recognized the concept of a trust. Because there was no legal basis for trusts under Swiss law, Switzerland began the process of considering the adoption of the Hague Convention on the Law Applicable to Trusts and Their Recognition, which was adopted by the Hague Convention on Private International Law on July 1, 1985. At the time it was originally adopted by the Hague Convention, the delegates recognized that the trust, as developed in courts of equity and common law jurisdictions and adopted with some modifications in other jurisdictions, was a unique legal institution. Therefore, desiring to establish common law provisions on the law applicable to trusts and to deal with the most important issues concerning the recognition of trusts, the convention adopted general principles applicable to the recognition of trusts. For purposes of the convention, the term "trust" was defined as referring to a legal relationship created, either inter vivos or on death, by a person, the settlor, when assets had been placed under control of the trustee for the benefit of a beneficiary or for a specified purpose. As such, the trust was recognized as having these three characteristics:

1. The assets constituted a separate fund and were not part of the trustee's own estate.
2. Title to the trust assets was in the name of the trustee or in the name of another person on behalf of the trustee.
3. The trustee had the power and the duty, in respect to which it is accountable, to manage, employ, or dispose of the assets in accordance with the terms of the trust and the special duties imposed on the trustee by law.

The flexibility provided by the convention is found in Article 6 regarding the law applicable to the trust. Specifically, Article 6 of the Hague Convention on Trusts provides that "a trust shall be governed by the law chosen by the settlor." However, while the convention provides significant detail regarding virtually all aspects of the trust, Article 9 of the convention specifically provides that in applying the convention on the law applicable to trust, "a severable aspect of the trust, particularly in matters of an administration, may be governed by a different law. The law applicable to the validity of the trust shall not determine whether that law or the law governing a severable aspect of the trust may be replaced by another law." In other words, different aspects of a trust may be governed by the law of different jurisdictions; all aspects of the trust do not have to be governed by a single jurisdiction. Thus, a settlor can literally pick and choose which law will govern various aspects of the trust so that a trust agreement could effectively be governed by the law of multiple jurisdictions.

After years of work on formulating law that would be acceptable to Switzerland, the Swiss parliament finally decided, on December 20, 2006, to authorize the Federal Council to ratify the Hague Convention on the Law Applicable to Trusts effective July 1, 2007. As such, upon the Hague Convention on Trusts becoming effective in Switzerland, a common law trust will, for the first time ever, be recognized as a separate legal institution in Switzerland.

Swiss Enabling Legislation

In connection with the ratification of the Hague Convention on Trusts, Switzerland enacted legislation to implement details regarding the recognition and operation of trusts within the country by adopting conforming amendments to Switzerland's Code on Private International Law. The law is the principal source of authority for the resolution of conflicts of law and of jurisdiction; it also governs the conditions and circumstances under which Switzerland will recognize a foreign court decision. While the Swiss Private International Law has included 13 separate sections governing various aspects of international law, the Code on Private International Law had no provisions to deal with trusts. Included in the revisions to the Private International Law are provisions allowing Swiss courts to have exclusive jurisdiction over trust disputes, if provided for in the underlying trust agreement. Legislation was also introduced to make the necessary amendments to the Swiss Debt Collection and Bankruptcy Act to underscore and codify the separation between assets of a trust versus the trustee's own assets, so that claims against a trustee will not reach trust assets under its control. This enabling legislation was required since Switzerland merely elected to recognize the existence of trusts pursuant to the Hague Convention on Trusts without actually adopting trust law of its own.

One of the most important revisions to the Private International Law provides details regarding the selection of the proper law to govern the trust or specific provisions of the trust. As allowed by the Hague Convention, a trust agreement can provide that the law of two or more particular jurisdictions will govern specific provisions of the trust agreement. Such flexibility allows the settlor to draft a trust agreement that will have Switzerland as its principal situs and provide for a managing trustee in Switzerland and, possibly most important of all, provide that any legal disputes associated with the trust shall be resolved exclusively by the Swiss courts. In this regard, it is absolutely crucial for a trust agreement to specifically state that Switzerland is selected as the forum for the resolution of any and all matters concerning the trust. Similarly, the trust agreement should provide that the administration of the trust shall occur in Switzerland. It also should probably provide that the Swiss trustee shall be the managing trustee of the trust, thereby allowing the Swiss trustee to have virtually exclusive authority with respect to all decisions regarding the trust.

The ratification by Switzerland of the Hague Convention on Trusts combined with the amendments to the Swiss Private International Law does not mean that Switzerland will have its own trust law. Thus, to utilize the benefits associated with the recent recognition of trusts in Switzerland and the adoption of conforming legislation, it is necessary to first form the trust in a jurisdiction that recognizes common law trusts. Typically this can be any common law jurisdiction, although certain civil law jurisdictions, such as Liechtenstein and Panama, also provide for common law trusts. In any event, by way of example, if an individual were to settle a trust to be managed by a Swiss trustee, the trust would be settled pursuant to the law of a jurisdiction that provides for common law trusts while the trust agreement would provide that the management of the trust shall lie exclusively in Switzerland with a Swiss trustee and with Swiss courts having exclusive jurisdiction over any disputes involving the trust.

Net Effect of "Swiss Trusts"

The net effect of Switzerland's ratification of the Hague Convention on Trusts and the adoption of conforming amendments to the Swiss Private International Law Act is effectively to allow an individual to design and implement a common law trust vehicle that will be managed by a Swiss trustee, with certain parts of the trust agreement governed by Swiss private law, including access to the Swiss courts for the resolution of any disputes, without Switzerland ever having actually adopted common law trust law for itself. While Switzerland could, like Liechtenstein and Panama, adopt its own common law-style trust law, there does not appear to be a significant movement in that regard. For one thing, since Switzerland is a civil law jurisdiction, it has no "common law" to fall back on. Thus, the same difficulties that Liechtenstein and other civil law jurisdictions face when their courts have to resolve disputes involving common law trusts formed in a civil jurisdiction are likely to be encountered. In many cases, such dispute resolution can be resolved only through an actual amendment of the applicable statutory trust law in question; otherwise, without common law to rely on, the courts would not have any guidance on how a dispute should be resolved.

It is likely that the hybrid legislative model adopted for Switzerland will allow Swiss courts, accustomed to the application of civil law, to resolve disputes involving common law issues by relying on the common law of the jurisdiction pursuant to which the trust was actually formed. By way of example, in the well- known case of W. K. Rey, the courts of the Canton of Zurich empaneled a five-man group of Guernsey advocates to advise the judges on how to apply Guernsey law, the law chosen to govern the trust involved in the case. Thus, much in the same way that a United States federal district court will apply the state law chosen by the parties to govern a particular transaction, a Swiss court will look at the common law of the jurisdiction selected by the settlor to govern the trust. Such a model adopts a clear mechanism by which disputes involving a common law trust can be resolved by Swiss courts.

While many questions still remain regarding the application of these recent developments to trusts in Switzerland, they nevertheless have the potential to provide significant opportunities for the design and implementation of a trust structure that is modeled after traditional well-known common law concepts while effectively domiciled in Switzerland. While drafting such a hybrid trust agreement is not an easy task, such agreements undoubtedly will develop into trust alternatives that will become popular with trust practitioners throughout the world, particularly those who prefer to benefit from the multiple advantages offered by traditional Swiss private banking traditions.

DRAFTING AN INTERNATIONAL TRUST

Many of the considerations applicable to the formation of any trust are also applicable to the formation of an international wealth preservation trust. Certain considerations, such as the choice of a trustee, are amplified when using a foreign trustee. Rarely is an individual comfortable with the prospect of having his or her assets and wealth subject to the control of an individual or trust company in a foreign jurisdiction. However, the competency of the trustee can have a significant effect on whether an international trust can achieve its desired goals. Moreover, the more the trust arrangement reflects a legitimate arm's-length arrangement with an independent trustee, the better the benefits to the client from an asset protection standpoint and, if so desired and provided for, an estate planning standpoint.

As with any legal document, a trust agreement for an international trust should be drafted to reflect the wishes of the settlor. Although such a trust instrument will include provisions that may not be typical in a client's home country, particularly a civil law jurisdiction, any professional advising his or her client on forming an international trust should first identify the settlor's overall wishes and goals. These desires then are incorporated into the international trust agreement just as they are incorporated into any agreement. Of course, any such provisions will have to comply with the law of the jurisdiction that has been selected for the trust. In addition, the trust should include these provisions:

- Self-settled trust
- Ability to change situs of trust
- Ability to change trustees
- Ability to move trust assets
- Use of a protector

Self-Settled Trust

Assuming it is permissible under the jurisdiction chosen for the situs of the trust, the trust agreement will usually provide that the settlor has and can retain a beneficial interest in the income or corpus of the trust. Great care should be used in selecting a jurisdiction for such a trust; not all offshore jurisdictions will recognize self-settled trusts.

Ability to Change Situs of Trust

It is not unusual for clients to respond unfavorably to the idea of establishing a trust in a jurisdiction that they had never heard of prior to consulting with an attorney. If settlors genuinely are creditor free or solvent, they may prefer to establish the trust in a better-known jurisdiction, such as the Cayman Islands, which may not have ideal legislation. This problem can be resolved by a provision in the trust agreement that authorizes the trustees to change the situs of the trust upon the occurrence of certain unfavorable events. Thus, for example, if a trust is established in Bermuda, a "flee clause" will authorize the trustee in Bermuda or the trust "protector" to change the situs of the trust to a more favorable offshore jurisdiction if it appears that the trust will come under attack in Bermuda as a result of unforeseen problems in the debtor's home country.

Ability to Change Trustees

The trust agreement should also provide that, upon the occurrence of certain events, the trustees of the international trust may be changed. This can become necessary in a variety of circumstances, not the least of which is a situation where the existing trustee may be found to come under the jurisdiction of an unfavorable legal environment. Should that occur, the trust agreement can provide for the automatic removal of the "tainted" trustee and the appointment of a new trustee or trustees.

Ability to Move Trust Assets

The trustees of an international trust typically should be given broad authority to move assets of the trust for specific enumerated reasons. So long as the trustees have a legitimate reason to continue to preserve and protect the assets of the trust, the trustees will owe a fiduciary duty to the trust and its beneficiaries to protect its assets by moving them, if necessary, to a more favorable jurisdiction should changed circumstances require such a move.

Use of a Protector

An important part of any international trust is the use of a trust protector. The legislation of most offshore jurisdictions recognizes the concept of the protector. A protector is the guardian angel of a trust. It is typically an individual or a company affiliated with a law firm or professional trustee. The particular powers that a protector have typically are provided for in the trust deed. Such powers usually include significant and well-defined veto powers over certain proposed actions of the trustee. For example, if a trustee in an offshore jurisdiction should receive a request from the grantor that is in clear contravention of the settlor's original wishes, the protector has the right to veto such request if the protector, in its sole and absolute judgment, believes that granting the request would be inconsistent with the settlor's original intent. Powers usually granted a trust protector include the power to:

- Remove a trustee
- Cause the trust to relocate to another jurisdiction
- Freeze benefits payable to beneficiaries who have encountered creditor, marital, or other problems
- Add beneficiaries, within parameters outlined by the settlor in his or her "Letter of Wishes"
- Authorize the amendment of the trust to update the document for changed circumstances including income or estate tax purposes

MANAGEMENT AND INVESTMENT OF TRUST ASSETS

A common misconception associated with international trusts relates to the location of trust assets. While a particular jurisdiction might be ideal for forming an international trust, it does not necessarily mean that assets contributed to the trust will be transferred and managed there. On the contrary, assets transferred to an international trust are managed where it is logical to do so, particularly liquid assets and investments that are usually managed in an offshore financial center such as the Cayman Islands, Switzerland, or Luxembourg.

Assets transferred into an international trust typically can be classified as either liquid or illiquid. If an individual transfers an interest in an illiquid asset such as real estate or a closely held business, typically there is very little that the international trustee is required to do on a day-to-day basis. For example, if the client were to transfer an interest in a limited liability company, closely held corporation, or family limited partnership, the role of the international trustee typically is limited to monitoring the interest of the trust in the underlying entity. If cash or other liquid assets are transferred into an international trust, however, those assets typically require close management by a professional asset manager or investment advisor.

Cash or Other Liquid Assets

If a large bank or other similar institution is used as trustee of the international trust, the trustee itself typically manages the assets for the trust. For example, if Bank of Bermuda were the trustee of the international trust, the investment branch of Bank of Bermuda would handle the day-to-day investment decisions involving trust assets.

A more typical scenario involves an international trust company that utilizes the services of a professional asset manager in a top financial center such as Switzerland to manage liquid trust investments. For example, a trust can first be formed in the Cook Islands using one of several reputable trust companies available in that jurisdiction. Once the liquid funds are transferred into the international trust, the trustee will arrange to have the funds transferred to a professional asset manager in a reputable financial center. That investment manager will then manage the investments on behalf of the trust. The authority of the asset manager is limited to investment decisions involving the management of trust assets. The trustee retains authority over all other trust decisions including the amount and timing of any distributions to the beneficiaries of the trust.

Even though the settlor of the international trust is typically also the beneficiary, the settlor will not have any control over the investment advisor. However, the settlor nevertheless will be authorized to have regular communication with the investment advisor in order to monitor the investment activities of the trust.

Obviously, a client contemplating the transfer of cash to an international trust will want to have some influence over how those assets are invested by the trust. Unfortunately, the settler typically loses that control when the assets are actually transferred into the trust. Therefore, it is usually advisable for the settlor to inform the trustee and investment manager of his or her investment preferences prior to formation of the trust. Thus, if the settlor prefers that the trustee limit investments of the trust to conservative blue-chip stocks and bonds, he or she can make those preferences clear prior to the formation of the trust. Moreover, although the trustee is not required to abide by the beneficiary's investment desires, the international trustee typically is authorized and encouraged to seek advice from trust beneficiaries as to their investment preferences. After all, the trust exists for the benefit of its beneficiaries, even if the beneficiary also happens to be the original settlor of the trust.

Home-Advised Offshore Account

Often persons recognize their need to seek the benefits of an international trust but are reluctant to abandon their financial advisor, who knows their investment goals and tolerances better than anyone. Their confidence in the advisor may be difficult to reestablish with an unknown foreign financial institution. In such cases, depending on several variables, the clients' planner may be able to design an international trust structure that allows for the offshore transfer of the portfolio but still allows the local financial planner an investment advisory role.

A home-advised offshore account is an investment account established by the trustee with an offshore financial institution that is managed by an investment advisor in the individual's home jurisdiction. In a typical situation, the liquid assets under management are deposited into a custodial account with a financial institution. Thus, the Swiss financial institution merely acts as the custodian of the deposited assets and has no investment authority. Instead, the investment authority is delegated by the trustee to the individual's local financial advisor. As such, the local advisor has full investment and management authority over the assets that are deposited in the Swiss financial institution. However, the local advisor's authority is strictly limited to investment management; he or she has no authority to disburse funds from the account. That authority is retained by the trustee.

The advantages of a home-advised offshore account are obvious. It allows the assets under management to be held in a protected offshore account while being managed by an advisor based in the client's home jurisdiction. Such an arrangement allows the settlor easier access to the investment managers of the trust account. Although the settlor retains no control over trust assets, having a local advisor allows the beneficiaries of the trust to remain better informed about trust investment strategies. Some settlors and beneficiaries also take comfort from the use of an investment advisor who may be more familiar to them.

Summary

Swiss annuities and Swiss life insurance products offer unique benefits and advantages not available anywhere else in the world. Their value to an individual, from a wealth preservation standpoint, can be enhanced when integrated into an international trust. In fact, use of a properly structured international trust will ensure that the assets of the trust remain free from any interference, including legal action, which may at a later date affect the individual who organized the trust for his or her benefit and for the benefit of family and heirs. Moreover, for those individuals contemplating an eventual move to the United States, significant tax savings can be achieved by establishing an international trust at least five years prior to becoming a U.S. citizen or U.S. resident. In fact, unique planning opportunities exist for foreign individuals contemplating a move to the United States, if they take certain actions before establishing their tax residency in the United States. Specifically, until such tax residency is established, individuals typically will not be subject to taxation in the United States except on U.S.-based income. As a result, individuals can undertake tax planning that might otherwise be taxable in the United States but for the fact that the individuals consummate such transactions prior to becoming U.S. citizens or U.S. residents.

Once the international trust is formed, the trustees can invest in Swiss annuities and Swiss life insurance policies, which, in many jurisdictions around the world, are entitled to deferral of taxation on investment income earned by the investments held by such policies, particularly a Swiss variable life insurance policy. Even after the death of the individual who established the trust, the trust can continue to provide benefits to his or her family and heirs by serving as a long-term dynastic trust, thereby preserving and protecting the assets of the trust from the world's volatile political and economic environment. By selecting Switzerland and its annuity or insurance products, the trust and its beneficiaries will have the comfort of knowing that the products are in the care of insurance companies that are part of what is arguably the world's leading private wealth management capitol.

CHAPTER 9

The Advantages of Liechtenstein Annuities and Life Insurance

Alexander T. Skreiner

*Former Managing Director, CapitalLeben,
Liechtenstein; Partner, DATS-Consulting,
Rankweil, Austria*

L iechtenstein is a young location for the insurance industry that can look back at a highly successful history not much longer than a decade. Today, 17 life insurance companies based in the principality offer internationally recognized and attractive annuity and life insurance solutions for demanding clients. These solutions have become established in the sector of private wealth management and are growing in importance. In its advisory and structuring capacity for specific provident solutions, the industry bases its activities on the principality's benefits associated with investment, tax, insolvency, discretion, and legal status.

INTRODUCTION

Seen from today's perspective, the development of Liechtenstein as an insurance center looks like a genuine success story. Although its history goes back no more than about 11 years, it shows that internationally recognized solutions can be successfully offered on the basis of the right local policies and the commitment of everyone involved, despite a tough and often highly competitive market environment.

In this chapter, Liechtenstein is first presented and analyzed as an insurance location whose details are a precondition for understanding the solutions that it offers. The local benefits—also known as the princely privileges—then are described and a number of products offered by individual providers and their application and structuring options are examined.

LOCATION

The principality of Liechtenstein extends over 160 square kilometers along the river Rhine. It is bordered to the south and west by Switzerland, to the north and east by Austria. These two countries have also had the greatest influence on the country over the course of history.

Most of the 11 municipalities comprising Liechtenstein are located in the west of the country along the river Rhine. Vaduz is the principal town and a well-known tourist attraction.

About 35,000 people live in Liechtenstein, almost 34 percent of them nonnationals originating mostly from Switzerland, Austria, and Germany. Of particular note is the large number of cross-border commuters who travel on a daily basis from the adjoining regions of Switzerland and Austria, and sometimes from Germany, in order to work there.

Liechtenstein is a sovereign state with a constitutional hereditary monarchy reigning on the basis of a parliamentary democracy. Government power is vested in the prince and the populace. This political system, which is probably unique and guarantees stability and continuity, has, together with the character of its population and their efforts, made Liechtenstein one of the world's wealthiest countries.

History

1699   Prince Johann Adam Andreas von Liechtenstein acquires the Schellenberg domain
1712   Prince Johann Adam Andreas von Liechtenstein acquires the county of Vaduz
1719   Union as the Principality of Liechtenstein and promotion to an imperial principality
1806   Membership of the Confederation of the Rhine, sovereignty of the Principality of Liechtenstein
1815   Joins the German Confederation
1852   Customs union with Austria
1862   Written constitution promulgated
1919   Dissolution of the customs union with Austria
1921   New constitution
1924   Introduction of the Swiss franc/customs and monetary union with Switzerland

1926 Law on Persons and Companies (PGR) comes into force
1950 Member of the International Court of Justice at the Hague
1960 European Free Trade Association (EFTA) membership represented by Switzerland
1975 Participant at the Conference on Security and Cooperation in Europe (CSCE)
1978 Member of the Council of Europe
1980 Currency union with Switzerland
1990 160th member of the United Nations
1991 Full member of the European Free Trade Association (EFTA)
1995 Joins the European Economic Area (EEA)
1995 Joins the World Trade Organisation (WTO)
1997 Direct insurance agreement with Switzerland

A more detailed appreciation of recent developments within Europe is needed to understand the country's economic boom and above all its emergence and development as an insurance center as a complement to its familiar role as a financial center (especially as a banking and fiduciary center) that has been established for many decades.

The customs agreement in force since 1852 between Liechtenstein and the Austro-Hungarian Empire became irrelevant after the collapse of the empire in 1918 and consequently was revoked by Liechtenstein in 1919. In October 1919, the government of Liechtenstein asked Switzerland to look after the country's interests and those of its citizens abroad through its embassies and consulates.

The customs union with Switzerland of March 29, 1923, laid the foundation for a new epoch in the country's economic development that owes much of its success to ever closer cooperation with its western neighbor.

The customs agreement stipulates that the entire corpus of Swiss customs legislation as well as the rest of Swiss federal legislation to the extent implied by the customs union is applicable to Liechtenstein. However, all regulations of Swiss federal legislation that involve contributions by the Swiss Federation are exempt from these stipulations. The customs agreement also means that all trade and customs agreements concluded by Switzerland with third-party countries also apply to Liechtenstein. Switzerland is also authorized to represent Liechtenstein in relevant negotiations and to conclude any associated agreements such that they also apply to Liechtenstein.

The customs agreement, which is in principle limited to goods traffic, was adapted to changing needs in 1991 and 1995. As a result, Liechtenstein can now act as a contracting state in international agreements and become a member of international organizations in the area covered by the customs agreement as long as Switzerland is also a signatory to these agreements and organizations. Liechtenstein may also conclude such agreements and join such organizations if Switzerland does not do so. In the latter case, Liechtenstein and Switzerland each conclude a special agreement, such as was necessary in 1994 to prepare Liechtenstein's accession to the European Economic Area (EEA).

In addition to its effect as an international agreement, the customs union is also of symbolic significance for the particularly close relationships between Liechtenstein and Switzerland. It created the basis for a legal approximation and harmonization in the sectors of commercial and social law extending widely beyond its domain of application. This close intermeshing is currently expressed in numerous agreements and treaties, especially in the fields of social security, occupational training, indirect taxation, and police cooperation across borders.

In 1980, a currency agreement was concluded between Liechtenstein and Switzerland according to which Liechtenstein, which has used the Swiss franc as its legal currency since 1921, was integrated into the Swiss currency area while in principle retaining its monetary sovereignty. The Swiss regulations on monetary, credit, and currency policy in the sense of the national bank law thus also apply in Liechtenstein.

International Context

Liechtenstein has been a member of the EEA since May 1, 1995. The EEA agreement extends the single internal market of the European Union (EU) by three of the four EFTA states, namely Liechtenstein, Iceland, and Norway. Although Switzerland is a member of the European Free Trade Association (EFTA), it is not a member of the EEA, having rejected membership in a referendum of December 1992. The EEA represents a market of more than 462 million consumers. It is characterized by freedom of movement of goods, services, capital, and persons (known as the four freedoms) within its area. The citizens of all 30 EEA member states (27 EU member states plus Liechtenstein, Iceland, and Norway) have the right to move freely within the entire EEA and can reside, work, establish businesses, invest, and acquire property throughout this area.

Within the framework of implementing the agreement, the EEA/EFTA states may participate in elaborating the relevant legislation. The EEA agreement excludes the EU's common taxation policy as well as its common agricultural and fisheries policy. As the EEA is not a customs union, trade policy with respect to third-party countries does not come within the scope of the agreement either.

In addition to the legal regulations concerning the single market, the EEA agreement contains both horizontal and flanking policies aimed at strengthening this market. These additional cooperative sectors include:

research and development, statistics, education, social policy, the environment, consumer protection, tourism, small and midsize businesses, culture, information services, and the audiovisual sector. The EEA/EFTA states take part in EU programs in these sectors and have, through their participation in the relevant committees, a codetermination right in the development and implementation of the programs involved.

Liechtenstein was a cosignatory to the founding agreement of the World Trade Organization (WTO) in 1994 in Marrakesh and joined the WTO on September 1, 1995. Although the WTO agreement does not imply a level of economic integration comparable to the EEA, it does offer an indispensable and reliable legal foundation for Liechtenstein's economy, a significant part of whose exports go to countries outside Europe. The WTO's dispute resolution system is of particular importance for protecting Liechtenstein's interests in international trade.

The customs agreement with Switzerland and the coming into force of the Law on Persons and Companies in 1926 have proved to be particularly significant for the development of the country as a financial center.

The changes in the legal framework conditions as a result of joining the EEA in 1995 and the associated acceptance of its entire corpus of framework conditions relating to insurance law represented the starting point for the development of Liechtenstein as an insurance center.

The framework conditions that favor the country's financial activities and insurance activities may be summarized in this way:

- Security and stability thanks to an assured legal system based on a long tradition
- AAA country rating by Moody's and Standard & Poor's
- Excellent infrastructure and optimum human resources
- Minimal bureaucracy
- Intimate links to the Swiss economic area
- Currency union with Switzerland/Swiss franc as legal currency
- Efficient banking system
- Member of the EEA with its four freedoms:
  1. Free movement of goods
  2. Free movement of services
  3. Free movement of capital
  4. Free movement of persons
- Extremely rigorous regulations on duty of care applicable to all participants in the financial services sector
- Legally protected bank and insurance secrecy
- No aid to tax authorities
- No tax harmonization
- Attractive tax legislation

Liechtenstein has organized its insurance services on the European model, thus giving its insurance companies direct access to the entire EEA. Liechtenstein concluded an economic agreement with Switzerland in 1997 that grants insurance companies based in Liechtenstein or Switzerland the right to establish themselves and operate services in the direct insurance sector in both countries. As a result, a company may now operate from Liechtenstein and offer its services directly both in the EEA and in Switzerland, a unique situation for insurance companies in Europe.

In view of the government's intention that the country's insurance sector should grow organically, the various EU directives for the insurance industry were adopted in order to build up this new sector. With a balance sheet total of CHF 16.8 billion, the insurance industry cannot yet compete seriously with the banks, but its latest growth rates are far above those of the other parts of the financial services sector. According to the 2006 annual report of the Financial Market Authority, assets worth a total of CHF 219.4 billion were managed in Liechtenstein at the end of 2006. The banks accounted for CHF 173.4 billion of this (growth of 26.6 percent over the previous year), investment companies for CHF 26.6 billion (up by 29.1 percent) and provident institutions for CHF 3.2 billion (up by 3.2 percent). The asset investments of the insurance companies rose to CHF 14.77 billion and thus reached a growth rate of 58.8 percent.

Liechtenstein's insurance companies focus on fund-linked life insurance. The indemnity insurers operate a niche business and specialize in particular insurance products, such as art insurance. Captives operate in the reinsurance sector: These insurance companies are owned by the parent company and underwrite the insurance needs of the parent's subsidiaries. Liechtenstein has positioned itself from the outset as a center for captives of first-class companies with a strong financial position. Companies such as Novartis, Syngenta, Swisscom, SBB, Schindler, and Rieter already use these location benefits.

The prospects for the fund-linked business in Europe are generally regarded as highly promising. An insurance contract is known as fund-linked when the savings performance is tied directly to the value of shares in investment funds or company-own internal funds and the investment risk is borne by the policy holder. Index-linked or index-oriented products (where the savings performance is linked to a share index, bond index, or other reference index) are included under this umbrella term. "*Fund-linked products*' are an interesting alternative to traditional contracts with guaranties for both the policyholder and the life insurer," writes the Swiss Re,[1] not least because the policy holders obtain a transparent product.

New business fields are being opened up in order to give the insurance center further opportunities for development. Against the background of the increasing importance of the growing market for company annuity insurance in Europe, Liechtenstein is aiming to position itself as an attractive location for cross-border facilities in this sector. To this end, the government commissioned a prospective study for setting up Liechtenstein as a pension fund center in 2005. It concluded that traditional contribution-financed annuity insurance systems have reached their limits. The demand for company annuity insurance would continue to grow in most European countries and thus create a new market potential in future. The government regards this market situation as an opportunity to diversify the insurance business. The pension fund law as well as its implementation regulation came into force on January 17, 2007.

Supervision

The Financial Market Authority (FMA) that was refounded at the beginning of 2005 also makes a very significant contribution to the stability of Liechtenstein as an insurance center.

The setting up of this comprehensive authority to supervise all activities of the finance industry was one of the demands of the International Monetary Fund in the final report on its Offshore Financial Centre Assessment in October and November 2002. This assessment was preceded by Liechtenstein's inclusion on the Blacklist of the Financial Action Task Force (FATF) in June 2000. This list comprises the designated Non-Cooperative Countries and Territories (NCCT). Liechtenstein consequently intensified its efforts to assure duty of care in the sector, which led to its being delisted in June 2001.

The FMA is entitled to supervise the insurance companies and is responsible for all supervisory activities at the national and international level.

Supervision of the private insurance companies is subdivided in this way:

- Authorization to operate as a business
- Supervision of business operations
- Special regulations for individual branches of the insurance business

Insurance companies must be able to fulfill their contractual obligations at all times. These requirements also include financial security. The ongoing supervision thus focuses particularly on the solvency and business plans of the insurance companies.

Liechtenstein insurance supervision applies in principle to companies that operate direct or reinsurance in the principality of Liechtenstein. Those companies that cover risks located within the country, or cover risks located in another country from a base in Liechtenstein, are regarded as operating direct insurance in the principality. Special regulations apply to companies with headquarters in an EEA state, Switzerland (according to the direct insurance agreement), or a third country. The supervision does not apply to insurance companies with headquarters abroad that merely operate reinsurance services in the principality of Liechtenstein.

In its capacity as the home-country authority, the FMA supervises all the activities of Liechtenstein insurance companies within the EEA and Switzerland. This principle of single-license or home-country control that applies within the EU and the EEA also guarantees that the product constitution and supervision take place exclusively by the Liechtenstein authority. This means that the insurance companies need not follow any local authorization procedures. In addition, the fact that Liechtenstein legislation involves no substantive supervision, but concentrates on the quality or solvency of the companies, has turned out to be a competitive advantage. As a result, the insurance companies do not have to submit their products inclusive of the tariffs and their general insurance conditions in advance to the FMA for inspection and approval in each case. This allows them to respond with great flexibility to their customers and the market. It is hardly surprising that most of them offer customized solutions.

PRINCELY PRIVILEGES

The success of the Liechtenstein insurance companies is based to a significant extent on the framework conditions known widely as the princely privileges that are offered by Liechtenstein. These are:

- Investment privilege
- Tax privilege
- Asset protection privilege
- Discretion privilege
- Arrangement privilege

Investment Privilege

In contrast to traditional insurance contracts in which the policy holder has no influence on or transparency and knowledge about the investments made by the insurance company, the fund-linked solutions that grant the policy holder significantly greater influence have been available since the beginning or middle of the 1990s.

Liechtenstein has developed a third-generation, or unit-linked, insurance in which the savings part of an annuity or life insurance policy may be invested not only in internal or external funds (at the request of the policy holder) but in any bankable investment.

The framework conditions required for this innovation are found in section 43 of the insurance supervision regulations.[2] They stipulate that in insurance contracts in which the policy holder bears the investment risk, the insurance company can in principle make use of any investment for which the policy holder is willing to accept the risk. The policy holder thus participates directly in the development of the investment.

The development of insurance products in Liechtenstein has led to the situation in which some providers now offer individualized premium reserve accounts. (See Figure 9.1.) The term "premium reserve" refers to assets that reflect the value of the policies of an insurance company. This means that the sum of all claims from the policies must be covered by the premium reserve of the insurance company, which is, in the case of traditional insurance products, solely responsible for investing in the premium reserve.[3] In fund-linked insurance products, however, the insurance company keeps in its premium reserve the sum of all those parts of the fund that it has acquired on the basis of the policy holder's specifications and assigns the shares to the individual policies. The policies then have an accounting par value and assignable but not assigned assets. This situation, which is not insignificant especially for private banking clients, is resolved by the individual premium reserve account solution offered by Liechtenstein providers.

An individual premium reserve account is differentiated with respect to each policy; that is, the insurance company effectively runs a designated securities deposit (including a clearing account) for each individual policy,

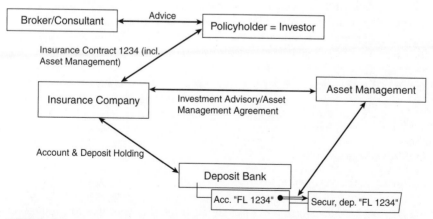

FIGURE 9.1 Individual Premium Reserve Account Solution

and most providers even allow several banks. But it also allows individual assets to be assigned quite specifically to individual policies and gives the policy holder greater say in structuring the premium reserve account of the policy. Thus he or she can determine the investment strategy, designate the external asset manager who implements the desired investment strategy, and select a depositary bank permitted by the insurance provider.

In conjunction with external asset managers, private banks, and private banking departments, such individual premium reserve account solutions allow highly individual solutions, completely in line with the client's preferences, specifications, and ideas. This makes such annuity or life assurance solutions an ideal instrument for structuring investment and pension assets.

The commissioned asset manager can now implement the desired investment strategy in these individual premium reserve accounts. The client's wishes and ideas may range from very conservative bond deposits all the way to dynamic share deposits with a mixture of private equity or alternative investments. However, investments may also be made in unquoted stocks. Only direct investments in real estate, in limited partnerships (the well-known KG model for closed-end funds), and in investments with the obligation to make additional contributions are excluded.

It should in general be noted that policy holders cannot make the investment decisions themselves but can only define the strategy and designate the asset manager or else select them from a specified number of options. These regulations are also known as owner-control rules.

Later in the chapter, in examining tax aspects, it is shown that national regulations may completely or at least partially restrict this freedom of investment.

Liechtenstein life insurance solutions are also very popular with private investors who are keen to avoid restrictions or constraints in their selection of investments and thus to optimize and extend their scope of action. Numerous jurisdictions place restrictions on alternative investments, particularly on hedge funds, private equity funds, and real estate funds. As a rule, clients can avoid these restrictions by acquiring a fiscally and legally recognized life insurance solution from Liechtenstein within the scope of which their designated asset manager may invest in funds of just this type.

Tax Privilege

Unlike capital investments, investments in fund-linked annuity or life insurance policies are associated in most European countries with tax benefits, which may be considerable. As a rule, such fiscal advantages are linked to specific criteria, such as minimum terms or assurance payable at death.

A distinction should be made between tax benefits that refer to the beginning of the insurance term (parts of the premium are tax-deductible or are promoted) or to its duration (tax-free saving phase or earnings retention) and those granted in connection with payments (tax-free or reduced-tax treatment).

The various national systems[4] cannot be treated in detail here, but the potential of such tax-compliant solutions will be shown on the basis of specific examples from Germany, Italy, and the United States.

Germany   For clients from Germany, annuity and life insurance policies represent one of the few remaining ways of tax optimization. The premiums are paid tax-free into the policy and earnings retention is completely tax-free during the saving phase. Various requirements must be observed at payout: In principle, differential taxation is applied (payout sum minus pay-in sum), although in the case of an endowment, where payment is made after a term of at least 12 years and after the beneficiary's sixtieth birthday, only half the difference sum is taxed. Annuity payments are also particularly attractive, as they allow very interesting yield taxation (tax on a low percentage of the annuities payment at the applicable personal tax rate).

Italy   For Italian clients, the life insurance solution offers the advantages of tax-free inclusion of premiums and tax-free earnings retention during the entire term as well as allowing all bankable investments (including hedge funds, private equity funds, and real estate funds). In the case of payment during life, there is 12.5 percent differential taxation on the value growth, whereas at payment upon death, the entire insurance benefit is available to the beneficiaries free of tax (neither income tax nor inheritance tax is payable).

United States   Taking out an annuity policy—better known as a deferred variable annuity (DVA)—or a life insurance policy—usually designated as a private placement life insurance (PPLI)—abroad[5] can be very attractive for persons liable to tax in the United States. Recognition of these products in the United States depends not on where the insurance company is based but on whether the U.S. product specifications can be fulfilled. Such product structuring is possible in Liechtenstein and is offered by at least one company.

In addition to the advantages of a free choice of investment already mentioned, a DVA is very attractive from a tax standpoint. Apart from 1 percent excise tax payable on premiums by the policy holder, no tax is liable during the term of the policy. In the event of payment during life, 35 percent income tax is liable when the policy holder is older than $59\frac{1}{2}$

years of age. The DVA is an interesting planning instrument for optimizing ongoing income tax on investments.

Tax on the PPLI is even more attractive during the term of the policy, because in addition to the 1 percent excise tax also payable on premiums by the policy holder, tax-free earnings retention applies as long as the assets are held in the policy. If the benefit is paid at the death of the insured person, the beneficiaries receive the sum free of income tax. Inheritance tax depends on the degree of relationship, the value of the policy, and the residence of the beneficiary.

International Advantages　　Quite apart from products adapted to national rules, Liechtenstein policies can be used even more frequently within the scope of international solutions. Special reference should be made at this point to relief from EU withholding tax[6] that has been payable since 2005 by EU nonresidents who hold accounts or deposits at banks in Switzerland, the principality of Liechtenstein, Austria, Luxemburg, Belgium, Monaco, San Marino, or Andorra. This EU withholding tax is in the first place applied to interest income and currently stands at 15 percent (since July 1, 2005), but will rise to 20 percent on July 1, 2008 and to 35 percent on July 1, 2011.

The term "interest" used in the relevant agreement[7] is in general defined very broadly. Thus it comprises interest paid into or credited to an account from debt claims of any kind (especially earnings from government securities, loans, and debt certificates), interest accrued or capitalized at the sale or repayment of debts or on periodic interest as well as interest payments on payouts from investment funds or realized at the sale or repayment of shares in investment funds as long as certain limits of interest-bearing investments are exceeded within the investment fund.

However, the term "interest" used here excludes payments such as dividends and other payments from equities as well as interest income from insurance policies and benefits from provident facilities. As a rule, this advantage alone already covers the extra annual costs associated with the conclusion of a Liechtenstein life or annuity insurance policy.

Neither is any tax paid on the earnings or value growth within the premium reserve account of the insurance policies offered by Liechtenstein insurance companies, so the profit retention on earnings within the policy is in fact tax-free.

Asset Protection Privilege

Quite generally, the topic of asset protection plays a very important role in the provident sector and is frequently the motivator for developing structured solutions for clients. Life and annuity insurance policies in particular enjoy various levels of protection from access by third parties in almost all jurisdictions. Two aspects are relevant here: Claims may be directed against the policy holder or against the insurance company itself. Liechtenstein assures a very high degree of asset protection in both cases.

As a rule, the asset protection privilege is initially considered from the client's perspective. To what extent is the value of the policy secured when he or she is subject to litigation? This is where the stipulations of Article 78 of the insurance contract law[8] come into effect: Its objectives and formulation are based on the relevant Swiss regulations, and its provisions are significantly broader than comparable regulations in other European countries, which often merely offer preferential access rights to the beneficiaries. The Liechtenstein rules stipulate that where the beneficiaries are close relatives (spouses, children, and cohabiting partners are explicitly mentioned), the policy is prohibited to access by third parties.[9]

Second, however, this privilege is seen from the perspective of the insurance company. To what extent is the value of the policy secured when the company is subject to litigation? At this point, reference is made both to what has already been said on the substantive supervision by the FMA and to the application of the stipulations of Article 59a of the law on the Supervision of Insurance Undertakings[10] that also refers to Article 45 of the insolvency regulations.[11] Accordingly, the assets in the cover stock are treated as a special estate that is used exclusively to satisfy insurance claims. Where providers offer the individual cover stock solutions outlined above (i.e., hold a specific securities deposit for each policy), this inevitably leads to segregated accounts (i.e., the policy holder is always paid specifically from the securities deposit or account that may be allocated to his or her policy). However, as the value of the policy results from the sum of these accounting facilities (securities deposit plus account), the cover will never be deficient.

It is precisely thanks to this segregated deposit facility that the policy holder is also granted a transparency that is rare for insurance contracts. It allows him or her to trace exactly how the cover stock had been invested within the specified investment strategy as well as when any insurance, bank, and asset-management fees were paid.

Discretion Privilege

Discretion has also become a key client requirement, and international studies have shown that whereas secrecy protection should apply to the legitimate interests of the individual,[12] they must not disregard the equally legitimate interests of the general public, such as measures designed to combat money laundering, action against terrorism, and organized crime. In this area, the discretionary regulations of Liechtenstein bank and insurance secrecy should also be understood as data protection and not as protection against actions.

The insurance secrecy rules in Article 44 of the law on insurance supervision[13] were based on the proven practice of bank secrecy and protect the legitimate private sphere of the insurance client, but not criminal practices. Thus insurance secrecy is lifted in cases of criminal prosecution, with the exception of violations of nonnational tax regulations.

The legal regulations make explicit provision for lifting insurance secrecy when the relevant information is indispensable for pursuing domestic or foreign criminal proceedings. In the case of foreign proceedings, the question of whether and to what degree such information is made available will depend on the provisions of the law on legal assistance. Although this procedure has now been made more rigorous, policy holders retain sufficient legal protection.

However, this strict insurance secrecy can be lifted when there is justified suspicion of money laundering on the basis of the transactions carried out.

In contrast, insurance secrecy remains fully enshrined in fiscal law, as the insurance companies are not permitted to give tax authorities any information at all. Liechtenstein does not provide any legal assistance to foreign states in tax matters either, so that insurance secrecy is maintained in this sector. In view of the particular circumstances, only the legal assistance agreement between Liechtenstein and the United States allows the granting of mutual assistance in cases of tax fraud but not of tax evasion.

Another aspect of discretion is the fact that life assurance companies are economically entitled to the assets they hold in the cover stock (irrespective of whether this is an individual or a joint cover stock). In the case of shares, for example, this means that the life assurance company rather than the policy holder whose policy contains these shares becomes a shareholder and must be recorded in a share register.

The resulting discretion with regard to the depositary bank must not be confused with anonymity or anonymous accounts. All Liechtenstein insurance companies are, like the banks, subject to the regulations of the due diligence legislation.[14] At the conclusion of an insurance contract, therefore, the life insurance companies must check the identity of the policy holder (the contractual partner) and the insured person and must check or credibly show economic entitlement to the assets as well as their origin. The identity of the beneficiary and his or her economic entitlement must also be determined and recorded at the time of payout. With the implementation of rigorous due diligence legislation in 2000, Liechtenstein decided to pursue a policy of quality[15] and cooperation with international efforts to combat money laundering.

Constitutive Privilege

If we were to ask why clients seek and set up international structuring solutions, a recurring answer involves their need for transferring and passing on assets. They require not only a tax-efficient structure but have a particular interest in questions of time, mode, and amount.

In general, it may be said that the generation responsible for the transfer has an interest in being able to influence the arrangements for as long as possible. This is certainly a completely legitimate and vital interest; after all, who wants to depend on others merely because the assets were transferred too early?

Life and annuity insurance solutions, depending on the life of one or several persons, are particularly suited to meet this requirement. An insurance contract becomes due either when its term has matured or when the insured event takes place. By selecting a long term, the maturity date can be significantly delayed. But what if the death of the insured person occurs too early? In such a case, the specification of several insured persons and the stipulation "Due at the death of the last insured person" allows the time of payment to be pushed far into the future.

If, in contrast, independently of the life of the insured persons, a specific term of the insurance contract is to be assured in every case, then a fixed term clause may be used. This clause stops the policy from maturing until a specific or specifiable date, such as a particular birthday of the beneficiary or the successful completion of his or her education. In the event of the death of the insured person, the benefit payout is postponed either until an exact day X or until the occurrence of a specified event. The insurance contract remains valid and continues to run up to that day.

As soon as the maturity date has been set, the conditions linked to the mode defined by the policy holder come into effect. Thus the policy holder may define the sequence of beneficiaries and also the percentage distribution between several beneficiaries of the same rank. Members of the next rank receive the insured sum only if all the members of the previous rank have predeceased them.

An annuity insurance policy may also allow a distinction to be made between annuity payments (to all or specific beneficiaries) and a complete or partial capital payment (to an individual or all beneficiaries). These payment variants may also be combined; thus the policy holder's daughter can receive a third of the policy value as a capital sum at his death, whereas his two sons receive "their" thirds only in the form of 10-year annuities.

Annuity insurance policies may also make provision for a full or partial transfer of an annuity from one beneficiary to another. These instruments are used particularly to assure several beneficiaries of the same age. For instance, the policy holder's son may receive an annuity for life, but if he dies, his widow receives 80 percent of the pension received up to that time, also for life. Annuity payments may also allow guarantee times to be agreed, so that the payment is made independently of the first beneficiary. This variant is usually selected when minors are to be assured. For example, a grandfather may conclude an insurance policy that grants his son a monthly annuity at his death, but if his son dies too soon, the annuity continues to be paid to his grandson at least up to the latter's thirtieth birthday (allowing him to complete his education or assuring him a certain livelihood).

If the options just outlined are insufficient due to a very complex initial situation or the distribution of the assets is subject to discretionary decision authorizations, it makes sense to appoint a foundation or trust as the sole beneficiary of the insurance contract and then use the instruments offered by these facilities to define the payment modes. This structure is also suited to clients from countries in which trusts or foundations may be used in a way that offers tax advantages.

Life insurance policies may be set up in conjunction with trusts, foundations, and other company types for tax reasons (various jurisdictions with different structuring options) or to meet additional discretionary needs of the client.

Regarding the benefits, it should be generally noted that both natural and legal persons may be designated as beneficiaries, either revocably or irrevocably. If a revocable arrangement has been made, then a single provision or even the entire benefit arrangement may be changed without the need for lawyers, quickly and flexibly, with merely the need to inform the insurance company in writing.

The question of who may act as a contractual partner of the insurance company also relates to the constitutive privilege. This partner will often be a natural person, especially when the life insurance is treated preferentially in its tax environment: The preferential conditions are then linked to this person. However, a legal person or a trustee may well act as the policy holder and conclude the insurance contract on behalf of the company. In contrast, it is obvious that only a natural person may be individually insured, and must be identified, as explained earlier, as well as give his or her written agreement.

SOLUTIONS FROM LIECHTENSTEIN

Not all providers use all the product structuring options described. Potential clients can check out providers by looking at the home pages of the Financial Market Authority or the Liechtenstein Insurance Association. Next we examine several providers and some of their offerings to present a fair sampling of the range of solutions on offer.[16]

The life assurance companies include both affiliates of insurance companies and banks with an international scope of operations as well as independent providers of niche solutions. Some applications for new concessions from the Financial Market Authority are still pending, so the range of products and offeringss is changing all the time.

Traditional and Fund-Linked Insurance Solutions

Fortuna Lebensversicherung AG (henceforth known as Fortuna) is a subsidiary of the Generali Group. It offers both fund-linked life and annuity insurance solutions, such as Invest Plan, Invest Plan Plus, and Fortuna-Vorsorge Plan, as well as a traditional annuity, the Invest Pension. For the fund-linked products, three different investment plans are available in three currencies (CHF, USD, and EUR): Income, Balanced, and Growth. The policy holder can choose the Basic or Active variants of these plans. The Active variant is constantly rebalanced (i.e., the rates of its individual investment categories are adapted in response to the market situation); thus the equity rate for Growth averages 40 percent but is repeatedly rebalanced in a bull market. In contrast, the rates of the individual investment categories are shifted with respect to each other in the Basic variant as their values change. Fortuna offers a minimum rate of interest as a special product feature, despite its fund-linked investment strategy.

UBS Global Life AG offers a series of fund-linked solutions backed up by the expertise of Switzerland's largest bank. Its range of products includes those financed with a single premium or with regular premium payments and allows the policy holder to choose his investment strategy at any time (UBS Life Funds). Alternatively, the UBS Life Funds MFP (Managed Fund Portfolio) also makes investment funds of leading third-party providers available and allows the policy holder to specify a guaranteed risk sum. All these products are available in CHF, USD, and EUR. The UBS Life Comfort product group comprises traditional mixed life insurance policies (with single premium or regular premium payments) with guaranteed capital payout at death or maturity; surpluses are also paid. UBS Life Vision is a classical annuity insurance that is offered in immediate and deferred versions. UBS Life Protect is a pure whole life insurance policy with no savings character and is designed purely for risk coverage: it allows the policy holder to select between constant capital (constant death benefit) and variable capital (death benefit may be adapted annually to changed requirements) variants.

Valor Life Lebensversicherungs-AG offers traditional solutions, such as pure risk insurance with a fixed or life term in which the defined capital is paid out at death: Versions with constant or annually recalculated premiums (depending on the state of health) are available. A mixed life assurance is also offered in which the accumulated surpluses are paid out in addition to a death benefit; both products are available in CHF, USD, and EUR. Other options are fund-linked products with single premiums (VipValor) or with regular premium payments (VipValor Plan) as well as solutions whose appreciation is linked to an index (Trendvalor) or to the price of individual stocks (Stockvalor).

UNIQA Lebensversicherung AG is the oldest insurance company in Liechtenstein. In the sector of classical insurance solutions, it offers not only endowment and term policies but a broad range of annuity solutions. The policy holder can choose between solutions with lifelong annuities, lifelong annuities with guaranteed capital repayment, lifetime annuities with joint-life provision, lifetime annuities with joint-life provision and guaranteed capital repayment, lifetime annuities with guaranteed duration, temporary annuities, temporary annuities with guaranteed duration, and temporary annuities with joint-life provisions.

Equity-Linked Insurance Solutions

All location benefits are exploited in the individual cover stock solutions just outlined. They are offered by several providers, including CapitalLeben Versicherung AG,[17] Credit Suisse Life & Annuities AG, Swiss Life (Liechtenstein) AG, Swisspartners Versicherung AG, UBS Global Life, UNIQA Lebensversicherung AG, Vienna-Life Lebensversicherung AG, and Valor Life Lebensversicherungs-AG.

The Liechtenstein Fund Life group of products offered by CapitalLeben was a pioneer of these solutions. The policy holder can freely select both the depositary bank and asset manager. The investment strategy defined for the latter may be changed at any time by the policy holder, who may also be granted a pure right of information vis-à-vis the depositary bank upon request. This gives the policy holder complete transparency as to what happens to the cover stock of the policy. The client can become a sole contractual partner of CapitalLeben or share the policy with up to four other policy holders, and up to five insured persons may also be specified. Full structural freedom in the designation of the beneficiaries is assured. The minimum term is in principle set at five years, but may be longer due to national tax regulations (e.g., Germany, 12 years; Austria, 10 years; United States, up to the age of $59\frac{1}{2}$). The longest possible term is recommended for optimum utilization, as the policy holder may terminate the policy at any time. CapitalLeben has built up an extensive network of partners in Europe over the years so that customers have an optimal selection of leading banks and experienced asset managers to choose from.

Swiss Life (Liechtenstein) AG also uses the benefits of the location for its Asset Portfolio product family (LAP in brief). Thanks to its membership in Switzerland's oldest and largest life assurance group, Swiss Life (Liechtenstein) AG can offer further unique benefits, such as namely complementary reinsurance options of particular interest to customers from the United States and the Asian region as well as a subsidiary in Luxembourg. This is another very attractive European location for innovative life assurance, which offers good solutions for France and Belgium, for example. Jointly with CapitalLeben, Swiss Life (Liechtenstein) AG is the market leader in the principality of Liechtenstein.

In addition to the traditional and fund-linked solutions already described, Valor Life also offers equity-linked or annuity insurance policies with an individual cover stock, VipValor Privatissimo (with a single premium) and VipValor Crescendo (with regular payment of premiums): These solutions also grant the policy holder a free choice of depositary bank and asset manager. These products, focusing principally on asset formation, can also be combined with additional death benefits, in some cases even without a health check. Desired annuity payments are calculated at the moment of conversion. Both these products have a minimum term of six years.

SUMMARY

Over the years, the life and annuity insurance business has gained a permanent place in the sector of provident planning. In recent years, it has also become possible to use flexible life and annuity insurance solutions (especially from Liechtenstein) as an alternative planning instrument for the tax planning and structuring of international assets.

Experts[18] recommend that before making a decision on complex structures, providers should clarify these questions:

■ How can clients fully understand the concept of a trust when their own legal environment is quite ignorant of such structures?
■ Is it desirable to find a solution whose planned result is achieved on the basis of a lack of transparency?
■ Will the solution be suitably modified if the client is or will be recognized as fully entitled to it in economic terms?

These topics show that the insurance contract—a familiar instrument used millions of times—offers an option based on trust specifically for clients who are unfamiliar with instruments such as foundations, trusts, or even offshore companies. In addition, insurance solutions enjoy tax benefits in almost all jurisdictions thanks to their provident character. International solutions can be structured in full compliance with national fiscal and legal regulations. Liechtenstein annuity and life assurance solutions offer an ideal instrument for this purpose.

CHAPTER 10

Asset Protection through Liechtenstein Annuities and Life Insurance

Johannes Gasser

Attorney at Law, Dr. Dr. Batliner and Dr. Gasser, Vaduz

Markus Schwingshackl

Attorney at Law

In recent years life insurance contracts under Liechtenstein law have become an interesting alternative to traditional vehicles for asset protection and estate planning like foundations or trusts. Such life insurance contracts offer several advantages. The policy holder is largely free to select the assets to cover the policy. At the same time, he or she benefits from customized estate planning in combination with asset protection in the case of bankruptcy or enforcement proceedings. The contract may be terminated at any time; even a partial surrender in order to withdraw cash is possible. The flexibility and tax advantages of life insurance contracts allow for tailor-made solutions that satisfy policy holders' various needs.

PRINCIPALITY OF LIECHTENSTEIN

Financial Services in Liechtenstein

Financial services represent an important economic sector in Liechtenstein. Due to the high-added-value intensity of this economic sector, persons employed in the financial services sector contribute a share of about 30 percent to Liechtenstein's gross domestic product. The services offered include in particular private asset management, international asset structuring, investment funds, and insurance solutions. As of the end of 2005, 16 banks, 164 domestic and 239 foreign investment undertakings, 31 Liechtenstein insurance companies, 41 pension schemes, and 1,314 other financial intermediaries (professional trustees, auditors, lawyers, patent attorneys, exchange offices, real estate brokers, dealers in high-priced goods and auctioneers, and other persons subject to due diligence) were working in the Liechtenstein financial center.

Liechtenstein has been a member of the European Economic Area (EEA) since May 1, 1995. Its EEA membership has important consequences for the development of the financial center. For example, it means that Liechtenstein financial intermediaries can profit from the freedom of establishment and movement of services when offering cross-border financial services within the EEA. At the same time, accession to the EEA came with the commitment to continuously implement all EEA-relevant legal acts of the European Union (EU) in the financial services sector into domestic law, in accordance with the provisions established by the EEA agreement.

With regard to supervision, the EEA triggers the commitment to comply with supervisory law standards and principles applicable to the entire EEA. The principles of mutual recognition of the equality of supervisory authorities apply. Thus the other EEA supervisory authorities recognize a priori the relevant Liechtenstein supervisory authority as an equal. This situation facilitates both approval conditions for EEA financial intermediaries and cross-border supervisory activities for the relevant supervisory authorities within the EEA.[1]

Liechtenstein Insurance Center

Insurance Supervision Act (ISA) After signing the EEA agreement in 1995, Liechtenstein initiated the Liechtenstein Insurance Center Project, establishing insurance supervision legislation in conformity with European standards. The law of December 6, 1995, the Insurance Supervision Act (ISA) on the supervision of insurance companies, and the ordinance of December 17, 1996, the Insurance Supervision Ordinance (ISO), entered into force on January 1, 1996, and January 24, 1997, respectively. The ISA circumscribes the organization and content of insurance supervision and in particular aims to protect insured persons and the confidence in the Liechtenstein insurance and financial system.

Insurance companies domiciled in Liechtenstein enjoy free access to the European market, which encompasses over 450 million inhabitants. Their business activities are subject to insurance supervision that conforms with European and internationally recognized standards.

Before Liechtenstein joined the EEA, only agencies of Swiss insurance companies were operating in the principality. After Liechtenstein joined the EEA, in order to create the same conditions for Swiss insurance companies as for the EEA insurance companies, Liechtenstein and Switzerland concluded a Direct Insurance Agreement, which has been in force since January 1, 1997. Insurance companies domiciled in Liechtenstein and Switzerland are granted freedom of establishment and services with respect to direct insurance activities in the territory of the other state. Thus it is possible to operate directly from Liechtenstein not only in the EEA, but also in Switzerland. This position is unique in Europe.[2]

As a result of EEA membership, the insurance agreement with Switzerland, and the insurance supervision legislation, which complies with the EEA standards, Liechtenstein is in an excellent position to continue to establish itself as an insurance location.[3]

Three principles govern the insurance law in the EEA:

1. Single license
2. Home country control
3. Supervision on solvency of the insurance companies[4]

Under Liechtenstein law, supervision is focused on the solvency of insurance companies rather than on material monitoring of products including tariffs and insurance terms and codifications. Insurance companies are very flexible in their product design, and the policy holders have the additional benefit of freely choosing their investment. The ISA is in full compliance with the European standard and offers the opportunity to provide innovative integral asset management solutions, in particular, in the field of life insurance contracts. Thus, Liechtenstein insurance companies are in the position to provide their clients with tailor-made solutions that take into consideration the clients' complete personal and financial situation. The fact that assets under control grew 84.3 percent from 2004 to 2005 confirms the attractiveness of Liechtenstein life insurance contracts.

For insurance companies whose head office is in the principality of Liechtenstein, the license under the ISA covers the territory of all member states of the EEA. Thus, direct insurance may be offered in another member state of the EEA by way of formation of a branch or cross-border provision of services. The insurance company must notify the home country supervisory authority where it intends to establish a branch. The same applies in the case of cross-border provision of services.

Due to its political and economic stability, location in the heart of Europe, close economic link to Switzerland, membership in the EEA, highly developed banking system, strict secrecy laws, and a sophisticated, fully integrated infrastructure, Liechtenstein has become an important insurance center for both corporate and individual clients.

International Insurance Contract Law   With the enactment on May 13, 1998, of the International Insurance Contracts Act (IICA), Liechtenstein has implemented the acquis communautaire in the field of international insurance contract law.

Insurance Contract Act   With the enactment on May 16, 2001, of the Insurance Contract Act (ICA), Liechtenstein took an important step closer to realizing the Liechtenstein Insurance Center Project whose goal is to attract insurance companies to the principality. The ICA governs the legal relationship between the insurance company and the policy holder. Before the enactment of the ICA, the Swiss Insurance Act was applicable in Liechtenstein. The ICA is based on the provisions of the Swiss Insurance Act. According to the principle of "law in action," the ICA, where it corresponds to the provisions of the Swiss Insurance Act, is to be construed in accordance with Swiss case law and doctrine. The ICA is seen as a masterpiece of the Europeanization of Liechtenstein law.[5]

LIFE INSURANCE

Life Insurance Contract

A life insurance policy is a traditional choice and a common form of capital investment. It provides a rate of guaranteed interest over the term of the policy as well as offering opportunities for asset protection, tax planning, and insolvency legislation. The parties to the insurance contract are the insurance company and the policy holder. The insurance company issues the policy in return for the payment of the premium while the policy holder receives coverage for him- or herself and/or other persons. The insurance covers the life of the policy holder or another natural person. The beneficiaries are the persons designated by the policy holder who may claim the benefits in the insurance contract upon occurrence of the insured event.[6]

It is also possible to use a life insurance policy as a credit instrument. This flexibility allows the policy holder to utilize it in different forms as capital investment and/or as a credit instrument. Each capital-forming insurance is not only a savings but also a financing instrument. If necessary, such capital may be used before maturity by loaning or pledging.[7]

For the assignment or pledge of life insurance claims to be valid, the assignment or pledge must be in writing and the policy must be handed over. This is thought to protect from precipitancy and for the preservation of evidence.[8] Thus, the policy is basically just a document of evidence. However, there are certain forms that make the policy similar to a security. This applies, for example, to life insurance contracts containing a bearer clause according to which the insurance company may pay benefits to the bearer. In such case the insurance company acting in good faith is authorized to consider any bearer entitled to the claim.

Since life insurance contracts are frequently effected for a long time period, Article 65 ICA grants a special right of cancellation to the policy holder who may cancel the life insurance contract if the premium has been paid for one year. The cancellation must be submitted in writing to the insurance company four weeks prior to commencement of a new insurance period. If the policy holder does not wish to pay any further premium, the insurance company shall, upon request of the policy holder, be required to convert in whole or in part any life insurance policy for which premiums have been paid for at least three years into a fully paid-up policy. The insurance contract may provide that the surrender value be paid in lieu of the desired conversion if the insurance sum or annuity resulting from the conversion would exceed an agreed amount. Moreover, the insurance company must, upon request of the policy holder, repurchase in whole or in part any life insurance for which the insured event is certain to occur, if the premiums have been paid for at least three years.

Unit-Linked Life Insurance Contracts

The unit-linked life insurance policy is basically a mixed life insurance that combines term coverage with a saving and an investment component. Unlike the traditional mixed life insurance, where the insurer bears the responsibility for the investment of the capital, in unit-linked life insurance contracts the policy holder decides how to invest the capital. Usually the policy holder may choose from a range of investment funds. By combining the funds, the policy holder decides on the investment strategy on his or her own, whether willing to take risks, balanced, or risk-averse. Many contracts allow policy holders to switch funds in order to adapt the investment to changes in the financial markets or to a new life situation. Since the policy holder chooses the portfolio strategy, a warranty for the maturity benefit does not apply. At maturity, the insurance company disburses the value of the shares in the fund but does not guarantee a certain capital as it does with traditionally mixed life insurances. In the case of death, the beneficiaries have a title in the preestimated and, in case of death guaranteed capital or the equivalent of the shares in the fund, if the amount is higher.[9]

Unit-linked life insurance contracts under Liechtenstein law combine the taxation benefits of insurance with the potential of gains on the capital market and allows policy holders complete freedom to select the portfolio options.

Asset Protection through Life Insurance Contracts

The term "asset protection" is generally used to refer to any arrangement designed and intended to protect assets from claims by creditors and others. It is a means of organizing one's affairs and assets in advance in order to safeguard against potential losses arising from some future calamity. Life insurance contracts, similar to trusts or foundations, usually form part of general estate planning. As such, many different considerations extending well beyond the protection of assets from potential creditors will be relevant and must be taken into account. Asset protection vehicles are essentially symptoms of a changing economic and legal environment. Not only in North America but also in Europe, an explosion in litigation, especially in professional malpractice suits and environmental claims, has occurred. These and other factors account for the appearance and growth of asset protection vehicles.[10]

Whoever seeks the benefits of asset protection vehicles in general benefits from Liechtenstein's banking secrecy. In addition, the Liechtenstein legal system offers insurance secrecy based on the strict banking secrecy. The Liechtenstein legal system protects the individual sphere of any person. The private sphere of a person also includes information relating to his or her financial affairs and personal fortune.[11] While confidentiality is still regarded suspiciously by a number of foreign authorities, it represents protection of privacy and discretion as a personal property based on Liechtenstein legal order in the financial sphere. Competitive financial products, outstanding services, and secrecy aspects make the financial center of the principality of Liechtenstein well suited to investors.

Liechtenstein legislation on due diligence aimed at the prevention of money laundering and terrorism financing today satisfies the highest international standards.[12] Therefore, the belief that only dishonest clients are in real need of confidentiality no longer applies. In particular, Liechtenstein's measures to prevent the abuse of insurance and banking secrecy as well as the confidentiality obligation of trustees contribute to the interest of honest clients who can rely on the fact that a maximum of due diligence permits the country to defend professional confidentiality in the financial area against fiscally motivated attacks from abroad.

The great importance of insurance secrecy is demonstrated in Article 44 ISA, according to which members of insurance companies and their employees, as well as other persons working on behalf of such companies, shall be required to maintain secrecy with respect to facts that are not publicly known and that have been entrusted to them or made accessible to them on basis of business connections with clients. The secrecy requirement is not time restricted. Furthermore, should representatives of authorities gain knowledge of facts that are subject to insurance secrecy, such facts are regarded as official secrets and remain confidential. A violation of the insurance secrecy may be punished with imprisonment of up to six months or with a fine of up to CHF 360,000. If the offense is committed negligently, the maximum penalties can be reduced by half.

Liechtenstein life insurance contracts offer the protection of the assets of the policy holder in two ways. The first way consists of the irrevocable designation of a beneficiary, while in the second scenario not only the policy holder but also the spouse or descendants are protected from creditors' claims if the policy holder has designated the spouse or descendants as beneficiaries.

Right of Disposal and Beneficial Interest

Right of Disposal According to Article 74 ICA, the policy holder shall be authorized to designate a third-party beneficiary without the consent of the insurance company. Both the policyholder and/or the beneficiary may be natural and/or juridical persons. Thus trusts or foundations may be beneficiaries of a life insurance contract. At any rate the insured person must be a natural one. Note that it is not possible to insure the life of a third party without the consent before signing the contract. Such a third-party insurance policy would continue to exist in the event of the demise of the policy holder and become part of his or her estate. The designation of a beneficiary may refer to the entire insurance claim or to a part thereof. An insurance company shall pay the benefit to the last person named pursuant to the beneficiary rules with debt-discharging effect.

This provision primarily refers to claims resulting from life insurance contracts that are due in the event of demise of the policy holder. The beneficiary acquires the beneficial interest directly, not through provisions of inheritance law. However, the provision is also applicable in the case of survival in an endowment policy where normally the policy holder is also the beneficiary. The life insurance policy with a third-party beneficiary is considered as a provision in favor of a third party.[13] The beneficiary will acquire the right to benefit from the insurance policy upon occurrence of the insured event.

The policy holder of a life insurance policy may, even if a third-party beneficiary has been designated, exercise free disposal of the payment requests resulting from the insurance among the living and in consequence of death. The right of the policy holder or his or her legal successor to revoke the designation of the beneficiary shall expire only if the policy holder has signed a waiver of his or her right in the policy and has handed over the policy to the beneficiary (Article 75 ICA).

Beneficial Interest   By naming of a beneficiary the policy holder disposes of the beneficial right resulting from the policy and a third party acquires the right of a reversioner. The beneficiary will obtain an independent right to the insurance claim as defined in the insurance contract only upon occurrence of the insured event. The beneficiary is then entitled to act in judicial proceedings in his or her own name against the insurance company (e.g., if the insurance company refuses payment). However, the policy holder may withdraw the designation of a beneficiary at any time as long as he or she has not expressly waived such right. Such revocation is not subject to any formal requirement. The instruction to the insurance company may even be given over the telephone.[14] Upon occurrence of the insured event—the demise of the policy holder—the sum payable will not form part of the estate but will be paid directly to the beneficiary. Thus, beneficiaries and family members of the policy holder with an interest in his or her estate may claim the insurance benefit even if they waive their right in a succession. This may be the case if the estate is encumbered by debt.

Life Insurance in Enforcement and Bankruptcy Proceedings

Irrevocable Designation of a Third-Party Beneficiary   In general, a life insurance policy may be subject to bankruptcy or enforcement proceedings concerning the policy holder. According to Article 77 ICA, the designation of the beneficiary shall expire if the insurance claim is charged in Liechtenstein or if bankruptcy is opened with respect to the policy holder in Liechtenstein. It shall revive if the charge expires or bankruptcy is lifted. If the policy holder has waived the right to revoke the designation of the beneficiary, the insurance claim arising from the designation shall not be subject to enforcement on behalf of the creditors of the policy holder. The waiver of the right to revoke the designation of the beneficiary triggers the loss of the insurance claim of the policy holder. Such claim is no longer part of his or her patrimony; thus his or her creditors may not seize this particular claim.[15]

However, the interest of the creditors of the policy holder shall prevail in the event of a revocable designation of beneficiaries. If the insurance event has not occurred, the designation shall expire and the policy may be seized by the creditors of the policy holder or be included in the bankruptcy estate of the policy holder. The right of the policy holder to revoke the designation of the beneficiary is considered as expired only if the policy holder has signed a waiver of his or her right in the policy and has handed over the policy to the beneficiary. Due to these special formal requirements, the policy holder shall be aware of the consequences of the decision, as after such waiver a new designation of a beneficiary shall not be admissible.[16]

If a third party has been irrevocably designated as beneficiary, neither the policy holder nor his or her heirs may ever become beneficiaries. The policy holder will never be entitled to the insurance claim, and thus the policy will not become part of his or her bankruptcy estate.[17] Furthermore, according to Article 210 (1) (d) of the Liechtenstein Execution Code (EC, LGBl. 1972/92 II), monetary claims, which due to legal provision are not seizable, may not be subject to enforcement proceedings. Thus the creditors of a policy holder who has waived the right to revoke the beneficiary will not be able to seize the policy.

In general, after occurrence of the insurance event, the insurance claim of the third-party beneficiary may be seized by his or her creditors or included in the bankruptcy estate of the third-party beneficiary.

Designation of the Spouse or the Descendants as Beneficiaries Pursuant to Article 78 ICA, if the spouse or the descendants of the policy holder are beneficiaries, then, subject to any liens, neither the insurance claim of the beneficiary nor of the policy holder shall be subject (i) to enforcement on behalf of the creditors or (ii) to the bankruptcy of the policy holder or the beneficiary. A person living in cohabitation with the policy holder shall be considered equivalent to a spouse. The designation of the beneficiaries will not expire, and thus the insurance claim will not become part of the patrimony of the policy holder again. The ownership of the insurance contract automatically transfers to the protected beneficiaries, and any order or instructions of the policy holder or on his or her behalf, including a court order, is ineffective.[18] It is irrelevant whether the designation is irrevocable or revocable. The insurance policy will continue to be protected from the creditors even if the designation of the beneficiaries is revocable.[19]

This provision aims to protect the financial security of the policy holder's family. The legislation also has taken into account social realities and has extended the protection to the person living in cohabitation with the policy holder, even if such person is of the same sex as the latter.[20] In such cases, contrary to the general rule and contrary to life insurance contracts governed by Swiss law, the protection extends also to the insurance claim of the beneficiaries. It may not be seized by their creditors and may not be included in their bankruptcy estate. However, if third parties have acquired any liens regarding the insurance policy, this provision will not affect their rights.

Succession Right of the Spouse and the Descendants   If the spouse or the descendants of the policy holder are beneficiaries of a life insurance contract, then they shall succeed to the rights and duties arising from the insurance contract as soon as the policy holder is subject to enforcement or bankruptcy, unless they expressly reject the succession. The beneficiaries shall be required to indicate the succession to the policy by submitting a certification of the district court regarding enforcement or bankruptcy to the insurance company. If there is more than one beneficiary, then they must designate a representative who shall receive the notifications from the insurance company (Article 79 ICA).

In the event of bankruptcy of the policy holder or enforcement proceedings instituted by his or her creditors, all rights and duties regarding the insurance contract pass to the spouse or descendants if designated as beneficiaries. The protection also extends to bankruptcy proceedings in foreign states and ineffective enforcement proceedings abroad.[21]

Rights of the Spouse and Descendants in the Case of Chargeable Insurance Claims   Claims arising from a life insurance contract that the debtor has concluded on his or her own life may be subject to utilization under enforcement or bankruptcy law. However, the spouse or the descendants of the debtor may, with the debtor's consent, demand that the insurance claim be transferred to them in return for reimbursement of the surrender price.

If such an insurance claim is charged and if it is to be utilized under enforcement or bankruptcy law, then the spouse or the descendants of the debtor may, with the debtor's consent, demand that the insurance claim be transferred to them in return for payment of the claim secured by the distraint or, if the claim is smaller than the surrender price, in return for payment of this price.

The spouse or the descendants must make their request prior to utilization of the claim before the district court or the trustee in bankruptcy. This provision may also apply if no beneficiaries have been designated.[22]

Reservation of Action for Rescission   The just-outlined provisions of the ICA concerning insurance contracts for the benefit of a third party are subject to the provisions of the Rights Protection Code governing actions for rescission.

In the event that a bankruptcy order is made, the debtor's trustee in bankruptcy has, by virtue of Article 70 of the Bankruptcy Code, the right to challenge all prior legal acts performed by the debtor subject to Articles 64 to 75 of the Rights Protection Code. These provisions explicitly set out the grounds for challenge by judgment creditors whose attempts at execution have gone wholly or partially unsatisfied or where there is a presumption that such execution will not lead to complete satisfaction of the judgment creditor's claim. However, if they are applied by reference in a bankruptcy situation, the trustee in bankruptcy has the sole right over such creditors with regard to contesting transactions undertaken prior to the bankruptcy order.

According to Article 65 of the Rights Protection Code, gratuitous dispositions or transactions for disproportionate consideration can be challenged if they were made one year before the issue of an execution or bankruptcy order. It is assumed that proper consideration has been given in the case of bilateral transactions and that the existence of fraud can be excluded.

Article 67 of the Rights Protection Code permits a challenge of transactions by the debtor (regardless of when undertaken) that have been undertaken with the intention (discernible by the other party) to defraud creditors or to pertain certain creditors.

APPLICABILITY OF THE LIECHTENSTEIN LIFE INSURANCE ACT TO INSURANCE CONTRACTS WITH FOREIGN POLICY HOLDERS

Choice of Liechtenstein Law

The rules of the IICA determine whether Liechtenstein law is the law governing an insurance policy that has a foreign policy holder not resident in Liechtenstein. According to Article 3 IICA, the insurance policy shall be subject to the law chosen by the parties if the risk is situated in the principality of Liechtenstein or in another state granting the free choice of law. Article 11 (3) (d) ISA states that the risk is situated in the state in which the policy holder usually lives or, if the policy holder is a legal person, the state where this legal person has been established or registered. Pursuant to Article 4 IICA, in the case of life insurance, if the prerequisites for free choice of law pursuant to Article 3 IICA are not fulfilled, then the parties may in any event make use of the options for choice of law granted by the state in which the risk is situated. If the policy holder is a natural person and if his or her habitual abode is in a different state than the state of citizenship, then the parties may also choose the law of the state of citizenship of the policy holder.

Due to the provisions of the IICA, it must be verified whether the state where the risk is located grants the free choice of law in order to validly choose Liechtenstein law for a life insurance contract between an insurance company and a foreign policy holder.

Limitations to a free choice of law under Liechtenstein legislation may arise out of the public policy rule, as contained in Article 6 of the September 19, 1996, Private International Law. According to this, the corresponding rule of Liechtenstein law shall apply if a provision in the foreign law applicable (according to the choice of law) is in conflict with fundamental values of the Liechtenstein legal system. Under Liechtenstein law, the parties to an agreement are not free to exclude Liechtenstein public laws; these laws include, for example, the Liechtenstein Bankruptcy Code (Konkursordnung) and the Liechtenstein Deed of Arrangement Act (Nachlassvertrag). Thus, should one of the parties become insolvent, a Liechtenstein court would uphold the parties' earlier choice of law as far as matters of private law are concerned. However, Liechtenstein bankruptcy and arrangement law and procedure would, automatically and necessarily, be applied by a Liechtenstein court.

Excursus: Choice of Liechtenstein Law in an Insurance Policy with an Austrian Policy Holder The Austrian Law on International Insurance Contracts in the European Economic Area (EVSG)[23] governs the law applicable to insurance policies with a nondomestic aspect if the risk is situated in a member state of the EEA. In the case of a life insurance contract, the risk is situated in the member state where the natural person has his or her habitual abode. Article 5 EVSG grants the free choice of law to the parties of a life insurance contract if the risk is situated in the ambit of the EVSG (Austria) or in another member state that grants the free choice of law. Thus, the choice of Liechtenstein law in an insurance contract between a Liechtenstein insurance company and an Austrian citizen would be valid and binding.

Article 9, paragraph 1 EVSG limits the choice of law in a contract, which has been stipulated in connection with a service directed to the stipulation of such contracts by an insurance company in a member state of the policy holder's domicile. Imperative provisions of such member state may not be excluded to the disadvantage of the policy holder. This provision aims to protect the policy holder. The imperative provisions of his or her state of habitual abode remain applicable if the provision of the law of choice should be to the disadvantage of the policy holder. However, the law of choice remains applicable if it is more advantageous or if imperative provisions do not conflict with such law.[24]

Bankruptcy Proceedings Concerning a Foreign Policy Holder

Until recently, Liechtenstein courts and authorities did not acknowledge or enforce any decision or judgment of a foreign court or administrative body in foreign bankruptcy or insolvency proceedings. Contrary to earlier decisions, on May 6, 2003 (2 CG 2001.68, LES 2004/28), the supreme court finally held that the international bankruptcy law of Liechtenstein is obliged to follow the principle of "ubiquity." Thus bankruptcy proceedings abroad are to be acknowledged and tangible assets located in Liechtenstein are to be surrendered and delivered to the foreign authority and trustee in bankruptcy, if:

- Any claims of third parties for release of the bankrupt's estate or, alternatively, any preferential claim or secured creditors are not impaired.
- No proper domestic insolvency proceedings have been instigated at the date when the Liechtenstein courts decide on such foreign request of delivery of Liechtenstein assets.
- The respective foreign state grants reciprocity.

Reciprocity does not mean that the foreign state is willing to acknowledge a Liechtenstein bankruptcy proceeding. The fact that the foreign requirements for recognition are not significantly more severe than the requirements under Liechtenstein law is decisive.

Thus, in a request for judicial assistance, the foreign court would request the delivery of the claim over the foreign bankruptcy estate. The district court would then request a binding decision from the superior court to determine whether reciprocity is given. The superior court will decide on a case-by-case basis whether the foreign state grants reciprocity according to its bankruptcy law. The court granting assistance such a request must subsequently order the third-party debtor (the insurance company) to release such assets in favor of the requesting party. Further, the insurance company will have to provide information regarding whether it holds such assets and, if so, how much and whether such assets were already claimed by other preferential creditors by order of the court. If the Liechtenstein insurance company, in its capacity as third-party debtor, fails to comply with such order, then it may be sued by the trustee in bankruptcy.

Under this new case law, which did not apply to life insurance contracts, it remains to be determined whether the Liechtenstein courts will deny the delivery of the insurance claim to a foreign bankruptcy estate on grounds of the limitations resulting from public policy (ordre public) applicable in

Liechtenstein. The bankruptcy privilege with regard to the beneficiaries of Liechtenstein foundations[25] is a fundamental value of the Liechtenstein legal system. The scope of the ordre public is to protect the Liechtenstein legal system from foreign legal principles that are not in compliance with the fundamental values of the Liechtenstein legal system. That beneficial rights in a foundation may not be charged is a long-established legal tradition in Liechtenstein. Even if the provisions granting the bankruptcy and enforcement privilege are absent among the provisions that according to Article 94 ICA may not be modified to the disadvantage of the policy holder or the beneficiary, the protection of the family's financial security is part of a long-established legal tradition. This tradition inter alia arises from the entailed estate, which, contrary to many other European jurisdictions, is still recognized in Liechtenstein.[26]

As outlined, the protection of life insurance extends to bankruptcy proceedings in foreign states and ineffective proceedings abroad. Seen in this context, there is no reason to assume that the legislation intended to grant the bankruptcy and enforcement privilege to Liechtenstein citizens only. If this was the case, it would result in a violation of the fundamental European freedoms and therefore be in a violation of EEA law.

The income a beneficiary receives from a foundation without valuable consideration ("quid pro quo") may be seized by the beneficiary's creditors by injunction, levy of execution, and writ or bankruptcy proceedings only if the said income is not required to cover the necessary living expenses of the beneficiary, the beneficiary's spouse, and the beneficiary's children without means. In the case of family foundations, the founder may stipulate that creditors must not deprive specifically indicated beneficiaries (other than the founder) of such gratuitously acquired benefits by injunction, levy of execution, and writ or bankruptcy proceedings.

The creditors of the beneficiary of a trust[27] may assert claims against the trust property only if the beneficiary him- or herself has a beneficial interest in the trust property and the settlor has not exercised power to exempt such interest from seizure, which power is explicitly provided for by the law. The settlor may thus stipulate that creditors must not deprive specifically indicated beneficiaries of their gratuitously acquired enjoyment of the trust property.[28]

Independent of the question of whether a Liechtenstein court would grant or deny legal assistance in foreign bankruptcy proceedings, it is advisable to ensure that the policy holder in his or her state of habitual abode benefits from the bankruptcy privilege too. Assuming the validity of the choice of law, many legal systems provide for the principle that bankruptcy may not include assets that by law cannot be distrained.

For instance, amounts due to the policy holder or the beneficiary are under Italian law (Article 1923, para. 1 of the Civil Code[29]) unchargeable and not liable to sequestration. This also applies in the event of the bankruptcy of the policy holder in accordance with Article 46 of Royal Decree 267/1942,[30] which specifies that the bankruptcy estate does not include assets that by law cannot be distrained. According to prevalent doctrine, Article 1923, paragraph 1 Civil Code must be construed in light of Article 46 bankruptcy law; thus the insurance claim will not be included in the bankruptcy estate.[31] When asked to state its position on this matter, the court of cassation[32] clarified the scope of validity of the above-mentioned provisions, confirming that the insurance claim is exempt from distraint and stipulating that only surrendered amounts (i.e., amounts requested by the policy holder prior to the insured event) are subject to enforcement or precautionary measures on the part of the policy holder's creditors.

Excursus: Bankruptcy of an Austrian Policy Holder

As outlined, Article 5 EVSG permits the parties of a life insurance contract the freedom to choose the governing law if the risk is situated in the ambit of the EVSG (Austria) or in another member state that grants the free choice of law.

The doctrine suggests that the insurance policy will not be included in the bankruptcy estate of the Austrian policy holder if the assets represented by the ducument are located in Liechtenstein. This is the case if the policy is physically deposited in Liechtenstein and requested for the insurance claim. If the policy is located in Austria, the insurance claim is generally to be considered as part of the bankruptcy estate. However, Article 77 seqq. ICA are of material rather than procedural character. An Austrian court will always apply Austrian procedural rules. The applicable material law is Liechtenstein law as lex causea. The bankruptcy privilege is a distinctive element of the life insurance policy under Liechtenstein law, which has to be applied inseparably with the other product-distinctive elements of the ICA. Thus, the life insurance policy under Liechtenstein law also extends its benefits to an Austrian policy holder subject to a bankruptcy proceeding. According to Article 77 seqq. ICA, under material law the insurance claim is not part of the estate of the policy holder. The application of foreign law is limited on grounds of Austrian public policy (ordre public). A foreign material provision may not be applied if it violates fundamental values of the Austrian legal system. Due to Article 77 seqq. ICA, no singular creditor is privileged, and therefore there is no violation of the fundamental principle of par conditio creditorum. Furthermore, the principle of protection of the financial security of the family of the policy holder is also in compliance with the Austrian ordre public. Article 77 seqq. ICA are to be seen as integrated elements of the ICA and thus to be respected in an Austrian bankruptcy proceeding as well.[33]

Enforcement of Foreign Judgments in Liechtenstein

Pursuant to Article 52 of the Execution Code (Exekutionsordnung), foreign judgments will be enforced by Liechtenstein courts only if, and to the extent that, reciprocity with the foreign country has been guaranteed by government policy statements or international treaties. Applicable enforcement treaties exist only with Austria and Switzerland. There is no possibility of registering a foreign judgment with the local court authorities either. The principality of Liechtenstein did not join the Lugano Convention on Jurisdiction and Enforcement of Judgments in Civil and Commercial Matters concluded in Lugano on September 16, 1988, despite its membership in the EFTA states. The Lugano Convention intended to elevate the international jurisdictional law and the international enforcement of judgment law of the EFTA member states to the same standards of the members of the European Union. The rationale for this decision was that accession to the Lugano Convention would have been tantamount to destroying the existence of the judiciary of the ministate of Liechtenstein.[34]

Provided that the venue court is not in Switzerland or Austria, a judgment creditor seeking to enforce a decision obtained in any other country except Switzerland or Austria may bring the claim by way of the so-called payment order proceedings.[35] The judgment creditor simply asserts the (pecuniary) claim, and the court will issue a payment order and serve it on the judgment debtor without a hearing. The judgment debtor has 14 days to lodge an objection (the so-called Rechtsvorschlag) with the court. If the judgment debtor does so (otherwise the claim becomes enforceable), the judgment creditor may apply for annulment of the objection in a summary proceeding called Rechtsöffnung. In such proceedings, the original foreign judgment or certified copy thereof is regarded as an official document evidencing a debt. After a hearing in which the judgment debtor is allowed to present evidence that he or she does not owe the judgment anymore, the court will issue a provisional enforcement decision to the judgment debtor, with the direction to file a suit (Aberkennungsklage) in order to invalidate the claim within 14 days. If he or she does so (otherwise the claim becomes enforceable), regular proceedings start and the judge presiding over the matter will summon the parties to a hearing. The debtor must assume the plaintiff's role, but the burden of proving the existence of the claim remains with the judgment creditor. For non-pecuniary claims the procedure is the same.

The summary proceeding could therefore end again in an ordinary proceeding, which would result in a Liechtenstein court deciding on exactly the same issue that had been already decided by any other than a Swiss or Austrian court. Even a foreign court decision that orders the forced realization of the policy or the revocation of the beneficiary designation would not be enforceable.

Once the creditor has achieved an enforceable title in Liechtenstein, a Liechtenstein court would have to respect Article 210 (1) (d) EC; this denies any request for the creditor in the case of insurance policies under Liechtenstein law being the subject of attempted forced realization. The insurance company as third-party debtor in the case of enforcement could cite the provision of Article 78 ICA, according to which the insurance claim of neither the beneficiary nor the policy holder shall be subject to enforcement if the spouse or the descendants of the policy holder are the designated beneficiaries.

CONCLUSION

The life insurance contract under Liechtenstein law offers a variety of benefits for the policy holder. One of the most convincing arguments for signing such a life insurance contract is asset protection in bankruptcy and enforcement proceedings, which extends not only to the policy holder but also to the spouse and descendants if designated as beneficiaries. Taxation benefits, flexible portfolio management, and insurance and banking secrecy complete the range of the impressive product characteristics. Due to modern legal provisions, life insurance contracts under Liechtenstein law provide tailor-made solutions that take into consideration the clients' complete personal and financial situation. The strong growth of the Liechtenstein life insurance market in the past few years confirms the attractiveness of the life insurance products under Liechtenstein law.

CHAPTER 11

Swiss Annuities versus Asset Protection Trusts

Maehala R. Nathan

*Director, Swiss Annuity Consulting
Group, Zurich*

Annuities are often viewed simply as investment vehicles. However, a closer look at annuities reveals that they play a more important role and are widely used by sophisticated international tax and estate practitioners and wealth planning advisors to structure their clients' assets in view of tax and estate planning considerations and for the protection such insurance contracts offer.

Specific provisions that protect life insurance and annuity contracts are known in many jurisdictions, including in several states in the United States. The laws in many countries afford similar protection. Switzerland and to some extent also Liechtenstein have what are arguably the world's strongest and most tested asset protection provisions that apply to annuities and life insurance.

Asset protection often has been viewed as synonymous with trusts. Indeed, trusts are not only traditional estate planning tools but often are used in asset protection planning since the key characteristic of a trust is the separation of legal ownership and beneficial interests in property, and this can work favorably to shield wealth from unjustified claims. Some countries even have passed specific legislation to make trusts established under the laws of their jurisdictions particularly suitable for asset protection purposes. Famous examples are the Cook Islands, a South Pacific island state associated with New Zealand, and Nevis, which is part of the Federation of St. Kitts and Nevis, an independent country in the Caribbean. Many other jurisdictions, for example the Bahamas and, more recently,

Antigua and Barbuda, have enacted specific legislation to attract such trust structures.

Trusts of course continue to play an important role in asset protection planning. But annuities and life insurance, and in particular Swiss annuities, are a viable alternative in many cases. Furthermore, in most cases the combination of both structures can result in benefits that go beyond that of a pure trust structure or a sole annuity.

The ability to stay in control is probably the most important reason why Swiss annuities should be considered in many cases. Unlike a trust, with a Swiss annuity or life insurance policy for asset protection, the policy owner does not actually have to give up control over his or her assets in order to protect them. Besides this factor, there are many other good reasons for considering a Swiss (or Liechtenstein) annuity instead of or in addition to a trust.

Furthermore, a trust is always a particular arrangement made in a specific setting where it can be construed that the legitimate aim was, at least partially, to remove assets from the reach of (potential) creditors or claimants. This, plus the fact that judges, particularly in the United States, generally see red flags when confronted with a foreign trust, make annuities and life insurance interesting alternatives. When properly set up, they are fully protected not on the basis of an individual arrangement and reliance on some offshore jurisdiction's laws and courts but, in the case of Swiss annuities, based on an insurance law with more than 100 years of history, clear precedents, and a politically and economically stable jurisdiction with an efficient legal system.

Swiss annuities and life insurance therefore represent interesting alternatives to more complex, more costly, and generally less secure trust arrangements. Swiss annuities and life insurance can also be interesting complementary elements where the flexibility of a trust is required to achieve particular benefits. Thus, Swiss annuities can be combined with trusts in sophisticated asset protection planning.

Indeed, both trusts and Swiss annuities can be understood as synonymous with asset protection.

ESSENCE OF A SWISS ANNUITY

Generally, an annuity is a contract whereby a person (in this context, normally an insurance company) will commit to pay an income for life or a specified period of time, or to pay a lump sum at a particular time in the future (in the latter case, the arrangement is called an endowment policy). (See Figure 11.1.)

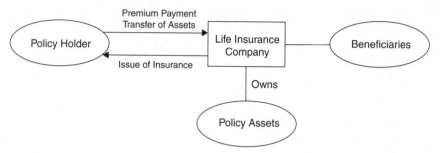

FIGURE 11.1   Overview of Contractual Relationships in an Annuity Arrangement

An annuity, in this context, normally involves four parties:

1. Insurance company
2. Policy holder
3. Insured person
4. Beneficiary (or beneficiaries if there is more than one)

It is a contractual arrangement whereby the policy holder enters into an agreement with the insurance company and receives coverage for self and/or other persons (beneficiaries) in return for either a lump-sum (one-time) premium, regular premium payments, or a combination of both. The policy holder may be a legal entity such as a company or foundation, and a trust can also be the policy holder. The insured person is the one whose life the insurance covers. This may or may not be the same person as the policy holder, but it must be a physical person.

The beneficiary is designated by the policy holder to receive the specified capital or annuity payments. The beneficiary can also be a legal entity or a trust and need not necessarily be a physical person.

The most important use of annuities in asset protection planning is to place and to accumulate wealth in a protected policy. Even if an annuity is set up with the primary goal of protecting the assets placed with the insurance company, in order to avoid negative tax consequences or to benefit from any tax advantages, the policy must comply with the tax regulations in the policy holder's and beneficiary's country of residence (i.e., where he or she has his or her main tax residence). For example, a certain minimum duration of the policy may be required, or the insurance must include a certain amount of life coverage besides the investment component.

Income and capital gains on assets placed in a life insurance policy in a Swiss or Liechtenstein life insurance company are not subject to any local taxes, not even to the Swiss 35 percent withholding tax on dividends and interest that normally applies on payments from practically all Swiss sources. In both countries, no tax is deducted from the policy proceeds (i.e., the proceeds are paid net to the beneficiary or back to the policy holder, as the case may be).

The assets paid into an annuity or life insurance policy do not constitute a gift as they are normally recognized as a premium payment. Furthermore, in some countries these assets will not form part of the policy holder's estate for inheritance purposes, since the nature of the policy holder's interest in the assets is not that of an owner or trust settlor but rather of a contractual partner and holder of an insurance policy.

Similarly, where there are wealth (net asset) taxes, often assets placed in a properly structured insurance policy will not be subject to these taxes either. Finally, capital accumulated in life insurance policies upon expiry is not subject to tax in some countries; even if it is, the tax is only at a very low rate.

SECURE INVESTMENT

In both Switzerland and Liechtenstein, the government regulates all insurance business by enforcing probably the strictest regulations known in the industry. Of particular relevance to international investors is the fact that life insurance companies are required to maintain a security fund that covers all their obligations plus an additional security margin. This fund is segregated from the company's operating assets. Therefore, even if a Swiss or Liechtenstein insurance company were to go bankrupt (which has so far never happened in history—a situation unique in the world), the funds placed in an annuity or life insurance will not be included in the bankruptcy and are safe and protected.

By contrast, assets placed in trusts are much more vulnerable since trust companies are generally less strictly regulated (or not regulated at all, depending on the country), and much depends on the trustees' sound management and integrity. Of course, if the trustee is carefully chosen and monitored (perhaps with an appropriate protector in place who will keep an eye on all activities within the trust, approve distributions, and has the right to veto certain decisions by the trustees), these potential problems can be largely avoided. However, this requires appropriate planning and a setup that is much more complex and more expensive to maintain than insurance.

ESSENCE OF A TRUST

A trust is a legally binding arrangement[1] whereby a person (the settlor) transfers assets to a trustee (or trustees) who is entrusted with and takes legal title to these assets, and holds them for the benefit of named individuals or groups (the beneficiaries). These may or may not include the settlor but will not include the trustees. The key characteristic is the separation of legal ownership and beneficial interests in property settled into the trust.

The primary trust document is the trust instrument, which can take the form of a settlement (settlor is named) or a declaration of trust (settlor is not named other than perhaps as a beneficiary). This document defines the respective rights and duties of the settlor and trustees. The trust instrument will provide that the trustees have the power to manage the trust assets in accordance with the trust instrument and the very strict obligations usually imposed on the trustee under the governing law.

Asset protection trusts usually are set up under a governing law (such as the law of Nevis, Cook Islands, the Bahamas, and similar jurisdictions) whose main feature is a particularly short statute of limitations regarding any challenges that can be brought against transfers of assets, which begins to run from the date of the transfer of assets into the trust, thus providing additional protection on these assets. Of course, fraudulent transfers would not be covered by such provisions, but the relevant laws are usually quite restrictive. In the Bahamas, for example, the Fraudulent Dispositions Act provides that every disposition of property at an undervalue and with an intent to defraud shall be voidable at the instance of a creditor thereby prejudiced. The fraud, however, must be "willful," the undervaluation must be "significant," and the burden of proof is on the creditor.

In every trust arrangement, it is essential that the legal title to the trust assets be vested in the name of the trustees who will be responsible for the administration of the trust. The trustees must be in full control, or else the trust may be attacked easily, asset protection may not be available, or the trust may even be found to be a sham. The trustees are required to act with due diligence as would a prudent person to the best of their ability and skill, and where professional trustees act, to a degree commensurate with their professional qualifications. All trustees must observe utmost good faith. The trustees must exercise their powers solely for the benefit and interest of the beneficiaries. The settlor should not have any direct influence or even control over the trustees.

NO NEED TO RELINQUISH CONTROL

The investor who is interested in protecting assets by placing them into a trust has no choice but to give up control over the assets in order for the asset protection of this trust arrangement to be effective. This is often a tough choice to make and a classic problem with trusts, as a trust can in principle be validly established only if the settlor effectively hands over the assets to the trustee and gives up ownership and control over the assets.

It appears that with trusts, retaining control over assets placed in trust and properly establishing an effective trust are mutually exclusive. This is absolutely essential for the trust to protect the assets placed in it.

Swiss and Liechtenstein annuities, however, are very different. When comparing annuities with trusts for asset protection, probably the most important difference is that the assets placed in an annuity remain, in principle, under the full control of the investor (policy holder), yet at the same time the effective protection is as strong as, or arguably even stronger than, in the case of a trust. The control is only somewhat diminished if beneficiaries are designated on an irrevocable basis; otherwise, the investor has full control over the policy and the underlying assets.

The investor can change beneficiaries or relinquish the policy at any time. Depending on the specific insurance product chosen, the investor can decide to receive a lump-sum payment or roll over the policy into a new one at maturity. He or she also may have a choice of switching currencies, deciding on investment strategies, designating an independent investment advisor to manage the assets in the policy, and so on.

Most of these choices are available while the applicable asset protection provisions remain in force and protect the underlying assets to the fullest extent. Clearly no trust structure can match this flexibility and the fact that the "owner" retains control.

ANTI-AVOIDANCE LAWS AND TAX EXEMPTIONS

Many countries today have anti-avoidance provisions in place regarding the taxation of assets placed into trusts and income derived from such trust assets. However, far fewer provisions like this concern annuity and life insurance policies.

The social benefits of insurance, such as the idea of protecting families from poverty at the time where widespread social security was not yet in place in developed countries, have caused governments around the world to support the use of life insurance and annuities by providing asset protection and tax benefits for policy holders and beneficiaries.

With trusts, one of the key problems is that the settlement of property into a trust often triggers gift taxes. Annuities and life insurance, however, are contracts and require the payment of premiums to insurance companies, which normally does not trigger gift taxes. Often the payout of the benefits is tax exempt; on the contrary, actual or deemed distributions from trusts are taxed, sometimes at prohibitive rates because distributions may be qualified as gifts from third parties or because of laws specifically designed to discourage the holding of assets through trusts.

WORLD'S MOST SOLID ASSET PROTECTION

The most important advantage of a Swiss annuity over an international trust is the strength of asset protection that comes with Swiss annuities. Although asset protection is particularly relevant to clients with U.S. exposure, more than ever successful individuals and families around the world are seeking to protect their wealth from unjustified lawsuits and claims. Business owners and professionals with high potential liabilities (e.g., medical doctors, surgeons, attorneys, and accountants), as well as developers and chief executives of publicly quoted companies, are practically forced to implement some form of asset protection planning as an essential part of their private wealth planning. Even in countries with less litigious societies and more balanced legal systems, where lawsuits are less common than in the United States, asset protection planning is becoming increasingly important.

Traditionally trusts have been the tool of choice in this regard, but as already shown, Swiss annuities are in fact also ideal vehicles for investors in need of effective asset protection solutions. Even if requirements are complex and involve more sophisticated planning, as in the case of large estates, tailor-made annuity and life insurance contracts can provide the same kind or even better flexibility than trusts, with generally stronger asset protection.

The asset protection provisions in Switzerland are similar to the ones in several U.S. states, which provide very strong protection of annuity policies. Historically, these protection provisions were introduced into law for the same social reasons, to provide a safe vehicle to safeguard nest eggs or family assets so that they are available in all circumstances (e.g., a bankruptcy of the breadwinner of the family). These provisions were introduced when a general social security system did not exist and there was a clear need to protect owners and beneficiaries of annuity and life insurance policies.

While these asset protection provisions protecting annuities are very strong in some U.S. states, from a U.S. perspective, a foreign or Swiss annuity, in particular, can prove to be more effective. For the most part, this is due to the simple fact that placing one's assets in a vehicle in a foreign jurisdiction in itself makes those assets much harder to reach and will involve searches abroad and the hiring of foreign attorneys.

This fact— which of course applies generally to any structure set up outside one's home country, including international trusts and bank accounts maintained abroad—itself acts as a strong deterrent.

Furthermore, the asset protection provisions in Switzerland relating to insurance contracts are based on federal law and have been tried and tested up to the highest court in Switzerland, the Federal Supreme Court in Lausanne. Switzerland, which has one of the world's most solid and reliable legal systems, is an almost ideal jurisdiction in which to place one's assets.

In Switzerland, full asset protection is provided if you purchase an annuity policy from a Swiss insurance company and designate your spouse and/or descendants as beneficiaries, or irrevocably designate any other third party (e.g., a legal entity or a trust) as a beneficiary. Swiss law then protects the annuity against any debt-collection procedures initiated by the policy holder's creditors and excludes it from any Swiss bankruptcy procedures.

Unlike the designation of another third party as a beneficiary, when a spouse and/or descendants are so designated, it is irrelevant whether the designation is irrevocable or revocable. The insurance policy will continue to be protected from the policy holder's creditors even if the designation of the spouse and/or descendants is revocable.

Creditors may seize a Swiss policy or have it included in the estate of the bankrupt party only if its purchase or the designation of the beneficiaries is regarded as a fraudulent conveyance within the meaning of Article 285 et seq. of the Swiss Debt Collection and Bankruptcy Act. This would be the case if the policy holder has designated the beneficiaries less than one year before the initiation of debt-collection proceedings, ultimately leading to a bankruptcy decree against the policy holder or to the seizure of the latter's assets.

The same applies if the beneficiary has been designated with the clear intent to damage creditors or to give some creditors preferential treatment and the designation was made within five years of the date of debt-collection proceedings resulting in a bankruptcy decree or the seizure of the policy holder's assets. These statutes of limitation are comparable with those applicable on transfers of assets into trusts and foundations in asset protection jurisdictions.

When the insurance policy expires, the policy holder usually will be able to collect the proceeds accruing from the policy, extend the existing policy, or roll the proceeds over into a new policy. Of course, the actual options open to the policy holder depend on the particular insurance contract, but generally both Swiss and Liechtenstein annuities are rather flexible in this regard.

If the policy holder becomes bankrupt, he or she continues to be protected because ownership is then automatically transferred to the beneficiaries. Any instructions from the original policy holder that are forced on him or her must now be ignored; now only the latter's beneficiaries, as the new owners, may instruct the insurance company. This single rule in Swiss law probably affords better protection than any other asset protection structure.

The Swiss law deems the rights under an insurance contract between a foreign person and a Swiss insurance company to be located at the latter's domicile. However, if the policy holder's and beneficiaries' rights are embodied in a policy (which can be considered as a security), a creditor could claim that the latter could be seized in accordance with the debt-collection and bankruptcy rules of the country in which it is deposited. After all, securities are normally subject to the debt-collection and bankruptcy law of the country where they are deposited.

However, this problem may be circumvented if the insurance policy is deposited in Switzerland, which is a simple procedure. It is easy to rent a bank deposit box in any Swiss bank. To fund a Swiss annuity or life insurance, it is advisable and in some cases necessary to establish a Swiss bank account. Once a bank account is established, renting a safety deposit box is just a matter of filling in a simple form.

All debt-collection and bankruptcy procedures taking place in Switzerland are based solely on Swiss bankruptcy rules. This means that life insurance policies are protected in accordance with Swiss law even if the debt-collection or bankruptcy law in the debtor's domicile would not afford him or her such protection.

Specifically, only the Swiss rules on fraudulent conveyance apply here. Creditors cannot avoid the designation of beneficiaries unless they prove that the conditions for fraudulent conveyance are met. This remains true even if the purchase or designation was a voidable preference under the rules relating to fraudulent conveyance applicable at the claimant's domicile.

Accordingly, the creditors of a non-Swiss resident may not—in Switzerland—seize or include in the bankrupt's estate any life insurance policies that are protected under Swiss law even if they have a judgment or a bankruptcy decree that is enforceable in Switzerland, unless they can prove that the designation of the beneficiaries of the insurance policies is a voidable preference under the Swiss rules relating to fraudulent conveyance.

A further important advantage of Swiss annuities is that they offer instant liquidity, directly accessible by the policy holder. All capital, plus all accumulated interest and dividends, is freely available. Again, with properly established and professionally managed trusts, normally it is impossible to "liquidate" trust assets or to have trustees distribute large parts of the trust assets immediately if required, although loans sometimes can be arranged, provided they are made at arm's length.

Depending on the type of annuity, only a minimal penalty in case of withdrawal applies, and only during an initial period, usually up to one

TABLE 11.1 Comparing Swiss Annuities and Asset Protection Trusts

Criteria	Swiss Annuity	Asset Protection Trust
Owner retains full control	Yes	No
Privacy	Yes	Yes
Foreign jurisdiction	Yes	Depends on where trust assets are invested
Tax on funding of trust/annuity	No	Often gift taxes apply
Tax on income/capital gains within trust/annuity	No	Generally yes
Tax on distributions	Generally no	Generally yes
Liquidity	Yes	Depending on structure and the investment decisions of the trustee
Tax-free locally	Yes	Generally yes
Subject to restrictive anti-avoidance rules	Generally no	Generally yes
Statutory asset protection provisions	Yes	Variable, depending on trust domicile, location of trustee and trust assets
Asset protection provisions tested by highest court	Yes	Depending on trust domicile, location of trustee and trust assets
Simple and inexpensive	Yes	No

year. If funds are needed quickly, they are available and not tied down for a fixed period of time; with certain types of trust structures, they may not be tied down at all.

In addition, and most interestingly, all Swiss banks will accept Swiss life insurance policies as collateral for loans, so funds can be mobilized quickly if needed without having to make a withdrawal or cancelling the policy.

Table 11.1 summarizes these distinctions.

CONCLUSION

The Swiss (and Liechtenstein) insurance industry's impeccable track record and sophisticated products—particularly Swiss annuities and life insurance—are attractive to international investors who are interested in protecting their wealth and constitute a good alternative to usually more complex and more costly asset protection trusts.

Furthermore, the combination of insurance and trusts can in many instances achieve benefits that go beyond the use of just a trust or just an insurance structure for asset protection and tax planning purposes. Annuities are attractive from various perspectives: Not only are they a very safe form of investment, but they offer truly unique asset protection, which is particularly relevant to American investors and also increasingly important to wealthy individuals and families elsewhere in the world who wish to protect their assets effectively.

Moreover, investments in Swiss annuities and life insurance may also offer tax advantages, depending on individual situations. All of these advantages are available in an environment of profound legal, economic, and political stability that Switzerland offers, a truly rare situation.

CHAPTER 12

Swiss Annuities in Self-Directed Retirement Plans

Marco Gantenbein
Managing Director, Swiss Annuity
Consulting Group, Zurich

Swiss annuities have gained increasing acceptance and popularity among U.S. residents over the past few years as an attractive investment alternative for self-directed retirement plans. Investors have been drawn to this type of investment due to its security and flexibility, and the added degree of diversity offered by investing in foreign currencies.

While the average investor might feel some apprehension about the complexities of investing in a foreign-based annuity policy, it is a relatively simple process. All that is required for a Swiss annuity to be purchased in many retirement plans is that the annuity contract be held in the U.S. by a plan administrator, or custodian such as a bank or a trust company.

SELF-DIRECTED RETIREMENT PLAN OPTIONS IN THE UNITED STATES

When it comes to putting money away for retirement, one of the key options U.S. residents generally have is self-directed retirement plans. Depending on their income level (as measured by adjusted gross income on their U.S. tax returns), marital status, and age, they can make annual contributions using "pre-" or "post-" tax dollars to an individual retirement account, or contribute "pre-" tax dollars through a traditional IRA sponsored by

The author wishes to thank Millennium Trust Company and Mr. Gene Meeker for their gracious help in writing this chapter.

their employer with the opportunity for matching contributions from the employer. Investment choices in these types of plans are very flexible and are determined by the account owner of the IRA.

One of the most recent additions to the self-directed arena has been the Solo 401(k) plan. Designed strictly for sole proprietors, these plans offer the opportunity to employ a combination of contributions and earnings to amass significant funds in a shorter period of time. Investment choices in these types of plans are typically determined by the plan sponsor, which in this case is the sole proprietor.

TYPES OF SELF-DIRECTED RETIREMENT PLANS

For millions of Americans, the self-directed IRA has become a primary means of investing for retirement on a tax-advantaged basis. As of the end of 2006, industry estimates value assets held in self-directed IRAs at more than $4 trillion, and that trend is expected to continue as the Baby Boomers near retirement.

Each of these self-directed retirement plans has unique features and restrictions, including how much can be contributed annually and how those contributions, earnings, and distributions are taxed. Experts recommend consulting with a tax advisor before deciding on an appropriate self-directed IRA.

Personal IRAs

Traditional IRA   As the first type of IRA created for an individual, the traditional IRA allows annual tax-deductible contributions that depend on the individual's modified adjusted gross income (MAGI) with set maximums, and the individual's participation in an employer's retirement plan. While withdrawals are taxed, earnings on principal and interest accumulate tax-deferred until funds are withdrawn from the account, penalty-free after age $59\frac{1}{2}$. Minimum required distributions are mandatory after age $70\frac{1}{2}$.

Among other considerations, a traditional IRA may be appropriate for individuals who anticipate that tax rates during retirement will be lower than their current rate, or whose tax strategy is to defer taxes until after retirement.

Roth IRA   The Roth IRA is an alternative to a traditional IRA with distinct tax benefits. Contributions, for example, are not tax-deductible, but can be made past age $70\frac{1}{2}$. Earnings accumulate tax-free, but unlike a traditional

TABLE 12.1   Individual Retirement Accounts

IRA Type	Key Distinctions
Traditional IRA	Tax-deductible contributions[1]
	Earnings taxed at withdrawal
	Investment choices made by account owner
Roth IRA	Qualified withdrawals not taxable
	Nondeductible contributions[1]
	Investment choices made by account owner

[1]Investors should consult with tax advisor with respect to annual contribution amounts, catch-up provisions, income restrictions, and so on.

IRA, withdrawals are free of tax and penalties, provided certain conditions are met. Those conditions include a five-year holding period and attainment of age $59\frac{1}{2}$, or if made for certain specific purposes.

Among other considerations, a Roth IRA may be appropriate for those who expect tax rates during retirement to remain the same or to be higher than their current tax rate. (See Table 12.1.)

While on the surface it may not seem as if there are any real differences between these two eligible IRAs, the type of plan chosen can have significant long-term impact on the tax treatment of the investment in a Swiss annuity. The most obvious example is a Roth IRA. Because Roth IRAs are funded with nondeductible contributions, withdrawals after age $59\frac{1}{2}$ are taken free of income tax. In the case of a retirement plan, designated beneficiaries of the annuity contract will inherit their interest in the contract free of any U.S. tax obligation other than estate tax.

Employer-Sponsored IRAs

Two types of employer-sponsored self-directed IRAs are available in the United States: the SEP IRA and the SIMPLE IRA. Small business owners should consider their IRA choices carefully to determine which makes the most sense based on the size of their business, the number of employees, and the amount of matching contributions they are comfortable offering to their employees.

Simplified Employee Pension   The Simplified Employee Pension (SEP) IRA allows employers to make contributions to their employees' retirement accounts of up to 25 percent of the employee's compensation, or $45,000, whichever is less. For 2007 there is a compensation cap of $225,000. With a SEP IRA there is no catch-up provision.

Savings Incentive Match Plan for Employees   The Savings Incentive Match Plan for Employees (SIMPLE) IRA enables employers with fewer than 100 employees to establish an individual retirement account for each participating employee. The SIMPLE IRA has requirements similar to a traditional IRA, but individual contribution limits are higher. The employer can match all or a part of the employee's contribution. With a SIMPLE IRA, there is a maximum deferral of $10,500 for 2007, plus a catch-up of $2,500.

PERMISSIBLE INVESTMENTS IN IRAs

Prohibited Transactions

While self-directed IRAs offer investors great flexibility in investment choices, the U.S. regulatory bodies responsible for overseeing these types of accounts have established certain limits on the types of transactions an owner is allowed to conduct within an IRA. Violations of these guidelines have become known as prohibited transactions.

Any transaction, for example, that can be construed as providing immediate personal financial gain to a self-directed account holder is not allowed; often such transactions are referred to as self-dealing. Examples of self-dealing would include borrowing money from your IRA, selling property to your IRA, receiving a current benefit outside the IRA from assets in the IRA, or using the IRA as security for a personal loan.

In addition, direct investments of self-directed funds in any of these categories are strictly prohibited:

- Life insurance
- Collectibles such as works of art, rugs, antiques, metals (other than gold, silver and palladium), gems, stamps, coins (except certain U.S. minted coins), alcoholic beverages, and other tangible property
- Subchapter S corporations or any other categories as may be defined by the Secretary of the Treasury

All other types of investments are permissible subject to the policy of the custodian/trustee of the self-directed retirement plan.

While a Swiss annuity has a life insurance component to it, it is not considered to be a life insurance policy on the life of the IRA owner. Therefore, it is not considered a prohibited transaction by the Internal Revenue Service (IRS).

Disqualifications

IRAs may not transfer plan income or assets; sell, exchange, or lease property; lend money; extend credit; furnish goods, services or facilities to disqualified people; or allow fiduciaries to obtain or use the income or assets for their own interest.

For IRAs, a disqualified person is:

- The IRA holder and his or her spouse
- The IRA holder's ancestors, lineal descendants, and their spouses
- The IRA holder's investment advisors and managers
- Any corporation, partnership, trust, or estate in which the IRA holder has a 50 percent or greater interest
- Anyone providing services to the IRA such as the trustee or custodian

A self-directed IRA owner who engages in disqualifying activities or transacts with a disqualified person on behalf of the IRA is subject to having the IRA's tax-deferred status disqualified. In such an instance, all the related assets in the IRA would be distributed to the IRA owner and subject to income tax and penalties in the current tax year.

FUNDING IRAs

Annual Contributions

IRAs are available to anyone who receives taxable compensation during the year. For IRA contribution purposes, compensation includes wages, salaries, fees, tips, bonuses, commissions, taxable alimony, and separate maintenance payments.

Husbands and wives are eligible to each have an IRA, even if one spouse is not working. An individual's annual contribution is limited to the lesser of total taxable compensation or to the yearly amount shown in Table 12.2. IRA account owners age 50 or older may make an additional "catch-up" contribution in the amounts indicated in the table.

There is no minimum or required IRA contribution amount, and all earnings on the amounts in a traditional IRA are not taxed until withdrawn. In the case of Roth IRAs, as contributions are not deductible, withdrawals

TABLE 12.2   Traditional and Roth IRA: Annual Contribution
Limits

Year	Normal Contribution	"Catch-up" Amount
2006	$4,000	$1,000
2007	$4,000	$1,000
2008	$5,000	$1,000
2009	Indexed[1]	$1,000

[1]Normal contribution limits will increase annually by $500 whenever cumulative inflation exceeds the next-higher $500 increment.

may be made on a tax-free basis provided certain conditions are met, including a five-year holding period.

Rollovers

A rollover begins with a distribution, followed by a recontribution of all, or a portion of, the assets to another plan. The distribution may occur between a qualified plan and an IRA. The rollover transaction must be completed within a 60-day period, or the assets' eligibility to be returned to a tax-advantaged account is lost. The distribution will then be taxed as ordinary income in the year it was received, and if the individual who received the distribution is under age $59\frac{1}{2}$, the IRS imposes a 10 percent penalty on the distribution, subject to certain exceptions.

It is important for retirement plan owners considering a rollover to take extra precautions that the transaction is completed on a timely basis, as all distributions are reported to the IRS. If the IRS does not receive confirmation of recontribution within the 60-day period, it will assume the transaction is a distribution and therefore taxable.

Rollovers are not permitted in these cases:

- More than one rollover in the same account, as in an IRA to an IRA, or more than one same-fund transfer within a 12-month period
- Rollovers from a SIMPLE IRA plan to a traditional IRA during the first two years of a SIMPLE IRA's plan participation
- After age $70\frac{1}{2}$, IRA or qualified plan rollover amounts that represent a taxpayer's required minimum distribution for that year
- Rollover from a Roth IRA to a traditional IRA or qualified plan

Direct Rollover

Unlike a rollover, a "direct" rollover always originates with assets in a qualified plan, traditional IRA, or SIMPLE IRA, and involves movement to a traditional IRA or another employer plan. At no time are the assets cashable or negotiable by the taxpayer. Also, while direct rollovers are reported to the IRS as distributions, a special code on the distribution report indicates the funds were transferred in a direct rollover to an IRA or employer plan and are, therefore, not taxable.

Transfers

Transfers are the most common funding method for a new or existing IRA. A transfer is the movement of IRA assets directly from one trustee or custodian to another. In IRAs, these types of transfers are unlimited since funds are transferred from one institution to another. The transaction is not reported to the IRS as a distribution.

SOLO 401(k) FOR SOLE PROPRIETORS

A Solo 401(k) account offers retirement planning options including enhanced contribution amounts and exceptional tax benefits for sole proprietors. And as with IRAs, there is opportunity to invest in both traditional and alternative investments (provided the custodian will hold alternative investments in these types of plans).

For sole proprietors, the Solo 401(k) offers the same plan options, contribution limits, and flexibility available in 401(k) plans for companies with multiple employees. As a result, single-owner businesses can put away more money for retirement in a shorter amount of time using a combination of salary deferral and profit-sharing contributions to fund the plan than with an IRA.

The advantages of opening a Solo 401(k) over other small-business-oriented retirement plans include:

- *Contribution flexibility.* The business owner decides each year whether to contribute, and how much.
- *Higher contribution limits.* Tax-deferred contributions can be up to three times that offered by other types of retirement plans.
- *Easy setup.* There are no complicated administrative requirements, if working with a good prototype plan and custodian/trustee.

- *Consolidation convenience.* Ability to consolidate assets from traditional IRAs or other retirement plans into a Solo 401(k).
- *Ability to borrow.* Owners can borrow up to the lesser of $50,000 or one-half of the Solo 401(k) balance. The loan can be used for any purpose and is tax-free and penalty-free, as long as it is paid back on time.

The benefits of the Solo 401(k) were recently enhanced by the passage of legislation by the U.S. Congress allowing Solo 401(k) contributions to be earmarked as nondeductible Roth 401(k) contributions. This law allows the opportunity for tax-free withdrawals and/or distributions after age $59\frac{1}{2}$, provided certain conditions and requirements are met.

Unlike IRAs, the Solo 401(k) permits investments in life insurance and "S" corporations.

Eligible Businesses

Solo 401(k)s may be ideal retirement plans for a variety of single-owner businesses, including sole proprietorships, limited liability companies, partnerships, and corporations. Candidates for these types of plans include real estate brokers, sole-practitioner CPA firms, consultants, contractors, entrepreneurs, attorneys, and tradespeople. While Solo 401(k)s are designed for single-owner businesses with no full-time employees, these exceptions are permitted:

- Spouses
- Part-time employees working fewer than 1,000 hours per year
- Employees with less than one year of service
- Certain union employees
- Certain nonresident/alien employees

Business owners should know that once a single full-time employee is added, the plan must be converted to a traditional employee-sponsored 401(k) plan, which is then subject to ERISA (The Employee Retirement Income Security Act of 1974, a federal law that establishes legal guidelines for private pension and employee benefit plans) rules.

Contribution Limits

As the employee and the employer, the business owner is permitted to make a combination of contributions, including salary deferral and profits from

TABLE 12.3 Contribution Limits for 2006 and 2007

		2006	2007
Employee	Annual Contribution	$15,000	$15,500
	50+ Catch-up Provision	$5,000	$5,000
Employer	Up to 25% of W-2 Compensation, if incorporated		
	Up to 20% of Self-Employment Income as Sole Proprietor		
Total Plan Contribution Limits	Lesser of 100% of compensation or...	$44,000	$45,000

the business. Also, if the business owner is age 50 or older, he or she is able to defer additional salary in the form of a "catch-up" provision.

The contribution limits for 2006 and 2007 are shown in Table 12.3.

Business owners should be aware that contribution limits, whether to a 401(k) or a Roth 401(k), are counted in the aggregate. The limits indicated are for the entire Solo 401(k). Were a plan to offer both options, exceeding the allowable limits for each or both components is not permitted.

Funding Sources

In addition to salary deferrals and profit sharing, Solo 401(k)s can be funded by rolling over or transferring funds from any of these types of retirement plans:

- Traditional IRA, SEP, and SIMPLE (after a two-year holding period)
- Qualified plans or Keoghs (profit sharing, money purchase pension, defined benefit)
- 401(k) plans
- 403(b) plans
- 457 plans

Each Solo 401(k) must be established no later than December 31 or fiscal year-end, whichever comes first, to be eligible for tax deductions for that year.

Roth Solo 401(k)

The Roth Solo 401(k) is not a separate type of account. Rather, it is an amendment to an existing Solo 401(k). The amendment allows the business owner to earmark, and track, contributions as Roth contributions. This Roth component of the Solo 401(k) combines the enhanced contribution limits of the Solo 401(k) with the tax advantages of the Roth IRA.

Unlike a Roth IRA, however, Roth contributions to a Solo 401(k) are not subject to any income limits. The business owner can contribute three times as much to a Solo 401(k) than to a Roth IRA. In fact, if the business owner is more than 50 years old and had maximized contributions into a Roth IRA, the Roth component of the Solo 401(k) could be used to put away up to $25,000 per year, or up to $50,000 if the owner is married to a working eligible spouse.

Business owners should be aware that contribution limits, whether to the Solo 401(k) or the Roth Solo 401(k) component, are counted in the aggregate. The limits indicated are for the entire Solo 401(k). Exceeding the allowable limits for each component, or the combination, is not permitted.

Important: The five-year holding period on Roth contributions generally starts on the date of the Roth IRA opening, not the first day of the Roth contributions to the Solo 401(k). In the case of a rollover of a distribution from a designated Roth account maintained under a section 401(k) plan to a Roth IRA, the period that the rolled-over funds were in the designated Roth account does not count toward the five-taxable-year period for determining qualified distributions from the Roth IRA. However, if an individual had established a Roth IRA in a prior year, the five-year period for determining qualified distributions from a Roth IRA that began as a result of that earlier Roth IRA contribution applies to any distributions from the Roth IRA (including a distribution of an amount attributable to a rollover contribution from a designated Roth account).

When contemplating a transfer of funds from a Roth 401(k) to a Roth IRA, it is advisable to consult with an attorney or tax professional to understand all the implications.

PROVIDERS OF IRAs AND SOLO 401(k)s

Self-directed retirement accounts, both personal and employer sponsored, can be held in custody by a variety of licensed financial institutions in the United States. Not all custodians, however, may permit the retirement account owner to hold Swiss annuities in the IRA or Solo 401(k).

Banks

Banks in the United States, state or nationally chartered, offer self-directed IRA owners the opportunity to custody the more traditional investments, such as stocks, bonds, mutual funds, and, of course, bank deposits, in their accounts.

Cash balances in bank accounts in IRA accounts that are owned by one person and titled in the name of that person's retirement plan are eligible for Federal Deposit Insurance Corporation (FDIC) insurance.

All deposits that an individual has in any retirement plans, if titled correctly, at the same insured bank are added together, and the total is insured up to $250,000. For example, if an individual has an IRA and a self-directed Keogh account at the same bank, the deposits in both accounts would be added together and insured up to $250,000.

The FDIC does not insure retirement money invested in stocks, bonds, mutual funds, annuities, or municipal securities, even if these products are purchased from an insured bank.

Banks often may not allow self-directed retirement account owners the opportunity to hold alternative investments, such as Swiss annuities, in their retirement accounts.

Brokerage Firms

Brokerage firms in the United States, both online and full service, offer self-directed retirement account owners the opportunity to hold registered investments, such as stocks, bonds, and mutual funds, in their accounts. Investors meeting certain qualifications criteria, in terms of income and net worth, may also hold certain registered securities that are not available to the general public, such as privately placed securities.

Investments in stocks, bonds, and mutual funds are not covered by any kind of "deposit" insurance, but the securities industry in the United States has created the Securities Investor Protection Corporation (SIPC) to handle claims of loss against a particular brokerage firm. SIPC insurance does not cover a decline in value of the investments themselves.

Most brokerage firms do not allow self-directed account owners the opportunity to hold alternative investments, such as Swiss annuities, in their retirement accounts; however, there are signs this may change in the future.

Trust Companies (Custodians)

Trust companies, like banks, are empowered to custody IRA accounts by Internal Revenue Code Section 408(n). Trust companies, like banks, may be empowered by the respective state they reside in or by the federal government.

In the United States, IRA custodians may be thought of as falling into one of two categories:

1. *Traditional custodians,* which permit account holders to hold only more traditional investments, such as stocks, bonds, and mutual funds
2. *Nontraditional custodians,* which, in addition to those traditional assets, permit account holders to hold a range of alternative investments, such as Swiss annuities, real estate, hedge funds, precious metals, promissory notes, and the like

Custodians offering only self-directed IRAs do not offer any form of advice to clients regarding management of the investments, tax consequences, or legal issues. The respective investments are held in custody for the benefit of the IRA holder. Management of the investments is the responsibility of the IRA holder or his or her investment advisor.

SWISS ANNUITIES

Eligible Annuities

While it may vary from custodian to custodian in the United States, both fixed and variable annuities may be held in a self-directed retirement account. A "fixed" annuity has the principal and a specified return on the investment guaranteed by the life insurance company. In a "variable" annuity, the value of the insurance policy is determined by the underlying investments.

While a Swiss annuity has a life insurance component too, it is not considered to be a prohibited life insurance policy investment. Therefore, purchase of a Swiss annuity is not considered a prohibited transaction by the IRS.

Premiums, Annuity Payments, and Distributions

When investing in a self-directed IRA, the general rule of thumb is that all expenses related to the investment must be deducted from the IRA itself and all income related to the account must be deposited back into the account. The only exceptions to this are the IRA fees, which may be paid by the account owner outside the IRA.

Therefore, no annuity premiums or payments should be made directly between the Swiss insurance company and the individual IRA account holder. The custodian will pay premiums to the insurance company from the IRA assets. The insurance company will pay annuity payments and benefits into the IRA through the IRA custodian. The account holder may request distributions from the assets of the IRA as desired subject to tax and penalty, depending on the circumstances and timing of the distribution request prior to age $59\frac{1}{2}$.

Registration

In a typical purchase of a Swiss annuity or life insurance contract, there are four parties involved in the transaction:

1. The insurer who issues the policy and provides coverage in return for payment of the annual premiums
2. The policy holder who enters into a contract with the insurer and receives coverage for themselves or other designated beneficiary, confirmed in the insurance policy
3. The insured person whose life is covered by the insurance
4. The beneficiary or beneficiaries who have been designated by the policy holder to receive the proceeds of the policy upon the death of the designated insured

When the purchase of the policy is done within a self-directed retirement account, the self-directed IRA becomes the owner and beneficiary of the annuity, and the owner becomes the insured.

Taxation

Swiss annuities can be legally purchased by U.S. citizens, and they can be placed in U.S. tax-deferred retirement plans such as IRAs.

Swiss annuities may have certain advantages for U.S. investors when it comes to tax reporting compared with other foreign investments. For example, a Swiss annuity is not a foreign bank account subject to the U.S. reporting requirements on IRS Form 1040 or the special U.S. Treasury form for reporting foreign accounts.

Normally, the IRS requires citizens to file Form 720 for 1 percent excise tax (which is 1 percent of premium paid) if they buy foreign held annuities. But the tax treaty with Switzerland eliminates this tax. The tax consequences for those who plan to withdraw payments from the annuity and the IRA before age $59\frac{1}{2}$ have been discussed. It is important that U.S. investors consult their tax advisor for more information before making an investment in a Swiss annuity in a self-directed retirement account.

Other Considerations

Self-directed retirement account investors may want to consider several unique qualities of typical Swiss annuities. These qualities include:

- Investments can be canceled at any time without loss of principal and with all principal, interest, and dividends payable if canceled after one year.
- All capital, plus all accumulated interest and dividends, is freely accessible. Depending on the type of annuity, a minimal penalty in case of withdrawal applies only to an initial period of up to one year, So, if funds are needed quickly, they are available in an IRA. After the IRA owner reaches $59\frac{1}{2}$, the proceeds can be withdrawn without penalty. Up until that age, distributions from the IRA will be subject to both U.S. current income tax and penalty.
- Swiss annuities can be tailor-made to suit most individual needs. For example, if substantial assets are to be invested in the annuitity, it is possible for a specific insurance plan to be set up that allows the underlying investments to be organized in individual portfolios through the existing investment manager. Such plans are also referred to as portfolio bonds or insurance wrappers.
- From a historical perspective, Switzerland, one of the world's most stable countries both politically and economically, also has the world's strongest insurance industry with a continuing history of success without a single failure—ever.
- A currency conversion option is most often available into any of the world's major currencies. A U.S. investor may therefore choose a Swiss franc annuity and convert it into U.S. dollars (or any another major currency) at almost any time.
- Swiss annuities usually would escape any forced repatriation under imposed exchange controls, because they are regarded as a pending contract between the investor and the insurance company.

Additional distinctive features may be available to investors depending on the insurance company underwriting the annuity.

Survey of Basic U.S. Federal Income Tax Considerations in Purchasing and Holding an Annuity or Life Insurance Contract Issued by a Swiss or Liechtenstein Insurance Company

Frederic J. Gelfond

Principal, Financial Services—Insurance,
Deloitte Tax LLP, Washington, DC

Life insurance and annuity products are generally afforded more favorable treatment under the U.S. federal income tax rules than many other types of investments or savings vehicles.[1] Increases in cash or policy values that build up inside of a life insurance contract generally are not subject to tax during the lifetime of the insured unless total distributions from the contract exceed amounts paid into the contract.[2] In addition, death benefits typically are excluded from taxable income.[3] Similar to a life insurance contract, earnings within an annuity contract are not included in income until amounts are received under the contract. To the extent that amounts distributed are received as part of an annuity stream, only a proportionate part of each payment is treated as taxable earnings, with the remainder deemed a nontaxable return of capital, or "investment in the contract."

Complicating Factors

Although the Internal Revenue Code[4] provides relatively taxpayer-favorable treatment for such contracts, there are many tax complexities involved in the holding of a life insurance or annuity contract. Complicating matters further, the Internal Revenue Service (IRS or Service) has been unable or unwilling to provide interpretative guidance on many insurance tax issues that practitioners and taxpayers have raised over the years. Some believe this is driven by IRS concern that drawing bright lines in certain areas will provide road maps for innovative industry participants to take advantage of the tax rules governing insurance in a manner that Congress did not intend.

A second complicating factor is that the rules that have been provided by Congress in this area—that is, the Code—are broadly crafted. As a result, they arguably do not consider specific product innovations that have occurred over the years. Several rules in place were enacted to limit the investment orientation of many insurance products relative to the net amounts at risk under the contracts. In other words, the rules have been designed to ensure that the products provide meaningful amounts of true insurance coverage in order for a holder to be able to enjoy the benefits of insurance tax treatment.

Threshold Question

This chapter provides an overview of many of the basic rules that one might want to consider relative to the purchase, holding, and other transactions that may occur with respect to an insurance policy.[5] Before one even gets to those issues, however, it must be established that the contract in question will be recognized, or qualify, as an insurance contract. That is, the threshold question with regard to an insurance policy is whether the contract itself satisfies the federal income tax definitional requirements.

Definition of Life Insurance

The rules for qualification as a life insurance contract are set forth in the Code under section 7702. Some contracts that satisfy the life insurance contract definition may be further characterized, under section 7702A, as modified endowment contracts (MECs). A holder of a life insurance contract that is characterized as a MEC will be entitled to some, but not all, of the tax benefits afforded a holder of a life insurance contract that is not a MEC.

Despite the importance of these rules in determining the tax treatment of life insurance contract ownership, it is probably safe to say that few people other than professionals who practice in the area are aware of, let alone are well versed in, these rules. Even though these are technically policyholder issues, they are virtually without exception managed by the issuing insurance company, not its policyholders. Certainly most policyholders would not even be able to state with direct, personal knowledge, if their contracts qualify. If anything, they would have to seek confirmation from the issuing insurance company.

Technical and Administrative Complexity

Depending on the type of contract, the calculations and processing involved in maintaining a product's compliance with these rules throughout its life cycle are both technically and administratively intensive for the insurance company, thus heightening the likelihood of a compliance issue among a large group of contracts being administered by the company. The consequences of a compliance failure to a policyholder can be a loss of many, if not all, of the benefits of insurance tax treatment, as well as exposure to potential tax penalties and interest.

Why is this important to a purchaser of a product issued by a Swiss or Liechtenstein company? First, regardless of where the issuing insurance company is located, the U.S. insurance tax rules will apply with respect to a policy held by a U.S. citizen or resident who is subject to the U.S. income tax rules. Second, most U.S. life insurance companies must make significant investments in managing the section 7702 and 7702A compliance processes. Clearly, an additional level of scrutiny is required when buying a contract from a foreign insurance company whose core business does not necessarily require compliance with U.S. insurance tax rules.

Even if the foreign jurisdiction where the insurance company is located has rules similar to the U.S. rules in terms of their intent to limit investment orientation, there is one thing that a policyholder can be certain of: The rules that apply in that jurisdiction are going to be different from the unique and mostly unforgiving rules that are in place in the United States. Hence, one should make certain, prior to entering into such a purchase, that the foreign company has received the appropriate level of technical tax scrutiny on the product design and has the systems and controls in place to monitor its products for compliance throughout their entire life cycle. While one would think that a company that is specifically targeting the U.S. market is aware of these rules, a healthy dose of skepticism, or certainly diligence, will be required that may, as a practical matter, not be as necessary with respect to a contract issued by a U.S. company.

Annuity Definitional Rules

The U.S. tax rules defining an annuity contract are not administratively complex. But then again, unlike the complicated provisions set forth in the

Code that establish what will qualify as a life insurance contract, there is no Code-based definition of an annuity contract. Instead, the concept of what will constitute or be accepted as an annuity contract for U.S. federal income tax purposes has evolved over the years through case law and administrative guidance. Certain characteristics are generally accepted in the marketplace and by the IRS as to what is necessary in order to have an annuity. By virtue of the nature in which the tax law in this area has evolved, however, there exist some uncertainties around what some of the true requirements might be.

Exceptions to this circumstance are found in sections 72(s) and 72(u), which set forth specific situations in which a contract will not be treated as an annuity. Section 72(s) deals with contracts that do not contain prescribed language requiring certain distributions upon the death of a contract holder. Section 72(u) limits the insurance tax treatment of certain contracts held by nonnatural persons.

In addition, and particularly relevant here, section 1275 provides certain requirements in order for the holder of an annuity contract issued by an insurance company, not subject to tax in the United States, to be able to enjoy the benefit of tax deferral on cash value buildup under the contract.

Additional Variable Contract Considerations

Finally, it is assumed that readers of this text are primarily interested in variable or separate account insurance products. These are life insurance or annuity contracts whereby the policyholder chooses the funds that premiums and cash values are to be allocated to. In turn, the policyholder receives a return on the contract based on the performance of those funds. It is likely that some readers also are interested in separate account products that are issued as part of private placement offerings. As such, there are two additional areas that they will need to be highly cognizant of.

The first is an IRS doctrine commonly referred to as the investor control doctrine. The second relates to a Code-based provision that requires that the assets held in the separate or, more precisely, segregated asset account(s) underlying the variable insurance contract be adequately diversified. The consequence of falling within the investor control doctrine is a loss of deferral of tax on inside buildup. A failure under the diversification requirements results in the product not qualifying as a life insurance or annuity contract during the period of nondiversification and, hence, a similar loss of deferral of tax on inside buildup.

The remainder of this chapter is divided into two main sections. The first discusses the definitional-, or qualification-type issues described in this introduction. The second section describes the primary federal income tax rules involved in the purchase and holding of a life insurance or annuity contract.[6] Each section separately discusses the rules relating to life insurance contracts and those relating to annuities. Where similar rules apply to both types of products, such fact is indicated.

DEFINITIONAL AND OTHER COMPLIANCE ISSUES

Background on the Modern Taxation of Life Insurance and Annuity Products

Historically, policyholders have never been taxed on investment earnings building up inside an insurance contract[7] until there has been some form of predeath distribution.[8] Over the past two and a half decades, however, there has been a constant discourse among the insurance industry, Congress, the Treasury Department, and the courts over what types of products will entitle policyholders to this insurance tax treatment.

One need only observe the interaction between the industry and Congress relative to the development of the federal income tax definition of "life insurance contract." Through the development of flexible premium contracts, such as universal life insurance, and other product innovations, insurers are able to offer potential policyholders the ability to significantly increase the investment orientation of a life insurance contract relative to the death benefits available thereunder. Thus, in 1982, Congress introduced section 101(f) as a stop-gap measure for limiting the investment features of certain flexible-premium life insurance contracts.[9] This section mandated certain relationships between policy cash values and death benefits. Two years later, Congress enacted section 7702, providing a permanent, and generally applicable, definition of a life insurance contract based on principles similar to section 101(f).[10]

Section 7702 alone, however, did not prevent the investment orientation that could be achieved through the use of single-premium and other limited payment contracts. Thus, Congress, through the subsequent enactment of section 7702A, eliminated some of the tax benefits available under a new class of life insurance contracts, known as modified endowment contracts.[11] The most prominent impact of such characterization is that distributions from MECs are taxed under the "income-first" rules similar to those applicable to annuities under section 72, rather than the more favorable "investment-first" distribution rules typically accorded life insurance contracts.

As a result of these iterative rounds of innovation and regulation, the insurance product tax landscape has evolved into a series of complex tax rules intended to prevent potential and perceived tax abuses. These rules, if violated, have a harsh effect on both the issuing insurance company and its policyholders.[12] Moreover, these rules must be applied in conjunction with numerous other federal and state laws and regulations.[13] Further, all of these rules, laws, and regulations must be complied with over the course of the entire natural life cycle of an insurance product.

Variable products—also referred to as separate account or segregated asset account products[14]—involve even more compliance issues, including the investor control doctrine and the so-called diversification rules contained in section 817(h) and the regulations thereunder. These products are a reflection of an ongoing evolution of life insurance products intended to meet consumer demands for investments yielding higher rates of return than traditional insurance company offerings. Separate account products achieve this higher level of performance primarily through product structures that promise returns similar to what can be generated through mutual fund or other noninsurance investments, as opposed to predefined returns typical of general account insurance products.[15]

The use of separate accounts was initially restricted to insurance company investments underlying pension and profit sharing plan contracts.[16] By using these accounts, insurance companies are able to avoid having to commingle the assets required to satisfy retirement plan obligations with those assets that were used to pay general account liabilities. In fact, because they can segregate these assets from their general accounts, they are able to escape from the substantial regulatory restraints that all states impose on general account investments.[17] Armed with the ability to make investments that are not available to general accounts, insurance companies are better able to compete with banks and other traditional pension plan providers.

Shortly after this innovation, insurers began to expand their use of separate accounts to support a wider variety of products, including life insurance and annuities.[18] Under a variable contract, a policyholder's return is based on the fluctuating value of the underlying separate account assets.[19] In contrast, the benefits under a general account product are based on fixed returns guaranteed by the issuer. In exchange for this potentially higher return of a separate account product, the policyholder assumes the investment risk from the insurer, while the insurer retains the mortality risk.[20]

Initial rulings issued by the IRS relative to these products reflected recognition of the insurance nature of these products. Fairly early in this evolution, however, the IRS took the position that certain separate account products did not differ sufficiently from other investments, such as a mutual fund, except of course for the more favorable tax treatment afforded insurance contracts versus other types of investments.[21] This occurred as the Service became cognizant of substantial growth in this market as well as the aggressive marketing by some producers who emphasized the tax treatment rather than the insurance benefits of these products.

The IRS's basic objection was that in many of these transactions, because of its factual findings in some cases that the policyholders retained significant control over how the funds paid into the contracts were to be invested, the policyholders rather than the insurance companies were the true owners of the underlying assets. As such, the IRS determined that the policyholders were the ones who should be taxed on the investment earnings.[22] Through a series of rulings in the late 1970s and early to mid-1980s, the IRS attempted to establish parameters over how much control a policyholder could exercise over a separate account investment and still defer recognition of inside buildup.[23] In 1984, the Eighth Circuit Court of Appeals weighed in on this issue in support of the IRS.[24]

In the 1984 act, Congress stepped in as well with legislation that, among other things, established objective diversification requirements for separate accounts other than those underlying pension plan contracts.[25] In addition, Congress authorized the Treasury Department to prescribe diversification standards via regulations for investments associated with separate account products. In authorizing the Treasury to prescribe the appropriate diversification standards, Congress sought to deny annuity or life insurance treatment for investments that were either available to the general public or made at the direction of a policyholder.[26]

The intent behind Congress's diversification requirements is similar to what the Service meant to accomplish through its investor control rulings. Nevertheless, there continues to be some question as to whether Congress also intended the diversification requirements to supersede those rulings. That is, whether mere satisfaction of the diversification requirements represents prima facie evidence of a lack of investor control or whether the investor control rulings continue to play a role in determining the ownership of separate account assets still is not clear.[27] The Service has taken the position that the investor control doctrine continues to be a viable theory upon which to challenge a transaction.

Two years after the 1984 Act, the Service issued proposed and temporary regulations[28] that addressed the minimum level of investment diversification appropriate for variable annuity and variable life insurance contracts. With the expectation that future regulations or revenue rulings would provide the necessary guidance on this issue, the preamble stated that the temporary regulations "do not provide guidance concerning the circumstances in which policyholder control of the investments of a segregated asset account may cause the contract holder, rather than the insurance company, to be treated as the owner of the assets in the account."[29] The final regulations incorporate some of the broad concepts from the investor control rulings.[30]

More recent guidance has been issued in the form of revenue rulings that provide some guidelines but do not fully address all of the questions that have been raised in this area and actually create some additional ones.[31] Thus, after all this interaction with the Service and various courts, separate account policyholders are still left with some lingering questions as to how much control can be exercised over the investments in separate account contracts without the policyholder being considered the owner of the underlying assets for federal income tax purposes.

Thus, the investor control rulings must continue to be considered in policy design. Further, policyholders and insurance companies now have to contend with an additional regulatory regime (i.e., the diversification rules) in order to maintain the viability of their products. The diversification requirements have increased the overall administrative complexity of separate account products. Therefore, not only does it appear that the diversification rules may not have fully eliminated the investor control issue, they have imposed additional restrictions on the investment of separate account assets for nonpension contracts. Satisfaction of these requirements, however, is vital to achieving favorable insurance tax treatment.

The discussion that follows provides some more precise detail on the various compliance requirements just introduced, including further information on the section 7702 and 7702A definitional rules as well as the section 817(h) diversification provisions. After that is a discussion of a revenue ruling that presents the IRS's most recent broadly applicable statement of what it indicates will qualify under its investor control theory; in effect, it provides "safe harbor" examples of a life insurance and an annuity contract with respect to this theory.

The section concludes with a discussion of the federal income tax requirements for an annuity contract. While section 7702 and 7702A apply only to life insurance contracts, the diversification rules and investor control doctrine also apply to annuity contracts. In fact, the investor control doctrine originated in an annuity context. As such, the discussion of investor control and diversification is not repeated in the annuity section.

Life Insurance Contract Definitional and Other Compliance Requirements

As noted, a contract must satisfy the federal income tax definition of a life insurance contract set forth in section 7702 in order to receive the full tax benefits of life insurance policy ownership. A failure to satisfy this definition will result in loss of the policyholder's ability to defer the recognition of income on increments to cash or policy values, commonly referred to as the inside buildup; however, the amount received by a beneficiary upon the death of the insured may still be received tax free.[32]

Moreover, to the extent that a life insurance contract that satisfies the section 7702 definition is characterized as a MEC under section 7702A, lifetime distributions from the contract will be taxed on an income-first basis. That is, amounts received will be deemed to come out of policy earnings to the extent of such earnings, before they will be treated as a return of capital, or the policyholder's investment in the contract. This is the opposite of the rule applicable to life insurance contracts that are not characterized as MECs. In addition, taxable amounts distributed from a MEC will also be subject to an additional 10 percent penalty on the taxable portion of any distribution. Finally, loans taken on the security of a MECs cash value—policy loans—are deemed to be distributions. This, too, is different from the rule applicable to non-MEC life insurance contracts, in which policy loans are considered to be a nontaxable event.

As further noted in the introduction, to the extent that the policy involved is a variable or separate account life insurance contract, the policyholder will need to ensure that the transaction does not violate the IRS investor control doctrine and, further, that the policy is adequately diversified under yet another complex set of Code provisions and regulations under section 817. Although questions have been raised regarding the sustainability of an IRS challenge under its investor control doctrine, a failure under either of these standards could also result in a loss of full insurance tax treatment.

Section 7702 Federal Income Tax Definition of Life Insurance Contract

Section 7702 imposes two requirements in order to satisfy the federal income tax definition of life insurance contract. First, the contract must be characterized as a life insurance contract under "applicable law." Next it must satisfy one of two actuarial, or mathematical, tests. These alternative tests are the cash value accumulation test (CVAT) and the guideline premium limitation and cash value corridor.

Section 7702 was added to the Code as a reaction to marketplace activity that involved sales of insurance that were deemed by Congress to be too heavily investment oriented and that effectively transferred relatively little or no insurance risk. To accomplish the desired result, the tests were designed to measure, or dictate, the relationship between the cash value growing inside of a life insurance contract and the face amount or death benefit that may be received in order for a policyholder to defer or avoid taxation on the contract's inside buildup.

The ultimate goal of both of the alternative actuarial tests is to make sure that there is a meaningful difference between the cash value and face amount.

This difference is referred to as the net amount at risk and constitutes the true insurance risk that is transferred to the insurance company. Over time, as the insured ages, the cash value of any cash value life insurance contract is expected to approach the amount of the death benefit and, in theory, equal the death benefit amount on the date the contract is expected to mature. Both tests under section 7702 allow for this but establish the rate at which the narrowing of this band may occur.

To the extent that there is a failure under one of the actuarial tests, the contract will effectively be bifurcated into its pure "term" insurance and cash value, or savings components.[33] The tax impact of such bifurcation is that earnings accruing on the cash value, or savings account will be currently taxable. In addition, any earnings on the contract that were generated prior to the time the contract failed to meet the provisions of section 7702 will also be currently taxable. In the event of the death of the insured, the amounts received under the pure insurance portion will still be excludable from federal income tax.[34]

Applicable law   The applicable law requirement is intended to refer to state, territorial, or foreign law. That is, the life insurance contract must be treated as such under the relevant local body of law regulating the issuance of the contract. The legislative history underlying this requirement refers to a contract that is treated as a "single, integrated life insurance contract." To the extent that a contract has a rider or other feature that provides benefits other than life insurance coverage, such as an annuity rider, the other feature will not be treated as part of the contract for performing the section 7702 actuarial tests unless it is considered part of the "single, integrated life insurance contract" under the controlling local law.[35]

For example, assume a policyholder held a policy that included a term insurance contract and premium deposit fund (albeit unlikely in today's market). The two elements, taken together, might look and perform economically very much like a typical whole life insurance policy. If the contract is not treated as a single, integrated contract of life insurance under local law, however, only the term insurance portion would be subject to qualification under section 7702. The premium deposit fund would be treated for federal income tax purposes as a separate noninsurance instrument that would not qualify for deferral of tax on any incremental earnings on the fund.

Insurable interest   Recently a great deal of attention has been focused on the concept of insurable interest. In the United States, every state has some requirement that the owner have an interest in the continued life of the insured. These rules have evolved since the late 1800s as the result of efforts among the states to avoid the moral hazards potentially involved in taking out insurance on individuals in situations where there is no pecuniary or other relationship among the parties that would be jeopardized in the event of the death of the insured.

The laws in this area and thus the standards that must be met to demonstrate an insurable interest vary by state. In some states, the rules are fairly broadly crafted. This is particularly true as it relates to a business being able to purchase insurance coverage on a large base of employees. This issue is relevant to the current discussion in that in some states, the question of whether an insurable interest exists may have an impact on whether a contract qualifies as a life insurance contract under that state's law (i.e., the applicable law, as referred to in section 7702). The question is whether the existence of an insurable interest is a requirement under the state's definition of life insurance contract or whether an insurable interest must exist merely as a prerequisite to a company's ability to sell a contract that otherwise meets the state's definition of life insurance contract.

While there has been much recent litigation in the insurable interest area, this precise question has not been addressed in either the tax or the nontax cases.

Mathematical tests

Cash value accumulation test   While either the CVAT or the guideline premium/cash value corridor test may be relied on for purposes of testing any contract, the CVAT is generally designed for purposes of testing more traditional contracts—as opposed to some of the more modern interest-sensitive contracts—in which there is a fairly predictable growth of cash or policy values relative to the death benefits. To meet this test, "by the terms of the contract, the cash surrender value . . . may not at any time exceed the net single premium which would have to be paid at such time to fund future benefits under the contract."[36] As such, the CVAT is a prospective test that examines whether, by applying the terms of the contract, it appears that the contract will not satisfy this requirement at any time throughout the life of the contract. If it appears that this might occur, then the contract would be deemed to have failed at the time of issue.

For purposes of determining the "net single premium," the Code provides for the use of an interest rate that is the greater of an annual effective rate of 4 percent or the rate or rates guaranteed on issuance of the contract[37] and "reasonable" mortality charges as of the time the contract is issued.[38] In addition, cash value is required to be determined without regard to any surrender charge, policy loan, or "reasonable termination dividend."

The term "future benefits" is a reference to death benefits and endowment benefits. These are essentially the benefits that are guaranteed to be provided each year under the contract. Death benefits include the entire amount payable by reason of the death of the insured. Certain "additional" benefits are not includible, but the charges for some additional benefits, known as qualified additional benefits, may be treated as future benefits.[39] Among other things, qualified additional benefits include accidental death or disability benefits and family term coverage.

The specific Code language setting forth the CVAT, as well as the guideline premium test to be described, contains many terms in addition to the ones just noted for which additional guidance would be useful. Moreover, one would generally require the services of an actuary to perform the required calculations. In simple terms, however, the test directs taxpayers to calculate a prescribed single premium amount, based on interest rate and other assumptions set forth in the Code that would fund the benefits payable, under the contract. Once this single premium is determined, it is compared to the contract's cash surrender value. So long as the cash surrender value does not exceed the prescribed net single premium amount at any point in time, then the contract will satisfy the CVAT.

It is difficult, but not impossible, to perform this test with respect to certain of the more modern product designs. Congress has also created, however, a two-part alternative guideline premium/cash value corridor test that taxpayers can use instead.

Guideline premium/cash value corridor test   The first part of this test, the guideline premium requirement, is satisfied under section 7702 if the sum of the premiums paid under a contract "does not at any time exceed the guideline premium limitation as of such time."[40] Unlike the CVAT, the guideline premium test cannot be applied on a prospective basis. It looks to amounts that have actually been paid into a contract. For this purpose, premiums paid are generally equal to premiums paid less certain policyholder dividends and other distributions and certain excess premiums returned to the policyholder. The guideline premium is the greater of the guideline single premium or guideline level premium, as those terms are defined in the Code.

The guideline single premium is defined as the "premium at issue" with respect to future benefits under the contract. The Code sets forth various assumptions for computing this amount, including assumptions as to the amount of reasonable mortality and other charges that may be considered, and an interest rate. The required interest rate is the greater of an annual effective rate of 6 percent or the rate or rates guaranteed on issuance of the contract.

The guideline level premium is similar to the guideline single premium, except that it is calculated assuming the premium is paid out over a period extending to at least the time the insured reaches age 95 and uses a 4 percent rather than a 6 percent interest rate.

Under the second part of this test, a contract will fall within the cash value corridor permitted under section 7702 if the "death benefit under the contract at any time is not less than the applicable percentage of the cash surrender value."[41] The applicable percentage changes with the age of the insured. Up to age 40, the applicable percentage is 250 percent. This means that at age 35, if the cash value of a contract is $100,000, the death benefit can be no less than $250,000. The applicable percentage then decreases incrementally until the insured reaches age 95, at which point the applicable percentage is 100 percent.

The cash value corridor operates independently of the guideline premium portion of the test, but both parts must be satisfied.

This chapter has discussed some of the basic concepts involved in section 7702 testing. As one might imagine, these tests get very complex due to the many types of innovative products in the marketplace, not to mention what happens when there are modifications to contracts. Such discussion is beyond the scope of this chapter, but before leaving the life insurance "definitional" area, potential policyholders should also be aware of the basic MEC testing rules set forth next.

Section 7702A 7-Pay Test for MEC Status   A MEC is a life insurance contract that fails to meet the "seven-pay test" set forth in section 7702A or is a contract that has been received in exchange for a MEC. The purpose of this test is to capture those contracts where policyholders are contributing large amounts in early policy years in order to benefit too much and too rapidly in the view of Congress from the tax-deferred growth of the cash value. Congress enacted this provision in 1988, just four years after it created section 7702, when Congress realized that section 7702 did not deter the investment orientation of many contracts in the manner it intended.

A contract fails to meet the seven-pay test if the accumulated amount paid under the contract at any time during the first seven contract years exceeds the sum of the net level premiums that would have been paid for paid-up future benefits after the payment of seven level annual premiums. For this purpose, "future benefits" refers to death benefits payable at the inception of the contract, and which are deemed to remain the same throughout the life of the contract. If there is a reduction in benefits during the first seven contract years, however, the test must be applied at the reduced benefit level. Death benefits that are scheduled to be reduced after the first seven contract years are ignored for this purpose.

In the event of certain types of "material changes" in a contract as the result of certain increases in death benefits or the addition of qualified additional benefits, the contract will be deemed to be newly issued, thus requiring a new seven-pay test. Section 7702A seven-pay testing also involves other complexities, such as may occur with respect to various other contract changes or exchanges.

Upon a failure of a contract to satisfy the seven-pay test and, hence, the characterization of a contract as a MEC, the primary tax impact is that lifetime distributions from the contract will become taxable in a manner that is more characteristic of the annuity distribution rules than the life insurance contract distribution rules. This means that funds will be deemed to be distributed on an income-first basis. For this purpose, policy loans will be treated as distributions, which is also different from the life insurance rules. To the extent that a distribution results in a taxable amount, the amount that is taxable will be subject to an additional 10 percent penalty tax.[42] There also exists an anti-abuse provision referred to as the MEC aggregation rule. This rule provides that, for purposes of calculating the taxable amount of distributions, all MECs issued to the same policyholder during the same calendar year must be aggregated.[43] This is intended to prevent policyholders from being able to avoid the impact of the income-first provision, as might be possible if a policyholder were to purchase several smaller MECs rather than a single large one.

For example, assume a policyholder purchases a MEC for $50, all of which goes immediately into the cash value.[44] After the first year, assume that the cash surrender value of the MEC is $100. If the taxpayer were to withdraw $15 after the first year, the taxable amount would be the entire $15 distribution. Next assume that the policyholder purchased five MECs on the same day from the same insurance company, with the premium for each policy being $10, and that after the first year, each contract had a cash surrender value of $20. Absent the MEC aggregation rule, if the taxpayer were to withdraw $15 from one of the MECs, the taxable amount would be $10 and the remaining $5 of the distribution would be a $5 return of capital. With the MEC aggregation rule, the policyholder would be required to consider the cash value growth on the other MECs, thus ensuring that the taxable amount would be $15, similar to the result in the first example.

In the event that a taxpayer does not anticipate making withdrawals, taking out policy loans, or otherwise entering into transactions that would be deemed to result in a distribution, there will be no practical tax impact of characterizing the contract as a MEC. For this reason, many policyholders, commonly banks, acquire coverage on large blocks of employees, and purchase contracts that they know will be characterized as MECs. While there is a practical loss of tax flexibility, such purchasers prefer the more substantial investment gains they believe the faster payment of premiums will provide. In the case of a corporate purchaser, the higher cash value buildup, even though noncurrently taxable, results in additional earnings for financial statement purposes.

Section 817(h) Diversification Rules

In order to be treated as an insurance product (life insurance, annuity, or endowment), a variable contract and its underlying separate account must satisfy the rigid series of definitional and mechanical requirements introduced to the Code as part of the 1984 Act. These rules primarily require that the underlying asset accounts be adequately diversified under at least one of three alternative tests:[45] a "basic test," a "safe harbor," and a third test whose availability is limited to life insurance contracts invested in government securities.

Alternative diversification tests   Under the basic test, the investments of a segregated asset account will be deemed to be adequately diversified if no more than (1) 55 percent of the value of the total assets of the account is represented by any one investment; (2) 70 percent of the value of the total assets of the account is represented by any two investments; (3) 80 percent of the value of the total assets of the account is represented by any three investments; and (4) 90 percent of the value of the total assets of the account is represented by any four investments. Thus, segregated asset accounts must have at least five investments.

The safe harbor is applicable to any fund that is at least as diversified as a regulated investment company, so long as no more than 55 percent of the assets consist of cash, cash items, government securities, or securities of other regulated investment companies. A regulated investment company will be considered to be adequately diversified if (1) at least 50 percent of the value of its total assets is represented by (a) cash and cash items (including receivables), government securities, and securities of other regulated investment companies; (b) securities of other issuers so long as such other securities from a single issuer do not exceed 5 percent of the total assets and 10 percent of the outstanding voting stock of such other issuer; and (2) not more than 25 percent of the value of the regulated investment company's total assets is invested in the securities of any one issuer (other than government securities or the securities of other regulated investment companies) or of two or more issuers which the taxpayer controls and which are determined to be in a similar or related business.[46]

Finally, a segregated asset account funding variable life insurance contracts (but not annuity contracts) will be deemed to be adequately diversified to the extent it invests in Treasury securities. Since the entire account must be adequately diversified, an adjustment must be made to the percentages under the basic test to determine whether the portion of the segregated asset account that is not represented by Treasury securities is also adequately diversified. Thus, each of the percentage limitations in the basic test must be increased by an amount equal to one-half of the percentage of the total assets of the account that are represented by Treasury securities. The resulting percentage limitations are applied to the other investments as though the account were not invested in the Treasury securities.

For example, assume a segregated asset account supporting a variable life insurance contract has a total value of $100,000, of which $60,000 is invested in Treasury securities. The 55 percent and 70 percent limitations under the first and second parts of the basic test would be increased in this instance to 85 percent (55 percent plus 0.5 times 60 percent value of account invested in Treasury securities) and 100 percent (70 percent plus 0.5 times 60 percent value of account invested in Treasury securities), respectively, before the percentage of any individual investment is compared to the limitations.

What is meant by the term "investment"?   Unlike some of the other definitions (or lack thereof) provided in this area, the regulations are quite specific about what constitutes a single investment for purposes of the diversification rules. All securities of the same issuer, all interests in the same real property project, and all interests in the same commodity are each treated as a single investment. The term "security" includes cash items and partnership interests registered under federal or state securities law.[47] Every U.S. government agency or instrumentality is to be treated as a separate issuer. A "government security" is any security issued, guaranteed, or insured by the United States or any of its instrumentalities. It also includes certificates of deposit of any such entities. If any of these instruments is only guaranteed or insured in part by the United States or its instrumentality, then it is to be treated as so insured or guaranteed to the same extent, with the direct obligor being treated as the issuer of the remaining piece. "Treasury securities" are securities in which the direct obligor is the U.S. Treasury. Thus, put and call options and interest rate futures on Treasury securities, as well as options on such contracts, are not Treasury securities since the direct obligor under such options is not the Treasury.

The term "interest in real property" includes ownership, leasehold rights to land, and land improvements as well as options to acquire such ownership or leasehold rights. "Interest in a commodity" refers to ownership, leaseholds, and options to purchase or sell any type of personal property other than a security.

Account that needs to be diversified   Earlier in this chapter, it was noted that the somewhat colloquial terms "variable" and "separate account" contracts would be used for ease of discussion of the products described herein. In order to properly apply the diversification rules, it is necessary to understand the more formal terms that Congress utilized to describe these products. That is, purchasers acquire a "variable contract." The contracts are supported by "separate accounts," or subaccounts, which are state law concepts. The Code, nevertheless, refers to "segregated asset accounts" in terms of what needs to be diversified. Congress and the Treasury have provided some guidance in this area, but they have also left several questions unanswered.

Variable contract   For example, for a policy to be a variable contract for tax purposes, it must contain three basic elements:

1. It must provide for the allocation of all or part of the amounts received under the contract to an account that, pursuant to state law or regulation, is segregated from the general asset accounts of the company.
2. It must provide for the payment of annuities or be a life insurance contract.
3. The amounts paid into or out of the contract, or the length or period of coverage under the contract, must reflect the investment return and market value of the "segregated asset account."

The initial impact of a contract's characterization as a variable contract has more of an impact on the insurance company than it does on the policyholder, as it directly affects the insurance company tax treatment of the arrangement. From a policyholder's perspective, the status as such, in and of itself, does not affect the tax treatment. It does, however, affect whether the diversification requirements will be applicable.

Segregated asset account   Observe that in setting forth which contracts would be classified as variable contracts, the Code indicates that the benefits under the contract must reflect the investment return and market value of a *segregated asset account*, as opposed to the investment return and market value of a "separate account." Although it may be convenient to equate these terms, doing so may result in an inaccurate depiction of legislative intent.

The term "separate account," typically defined under state law, has been a part of industry parlance for several decades. Yet nowhere does Congress use this term. Unfortunately, neither the Code nor Treasury regulations provide a definition of the term "segregated asset account."[48]

The regulations provide limited guidance in this area:

> *For purposes of section 817(h) and this section, a segregated asset account shall consist of all assets the investment return and market value of each of which must be allocated in an identical manner to any variable contract invested in any of such assets.*

By way of example, the Service illustrated that where policyholders were able to allocate premiums among two groups of assets, there were two segregated asset accounts. In a second example, policyholders did not have the ability to decide how to allocate premiums between two investment options. Here the Service found instead that there was only one segregated asset account.

Significantly, adding to the lack of clarity in this area is the fact that the regulations used neither the term "separate account" nor the term "subaccount." Instead they curiously refer to "groups of assets."

Look-through rules Under the application of a look-through rule, there are situations where an investment in a single asset can result in satisfaction of the diversification requirements. This can occur where the investment is in another entity—including regulated investment companies, real estate investment trusts, partnerships, and grantor trusts—and a pro rata portion of the assets held by such other entity, rather than the single investment in the entity itself, may be used for diversification test purposes.

The regulations provide four scenarios in which an interest in the investment company, partnership, or trust may be possessed by an entity other than a segregated asset account without precluding application of the look-through rules:

1. Such an interest is held by the general account of a life insurance company (or a corporation related to a life insurance company). Under this scenario, the return on the general account interest must be computed in a manner similar to the mode of calculating the investment return for the segregated asset account; there must be no intent on the part of the general account to sell the interest to the public; and a separate account of the insurance company also must possess a beneficial interest in the entity.

2. A rule similar to item 1 applies in the case of an interest held by a manager (or a party related to a manager) of the investment company, partnership, or trust. In this situation, the holding of such interest must be in connection with the creation or management of the subject entity. Further, the same conditions in effect with respect to a general account interest regarding the calculation of the return on the manager's interest and intended sales to the public also apply.

3. An interest may be held by the trustee of a qualified pension or retirement plan.

4. If there are publicly held interests in the investment company, partnership, or trust, or such interests are deemed to be held by policyholders under Revenue Ruling 81-225 (one of the investor control rulings

discussed earlier), the look-through rules still will apply if either the availability of such interests were closed to the public after December 31, 1981, or all the assets of the segregated asset account are attributable to premium payments made by policyholders prior to September 26, 1981, to premium payments made in connection with a qualified pension or retirement plan, or to any combination of such premium payments.

There are, however, limitations:

1. All of the beneficial interests in the investment company, partnership, or trust must be held by one or more segregated asset accounts of one or more insurance companies, and
2. Public access to the subject entity can be made available only through the purchase of a variable contract.

The regulations also provide a look-through rule for trusts in which substantially all of the assets consist of Treasury securities. Here the Treasury securities still will be treated as such even though they are held through a trust. Recently the Service has provided guidance with respect to the application of the look-through rules in situations involving tiered entities. Under this guidance, "double" look-through would be permitted with respect to funds that invest in other funds, so long as certain requirements are met.

Required diversification periods   The diversification requirements must be satisfied on the last day of a calendar quarter, or within 30 days thereafter, in order for the account to be deemed adequately diversified for the quarter. Segregated asset accounts other than real property accounts are deemed to be diversified up until their first anniversary. In the case of a segregated asset account that qualifies as a real property account on its first anniversary, the diversification rules will be deemed to be satisfied up until its fifth anniversary or the first anniversary after it ceases to be a real property account. Accounts that satisfy the diversification requirements on the date a plan of liquidation is adopted shall be treated as being diversified for a period of one year beginning on such date (two years in the case of real property accounts).

Consequences of failing the diversification tests   A variable contract that fails to satisfy the diversification requirements will not be treated as an annuity, endowment, or life insurance contract, for either insurance company or policyholder tax purposes, for any period beginning with the first period it is not adequately diversified.[49] In the event of such a failure, the contract holders lose the benefit of tax-deferred investment earnings.

As set forth above, section 817(h)(1), on its face, states that a contract that fails the diversification requirements shall not be treated as a life insurance or endowment contract for purposes of the section 7702(a) definition of life insurance contract. To the extent a contract ceases to meet the section 7702(a) definition of a life insurance contract, the income on the contract for all prior years shall be treated as received or accrued during the taxable year in which the failure occurred.[50] The regulations follow suit and mandate that similar treatment is appropriate for annuities that fail the diversification tests.

In the event of an inadvertent failure to satisfy the diversification requirements, the subject investments will still be deemed to be adequately diversified if (1) either the contract issuer or the policyholder demonstrates that the failure was inadvertent; (2) the investments satisfy the diversification requirements within a reasonable time after the discovery of the failure; and (3) either the issuer or the policyholder agrees to make adjustments or to pay the taxes that would have been owed had the policyholder actually received the income earned on the contract during the period(s) the account was not adequately diversified. In addition, the Service has indicated that it will waive civil penalties for the failure to satisfy the reporting, withholding, and deposit requirements for any income that would have been deemed to be received under section 7702(g) if the insurance company satisfies these three requirements.[51]

Investor control   The origins of the investor control doctrine are set forth at the outset of this section. The following discussion describes some more recent guidelines the IRS has provided taxpayers seeking to structure transactions in light of this doctrine.

As previously noted, the general reason the Service provides for applying this doctrine is to determine who should be treated as the owner of the assets underlying the subject insurance contract. In other words, it is an inquiry as to whether a policyholder is exercising so much dominion and control over the assets that the policyholder, rather than the insurance company, should be treated as the owner of the assets and be subject to current tax on the investment earnings. By denying policyholders the ability to defer recognition of income on investments only nominally purchased through an insurance contract, the Service is seeking to treat them like similarly situated taxpayers who invest in such assets directly.

Treasury and the Service, however, have never specifically articulated a precise standard for determining whether a transaction involves undue investor control. Rather, over the years, they have provided examples that generally illustrate types of transactions to which the doctrine would be applied. These have included situations where the policyholder purportedly actively managed the assets underlying the product or where the assets could be acquired by means other than through the purchase of an insurance contract.

See, for example, Revenue Ruling 77-85, where the policyholder was able to direct the custodian of an account underlying a variable annuity to sell or purchase specific securities, and Revenue Ruling 80-274, where the policyholder was able to select and control certificates of deposit supporting the contract. In both of those cases, the policyholder was deemed to be the owner of the assets. However, the Service held in Revenue Ruling 82-54 that the policyholder was not exercising undue control where it was permitted to allocate premiums among funds representing three general investment strategies.

On the public availability front, the IRS found in Revenue Ruling 81-225 that the investor control doctrine applied in various situations involving investments in publicly available mutual funds.

Due to the heightened insurance industry awareness of the IRS's prior application of this doctrine, most commercially available variable, or separate account, insurance products are carefully designed to steer clear of any potential challenges in this area. Nevertheless, questions have continued to linger over the years as to exactly how the Service might seek to apply the doctrine. For example, product designers have wondered whether the Service would contest an arrangement based on the number of subaccounts to which a policyholder might allocate its funds or how often a policyholder might be permitted to reallocate such amounts. Further, there is an element of uncertainty as to what sort of contact a policyholder could have with the insurance company or other personnel responsible for managing the assets in the accounts. Finally, given that all of the previous public guidance in this area has dealt with annuity contracts, some have even wondered whether the Service would—or could effectively—seek to apply the doctrine in the context of a life insurance arrangement.

Thus, despite the previous public guidance, the investor control doctrine continues to be a source of potential issues that taxpayers must carefully manage. This is true for both the insurance companies that are deeply experienced in this area as well as for the growing numbers of investment advisors—perhaps less familiar with the insurance terrain—seeking to move their clients toward what they believe to be more tax-efficient ways to invest.

Revenue Ruling 2003-91 is helpful in that it provides a somewhat comprehensive set of facts—some new, but many of which have been the subject of previous rulings—indicating what some might consider a "safe harbor" transaction from an investor control perspective. The problem is that while the revenue ruling provides some further guidance, it remains unclear how rigidly the boundaries illustrated in the ruling are intended to be interpreted. The following discussion sets forth in detail what these facts are and provides some commentary, if not additional questions, raised by each.

- The doctrine applies to life insurance arrangements.

  The first of the two factual scenarios set forth in the ruling represents the first public pronouncement by the Service indicating that the investor control doctrine applies to a life insurance arrangement. Although the Service was asked in a private letter ruling, LTR 9433030, to analyze a life insurance arrangement under the investor control doctrine, that ruling provided only private guidance applicable to the taxpayer that requested the guidance.[52] All previous revenue rulings in this area have involved annuity contracts. Revenue rulings are a higher level of guidance that is applicable to taxpayers generally.

- Interests in the subaccount are not available for sale to the public; rather, they are available solely through the purchase of an insurance contract.

  This factor has been described before (see Revenue Ruling 81-225, noted earlier). Ever since that ruling, however, there has been some question as to what it means for an asset to be publicly available or available to the general public. Revenue Ruling 2003-92, released the same day as Revenue Ruling 2003-91, indicates that the Service will treat an asset as being available to the public even when the class of people who can purchase the asset is narrowly defined. In that case, the Service found that the investor control doctrine applied where interests in partnerships acquired by the subject separate account could also be purchased by qualified or accredited investors, a limited class of investors identified under federal securities laws.

- No influence over investment advisors or investment officers.

  As described in Revenue Ruling 2003-91, the insurance company engaged the investment advisor who was responsible for managing the investment activities of each subaccount. The term "investment officer" was defined by the Service for this purpose as anyone whose responsibilities include giving investment advice or making investment decisions relating to assets held in a subaccount and anyone who directly or indirectly supervises the work performed by such individual. Further, here, the insurance company, in its sole and absolute discretion, made all decisions regarding the choice of, or changes to, the investment advisor or choice of, or changes to, any of the insurance company's investment officers involved in the investment activities of the separate account or any of the subaccounts. In fact, the policyholder was not even permitted to communicate—directly or indirectly—with the insurance company concerning the selection or substitution of the advisor or the choice of any investment officers involved in the investment activities of the separate account or subaccounts.

While it is clear that there is no influence over the investment advisor or officer in this set of facts, it is not clear if this example is meant to be a safe harbor. The restrictions in the insurance contract described in Revenue Ruling 2003-91 appear to be tighter than what the Service has previously found permissible. For example, in LTR 9752061, another case in which the Service was seeking to determine the proper owner of assets underlying an insurance contract, the policyholder was able to select an investment advisor from among a pool of advisors approved by the insurance company. In that case, the Service found that the insurance company owned the assets. Thus, there remains some question as to whether the ruling represents a safe harbor on this issue or a retracted limitation.

- No control over investing activity.

In this situation, there was no arrangement, plan, contract, or agreement between the policyholder and either the insurance company or the advisor regarding the availability of a particular subaccount. Other than the right to allocate funds among subaccounts, all investment decisions at the subaccount level were made by the insurance company or the investment advisor in their sole and absolute discretion. The policyholder was not permitted to select or recommend any particular investments or investment strategies. Nor was the policyholder allowed to communicate directly or indirectly with any investment officer of the insurance company or its affiliates, or with the investment advisor regarding the selection, quality, or rate of return of any specific investment or group of investments held in a subaccount.

The Service has previously found that a policyholder's involvement, on a very limited basis, in the determination of investment strategies relating to a separate account did not result in the policyholder retaining ownership of the underlying assets. Again, see LTR 9433030, where the Service recognized that prior to purchasing the subject life insurance policies, the "Insurer and Policy Owner agreed on the broad investment guidelines. . . . ." LTR 9433030 involved a single policyholder separate account. One is left to wonder whether the Service has changed its position on this issue and, if so, what input, if any, a policyholder might have in negotiating such arrangements.

Intuitively, there is no practical difference between an insurance company marketing a product supported by X types of subaccounts and a situation where a potential policyholder indicates to an insurance company that it might purchase a product supported by Y types of subaccounts. The key factor should be whether there is subsequent involvement in the investment process by the policyholder.

It is undeniable that operational control over the investment assets goes to the heart of the investor control doctrine. The question remains, however, as to how much flexibility a product designer can offer policyholders.

- There will never be more than 20 subaccounts available under the contracts.

Revenue Ruling 82-54 described a situation involving 3 investment options; Revenue Ruling 2003-91 entails 20 investment options. There are currently many products on the market that offer significantly more than 20 investment alternatives, a circumstance that is driven by the demands of a competitive market. Does the ruling's maximum number of subaccounts merely state a fact, or does it indicate a concern that as the number of choices increases, the investment strategies themselves might appear to become too narrowly defined—and thus less representative of the types of general investment choices described in Revenue Ruling 82-54?

Any concern on the IRS's part that the integrity of the investor control doctrine requires such a severe restriction on the number of investment strategies is not warranted. That is, Revenue Ruling 2003-91 indicates that the subject arrangement currently provides several investment strategies, including the following:

- Bond fund
- Large company stock fund
- International stock fund
- Small company stock fund
- Mortgage-backed securities fund
- Health care industry fund
- Emerging markets fund
- Money market fund
- Telecommunication fund
- Financial services industry fund
- South American stock fund
- Energy fund
- Asian markets fund

No additional detail is provided regarding the investing strategies of these accounts. Based solely on these descriptions, however, one can certainly envision many more similarly general investment strategies that could be added to this menu.

- Policyholders can make one—but only one—transfer per 30 days without charge.

  At the time of purchase, the policyholder could specify the allocation of its premiums among the subaccounts and could change the allocation of its funds at any time thereafter. This right to reallocate, however, is not completely unfettered. To the extent there is more than one transfer per 30-day period, the policyholder is subjected to a fee assessed against the cash value of the contract.

  The ruling does not state what the magnitude of the fee is. The presence of this fact in the ruling, however, appears intended to signal that the frequency of transfers among subaccounts is a factor that will be examined in determining whether a policyholder is exercising dominion and control over the assets.

- Policyholders can have no interest in the assets held by the subaccount.

  The policyholder can have no legal, equitable, direct, or indirect interest in any of the assets held by the subaccount. Moreover, the policyholder can have nothing more than a contractual claim against the insurance company to collect cash from the insurance company in the form of death benefits or cash surrender values under the contract. Typical commercially available products will satisfy these standards. Those involved in establishing more privately structured transactions, however, should use caution regarding the potentially amorphous nature of the term "indirect interest."

  Revenue Ruling 2003-91 sets forth a template that is presumably intended to illustrate the Service's view of a "pristine" transaction from an investor control perspective. As such, one would expect that the Service would not seek to challenge a transaction that squares entirely with the facts set forth in the ruling. However, whether a given transaction involves undue investor control typically has been viewed as a matter of facts and circumstances. One would, therefore, expect that a transaction could reasonably deviate from at least some of these facts without causing an investor control issue. The consequences of doing so, however, and falling on the wrong side of the analysis, can be quite significant.

Annuity Contract Definitional and Other Compliance Requirements

As discussed, there is no statutory definition of an annuity contract. The regulations provide only limited help, indicating that a contract will be treated as an annuity contract if it is "considered to be an annuity contract

in accordance with the customary practice of life insurance companies."[53]
Various courts and other authorities have interpreted an annuity contract as
being such for federal income tax purposes to the extent that it is an insurance
policy that promises to make a series of payments for a fixed period or over
someone's lifetime.[54] A further position has also been asserted that the
payments must systematically liquidate the amount paid into the contract
plus interest.[55] In conducting these analyses, the authorities have looked at
such things as whether the amount payable after the term of the annuity is
substantially equal to or larger than the aggregate amount of premiums or
other consideration; essentially, the contract cannot be one that is merely an
agreement to pay interest.[56]

Yet another factor to consider is whether the annuity will commence at
too late of an age. That is, whether it is contemplated that the contract will
ever annuitize.

In general, an "annuity," as opposed to an "annuity contract," is any
payment that will liquidate a principal sum, and includes payments based on
a life contingency as well as amounts covering a fixed period or fixed amount.
In the discussion that follows, with respect to section 1275, dealing with
annuities purchased from foreign insurers, an annuity payment stream from
a Swiss or Liechtenstein contract will need to be based on a life contingency
in order to be subject to deferred tax treatment on the inside buildup.

Although the Code and regulations do not provide definitive guidance
as to what an annuity is, it does describe certain situations in which a
contract will not be treated as an annuity. These include section 72(s), which
requires that certain language be set forth in an annuity contract regarding
distribution requirements upon the death of the holder of the contract; and
section 72(u), which limits, with certain exceptions, annuity tax treatment
for nonnatural persons that own an annuity. Section 817(h), as discussed,
states that a variable annuity will not be treated as an annuity for any tax
purpose if the segregated asset accounts underlying the contract are not
adequately diversified. Further, section 1275 provides strict requirements
with respect to an annuity purchased from an insurance company not subject
to tax under subchapter L, the insurance company tax provisions of the
Code; essentially, a company that is not subject to tax in the U.S. As also
discussed, a policyholder will lose the ability to defer tax on inside buildup
under the contract if the investor control doctrine is not satisfied.[57]

Section 72(s) Requirements Relating to Distributions upon the Death of the Holder

the Holder   Section 72(s) requires that an annuity contract contain language
that provides for distributions upon the death of the holder of the contract.
The purpose of these rules is to ensure that annuities are not utilized as a

means to transfer wealth as opposed to providing income for an individual, for example, as a retirement vehicle. The subsection effectively limits the amount of deferral of tax that may be achieved through annuity ownership.

Section 72(s) states, in pertinent part, that:

> *72(s)(1)—A contract shall not be treated as an annuity unless it provides that—*
>
> > *72(s)(1)(A)—if any holder of such contract dies on or after the annuity starting date and before the entire interest in such contract has been distributed, the remaining portion of such interest will be distributed as least as rapidly as under the method of distribution being used as of the date of his death, and*
> >
> > *72(s)(1)(B)—if any holder of such contract dies before the annuity starting date, the entire interest in such contract will be distributed within five years after the death of such holder.*

Under a strict interpretation, one might reason that the exact Code language contained in section 72(s)(1)(A) and (B) must appear in the contract. Even if a less strict reading of the subsection is sufficient, it is clear that whatever language is utilized, it must provide terms that are at least consistent with the section 72(s) language.

In setting forth such language, care must be taken not to lose sight of certain nuances within the language. For example, the Code requires that distributions upon the death of the holder or owner refers to "any" owner, not "the" owner. This reflects a technical correction to the Code to specifically capture situations where there is a joint owner or joint annuitants in situations where the owner is a nonnatural person. That is, the triggering event is the death of the first owner.

Second, the triggering dates under the Code refer to a death "on or after the annuity starting date" and "before the annuity starting date."

Also note that section 72(c)(4) provides, in pertinent part, that, "For purposes of this section, the annuity starting date in the case of any contract is the first day of the first period for which an amount is received as an annuity under the contract; . . .." Regulation section 1.72-4(b)(1) provides further that the annuity starting date is the later of the date on which the obligations under the contract become fixed, or the first day of the period that ends on the date of the first annuity payment.

The practical result here should probably be to ensure that whatever term is used to establish the starting date, it references the one that describes the date upon which the annuity value that is to be distributed is finally determined. The definition just noted is contained in the regulation section that deals with determination of exclusion ratio (a concept that will be discussed in the next section of this chapter). It is described in that section for the purpose of determining the amount of the holder's investment in the contract (another concept that will be discussed in the next section). Since the purpose of section 72(s) is to prevent unlimited deferral, it would seem appropriate that the date referred to in section 72(s) is the one that refers to the date that the investment in the contract, and thus the amount of income to be captured in income, is determinable.

With respect to the distribution rules themselves, there are significant exceptions to the death before annuitization rule that requires a distribution within five years of the date of death.

The primary exception provides that interest in the contract may instead be payable to or for the benefit of a designated beneficiary,[58] so long as the payments begin within one year of death of the holder and the period it is payable does not extend beyond the life expectancy of such individual. If the designated beneficiary is the surviving spouse of the holder, the spouse may effectively "step into the shoes of" the holder. That is, the above provisions will be applied as though the surviving spouse is the holder, and thus they will not come into effect until the surviving spouse dies.[59]

If the annuity is held by a corporation or other "nonindividual," the holder of the contract, and thus the individual upon whose life the provisions of section 72(s) operate, is the "primary annuitant." The primary annuitant is the individual whose life is of primary importance in affecting the timing or amount of the payout under the annuity contract. The provisions of section 72(s) will be triggered if there is a change in the primary annuitant, as such change will be treated as the death of the holder.

There is relatively little guidance governing the provisions of section 72(s), but there are clearly questions, including those already noted, that arise under this provision. Although it has not garnered much authoritative guidance, the consequences of a failure to comply with these provisions are significant, as the policy would not be treated as an annuity contract for federal income tax purposes. This would apply for both insurance company as well as policyholder tax purposes.

Section 72(u), discussed next, deals with annuities that are held by nonnatural persons. In contrast to section 72(s), the consequence of falling within section 72(u) is that a contract will not be treated as an annuity for policyholder tax purposes but will still be treated as an annuity for insurance company tax purposes.

Section 72(u) Nonnatural Owner Rules   Section 72(u) states that a contract that is owned by a nonnatural person shall not be treated as an annuity for policyholder tax purposes unless the nonnatural entity—for example, a trust—holds the contract as an agent for an individual. Thus, where the nonnatural person does not hold the contract as an agent for a natural person, taxation of inside buildup may not be deferred. Instead, the annual "income on the contract" must be treated as ordinary income received or accrued by the nonnatural entity each taxable year it holds the contract.

The income on the contract for a given year is measured by first adding the net surrender value of the contract as of the close of the taxable year and any distributions that the policyholder may have received during taxable year or any prior year. The taxable amount for the year is then determined by reducing the above sum by the total amount of net premiums[60] it paid during the year as well as by any amounts that were includible in taxable income from prior years with respect to the contract. In short, this calculation generally effectively results in the current inclusion of income each year of increases in the contract's net surrender value.

It is fairly common for an annuity to be held in trust for an individual, often a grantor trust. In cases such as this, where the entity holding legal title to the annuity contract is essentially the alter ego of the holder, the section 72(u) rules will not apply.

This subsection will also not apply in situations where the contract is:

- Acquired by the estate of a decedent by reason of the death of the decedent
- Held under or purchased in connection with certain retirement plan transactions
- A qualified funding asset with respect to certain structured settlements, or
- An immediate annuity

The Code provides a special definition for immediate annuity for purposes of the latter exception. Under this definition, the immediate annuity must be purchased with a single premium, have an annuity starting date that commences no later than one year from the date the annuity is purchased, and provide for a series of substantially equal periodic payments that occur no less frequently than once per year, throughout the entire annuity period.

Section 1275 Rules for Annuities Purchased from an Insurance Company Not Subject to Tax in the United States Annuity contracts issued by foreign insurance companies may not be treated as annuity contracts for U.S. tax purposes. Instead, those annuity contracts could be treated as debt instruments. In such cases, the contracts would be subject to the original issue discount rules, thus resulting in the current accrual of income on the contract by the contract holder.

Section 1275, however, provides two exceptions to this general rule. The exceptions would apply to a contract that meets the definition of an annuity contract and:

- Depends, in whole or in substantial part, on the life expectancy of one or more individuals; or
- Is issued by an insurance company that is taxed as a life insurance company for U.S. tax purposes.

In addition, the contract must be purchased with cash or another similar annuity contract.

With respect to the first exception, the annuity payments under the contract must be made at least once a year over the life of the individual, and the terms of the contract must allow for the possibility that the distributions/annuity payments are tied to the longevity of the annuitant(s) and can increase over time.[61]

There are certain provisions in a contract that would, under regulations, necessarily negate its treatment as an annuity. For instance, either the availability of a cash surrender option or the ability to take out a loan secured by the contract would be deemed to significantly reduce the probability that the total distributions would increase commensurately with the longevity of the annuitant. Underlying these proscriptions is the belief that either a cash surrender option or the ability to take a loan on the security of the contract would reduce the number or amount of the distributions, which would thus decrease the total distributions, not increase them. This would cause the contract to fail in meeting the first exception and result in it being taxed as a debt instrument, not an annuity contract.

Certain provisions in a contract for minimum and maximum payouts would cause a similar tax result. A term-certain annuity, which by its definition would limit the payout, however, could still meet the first exception if the period of time from the annuity starting date to its termination date is at least twice as long as the period from the annuity starting date to the expected date of terminating death.[62]

A variable annuity whose distributions may increase or decrease would not be considered to significantly reduce the probability that the total distributions would increase over time, corresponding to the longevity of the annuitant(s).[63]

The second exception would apply to annuity contracts issued by foreign insurance companies that have business operations in the United States. In this instance, the foreign insurer would be treated as though it was a U.S. insurer, and the contracts would be treated as annuity contracts, not debt instruments. The exception would also apply in a case where a foreign insurance company that is owned by a U.S. parent corporation is treated as a U.S. insurer as the result of an election to be taxed as a U.S. insurance company.

Any additional investment in a contract issued by a foreign insurer that was purchased prior to the enactment of these rules would be treated as the purchase of a new contract and, therefore, subject to the rules already explained.

BASIC TAX RULES ASSOCIATED WITH THE PURCHASE, HOLDING, AND OTHER TRANSACTIONS THAT MAY OCCUR ON, UNDER, OR WITH RESPECT TO AN INSURANCE POLICY

The structure of the general tax scheme relative to the taxation of transactions that occur with respect to life insurance and annuity products is designed in a manner that (1) distinguishes between the capital that a policyholder pays into a contract and the investment earnings or other amounts that are credited to the contract by the insurance company; and (2) establishes when, or if, the earnings component will be subject to federal income tax. Rules have also evolved over the years that are designed to limit arbitrage opportunities related to the ability to generate income on insurance contracts in a tax-deferred or tax-free manner, and, in certain other circumstances, to impose penalties.

While there are significant differences in the manner in which transactions relating to life insurance and annuity contracts are taxed, there are some fundamental concepts that are common to both and are key to understanding how many of the tax rules around these products work.

These include such things as the treatment of payments to purchase a contract, the concept of "investment in the contract," indicating what amounts might be received without being taxed during the lifetime of the insured, and how to measure "income on the contract," or the amounts that are subject to tax upon receipt. The remainder of this chapter takes the reader through the more significant of these rules, beginning with the rules governing the purchase transaction, what happens when certain transactions occur during the life of a contract, and the tax results upon contract maturity.

Purchase Transaction

Premiums paid for life insurance or annuity policies are generally not deductible in situations where the policyholder is directly or indirectly the beneficiary under the contract.[64]

In addition, interest expense on debt incurred to purchase or carry such contracts may not be deducted except in limited circumstances.[65]

The limited circumstances include situations where a business purchases life insurance coverage on "key persons," so long as the aggregate amount of debt per contract does not exceed $50,000, and with respect to cases involving contracts purchased by a business prior to June 21, 1986.[66] Even in those cases, however, interest will still not be deductible if the contract is either a single-premium contract or the arrangement involves a plan of purchase that contemplates the systematic borrowing of increases in cash value.[67]

With respect to the first of these exceptions, a contract will be deemed to be a single-premium contract if either (1) substantially all the premiums on the contract are paid within four years of the date on which the contract is purchased, or (2) a deposit is made with the insurer for a substantial number of future premiums.[68]

The exceptions to the permitted key man and pre-1986 contract interest deduction rules will not apply in any of these four circumstances:

1. If no part of four of the annual premiums due during the seven-year period (beginning with the date of the first premium on the contract to which the plan relates was paid) is paid through the use of debt. If there is a substantial increase in any annual premium, however, a new seven-year period begins.
2. The interest paid or accrued is $100 or less per year.
3. Interest on indebtedness incurred because of unforeseen substantial loss of income or a substantial increase in financial obligations by the policyholder.
4. If indebtedness is incurred by the policyholder in connection with a trade or business to finance business obligations, not life insurance.[69]

For purposes of the key person exception, a key person is essentially an officer or 20 percent owner of the corporation or business. The maximum number of individuals who can be considered key persons is the greater of five individuals or the lesser of 5 percent of the total officers and employees of the business or 20 individuals. A 20 percent owner is a person who owns directly 20 percent or more of the outstanding stock of the corporation or stock possessing 20 percent or more of the total combined voting power of all stock of the corporation. If the policyholder is not a corporation, a 20 percent owner would be any person who owns 20 percent or more of the capital or profits of the enterprise. When applying the key person exception, all corporations with common ownership are looked at as a single group. This applies to the $50,000 policy limit per key person as well as how to identify a key person.

As a result of a provision that was added to the Code in 1997, a business that purchased life insurance contracts subsequent to the effective date of that legislation must now also be cognizant of a limitation that would prevent them from deducting certain interest on their general business debt, unrelated to their insurance contracts. This rule establishes a pro rata interest disallowance rule based on a ratio, generally, of a company's unborrowed life insurance policy cash values to its total assets. A significant exception to this rule applies for policies covering the lives of 20 percent owners, officers, directors, and employees.

Distributions and Other Transactions during the Lifetime of the Contract Holder

As discussed, the Code generally provides holders of both life insurance and annuity contracts the ability to defer tax on earnings credited to their contracts, so long as there has not been a distribution from their contracts.[70] As a general matter, the tax scheme for distributions from these contracts is dependent on whether the amount received is an "amount received as an annuity" or an "amount not received as an annuity." The latter category may include such things as withdrawals, partial or full surrenders, policyholder dividends, and policy loans.

These items are each governed under rules that are generally applicable to all such contracts, with the differences that provide more favorable treatment for life insurance contracts handled through exceptions to the general rules. Perhaps the most significant difference relates to the ordering rules between amounts distributed from a life insurance contract other than a MEC and amounts distributed from an annuity or life insurance contract that is a MEC.

Distributions from and Other Lifetime Transactions Involving Non-MEC Life Insurance Contracts
In the case of both life insurance and annuity contracts, the portion of any such distribution that is not subject to tax is referred to as the "investment in the contract." Investment in the contract is essentially equal to the amount of premiums that the policyholder paid into the contract, less the amount of any distribution from the contract that may have been received that was not subject to tax.[71]

Distributions in general   In the case of a life insurance contract other than a MEC, distributions are deemed to be received first out of funds representing investment in the contract.[72] Any amounts received in excess of the investment in the contract—that is, the income on the contract—are deemed to be taxable income. That is, the policyholder is not taxed on any earnings in the contract until the entire investment in the contract has been recovered.

These rules apply to both withdrawals and partial surrenders. In the event of a full surrender or other complete termination of a contract whereby the entire cash surrender value of a contract is distributed to the policyholder, the policyholder is only subject to tax to the extent that the entire distribution exceeds the investment in the contract.[73] This might not make a difference to the extent that a policyholder cannot make a withdrawal that exceeds the cash surrender value of a life insurance contract due to the investment first rule. It does make a difference, however, in the case of an annuity or MEC, in which the distribution ordering rules are reversed. This is due to a nuance in the Code that requires a taxpayer to measure the potential taxable amount on a partial surrender or withdrawal based on the cash value unreduced by potential surrender charges. As such, in the case of an annuity or MEC, there is a greater amount of potential gain that might be recognized than would occur under a full termination of the contract.

Policyholder dividends Policyholder dividends received on a life insurance contract are deemed to be distributions that similarly come first out of investment in the contract. Under state law, however, there are several ways a policyholder can elect to receive a dividend. These usually include payment of the dividend in cash, having them applied directly to cash value, using them to purchase paid-up additional insurance, and having them applied directly towards the payment of premiums.

To the extent that the policyholder dividends are retained by the insurance company, they will not result in taxable income to the policyholder.[74] This drives home another point: Effectively, holders of a life insurance or annuity contract are put on a cash basis with respect to their contracts and hence generally do not become subject to tax on the earnings thereunder unless there is a receipt of a payment from the contract that exceeds the investment in the contract.

Policy loans Loans taken out on the security of a non-MEC life insurance contract are not treated as distributions from a life insurance contract. A similar rule is provided with respect to assignments or pledges of life insurance contracts.

Upon surrender, lapse, or other termination of a life insurance contract, the policyholder will be taxed to the extent the cash surrender value exceeds the policyholder's investment in the contract, even if there is a loan outstanding at that time and the funds that would otherwise be paid to the policyholder are instead used to pay off the loan to the insurance company.

Amounts held at interest Interest on amounts held on behalf of a policyholder by an insurance company are subject to current taxation, regardless of whether such amounts are actually received by the policyholder.[75] This holds true both for amounts held within a premium deposit fund as well as benefits payable to a policyholder that are either held pursuant to an agreement between the policyholder and insurance company, or claims or dividends or other amounts that have simply not yet been actually distributed to a policyholder.

Exchanges of life insurance contracts Under certain circumstances, a life insurance contract may be exchanged for another life insurance contract with no gain or loss recognized by the policyholder.[76] Such tax-free exchanges are commonly referred to as 1035 exchanges; they are so-named after the Code section under which they are available.

The rules that permit tax-free exchanges of insurance contracts are based on the like-kind exchange rules applicable to other, noninsurance assets. Both the old and new life insurance contracts must have the same insured. If cash or other property is received in the exchange of the contracts, then gain, if any, will be recognized only up to the value of the cash and property received. To the extent that there was an outstanding loan on the policy that was exchanged, the amount of the loan will be treated as property received if the new contract does not contain a similar loan.

The investment in the contract of the new contract, as well as the basis in the new contract, will be the same as the respective investment in the contract and basis in the old contract.

Sales of existing life insurance contracts/transfers for value

Seller's perspective Upon the sale of an existing life insurance contract by a policyholder,[77] income is required to be recognized by the policyholder to the extent the cash surrender value is greater than the policyholder's basis in the contract.[78] As will be noted, an issue exists as to whether a policyholder is required to reduce basis by the cost of insurance charges incurred during the time the policyholder held the contract.

In addition, IRS representatives have suggested that it is not possible to take a loss for tax purposes upon the sale or surrender of a life insurance contract. This position is based on a view that a life insurance contract is a personal expenditure, and hence a deductible loss does not arise.

If the consideration received upon the sale of a contract is greater than the cash surrender value, there is also some uncertainty whether this portion of the gain would be ordinary or capital in nature.

Amounts received upon certain sales of life insurance contracts, or viatical settlements, that satisfy very stringent Code requirements may be excluded from income. Among other requirements, in order to receive such treatment, the insured under the contract must be terminally or chronically ill, as those terms are defined in the Code for this purpose. Similar treatment is accorded certain accelerated death benefits that meet similar types of requirements.[79]

Purchaser's perspective   The Code does not distinguish between purchasers and sellers of existing life insurance contracts relative to the treatment of transactions relating to a contract, except with respect to the measurement of basis, or investment in the contract. The purchaser's investment in the contract is effectively measured by the amount the purchaser pays to the seller for the contract, together with any amounts paid subsequent to the purchase. Recall that the seller's investment in the contract is based, generally, on the amount of premiums the seller paid to the insurance company while it held the contract. In addition, under the transfer for value rules, described in more detail later, death proceeds will not be excludable from taxable income except in certain circumstances outlined in the Code.

Distributions from and Other Lifetime Transactions Involving Life Insurance Contracts Characterized as MECs   Holders of MECs do not get the benefit of the investment first ordering rules that are available to holders of non-MEC life insurance contracts.[80] Also unlike the rules applicable to life insurance contracts, policy loans, assignments, and pledges of MECs are treated as distributions.[81]

The Code also contains an anti-abuse provision relating to MECs that requires, for purposes of determining the taxable amount of any gains upon a distribution during a taxable year, that all MECs issued by the same insurance company to the same policyholder during any calendar year be treated as a single contract.

Furthermore, the policyholder must pay a 10 percent penalty tax on the amount of the distribution includible in gross income. The penalty will not apply to any distribution made on or after the policyholder attains the age of 59 1/2, due to the policyholder becoming disabled, or is part of a series of substantially equal periodic payments made for the life or life expectancy of the policyholder or the joint lives or life expectancies of the policyholder and the policyholder's beneficiary.[82]

These rules apply to contracts issued after June 20, 1988, or a contract received in exchange for a MEC. A contract that is materially changed after this date will be deemed to be a newly issued contract subject to these rules. For this purpose, a material change is, with certain exceptions, any increase in a death benefit or qualified additional benefit.[83]

Distributions from and Other Lifetime Transactions Involving Annuity Contracts Nonannuity distributions, or "amounts not received as an annuity" from an annuity contract, are deemed to be received on an income-first basis.[84] This is the opposite of what occurs with respect to a non-MEC life insurance contract. In addition, unless one of several exceptions apply, the taxable portion of such distributions may be subject to an additional 10 percent penalty tax. Loans taken out on the security of an annuity are considered to be taxable distributions, and are taxed and subject to penalty in the same manner as nonloan distributions from these contracts. Further, for purposes of calculating currently includible income upon a distribution, annuities are subject to an aggregation rule similar to that applicable to MECs. That is, multiple annuities issued by the same insurer to the same policyholder during the same calendar year are treated as a single contract.

Amounts that are received as annuity payments, and which, by the definition described earlier, liquidate the "principal amount" of the annuity contract, are deemed to be a combination of a return of investment in the contract and a distribution of income. As such, only a proportionate part of each annuity payment is subject to current tax.

As one might expect, there is a great deal of detail to be considered in applying these basic rules. The discussion that follows describes the federal income tax treatment of amounts not received as annuities. The treatment of amounts received as an annuity is described in the latter part of this section dealing with contract maturity.

Amounts not received as annuities In addition to the actual annuity installments paid over time, an annuitant may receive other types of distributions, referred to and taxed under the Code as "amounts not received as an annuity." This would include such things as policyholder dividends, withdrawals, loans, dividends, and surrenders. Such transactions may occur both prior to the time a contract matures, or annuitizes, or subsequent to the time annuity payments begin. In the latter case, the entire nonannuity amount received is currently included in taxable income. In the former situation, the amounts received are treated as discussed next.

General rule for nonterminating distributions As a general rule, amounts received prior to the "annuity starting date" are included in gross income to the extent of earnings, or income on the contract. The amount that must be included in income is measured by the excess of the cash value of the contract, without regard to surrender charges, over the investment in the contract.[85] If the distribution is larger than the amount of income on the contract, the remainder is treated as a nontaxable return of investment in the contract.

Full surrenders and other distributions related to the termination of a contract   In the event of a full surrender or other termination of the contract, the cash surrender value or proceeds actually received are included in the gross income of the recipient to the extent that this payment, when added to amounts previously received under the contract and excluded from gross income at the time of receipt, exceeds the premiums and other consideration paid for the contract. Essentially, the policyholder includes these amounts in income on an investment first, or cost recovery, basis.

As mentioned in the discussion dealing with distributions from a non-MEC life insurance contract, although this rule appears similar to the rule for nonterminating distributions, the impact of not considering surrender charges in the nonterminating distribution scenario might result in a policyholder being currently taxed on a greater amount of income than might occur if the contract is fully surrendered.

This may be illustrated by the following example. Assume that a policyholder had an investment in the contract of $100, with a cash value equal to $180 and a cash surrender value of $150.

If the policyholder were to make a withdrawal of $140, then the taxpayer would have taxable income of $80. This is because the first $80 of the withdrawal represents taxable income on the contract. The remaining $60 received is deemed to be a return of investment in the contract. If the policyholder had instead undertaken a full surrender, the policyholder would have had only $50 of taxable income, the amount by which the distribution exceeds the investment in the contract.

A refund of the consideration paid for a contract in full discharge of that contract would have similar tax consequences as a payment received upon a surrender of the contract. In such case, however, the payments would truly need to be in the nature of a refund, even if payable in more than a single lump sum, as opposed to, for example a continuation of payments under an annuity stream. The refund would be included in income to the extent that it, when added to amounts previously received under the contract which were excluded from gross income, exceeds the premiums and other consideration paid. The same result would occur with respect to amounts payable to a beneficiary after the death of the annuitant.

Policyholder dividends   Policyholder dividends are taxed in a manner similar to other amounts not received as an annuity, but only when such amounts are actually paid to the policyholder. That is, when policyholder dividends are retained by the insurer to pay premiums or other consideration for the contract, they are not included in income. When the dividends are used in such fashion, there is no net change in the investment in the contract.

Policy loans   Loans, assignments, and pledges of any portion of an annuity contract are considered amounts not received as an annuity. As such, the same general rules for income inclusion just described apply. The amount included in income will increase the policyholder's investment in the contract.

Unplanned increases in periodic payments   The increase in amount of the periodic payments after a contract's annuity starting date is an amount not received as an annuity if the increase was not provided for under the terms of the contract, and will be taxed accordingly. The exclusion ratio would still apply, however, to the original annuity payment amount.

Decreases in periodic payments   In the case of a partial surrender, where a lump-sum payment is received and the future annuity payments are reduced, the lump sum will be treated as an amount not received as an annuity. A portion of the lump-sum payment will be excluded from income based on a ratio equal to the reduction in future annuity payments to the original annuity payments multiplied by the remaining investment in the contract, after adjustment for excluded portions of annuity payments already received. The reduced annuity payments will be subject to the same exclusion ratio as in the past, as long as the term and life or lives on which the contract was based remain the same.

Annuities transferred as gifts   In the event the holder of an annuity transfers it without full and adequate consideration, the original holder of the annuity will recognize income to the extent the cash surrender value exceeds the investment in the contract. The investment in the contract for the new holder of the contract will be the same as that for the original holder, but increased by the amount of income recognized by the original holder as a result of the transfer. This recognition of income does not apply to transfers among spouses or incident to a divorce.[86] The exclusion ratio will remain the same for the new holder of the annuity unless the terms of the contract are modified.

Transfers of annuity contracts for valuable consideration   When an annuity contract is transferred for valuable consideration, it is treated as a new contract starting on the first day of the first period an annuity payment was received by the new annuitant. The investment in the contract for the new owner is the value of the consideration paid to transfer the contract plus the amount of premiums and other consideration paid after the purchase. A new exclusion ratio must be calculated to determine the amount that is not included in income.[87]

Upon the sale of an annuity contract, the seller will recognize any gain as ordinary income. The amount of gain is determined using the same methodology as with a surrender. Income would be recognized to the extent the proceeds from the sale exceed the policyholder's investment in the contract. If the annuity contract is sold after maturity of the contract, the investment in the contract for this purpose must be reduced by the excluded portion of all annuity payments already received, but such amount cannot be reduced below zero.

In the event of a loss on a sale, the loss would be ordinary. Unlike what occurs with respect to a life insurance contract, the IRS has recognized that an annuity contract may be purchased for profit or investment purposes. As such, it has acknowledged that taxpayers may be able to recognize losses with respect to annuity contracts.

Tax-free exchanges   Under certain circumstances, an annuity contract can be exchanged in a 1035 exchange for another annuity contract, with no gain or loss recognized by the contract holder upon the exchange. Both the old and new annuity contracts must have the same annuitants and the same obligees. As discussed with respect to 1035 exchanges of life insurance contracts, these rules are based on the like-kind exchange rules applicable to other assets. If cash or other property is received in the exchange of the contracts, then gain, if any, will be required to be recognized up to the value of the cash and property received. Losses may not be recognized.

Penalty tax on early distributions   In order to discourage the use of annuities for short-term tax deferral, tax penalties are imposed on "premature" annuity distributions. In such cases, the annuitant will be subject to a penalty tax of 10 percent of the amount of a distribution that is includible in gross income if the taxpayer receives such amount under an annuity contract and one of the following exceptions does not apply. These exceptions include distributions:

- Made on or after the date when the taxpayer attains age $59\frac{1}{2}$
- Made on or after the death of the holder, or, in a case where the holder is not an individual, the death of the primary annuitant
- Due to the taxpayer becoming disabled
- That are a part of a series of substantially equal periodic payments, payable at least annually, made for the life, or life expectancy, of the taxpayer or the joint lives, or joint life expectancies, of the taxpayer and his designated beneficiary
- Made from a plan, contract, account, trust, or annuity from a qualified retirement plan

- Allocable to investment in the contract before August 14, 1982
- Under an immediate annuity contract purchased with a single premium or consideration, the starting date of which begins no later than one year from the date of purchase of the annuity, and which provides for substantially equal periodic payments that are payable at least annually
- From a qualified funding asset as a result of a requirement to make periodic payments for damages or other types of agreements
- From an annuity purchased by an employer upon termination of a qualified plan which is held by the employer until the employee separates from service

If the 10 percent penalty tax is avoided because the distributions are part of a series of substantially periodic payments, but the payments are subsequently modified, other than by reason of death or disability, the penalty tax that had been avoided would be imposed with interest as of the date of the modification. The recapture provisions would come into play if the modification to the periodic payments occurs before the annuitant reaches age $59\frac{1}{2}$ or even if the annuitant has already reached age $59\frac{1}{2}$, if the modification occurs within the five-year period beginning on the date of the first payment.

Contract Maturity

Life Insurance Contract Death Benefits   Generally, death benefits, or amounts received under a life insurance contract due to the death of the insured, are not includible in gross income.[88] However, a terminally ill or chronically ill policyholder may receive an accelerated death benefit that will be excluded from income as though it were an amount received due to the death of the insured. Amounts received upon the sale or assignment of a life insurance policy to a viatical settlement provider can similarly be treated as amounts received due to the death of the insured. In order to receive such treatment, however, very stringent requirements would need to be satisfied. These requirements relate to such things as the condition of the insured that triggered the benefits and the satisfaction of certain state- or NAIC-[89]defined consumer protection standards that have been incorporated into the Code.

If the death benefits of a life insurance contract are subject to an agreement to pay interest, the interest payments or credits to the beneficiary are included in the beneficiary's gross income.

This might occur, for example, if the beneficiary elects not to receive the life insurance proceeds immediately after the death of the insured. If the amount payable at a later date does not exceed the amount payable immediately upon death, the amount will be fully excluded from income whenever it is received. In most cases, however, pursuant to state law, if life insurance proceeds are paid at a date later than death, the payment must include at least some minimum amount of interest.

It may also be possible for the beneficiary to elect—or through the payment of a settlement option in the contract—to have death proceeds payable in the form of an annuity. If such methodology is chosen, then the annuity payments would be subject to tax under rules similar to other annuity payments, with the amount of the death benefit effectively serving as the beneficiary's investment in the contract, a piece of which is included in each of the annuity payments, until the death benefit amount has been exhausted.

If a life insurance policy is transferred for valuable consideration, the death benefit is not excluded from income. Instead, the death benefit will be taxable to the extent it exceeds the consideration paid to transfer the policy and the premiums and other amounts paid by the purchaser after the transfer. Basis in the policy will be further increased for interest paid on indebtedness related to the policy that was not deductible pursuant to certain of the rules discussed above that limit the deductibility of interest on debt associated with the purchase or carrying of a life insurance contract. This "transfer for value" rule, however, does not apply when the life insurance policy is transferred to the insured, a partner of the insured, a partnership in which the insured is a partner, or a corporation in which the insured is a shareholder or officer. In such cases, the death benefit remains fully excludable.

The death benefits on a policy transferred as a gift or to a spouse would generally not be taxable.

Death benefits on employer-owned life insurance   The COLI Best Practices Act, recently enacted as part of the Pension Protection Act of 2006,[90] sets forth a general rule that would deny an exclusion from income for the full amount of death benefits on a life insurance contract that is owned by an employer and covers the lives of employees, officers, and directors. For such contracts, the amount that would be excludable would be limited to the sum of the premiums and other amounts paid by the employer for the contract

The full amount of the death benefit, however, will be excluded from income if, in addition to satisfaction of the new notice and consent requirements set forth below, the contracts involve:

- Either the insured was an employee of the policyholder at any time during the previous 12-month period before his or her death; or
- At the time the contract is issued, the insured is a director, a highly compensated employee, or a highly compensated individual.[91]

For this purpose, a "highly compensated employee" means an employee who was a 5 percent owner at any time during the year or preceding year or, for the preceding year, had compensation from the employer in excess of $100,000. A highly compensated individual is one of the five highest paid officers, a shareholder who owns more than 10 percent in value of stock of the employer, or is among the highest paid 35 percent of all employees.

The new notice and consent requirements include notification to the employee by the employer, in writing, of the employer's plans to insure the employee's life, including disclosure of the maximum face amount for which the employee could be insured at the time the contract is issued, as well as the fact that the employer/policyholder will be the beneficiary of any proceeds payable upon the death of the employee. In addition, the employer must receive written consent from the employee to the coverage and that the coverage may continue after the insured terminates employment.

Employers purchasing such coverage will also be required to satisfy a new regime of recordkeeping and reporting requirements associated with the contracts.

Amounts Received as an Annuity   When an annuity contract matures, or annuitizes, the annuity payments received are deemed to be both a return of investment in the contract and a payment of income on the contract. In order to determine the portion of each annuity payment to exclude from gross income, an exclusion ratio is calculated. The remainder of the annuity payment is included in income. The exclusion ratio is calculated at the annuity starting date and is based on the policyholder's investment in the contract and the earnings or income expected to be distributed in the life of the annuity stream.[92] The exclusion ratio will remain the same for the life of the annuity unless there is a change in ownership or a termination of the annuity. If, at some point, however, the total amount excluded from gross income equals the investment in the contract, the exclusion ratio will cease to apply and all remaining payments under the contract will be currently includible in taxable income, in full. In the case of a single contract with two or more annuitants, only one exclusion ratio is calculated for the contract as a whole.

Investment in the Contract   The investment in the contract is generally the total of premiums or other consideration paid for the contract as of the annuity starting date or the date on which an annuity payment is first received. Any returns of premium or dividends received, including unrepaid loans or dividends applied against the principal or interest on such loans, prior to the start of the contract would reduce the investment in the contract. In addition, if the annuity contract has a life contingency, the contract provides for payments to be made to a beneficiary when the annuitant dies, and such payments are in the nature of a refund, the value of these payments will be discounted, and the resulting amount will be used to reduce the investment in the contract as otherwise determined. Dividends (including excess interest) not received in cash that are credited to the cash value of the contract are not included in the investment in the contract.

Expected Return   Expected return is the total value of annuity payments expected to be paid under the annuity contract. If the payments are dependent on the life expectancy of an individual or individuals, as in the case of a joint or survivor annuity, actuarial tables must be used to calculate the expected return. Otherwise, with no life contingency, this amount is simply the aggregate of all amounts anticipated to be received under the contract as annuity payments.

In the case of a variable annuity, where the annuity payments may vary in amount, the determination of the taxable and nontaxable pieces of such payments is determined through a different approach. In this instance, the exclusion amount must be calculated differently since the return on the contract cannot be determined. The nontaxable piece of each payment is simply the investment in the contract divided by the number of years, or the expected number of payments under the contract. If the term is based on the life or lives of the annuitant(s), prescribed actuarial tables are used to estimate the term of the contract and the related exclusion amount.[93]

This amount is subtracted from each payment, with the remainder of each payment being includible in gross income. Due to the nature of a variable annuity, it is possible for the annuity payment to be lower than the exclusion amount for a particular period. Should this occur, the annuitant has the option of electing to redetermine the excludable amount in a later year to take into consideration the unused exclusion amount from a previous year.

Annuity Starting Date   The annuity starting date is the first day of the first period for which an amount is received as an annuity. This would be the later of the date when the obligations under the contract become fixed, or the first day of the period that ends on the date of the first annuity payment.[94]

Under limited circumstances, the annuity starting date may change. This could occur, for example, when there is a change to the contract that effectively results in a new annuity contract or an exchange that actually results in a new annuity contract. A new annuity starting date also may occur if there is a change in the holder of the contract (e.g., if there is a transfer for a valuable consideration).

When a new payee begins receiving annuity payments as the result of the death of the original annuitant under the contract, the previously determined exclusion ratio will continue to apply.

To the extent the investment in the contract is not fully recovered as the result of the premature death of the annuitant, the annuitant's estate is permitted to take a deduction for the unrecovered investment in the contract on his or her last income tax return.[95]

Lump-sum payments received upon deemed exchanges When the terms of a contract are modified after the annuity has already begun, the contract will be deemed to have been exchanged.[96] Regardless of whether there was an actual exchange to bring about the new terms or an exchange is simply deemed to occur, a new annuity starting date for the exchanged contract will be established: the first day of the first period for which the new annuity amount is received. As a new contract with a new start date, a new exclusion ratio must also be calculated. To the extent a lump-sum payment is received, the investment in the contract for purposes of calculating the new exclusion ratio will not reflect this amount, because it will be treated as an amount not received as an annuity before the new annuity's starting date for the contract obtained in the exchange.

CHAPTER 14

U.S. Estate and Tax Planning Aspects of Life Insurance and Annuities

Paul A. Ferrara
Associate, Alston & Bird LLP, New York

Glenn G. Fox
Partner, Alston & Bird LLP, New York

Life insurance and annuities can be useful estate planning tools for individuals with citizenship, residency, or other connections to the United States. In this chapter, we describe: the different types of life insurance; various estate planning uses of life insurance; taxation issues with regard to life insurance; irrevocable life insurance trusts; life insurance settlement agreements; special issues for nonresident aliens with regard to life insurance; and estate planning uses and taxation of annuities.

LIFE INSURANCE: DEFINITION AND TYPES

Life insurance is a contract by which a company (the insurer) in return for the purchase price of the policy (the premium) promises to pay a certain amount (the face value of the policy) to one or more individuals or entities (the beneficiary or beneficiaries) upon the death of an individual (the insured). The beneficiary usually must have an insurable interest in the life of the

The authors wish to thank Guy A. Reiss, Esq., of Wuersch & Gering LLP for his gracious review of and helpful comments on this chapter.

insured—that is, the relationship of the beneficiary to the insured should be such that the death of the insured would have an adverse economic effect on the beneficiary. For example, such a beneficiary could be a family member, a partner of the insured in a partnership, or a company managed by the insured. The policy reason behind this rule is to keep life insurance contracts from becoming essentially vehicles for gambling.

There are several different types of life insurance, ranging from "pure" insurance—that is, providing only a fixed death benefit—to policies that combine insurance with an investment, or "cash value," component. The U.S. government looks askance at policies that are not really insurance at all but rather use the guise of insurance to cloak what are essentially investment vehicles. As life insurance generally gets favorable tax treatment under U.S. law, the prospective purchaser of a life insurance policy, especially of a policy that combines insurance and investment characteristics, should get written confirmation from the issuer of the policy that it will be treated as life insurance for U.S. tax purposes.

Some of the most common types of life insurance are described below.

Term Life Insurance

Term life insurance provides the beneficiary with a payout if the insured dies within a fixed time, which is called the "term" of the policy. The term of such policies is often one year. Term life insurance contains no investment component; the premiums paid cover only the administrative costs of maintaining the policy and the actual cost of the insurance coverage. Thus, such policies contain little if any "cash value"—that is, the owner will get little or no return for terminating and cashing in the policy before the end of the term. The policy is often renewable for successive one-year terms, with the premium increasing each year to reflect the greater probability of death as the insured ages. Alternatively, some life insurance companies guarantee their rates for more than one year, while others allow the insured to pay several years' premiums at the issuance of the policy, offering a discount on the premiums that otherwise would be due. Term policies are often a good choice for younger individuals in that such insurance can provide a degree of financial protection at a relatively low price. As the insured ages and his or her risk of death increases, however, the cost of term insurance can become prohibitive.

Whole Life Insurance

Whole life insurance combines pure insurance with an investment component managed by the issuer. The term of a whole life policy is generally the lifetime of the insured, though the policy may be canceled by the owner in return for its cash value or by the insurance provider in the event of non-payment of premiums. The premium payments on such a policy generally remain the same until the insured reaches a certain age, at which time the policy is considered "paid up" (i.e., no further premium payments will be needed in order to maintain the policy). As the insured ages, the appreciation on the investment component goes partly toward keeping the premium payments level, even as the cost of the insurance component of such payments goes up due to the increasing likelihood of death on the part of the insured. At the point that the policy is paid up, the expected income on the policy's cash value will be sufficient to provide for all future premium payments.

Variable Life Insurance

Variable life insurance is a form of whole life insurance. Like whole life insurance, it contains both an insurance component and an investment component, with a goal of maintaining level premium payments for the life of the insured. With variable life insurance, however, the owner (rather than the insurance provider) controls the investment portion. Upon the death of the insured, the beneficiary receives not only the face value of the policy but also the value of the investments at that time. Thus, variable life insurance can be thought of as life insurance plus a mutual fund, with the owner bearing the risks and rewards of his or her investment strategy. The investment component of variable life insurance has the advantage, however, of growing tax free, unlike investment in a mutual fund. Because the U.S. Internal Revenue Service (IRS) carefully scrutinizes variable life insurance policies to ensure that they are not merely investment vehicles masquerading as life insurance, it is important that the owner of such a policy procure a letter from the provider stating that the policy complies with IRS rules for life insurance.

Universal Life Insurance

Universal life insurance also is a form of whole life insurance. Like whole life, it has a lifetime term but can be terminated by the owner in return for its cash value or canceled by the provider for nonpayment of premiums. Like variable life, the death benefits are flexible. But with universal life insurance, the premiums are flexible as well, as long as the total cash paid to the insurer covers the cost of the insurance component and administrative expenses each year. For example, the owner may choose to make a large premium payment at the beginning of the term with an eye toward eliminating future premium payments. Or the owner may make a series of large payments, with the goal of increasing the death benefit. As the excess payments earn interest tax free, a universal life insurance policy can be thought of as life insurance plus a savings account with tax-free growth.

Second-to-Die Life Insurance

Second-to-die life insurance is a form of life insurance in which there are two insureds, with the death benefit payable upon the death of the second insured. Premiums for second-to-die policies are generally lower than those on the life of a single insured, as the risk of mortality is lower for two people than for one person. Second-to-die policies are often useful in the estate planning context where the individuals are married and, because of the unlimited estate-tax marital deduction for U.S. citizens, liquidity is needed for estate taxes only on the death of the second spouse.

USES OF LIFE INSURANCE IN ESTATE PLANNING

Life insurance can be used in a variety of ways in estate planning. Some of the benefits that it conveys are discussed in the subsections that follow.

Income Replacement

The most basic use of life insurance is to provide income replacement for the dependents of the insured upon his or her death. For example, if the insured has a family and is paying off a mortgage on a residence, life insurance benefits can be used to pay off the mortgage. Alternatively, the benefits can be invested in order to provide a steady stream of income for the insured's family.

Liquidity

As life insurance can be a nonprobate asset—that is, it will not pass via a will and will not be subject to the potential delays of the estate administration process if the intended beneficiary (other than the insured's estate) is designated as such on the beneficiary designation form for the policy—the death benefit typically is available much more quickly than assets passing through a will or intestacy. Thus, life insurance can provide liquidity in the first few months after the death of the insured for his or her funeral expenses or unpaid debts. Life insurance benefits also can be used to pay off tax on the decedent's estate, if the estate is large enough to be subject to state or federal estate tax. This is especially important where the decedent's assets are mostly illiquid—caught up in a residence or business, for example—or where it would be difficult or disadvantageous to sell off part or all of the decedent's assets.

Business Planning

Life insurance can be useful in compensating a business on the death of a key employee, thus buying the business time until it is able to dissolve or to find an appropriate substitute employee. The purchase of life insurance is also integral to most "buy-sell" agreements. In a typical buy-sell agreement, each of the partners of a partnership or each of the owners of a closely held company agrees (i) that he or she will buy out—directly or through the company—the interest of another partner or owner upon that partner's or owner's death, and (ii) that upon his or her death his or her estate will sell to the surviving partner(s) or owner(s) his or her interest in the entity. In essence, buy-sell agreements are designed to prevent outsiders from attaining ownership of a business and having a say in its future conduct; in other words, they enable the surviving partner(s) or owner(s) to continue to control the business. The life insurance proceeds provide the liquidity necessary to effect the purchase.

Equalizing Distributions

Life insurance proceeds often are used to ensure that a decedent's beneficiaries are treated fairly. Suppose, for example, that the owner of a business dies and leaves two children, only one of whom is interested in participating in the business. The decedent could leave the entire business to the child who is interested in the business and name the other child as the beneficiary of a life insurance policy similar in value to the business.

Planning in the Case of a Second Marriage

Suppose an individual having children from a prior marriage subsequently remarries. A common estate planning solution in such a case is for that individual to leave his or her assets to the surviving spouse in the form of a QTIP trust[1] naming the individual's children as remaindermen. Unfortunately, such a plan can lead to squabbles regarding the management of the trust, as the spouse and children have interests adverse to each other: The spouse, who under the QTIP rules must receive all of the income of the trust, will want trust assets invested to produce maximum income, while the children will want trust assets invested for maximum growth. If the surviving spouse and the children do not get along, it might be advantageous for such an individual to leave his or her assets to the children and to provide for the surviving spouse by way of a life insurance policy naming the spouse as beneficiary.

Creditor Protection

In certain U.S. states, such as New York,[2] an interest in a life insurance policy cannot be attached by the insured's creditors, and life insurance proceeds payable to named beneficiaries cannot be attached by the creditors of the insured's estate. The degree of protection likely will depend on the residence of the insured at the time the creditor attempts to attach the property.[3] That said, if a policy is acquired (or cash is paid into a policy) with the intention of defrauding creditors, all or part of the policy or its proceeds probably will not be protected from the creditors of the insured or of the insured's estate.

INCOME TAXATION OF LIFE INSURANCE

Taxation of Owner

As mentioned above, life insurance is a tax-advantaged instrument both from an income tax and an estate tax point of view. As long as a policy falls within the federal definition for life insurance, any increase in the cash value of the policy during the life of the insured will occur free of income tax. Thus, investment in a variable life insurance policy, which, as mentioned above, is akin to investing in life insurance plus a mutual fund, is actually superior to separate investments in, say, a term policy plus a mutual fund, in that the annual increases in value in the mutual fund are subject to income tax whereas the increases in the cash value of the variable life policy are not. Investment in a universal life insurance policy, which is akin to investing in life insurance plus a savings account, is similarly advantaged: Once again, the annual increases in the value of a savings account will be subject to income tax, whereas the increase in the cash value of the universal life policy will not. (If in either case the owner surrenders the policy for its cash value, the owner will pay at that point income tax on the appreciation, under Internal Revenue Code [IRC] Section 1001.)

Taxation of Beneficiary

Under IRC Section 101(a), the beneficiary of a life insurance policy generally receives the proceeds of the policy free from income tax. The only exception to this rule is if consideration has been paid to any party other than the insurance company in exchange for ownership of the policy. This exception, known as the "transfer for value rule," is enshrined in IRC Section 101(a)(2). The rule does not apply, however, if the beneficiary is the insured, the insured's estate, a partner of the insured, a partnership in which the insured is a partner, or a corporation of which the insured is a corporation. If the transfer for value rule applies, then the beneficiary will be taxed on the value of the proceeds received minus the sum of (i) the consideration paid by the transferee and (ii) the value of the premiums paid by the transferee.

ESTATE TAXATION OF LIFE INSURANCE

Although proceeds from insurance on the life of the insured are not subject to income taxation, they are subject to taxation in the insured's estate in three cases:

1. If the proceeds are payable to or for the benefit of the insured's estate
2. If the insured possessed incidents of ownership in the policy
3. If the insured transferred ownership of the policy within three years of death

These three scenarios are discussed in the following subsections.

Proceeds Payable to or for the Benefit of the Insured's Estate

IRC Section 2042(1) provides that "[t]he value of the gross estate shall include the value of all property...[t]o the extent of the amount receivable by the executor as insurance under policies on the life of the decedent." Treasury Regulation Section 20.2042-1(a)(1) clarifies this provision, explaining that "[i]t makes no difference whether or not the estate is specifically named as the beneficiary under the terms of the policy"—that is, if the beneficiary is legally bound to pay obligations of the estate from the proceeds, then the proceeds, to the extent of the beneficiary's obligation, will be taxable in the insured's estate.

Insured Possessed Incidents of Ownership

Under IRC Section 2042(2), even if the life insurance proceeds are not payable to or for the benefit of the insured's estate, they still will be subject to estate tax if the insured at death possessed "incidents of ownership" in the policy. Treasury Regulation Section 20.2042-1(c)(2) provides that "the term 'incidents of ownership' is not limited in its meaning to ownership of the policy in the technical legal sense"; rather, "it includes the power to change the beneficiary, to surrender or cancel the policy, to assign the policy, to revoke an assignment, to pledge the policy for a loan, or to obtain from the insurer a loan against the surrender value of the policy...." That it might be impossible for the insured to exercise incidents of ownership—because of his or her incapacity, for example—is irrelevant.[4]

Incidents of Ownership under Treasury Regulation Section 20.2042-1(c)(2)   Treasury Regulation Section 20.2042-1(c)(2) goes on to list various powers that can constitute incidents of ownership:

- Power to change the beneficiary
- Power to surrender or cancel the policy
- Power to assign a policy or to revoke an assignment
- Power to pledge the policy for a loan or to obtain from the insurer a loan against the surrender value of the policy

Reversionary Interests   The Internal Revenue Code and Treasury Regulations detail other possible incidents of ownership as well. IRC Section 2042(2) provides that in certain cases a reversionary interest in a life insurance policy will be deemed an incident of ownership. Treasury Regulation Section 20.2042-1(c)(3) states that a "'reversionary interest' includes a possibility that the policy or its proceeds may return to the decedent or his estate and the possibility that the policy or its proceeds may become subject to a power of disposition by him." IRC Section 2042(2) specifies that it is irrelevant whether the reversionary interest arises under the express terms of the policy, under another instrument (such as, e.g., a divorce decree or trust agreement), or by operation of law. The statute limits its reach to reversionary interests exceeding 5 percent of the value of the policy immediately before the death of the insured, as calculated pursuant to the mortality tables issued by the IRS.

Suppose, for example, that under the terms of a settlement agreement, the insured must purchase and pay the premiums on a policy for the benefit of her former companion. The companion is to be owner and beneficiary of the policy unless she predeceases the insured, in which case ownership will revert to the insured. As it happens, the insured predeceases her companion, who receives the proceeds of the policy. Even though the insured does not own the policy at the time of her death, the proceeds will be included in her taxable estate if it is found that her reversionary interest exceeds 5 percent of the value of the policy immediately before her death.

Joint Powers IRC Section 2042(2) provides that the insured will be considered to possess incidents of ownership whether the powers constituting such incidents are exercisable alone "or in conjunction with any other person." The IRS has interpreted the statute to include among incidents of ownership not only those cases where the insured needs to act together with another individual or entity in order to exercise such a power but also (i) where it is necessary that the insured consent to the exercise of such a power and (ii) where the insured has power to veto the exercise of such a power.[5]

Special Issues in the Trust Context Under Treasury Regulation Section 20.2042-1(c)(4), a decedent is deemed to possess an incident of ownership in an insurance policy held in trust on his or her life if, under the terms of the policy, the insured has the power, either alone or in conjunction with another person or persons, and as trustee or otherwise, "to change the beneficial ownership in the policy or its proceeds, or the time or manner of enjoyment thereof, even though the decedent has no beneficial interest in the trust." The IRS has specified further that powers held by an insured in a fiduciary capacity (e.g., as trustee of a trust) will not constitute incidents of ownership in the policy where (i) such powers cannot be exercised for the insured's own benefit, and (ii) the insured is not the transferor of the policy and does not provide consideration (e.g., premium payments) for maintaining the policy.[6]

However, that the trustee is a beneficiary of a trust holding a policy on the trustee's life does not necessarily mean that the proceeds of the policy will be included in the taxable estate of the insured/trustee. In a Private Letter Ruling,[7] the IRS held that the insured did not possess any incidents of ownership in a policy where:

- The insured was trustee of an irrevocable trust holding a life insurance policy on the trustee's life.
- The insured was not the transferor of the policy to the trust.
- Under the terms of the trust, income and principal could be "distributed to the insured and the insured's husband's descendants, as necessary or advisable for their health, education, maintenance, or support, as long as the payments" did not "discharge the insured's or the trustee's support obligations."
- The trust further provided that any individual trustee, whose life was insured by a policy held as trust property, was "prohibited from exercising any power conferred on the owner of that policy."

- The insured also held "a special power of appointment over all the corpus except for the policy."
- The insured had "the power to remove the trustee without reason by written notice."

In ruling that the insured did not possess any incidents of ownership over the policy and that the policy proceeds thus would be excluded from her taxable estate, the IRS reasoned that, as trustee, the insured was "specifically prohibited from exercising powers typically conferred on the owner of a life policy" and that the insured's special power of appointment did not cover the policy. Notwithstanding the favorable ruling received by the taxpayer in this case, caution should be exercised where a trust holds insurance on the life of a nongrantor trustee: The trustee's powers should be limited as described above, and, if possible, an advance ruling regarding inclusion of the proceeds in the insured's estate should be obtained from the IRS.

Further issues involving life insurance held in trust will be discussed in the section entitled "Life Insurance Trusts."

Transfer of Ownership within Three Years of Death

Under IRC Section 2035(a), any property transferred by the insured within three years of death that otherwise would have been subject to taxation in his or her estate under IRC Section 2042 (or certain other sections of the Code) will nonetheless be subject to taxation, even if the insured at death retained none of the incidents of ownership described above.[8] The only exception to this rule is for transfers in connection with "a bona fide sale for an adequate and full consideration." Thus, in effect the rule applies to all gifts of life insurance policies made by the insured within three years of death.

What if the insured transfers the policy by gift more than three years before his or her death but continues to pay the policy premiums through the year of his or her death? The IRS has decided that in such a case the face value of the policy will not be included in the insured's taxable estate.[9]

To illustrate these rules, suppose that in 2005 the insured gifts a policy with a face value of $300,000 to her daughter, who is the beneficiary of the policy. The insured dies in 2007. Because the insured died within three years of the transfer of the policy, the policy's proceeds of $300,000 will be included in the insured's taxable estate. Now suppose instead that the insured transferred ownership of the policy to her daughter in 2003 but continued to pay the premiums on the policy. The insured dies in 2007. Because the insured died over three years after the transfer of the policy, the policy's proceeds of $300,000 will not be included in the insured's taxable estate. That the insured continued to pay the premiums on the policy is irrelevant.

LIFE INSURANCE TRUSTS

Types of Life Insurance Trusts; Advantages of ILITs

Life insurance policies may be held by inter vivos revocable trusts, inter vivos irrevocable trusts, or testamentary trusts. If the insured transfers a policy on his or her life to a revocable or testamentary trust, however, the proceeds of the policy likely will be includible in the insured's taxable estate under IRC Section 2042, as the insured at death will have continued to possess incidents of ownership over the policy.[10] Some individuals will prefer nonetheless to transfer their policies to such trusts in order to retain until death the power to change the type of policy, borrow against the cash surrender value of the policy, terminate the policy, or change the beneficiaries of the policy. For such individuals, having the flexibility to take such actions will outweigh the tax advantages of having a properly structured irrevocable trust own the policy.[11]

That said, the irrevocable life insurance trust, or "ILIT," is the type of trust most often used to hold life insurance policies and is the most common mechanism employed to prevent life insurance proceeds from being included in the insured's taxable estate. Indeed, if the insured is married and wishes the surviving spouse to benefit from the proceeds of the policy, a properly structured ILIT will keep the proceeds from being taxed not only in the estate of the insured but also in the estate of the insured's spouse. We will limit our discussion here to ILITs in view of their tax advantages over other types of insurance trusts.

The insured may establish an ILIT to which he or she will transfer an already existing policy on his or her life; alternatively, the ILIT may acquire the policy on the insured's life directly. In either case, the ILIT should be named both the owner and the beneficiary of the policy. The trust instrument itself will govern the disposition of the policy proceeds. As discussed further below, the ILIT should be structured (i) to ensure that proceeds of the life insurance policy held by the trust are not includible in the insured's taxable estate and (ii) to take full advantage of the "annual exclusions" for the gift and generation-skipping transfer tax with regard to the transfer or acquisition of the policy and the payment of premiums on it.

ILITs: Gift Tax Issues

Any transfers made by the insured to a properly structured ILIT ("properly structured" meaning, among other things, that the insured retains no power to designate new beneficiaries or affect their beneficial enjoyment of trust assets) will constitute completed gifts and thus may be subject to federal gift tax. IRC Section 2503(b), however, provides that the first $12,000 (or $24,000 if the donor is married and elects to "split gifts" with his or her spouse pursuant to IRC Section 2513) of "present interest" gifts to any donee during the calendar year will be excluded from gift tax.[12] This amount generally is referred to as the "annual exclusion" for gift tax purposes. In order for the ILIT to be as tax-efficient a vehicle as possible, it should be structured in such a way that transfers to it will qualify for the gift tax annual exclusion.

Crummey Powers   Note that the annual exclusion pertains only to "present interest" gifts. Treasury Regulation 25.2503-3(b) defines a "present interest" as an "unrestricted right to the immediate use, possession, or enjoyment of property or the income from property." Thus, if an ILIT provides for discretionary payments of income or principal to trust beneficiaries, transfers to the ILIT generally will be considered gifts of a future interest[13] and thus will not qualify for the gift tax annual exclusion.

If trust beneficiaries, however, have the power to withdraw the value of the contributed property for a reasonable period of time (generally considered to be not less than 30 days),[14] then the beneficiaries will be treated as having a present interest in the property contributed. The contribution will qualify for the annual gift tax exclusion, whether or not the beneficiaries actually exercise their right to the immediate use, possession, or enjoyment of the property contributed.[15] A beneficiary's withdrawal power is known as a Crummey power, after the landmark case approving the use of such a power.[16]

To illustrate, suppose that the insured sets up an ILIT for the benefit of his wife and descendants and gives each descendant a Crummey withdrawal power. The insured currently has two children and three grandchildren. He gifts to the trust a life insurance policy having a current cash value of $120,000, and the trustee of the ILIT sends out Crummey notices (discussed below) for each descendant. The insured and his wife elect to split gifts on their gift tax returns for the year of the transfer of the policy to the ILIT. Assuming that the insured and his wife made no other gifts in that calendar year to any of his descendants, he will be able to use annual gift tax exclusions totaling $120,000—that is, $24,000 for each of the five descendants having Crummey withdrawal powers—which will cover completely the gift of the policy to the ILIT. He will owe no federal gift tax on the transfer, nor will he use up any of his $1 million lifetime gift tax exemption amount.

The Crummey power must not be illusory. The beneficiaries must be made aware that the power to withdraw the contributed property exists, and they must have sufficient time to exercise such power.[17] This is normally accomplished by means of a letter known as a "Crummey notice," sent by the trustee to each trust beneficiary having a current withdrawal power. While any beneficiary of the ILIT is a minor, any notice required to be given to him or her should be given to the minor's court-appointed guardian or, if none, to the minor's parent as "natural guardian." The guardian for such purposes should not be anyone who has made a contribution to the trust. For example, suppose the insured creates an ILIT and contributes a premium payment to the trust, under the terms of which the insured's minor daughter has a Crummey withdrawal power. The trustee should *not* send the Crummey notice to the insured as natural guardian for the daughter; otherwise, the resulting power of the insured to exercise (or not) a withdrawal power on the daughter's behalf could be deemed a power to affect the beneficial enjoyment of the contribution, thus making it subject to taxation in the insured's estate under IRC Section 2036.[18] The trustee should send each Crummey notice by certified mail to document that he or she has complied with the notice requirements in a timely manner. In case of an audit, the trustee should maintain a record file containing (i) evidence that Crummey notices were provided to and received by each of the beneficiaries having a withdrawal power; (ii) copies of all statements and checks relating to payment of premiums; and (iii) copies of all documentation and correspondence related to the ILIT.

Lapse of Crummey Powers   The terms of the ILIT should state that the beneficiary's withdrawal power is noncumulative and will lapse automatically if not exercised. Obviously, it is hoped that the beneficiary will not exercise the withdrawal power, that the power will lapse, and that the contribution on the part of the insured to cover (for example) a premium payment actually will go to pay the premium on the life insurance held by the trust. There can be no prearranged understanding, however, that the beneficiary will not exercise the Crummey power, nor can there be any implied threat that he or she will be punished for doing so. If facts and circumstances show that this is, indeed, the case, then the IRS will not allow the gift tax annual exclusion to apply to contributions to the ILIT.[19]

It is possible that the lapse of a Crummey power will have adverse tax consequences for the beneficiaries. For example, such a lapse can be deemed in certain situations a taxable gift made by one beneficiary to the other trust beneficiaries: Under IRC Section 2514, the right to withdraw property is considered a general power of appointment, the release of which is treated, for gift tax purposes, as a transfer of such property. IRC Section 2514(e), however, provides an exception to this rule: In the ILIT context, the rule will not apply to the extent that the property subject to the lapsed Crummey power exceeds the greater of $5,000 or 5 percent of the property held in the trust. Thus, the ILIT should be drafted to take advantage of this "five and five" exception. If it is anticipated that premium payments will be covered vis-à-vis the annual exclusion by limiting each beneficiary's withdrawal right to the greater of $5,000 or 5 percent of the value of the trust corpus, such a limitation should be included in the terms of the ILIT. If the premium is too large to be covered by such an amount, the beneficiaries may be granted so-called "hanging" powers, by which each beneficiary's right of withdrawal lapses only to the extent of the greater of $5,000 or 5 percent of the value of the trust principal.[20]

ILITs: Estate Tax Issues

The ILIT must be carefully drafted so as to ensure that the proceeds of the life insurance policy, of which it is both owner and beneficiary, will not be includible in the insured's taxable estate. In particular, the insured must be careful not to retain any of the incidents of ownership described in IRC Section 2042(2).[21] Furthermore, the insured must be sure to part with any and all incidents of ownership more than three years before his or her death, so as to avoid inclusion of the proceeds in his or her taxable estate under IRC Section 2035(a).[22] In order to remove the IRC Section 2035(a) issue, it is preferable (if at all feasible) for the ILIT to purchase a new policy on the insured's life rather than for the insured to transfer to the ILIT an existing policy. Doing this will avoid application of the three-year look-back rule. Finally, if the insured is married, care should be taken to ensure where possible that the insurance proceeds are excluded from the taxable estate of the spouse.

Designating a Trustee   Choosing the wrong individual as trustee can destroy the tax advantages of the ILIT. If the proceeds of the life insurance held by the ILIT are to be excluded from the insured's taxable estate, the insured should not be a trustee of the ILIT.[23] Although the IRS provides some leeway where the terms of the ILIT prevent the trustee from exercising powers for his or her own benefit and the insured is not the transferor of the policy and does not provide consideration for maintaining the policy,[24] in practice this is seldom the case: Normally it is the insured who is establishing the trust and who will be making contributions to maintain the policy. Similarly, if the ILIT holds a second-to-die policy, neither insured spouse should serve as trustee of the trust. Indeed, any individual who potentially may contribute to the ILIT should not be designated as trustee, because the powers held by the trustee will cause all or a portion of the trust assets to be includible in that individual's taxable estate under IRC Sections 2036 and 2038. The ILIT should contain explicit provisions barring the insured(s) and contributors to the trust from acting as trustee.

Trustee Powers   ILITs often contain "sprinkle" provisions (i.e., provisions granting the trustee the power to "sprinkle" trust income and/or principal among various beneficiaries in the trustee's discretion). If the surviving spouse or a beneficiary of the ILIT is a sprinkle beneficiary as well as a trustee, he or she may be prevented under state law from exercising his or her sprinkle power.[25] Where this is not prevented, the trustee may be deemed to hold a general power of appointment over the trust assets, which could be includible in the trustee's taxable estate under IRC Section 2041. In either case, the ILIT should expressly forbid the surviving spouse or beneficiary from participating in the exercise of any sprinkle power. Alternatively, these problems may be avoided if the discretionary power to invade income or principal is limited to an "ascertainable standard," such as a power to distribute income or principal for the health, education, maintenance, or support of the beneficiary.[26] Powers limited by such a standard will not be considered general powers of appointment and thus will not cause inclusion of trust assets in the taxable estate under IRC Section 2041(b)(1).

Legal Obligations of the Insured   IRC Section 2036(a) provides that property transferred by a decedent to a trust under the terms of which he or she is able to retain "the possession or enjoyment of, or the right to the income from, the property" during his or her lifetime will be includible in the decedent's taxable estate. Under Treasury Regulation Section 20.2036-1(b)(2), the "use, possession, right to the income, or other enjoyment of the transferred property" is deemed retained by the decedent to the extent it "is to be applied toward the discharge of a legal obligation of the decedent," such as a legal obligation to support a dependent during the decedent's lifetime. Thus, in order to help prevent the assets of the ILIT from being included in the insured's taxable estate, the ILIT should contain a provision stating that nothing in it should be construed as requiring the trustee to use trust assets in satisfaction of any legal obligation of the insured.

ILITs: Generation-Skipping Transfer Tax Issues

Generation-skipping transfer (GST) tax issues with respect to ILITs are extremely complex. Even a superficial explanation of the most important issues would require more space than is available here. That said, we wish to explore briefly two particular topics with respect to GST taxation of ILITs: the GST tax annual exclusion and allocation of GST exemption.

GST Tax Annual Exclusion   One of the circumstances under which GST tax is imposed is where there is a "direct skip." In the ILIT context, a "direct skip" generally occurs where a gift is made to an ILIT, all the beneficiaries of which are "skip persons" (i.e., persons two or more generations below the donor's generation).[27] Suppose, for example, that the insured creates an ILIT solely for the benefit of her grandchildren or more remote descendants. The insured then gifts to the ILIT a policy on her life. The transfer is a direct skip and thus is subject to GST tax.

As with the gift tax, there is currently a $12,000 GST tax annual exclusion per donee (or $24,000 if the donor is married and elects to split gifts with his or her spouse) with respect to gifts of present interests.[28] The rules for application of the GST tax annual exclusion to trusts, however, differ in part from those for the gift tax annual exclusion. Eligibility for the gift tax annual exclusion is only the starting point in the analysis of whether a gift is eligible for the GST tax annual exclusion: indeed, under IRC Section 2642(c)(3), the GST tax annual exclusion will apply only in those cases where the gift tax annual exclusion applies.[29] Let us return to the ILIT mentioned in the previous paragraph, created by the insured for the benefit of her grandchildren and more remote descendants. If our sample ILIT contains provisions for Crummey powers, then gifts to it will be of present interests to the extent that the beneficiaries have a right to withdraw the gifts. As the gift tax annual exclusion will apply in this case, so potentially may the GST tax annual exclusion.

Next, IRC Section 2642(c)(2) provides that the GST tax annual exclusion will apply only to direct skips as required by IRC Section 2642(c)(1). We have already concluded that our sample ILIT is a skip person and that transfers to it are direct skips. (If the sample ILIT were created for the benefit of the insured's *children* or more remote descendants, however, it would not be a skip person, since the children are only one generation below the insured. Transfers to the ILIT would not be direct skips, and thus the GST tax annual exclusion would *not* apply, even thought the gift tax annual exclusion would apply.)

IRC Section 2642(c)(2) establishes a further requirement: There may be no more than one skip person beneficiary of the trust. Alas, our sample ILIT does not meet this final portion of the test, as its beneficiaries consist of multiple skip persons. If the insured wishes to be able to use her GST tax annual exemption for gifts in trust to her grandchildren and more remote descendants, she will have to create a separate trust for each beneficiary.

Allocation of GST Exemption   Most ILITs are for the benefit of multiple beneficiaries of various generations and thus will not enjoy the protection of the GST tax annual exclusion. Thus, GST tax will be due on gifts that are direct skips or, where the trust in question is not a skip person, on the eventual termination of an interest in the trust in favor of a skip person (a "taxable termination")[30] or an eventual distribution from the trust to a skip person (a "taxable distribution").[31] Under IRC Section 2631(c), however, every individual is allowed a lifetime GST tax exemption amount, which is currently $2 million.[32] It is generally to the donor's advantage to allocate part of his or her lifetime exemption amount to transfers to ILITs where GST tax eventually may be due: If GST exemption is allocated to the initial transfer and all premium payments to an ILIT, the proceeds of the policy held by the ILIT will pass completely free of GST tax.

Under IRC Section 2632(b)(1), direct skips automatically have GST exemption allocated to them, to the extent that the GST tax annual exclusion does not apply. Under IRC Section 2632(c), GST exemption is automatically allocated as well to transfers to certain "GST trusts." Unfortunately, the definition of such trusts is sufficiently complicated to make it unwise to rely on the deemed allocation rule to determine whether a specific trust meets the statutory definition. Thus, each year a contribution is made to an ILIT with potential GST tax issues, the donor should submit a gift (and generation-skipping transfer) tax return and affirmatively allocate GST exemption to the ILIT or, if appropriate, elect out of the automatic allocation rule.

ILITs: Income Tax Issues

Typically, ILITs are treated as "grantor" trusts for income tax purposes, inasmuch as IRC Section 677(a)(3) provides that a trust will be a grantor trust if trust income can be used to pay premiums on the life of the grantor or the grantor's spouse. Under the grantor trust rules, the ILIT will be disregarded as an entity for income tax purposes, and all income, deductions, and credits associated with the trust will be attributed directly to the insured.[33] The IRS also takes the position that the lapse of a beneficiary's Crummey withdrawal power, including any hanging power,[34] will be taxed as income to the beneficiary under IRC Section 678(a)(2).

Generally, ILITs hold little besides life insurance policies, and the growth on such policies is exempt from income tax unless they are cashed out. Thus, in practical terms, the grantor trust status of an ILIT should have little effect on either the insured or the beneficiaries, as ILITs generate little if any income.

SETTLEMENT TRANSACTIONS

Viatical Settlements

A viatical settlement is the sale of an existing insurance policy on the life of a terminally or chronically ill individual. For purposes of such transactions, a "terminally ill" individual is defined under IRC Section 101(g)(4)(A) as one "who has been certified by a physician as having an illness or physical condition which can reasonably be expected to result in death in 24 months or less after the date of certification." Under IRC Section 7702B(c)(2), a "chronically ill" individual is defined as one who is unable to perform (without substantial assistance from another individual) at least two activities of daily living for a period of 90 days due to a loss of functional capacity, or requires substantial supervision in order to be protected from threats to his or her health and safety due to severe cognitive impairment.

Viatical settlements are often used to provide liquidity for an individual to pay for healthcare costs or lifestyle choices. Qualifying viatical settlements should result in a cash offer of from 50 to 80 percent of the policy death benefit.[35] Under IRC Section 101(g)(2)(A), the proceeds of the viatical settlement are exempt from income tax.

Life Settlements

A life settlement is the sale to a third-party purchaser of an existing life insurance policy for its fair market value, which generally is somewhere between the cash value of the policy and its death benefit. The insured is neither terminally nor chronically ill (as defined above) and thus has a longer life expectancy than an individual seeking a viatical settlement. The insured may be willing to give up the policy because it is no longer needed or because the premium payments have become too much of an economic burden.

The IRS has not yet provided any guidance on the taxation of life settlement proceeds. Many authorities, however, assume that the excess of the settlement amount over the seller's cost basis in the policy will be subject to income tax, though there is some disagreement as to whether the excess will be treated as ordinary income or capital gain.[36]

Investor-Initiated Life Insurance

Programs referred to variously as "stranger-owned life insurance" and "investor-owned life insurance" have sparked considerable controversy within the life insurance and legal communities. These investment vehicles differ from traditional life settlement transactions in that they involve the purchase of a new policy solely as a speculative investment. In marketing such plans, promoters promise "free" life insurance coverage for two years (owing to a third-party recourse or nonrecourse loan) and the subsequent possibility of sharing in the profits when the policy is sold to a life settlement company.

Various states have already declared that the third-party investors in such transactions lack an "insurable interest."[37] Other objections have been raised over promoters' offering prohibited inducements or rebates in marketing such plans. Finally, some insurers have indicated that they will refuse to issue insurance for such plans or rescind policies purchased under such programs. Individuals contemplating the purchase of insurance under these plans should tread cautiously.

LIFE INSURANCE: ISSUES FOR NONRESIDENT ALIENS

The IRC Section 2042 rules on includibility of life insurance proceeds in a decedent's estate apply equally (i) to U.S. citizens and (ii) to non-U.S. citizens holding U.S. residency. Proceeds from an insurance policy on the life of a nonresident alien, however, are not subject to U.S. estate tax, even if the insured possesses all of the incidents of ownership in that policy: under IRC Section 2105, proceeds from an insurance policy on the life of a nonresident alien are not deemed U.S.-situs property, and under IRC Section 2103, only that part of a nonresident alien's estate situated in the United States is subject to U.S. estate tax. Because of the favorable tax treatment of policies on the life of a nonresident alien, the terms of a trust holding such policies can be much more flexible than those of an ILIT. Indeed, the trust need not be irrevocable at all, and the insured may freely reserve the right to change the beneficiaries of the trust.

ANNUITIES

Definitions and Characteristics

An "annuity" is a contract by which an entity or individual (the issuer), in return for a principal sum (i.e., the purchase price or cost of the annuity), makes periodic payments to one or more individuals (the recipient or recipients) for a fixed time period (the term) and/or the life of one or more individuals (the annuitant or annuitants). (As the recipient and the annuitant are, in the great majority of cases, the same individual, we shall assume such in this chapter.)

Annuities making payouts for a fixed period of time are called "fixed-period annuities." Annuities calling for payouts over one lifetime are known as "life annuities" or "single life annuities." Annuities providing for payouts over the lifetime of one annuitant and then over the lifetime of a second annuitant are termed "joint-and-survivor annuities." (Under a joint-and-survivor annuity, the amount paid to the second annuitant may differ from that paid to the first annuitant.)

The first day of the first period for which an annuity payment is received under the contract or the date on which the obligation under the contract becomes fixed, whichever is later, is referred to as the "annuity starting date." On occasion, the annuity contract will call for payment to an individual or individuals (the beneficiary or beneficiaries) upon the expiration of the term or life interest. An annuity can be "fixed" (i.e., each payment to the recipient is a sum certain) or "variable" (i.e., the amounts received may depend on cost-of-living indexes, profits earned by the annuity fund, or earnings from a mutual fund).

Annuities can be categorized also by issuer. Issuers include charitable entities, lotteries, employers, commercial entities (such as insurance companies and financial institutions), and individuals. An annuity purchased from a commercial entity in the business of selling annuities is known as a "commercial annuity." A sale of property by an annuitant to an individual—which individual is not in the business of selling annuities—in exchange for that individual's unsecured promise to make specific, periodic payments to the annuitant for a term of years or (as is more often the case) for the rest of the annuitant's life is known as a "private annuity." In this chapter we shall limit our discussion to commercial and private annuities, as these are the types most often employed in estate planning.

Commercial and private annuities belong to a class referred to as "nonqualified plans." Generally, "qualified plans" are annuities or pensions issued by employers for the benefit of their employees or beneficiaries pursuant to specific requirements outlined in the Internal Revenue Code. Nonqualified plans do not meet these requirements and are taxed differently from qualified plans.

Uses of Annuities in Estate Planning

Though commercial annuities can be used in estate planning, they are employed more often in retirement planning. A typical commercial annuity will provide for regular payments beginning with the date of the annuitant's retirement and lasting until his or her death, after which annuity payments will cease. In other words, the annuity is a vehicle by which the annuitant can ensure that he or she will receive adequate income during retirement. Some commercial annuities, however, provide for payouts after the death of the annuitant, thus combining both retirement planning and estate planning characteristics. Private annuities, on the other hand, are employed almost exclusively in the estate planning sphere.

Commercial Annuities   Although commercial annuities are essentially a vehicle for retirement planning, certain commercial annuities do allow for the term of the annuity to extend beyond the life of the annuitant, thus providing some of the same planning possibilities as those mentioned above for life insurance (e.g., liquidity, income replacement for a dependent, and provision for equalizing distributions). For example, a joint-and-survivor annuity by definition provides for retirement income for the first annuitant and then provides a steady stream of income for the surviving annuitant (who is often the first annuitant's spouse or child). A life annuity with a single payout to a beneficiary upon the annuitant's death can provide such beneficiary with quick cash for the annuitant's funeral expenses. Unlike insurance proceeds, however, at least a portion of (and sometimes all) annuity payments resulting from the death of the annuitant are subject to federal income tax (see discussion below). Thus, from an income tax perspective, annuities are a less efficient vehicle than life insurance for the transfer of assets.

Private Annuities   Unlike commercial annuities, private annuities almost always are purchased for estate planning reasons. In a typical private annuity scenario, the annuitant will transfer an asset to a child in exchange for a promised regular stream of income. Because such transactions are often made within the family unit, private annuities are useful as a vehicle to maintain family control of the transferred asset (e.g., a closely held business). As part of a family succession plan, a private annuity can be used to transfer management, control, and future appreciation of a family business to a relative of a succeeding generation while relieving the annuitant of the risks and cares of management. Furthermore, as described below, private annuities often are employed as a means to deplete the annuitant's taxable estate.

Private annuities thus differ from commercial annuities in that their value as an estate planning vehicle is based not on the possibility of their providing a stream of income or a lump-sum payment after the annuitant's death but rather on the opportunity they provide to distribute assets during the annuitant's life in a manner that is advantageous from a business or tax perspective.

Purchase of a private annuity may prove most useful in depleting the annuitant's taxable estate where the annuitant is in poor health and is not expected to survive for his or her life expectancy under the actuarial tables prescribed by the Treasury Regulations, provided that he or she is not so unwell as to be classified as "terminally ill" under Treasury Regulation Section 25.7520-3(b)(3), which defines an individual as "terminally ill" where there is at least a 50 percent chance that he or she will die within one year.[38] Suppose, for example, that an annuitant in poor health owns a closely held business that she would like to transfer to her son. The annuitant's physicians have certified that there is a greater than 50 percent chance that she will survive one year but less than a 50 percent chance that she will survive four years. According to the tables prescribed by the Treasury Regulations, the annuitant's life expectancy is 10.1 years, and the interest rate for annuities under IRC Section 7520 is 3.5 percent. The annuitant sells property worth $3 million to her son in exchange for his promise to pay the annuitant $360,000 annually until her death. The annuity has a fair market value equal to the value of the property transferred, so there are no gift tax consequences arising from the transaction. The annuitant uses the annuity payments to finance her living expenses. The annuitant dies three years later. Her estate does not include either the transferred property or the private annuity (except to the extent that she had not yet consumed any of the annuity payments previously paid to her). In effect, she has depleted her taxable estate by almost $2 million ($3 million minus the three payments of $360,000 made to her by her son). If the annuitant lives well beyond her life expectancy, however, such a transaction will have negative results both for her (from a transfer tax perspective) and for her son (who will wind up paying back to his mother more than the fair market value of the annuity).

Income Taxation of Annuities

Taxation of Periodic Payments Treasury Regulation Section 1.72-2(b)(2) provides that "amounts received as an annuity" must be periodic in nature, that is, they must be payments made at regular intervals (e.g., monthly or yearly) and for a period exceeding one year.

Under Revenue Ruling 69-74,[39] each annuity payment is divided into three parts: (i) recovery of capital, (ii) gain on capital, and (iii) ordinary annuity income. The "recovery of capital" portion generally is excluded from taxation as the return of the annuitant's adjusted basis in the property with which the annuity was purchased. The "gain on capital" portion is taxed to the annuitant as capital or ordinary gain on the transaction. The "annuity" portion is taxed to the annuitant as ordinary income.

The Revenue Ruling provides this example: An annuitant transfers to his son a capital asset having a fair market value of $60,000 and an adjusted basis of $20,000 in return for a life annuity of $7,200 annually, paid in equal monthly installments. According to the tables prescribed by the Regulations, the annuitant's life expectancy is 10.1 years, and the interest rate applicable to annuities is 3.5 percent.

Under the Revenue Ruling, recovery of capital is based on the calculation of an "exclusion ratio." The exclusion ratio is the "investment in the contract" divided by the "expected return" on the annuity. The "investment in the contract" is defined as the annuitant's adjusted basis in the property,[40] and the "expected return" is defined as the product of the annuitant's life expectancy and the annual proceeds of the annuity, without regard to present value calculations. Once the exclusion ratio has been established, it applies to each payment received by the annuitant until the adjusted basis has been fully recovered, after which time it becomes irrelevant.

With respect to the example just cited, the exclusion ratio is 27.5 percent: exclusion ratio = adjusted basis/expected return = \$20,000/(\$7,200 × 10.1) = \$20,000/\$72,720, = .275. Thus, 27.5 percent of each payment will be excluded from taxable income as a recovery of capital. Of the \$7,200 received by the annuitant annually, \$1,980 (i.e., 27.5 percent of \$7,200) will be excluded from taxable income as a recovery of capital, up to the point that the entire adjusted basis of \$20,000 has been recovered.

Annual gain on capital is calculated by dividing the difference between the present value of the annuity and the adjusted basis by the annuitant's life expectancy. With regard to the example cited, annual gain on capital will be \$2,743.87: gain on capital = (present value – adjusted basis)/life expectancy = (\$47,713.08 – \$20,000)/10.1 = \$27,713.08/10.1 = \$2,743.87. As the property transferred by the annuitant is capital property, the annuitant will report \$2,743.87 of capital gains annually with regard to the annuity until the entire \$27,713.08 of capital gain has been reported.

Ordinary annuity income in any year is the difference between the annuity payment and the sum of recovery of capital and gain on capital for that year. In the example cited, ordinary annuity income will be \$2,476.13 annually until the entire adjusted basis has been recovered and the total gain on capital has been reported: ordinary annuity income = annual annuity payment – (recovery of capital + gain on capital) = \$7,200 – (\$1,980 + \$2,743.87) = \$7,200 – \$4,723.87 = \$2,476.13. After the entire adjusted basis has been recovered and the total gain on capital has been reported, each payment of \$7,200 will be considered ordinary annuity income and taxable to the annuitant accordingly. (If the annuitant dies before all of the adjusted basis has been recovered, and there is no successor annuitant, then, pursuant to IRC Section 72(b)(3)(A), any unrecovered capital at the annuitant's death is allowed as a miscellaneous itemized deduction on the annuitant's final income tax return.)

The excess of the fair market value of the property transferred by the annuitant over the present value of the annuity (i.e., \$12,286.92) will be deemed a gift by the annuitant to his son, which will be subject to the federal gift tax rules: gift = fair market value of asset – present value of annuity = \$60,000 – \$47,713.08 = \$12,286.92.

Regulations[41] proposed by the IRS, however, would dramatically lessen the appeal of annuities by requiring that the gain on capital be realized in the tax year of the initial transaction rather than deferred for the expected lifespan of the annuitant as under Revenue Ruling 69-74. In the example cited from Revenue Ruling 69-74, the effect of Proposed Treasury Regulations Sections 1.72-6(e) and 1.1001-1(j) would be to place the annuitant in the same position as one who had sold his capital asset to a third party for cash and then purchased the annuity with the proceeds. As a result, in the tax year in which the annuity is purchased, he would need to report and pay tax on $27,713.08 (i.e., the difference between the fair market value of the transferred asset and its adjusted basis).

Though the Proposed Regulations apply to both commercial and private annuities, they probably will have a greater effect on the latter, as the former generally are purchased for cash and thus do not present capital gain issues.

Death Benefits   A beneficiary who receives periodic annuity payments on the death of the annuitant will step into the shoes of the original annuitant and pay tax on the distributions as described above. If the beneficiary is entitled to a lump-sum distribution on the death of the annuitant, the distribution generally will be taxable only to the extent it exceeds the unrecovered cost of the annuity contract, pursuant to IRC Section 72(e)(5)(E).

Taxation of Nonperiodic Payments   Cash withdrawals, distributions of current investment earnings (e.g., dividends), loans, and the value of annuity contracts transferred without full and adequate consideration are "nonperiodic payments" and thus do not fall under the definition of "amounts received as an annuity" under Treasury Regulation Section 1.72-2(b)(2).

If the nonperiodic distribution is made on or after the annuity starting date, the entire payment generally is included in the annuitant's gross income, pursuant to Treasury Regulation 1.72-4(d)(3)(i). For example, a cost-of-living increase after the annuity starting date is not considered an amount received as an annuity and thus is fully taxable.

If the nonperiodic distribution is made before the annuity starting date, it is allocated pursuant to IRC Section 72(e)(2)(B) and (3) first to earnings (the taxable portion) and then to recovery of the cost of the contract (the tax-free portion). As a result, the annuitant must include in gross income the smaller of (i) the nonperiodic distribution or (ii) the amount by which the cash value of the contract (calculated without considering any surrender charge) exceeds the investment in the contract immediately before the receipt of such distribution.

Under certain circumstances, cash withdrawals may be subject to a tax penalty of ten percent, pursuant to IRC Section 72(q).

One exception to the rules regarding nonperiodic payments applies where a distribution that fully satisfies the issuer's obligation under the contract is made to the annuitant. In such a case, whether the distribution is made before, on, or after the annuity starting date, the distribution is taxable only to the extent it exceeds the unrecovered cost of the contract, pursuant to IRC Section 72(e)(5)(E).

Deduction for Estate Tax Paid   Under IRC Section 691(d), the surviving annuitant under a joint-and-survivor annuity can deduct from income the portion of total federal estate tax based on the annuity, provided that the decedent died after his or her annuity starting date. Under Treasury Regulation Section 1.691(d)-1, the deduction is made in equal amounts over the survivor's remaining life expectancy.

Guaranteed Payments   As mentioned above, surviving annuitants and beneficiaries generally pay income tax under the same rules as those discussed above for the initial annuitant. One exception applies, however, where the recipient is guaranteed payments under the decedent annuitant's life annuity contract. In such a case, the recipient will not include in taxable income any distributions made to him or her until the value of such distributions plus the tax-free distributions received by the life annuitant equal the cost of the contract, pursuant to Treasury Regulation 1.72-11(c). All further distributions are fully taxed to the recipient.

Estate Taxation of Annuities

If an annuity provides for no further distributions after the death of the annuitant, then the annuitant's interest ends at his or her death, and the annuity is not taxable in the annuitant's estate under IRC Section 2039. If, however, (i) an annuity provides for distributions to a beneficiary _after_ the death of the annuitant and by reason of surviving the annuitant, and (ii) the annuity was payable to the deceased annuitant (or the deceased annuitant "possessed the right to receive" the annuity) either alone or in conjunction with another for a period not ascertainable without reference to the annuitant's death or for any period that did not in fact end before the annuitant's death, then IRC Section 2039(a) provides that all or a portion of the value of the annuity will be includible in the annuitant's taxable estate. For example, in the case of a joint-and-survivor policy providing for payments to end on the death of the surviving annuitant, the value of the annuity to the survivor will be taxable in the estate of the first annuitant to die,[42] but the value of the annuity will not be includible in the taxable estate of the surviving annuitant upon his or her death. Under Treasury Regulation Section 20.2039-1(b)(1)(ii), the "right to receive" an annuity includes any enforceable right to receive annuity payments in the future, even if the decedent at the time of death did not have a present right to receive such payments.

Under IRC Section 2039(b), if the value of an annuity is otherwise includible in the annuitant's taxable estate, and if the annuitant contributed only a portion of the cost of the contract, then only that portion of the value of the annuity corresponding to such contributed portion is includible in the annuitant's taxable estate. For example, if the annuitant had contributed two-thirds of the cost of the contract, and the value of the annuity for the beneficiary is $30,000, then $20,000 is includible in the annuitant's estate.

Facts and Figures

The figures for the top 13 life insurance players in Switzerland were taken from the official statistics for 2005 issued by the Swiss Federal Office for Private Insurance (FOPI) and relate to the direct business of the insurers in Switzerland. We base our analysis of the Swiss market in Chapter 3 on these figures. As the FOPI publishes the figures of a financial year at the end of the following year, we had to rely on the figures for 2005, the most current ones available at the time of printing.

TABLE A.1 Life Insurance Industry of Switzerland in Figures, 2005

	Gross Premiums CHF mio.	Market Share	Group Life CHF mio.	Group Life %	Individual Life CHF mio.	Individual Life %	Straight Life CHF mio.	Market Share	Annuities CHF mio.	Market Share	Unit-linked CHF mio.	Market Share	% of Individual in CH	Staff in CH	Premiums per Capita CHF mio.
1 Swiss Life	7,949	27%	6,121	77%	1,828	23%	1,208	22%	506	40%	113	3%	6%	3,049	2.6
2 AXA/Winterthur	7,206	24%	5,965	83%	1,241	17%	882	16%	125	10%	56	2%	5%	1,290	2.1
3 Basler Leben	2,655	9%	1,814	68%	841	32%	634	11%	151	12%	57	2%	7%	1,354	1.6
4 Zürich Leben	2,200	7%	1,531	70%	669	30%	541	10%	94	7%	34	1%	5%	963	2.3
5 Helvetia Patria	2,179	7%	1,530	70%	649	30%	426	8%	129	10%	93	3%	14%	963	2.3
6 UBS Life	1,601	5%	—	0%	1,601	100%	5	0%	—	0%	1,596	48%	100%	25	64.0
7 Allianz Suisse Leben	1,587	5%	961	61%	626	39%	337	6%	69	6%	219	7%	35%	361	4.4
8 Generali Personenvers.	1,100	4%	44	4%	1,056	96%	319	6%	8	1%	728	22%	69%	686	1.6
9 PAX	870	3%	514	59%	356	41%	192	3%	33	3%	130	4%	37%	340	2.6
10 Genevoise Vie	696	2%	481	69%	215	31%	157	3%	51	4%	7	0%	3%	409	1.7
11 Mobiliar Leben	654	2%	348	53%	306	47%	234	4%	3	0%	68	2%	22%	286	2.3
12 National Leben	430	1%	233	54%	197	46%	161	3%	35	3%	1	0%	1%	271	1.6
13 Vaudoise Vie	218	1%	—	0%	218	100%	157	3%	31	2%	29	1%	13%	63	3.5
AXA Vie	179	1%	47	26%	132	74%	126	0	—	—	6	0	5%	45	4.0
Others	249	1%	77	31%	172	69%	158	3%	19	2%	180	5%	105%	222	1.1
TOTAL	29,773	100%	19,666	66%	10,107	34%	5,537	100%	1,254	100%	3,317	100%	33%	9,364	3.2

Important Contact Information

EDITORS AND AUTHORS

Marco Gantenbein, TEP
Partner
Swiss Annuity Consulting Group
Schifflände 26
8001 Zurich
Switzerland
Tel: +41 44 266 22 40
Fax: +41 44 266 22 41
marco.gantenbein@sacg.ch
www.sacg.ch

Mario A. Mata, TEP
Partner
Cantey & Hanger, LLP
1999 Bryan Street
Suite 3330
Dallas, Texas 75201
United States
Tel: +1 214 978 41 00
Fax: +1 214 978 41 50
mmata@canteyhanger.com
www.canteyhanger.com

Christian H. Kälin, MLaw, TEP
Partner
Henley & Partners AG
Kirchgasse 22
8001 Zurich

Switzerland
Tel: +41 44 266 22 22
Fax: +41 44 266 22 23
christian.kalin@henleyglobal.com
www.henleyglobal.com

Professor Clive H. Church, PhD
Emeritus Professor of European Studies
Centre for Swiss Politics
University of Kent
c/o 72A New House Lane
Thanington Without
Canterbury CT4 7BJ
United Kingdom
Tel: +44 1227 458437
Mobile: +44 7950 666488
Fax: +44 1227 827033
chc@kent.ac.uk
maandchchurch@qtxnet.co.uk
www.kent.ac.uk/politics/research

Peter Fierz, PhD
Knowledge Manager FS
PricewaterhouseCoopers AG
Birchstrasse 160
8050 Zurich
Switzerland
Tel: +41 58 792 44 00
Fax: +41 58 792 44 10
peter.fierz@ch.pwc.com
www.pwc.ch

Peter Lüssi
PricewaterhouseCoopers AG
Birchstrasse 160
8050 Zurich
Switzerland
Tel: +41 58 792 44 00
Fax: +41 58 792 44 10
peter.luessi@ch.pwc.com
www.pwc.ch

Dr. Monica Mächler
Director
Swiss Federal Office of Private Insurance FOPI
Schwanengasse 2
3003 Bern
Switzerland
monica.maechler@bpv.admin.ch
www.bpv.admin.ch

Professor Dr. Moritz W. Kuhn
Attorney at Law
Meyer Müller Eckert Partners
Kreuzstrasse 42
8008 Zurich
Switzerland
Phone: +41 44 254 99 66
Fax: +41 44 254 99 60
kuhn@mme-law.ch
www.mme-law.ch

PD Dr. Joachim Frick, LLM
Baker & McKenzie Zürich
Zollikerstrasse 225
PO Box
8034 Zurich
Switzerland
Tel: +41 44 384 14 14
Fax: +41 44 384 12 84
joachim.g.frick@bakernet.com
www.bakernet.com

Dr. Alexander T. Skreiner
Former Managing Director, CapitalLeben Liechtenstein
Partner
DATS-Consulting
St. Gerold Weg 5
A-6830 Rankweil
Austria
Tel: +43 676 354 49 48
Fax: +43 5522 31 0 77
a.skreiner@gmx.net

Dr. Johannes Gasser, LLM
Attorney at law
Advokaturburo Dr. Dr. Batliner & Dr. Gasser
Marktgass 21
FL-9490 Vaduz
Liechtenstein
Tel: +423 236 04 80
Fax: +423 236 04 81
gasser@batlinergasser.com
www.batlinergasser.com

Maehala R. Nathan
Director
Swiss Annuity Consulting Group
Schifflände 26
8001 Zurich
Switzerland
Tel: +41 44 266 22 40
Fax: +41 44 266 22 41
maehala.nathan@sacg.ch
www.sacg.ch

Frederic J. Gelfond, JD, LLM, MBA
Principal, Financial Services—Insurance
Deloitte Tax LLP
555 12th Street, NW
Washington, D.C. 20004
United States
Tel: +1 202 220 2017
fgelfond@deloitte.com
www.deloitte.com

Glenn G. Fox, Esq., JD., LLM, TEP
Partner
Alston & Bird LLP
90 Park Avenue
New York, NY 10016
United States
Tel: +1 212 210 9544
Fax: +1 212 210 9444
glenn.fox@alston.com
www.alston.com

Paul A. Ferrara, JD., LLM, PhD
Associate
Alston & Bird LLP
90 Park Avenue
New York, NY 10016
United States
Tel: +1 212 210 9517
Fax: +1 212 922 3867
paul.ferrara@alston.com
www.alston.com

SWISS AND LIECHTENSTEIN LIFE INSURANCE COMPANIES

Life Insurance Companies in Switzerland

AIG Life Insurance Company (Switzerland) Ltd.
Via Camara 19
PO Box 132
6932 Breganzona
Switzerland
Tel: +41 91 960 48 48
Fax: +41 91 967 25 15
www.aiglife.ch

Allianz Suisse Life Insurance Company
Bleicherweg 19
PO Box
8022 Zurich
Switzerland
Tel: +41 44 209 51 11
Fax: +41 44 209 51 20
www.allianz-suisse.ch

AXA-Winterthur Life Insurance Company
Paulstrasse 9
PO Box 300
8400 Winterthur
Switzerland
Tel: +41 52 261 11 11
Fax: +41 52 213 66 20
www.axa-winterthur.ch

Basler Life
Aeschengraben 21
PO Box 176
4002 Basel
Switzerland
Tel: +41 61 285 85 85
Fax: +41 61 285 70 70
www.baloise.ch

Convia Life Insurance Company
Pilatusstrasse 23
PO Box 2565
6002 Luzern
Switzerland
Tel: +41 41 227 50 80
Fax: +41 41 227 50 88
www.convia.ch

Forces Vives
Rue Caroline 11
P.O. Box 288
1001 Lausanne
Switzerland
Tel: +41 21 348 31 11
Fax: +41 21 348 23 96
www.forcesvives.ch

Generali Life
Soodmattenstrasse 10
PO Box 1040
8134 Adliswil 1
Switzerland
Tel: +41 44 712 44 44
Fax: +41 44 712 55 55
www.generali.ch

Groupe Mutuel Life GMV
Rue du Nord 5
1920 Martigny
Switzerland
Tel: +41 848 803 111
Fax: +41 848 803 112
www.groupemutuel.ch

Helvetia
St. Alban-Anlage 26
PO Box 3855
4002 Basel
Switzerland
Tel: +41 58 280 1000
Fax: +41 58 280 1001
www.helvetia.ch

Mobiliar Life Insurance Company
54, Ch. de la Redoute
PO Box 302
1260 Nyon
Switzerland
Tel: +41 22 363 94 94
Fax: +41 22 361 78 28
www.mobi.ch

Pax Life Insurance Company
Aeschenplatz 13
4002 Basel
Switzerland
Tel: +41 61 277 66 66
Fax: +41 61 277 64 56
www.pax.ch

Phenix Life Insurance
4, Avenue de la Gare
PO Box 1200
1001 Lausanne
Switzerland
Tel: +41 21 340 04 04
Fax: +41 21 340 04 05
www.phenix-assurances.ch

Skandia Leben AG
Bellerivestrasse 30
PO Box 380
8034 Zurich
Switzerland
Tel: +41 44 388 28 28
Fax: +41 44 388 28 38
www.skandia.ch

Swiss Life
General Guisan-Quai 40
PO Box 4338
8022 Zurich
Switzerland
Tel: +41 43 284 33 11
Fax: +41 43 284 63 11
www.swisslife.ch

Swiss National Life Insurance Company
Wuhrmattstrasse 19
PO Box
4103 Bottmingen BL
Switzerland
Tel: +41 61 425 80 00
Fax: +41 61 425 80 01
www.nationalesuisse.ch

UBS Life
Birmensdorferstrasse 125
PO Box
8098 Zurich
Switzerland
Tel: +41 44 236 99 11
Fax: +41 44 235 47 65
www.ubs.com

Vaudoise Life Insurance Company
Place de Milan
PO Box 120
1001 Lausanne
Switzerland
Tel: +41 21 618 80 80
Fax: +41 21 618 81 81
www.vaudoise.ch

Zenith Life
Avenue Tribunal-Fédéral, 34
1005 Lausanne
Switzerland
Tel: +41 21 721 7000
Fax: +41 21 721 7120
www.zenithvie.ch

Zürich Life
Austrasse 46
8036 Zurich
Switzerland
Tel: +41 44 628 28 28
Fax: +41 44 628 29 29
www.zurich.ch

Life Insurance Companies in Liechtenstein

American Security Life
Landstrasse 38
9494 Schaan
Liechtenstein
Tel: +423 237 68 88
Fax: +423 237 68 89
www.aslife.com

Aspecta
Landstrasse 124
PO Box 101
9490 Vaduz
Liechtenstein
Tel: +423 239 30 30
Fax: +423 239 30 33
www.aspecta.com

Credit Suisse Life
Mühleholz 3
9490 Vaduz
Liechtenstein
Tel: +423 230 17 60
Fax: +423 230 17 62
www.cslife.li

FinterLife
Heiligkreuz 43
9490 Vaduz
Liechtenstein
Tel: +423 237 15 65
Fax: +423 237 15 69

Fortuna Life
Städtle 35
9490 Vaduz
Liechtenstein
Tel: +423 236 15 45
Fax: +423 236 15 46
www.fortuna.li

PKRück
Landstrasse 104
9490 Vaduz
Liechtenstein
Tel: +423 230 19 30
Fax: +423 230 19 31
www.pkrueck.com

Plenum Prudential AG
Zweistäpfle 6
PO Box 320
9496 Balzers
Liechtenstein
Tel: +423 230 16 03
Fax: +423 230 16 05
www.plenum.ch/pp

PrismaLife AG
Industriestrasse 416
9491 Ruggell
Liechtenstein
Tel: +423 237 00 00
Fax: +423 237 00 09
www.prismalife.com

Quantum Life AG
Städtle 17
9490 Vaduz
Liechtenstein
Tel: +423 236 19 30
Fax: +423 236 19 31
www.quantum.li

Skandia Life (FL) AG
Im Hasenacker 32
9494 Schaan
Liechtenstein
Tel: +423 233 48 28
Fax: +423 233 48 27
www.skandia.li

Swiss Life (Liechtenstein) AG
In der Specki 3
9494 Schaan
Liechtenstein
Tel: +423 377 70 00
Fax: +423 377 70 99
www.swisslife.li

Swisspartners Versicherung AG
Feldstrasse 16
9490 Vaduz
Liechtenstein
Tel: +423 239 79 79
Fax: +423 239 79 80
www.sp-versicherung.li

UBS Global Life AG
Zollstrasse 34
9490 Vaduz
Liechtenstein
Tel: +423 239 11 66
Fax: +423 239 11 67
www.ubs.com

Uniqa Life
Neugasse 15
9490 Vaduz
Liechtenstein
Tel: +423 237 56 30
Fax: +423 237 10 19
www.uniqa.li

Valorlife
Heiligkreuz 43
9490 Vaduz
Liechtenstein
Tel: +423 399 29 50
Fax: +423 237 50 19
www.valorlife.com

Vienna-Life
Wagnerweg 6
9494 Schaan
Liechtenstein
Tel: +423 235 0660
Fax: +423 235 0669
www.vienna-life.li

AUTHORITIES AND ORGANIZATIONS

Berufsbildungsverband der Versicherungsgesellschaft (VBV)
Bubenbergplatz 10
PO Box 8625
3001 Bern
Switzerland
Tel: +41 31 328 26 26
Fax: +41 31 328 26 28
vbvinfo@vbv.ch
www.vbv.ch

Federal Office of Private Insurance (FOPI)
Schwanengasse 2
3003 Bern
Switzerland
Tel: +41 31 322 79 11
Fax: +41 31 323 71 56
info@bpv.admin.ch
www.bpv.admin.ch

Federal Office of Public Health (FOPH)
3003 Bern
Switzerland

Tel: +41 31 322 21 11
Fax: +41 31 323 37 72
info@bag.admin.ch
www.bag.admin.ch

Federal Social Insurance Office
Effingerstrasse 20
3003 Berne
Switzerland
Tel: +41 31 322 90 11
Fax: +41 31 322 78 80
info@bsv.admin.ch
www.bsv.admin.ch

Liechtenstein Insurance Association
c/o Fortuna Life Insurance Company
Städtle 35
9490 Vaduz
Liechtenstein
Tel: +423 236 15 45
Fax: +423 236 15 46
office@versicherungsverband.li
www.versicherungsverband.li

Liechtenstein Financial Market Authority
Heiligkreuz 8
Postfach 684
9490 Vaduz
Liechtenstein
Tel: +423 236 73 73
Fax: +423 236 73 74
info@fma-li.li
www.fma-li.li

Money Laundering Control Authority
Christoffelgasse 5
3003 Bern
Switzerland
Tel: +41 31 323 39 94
Fax: +41 31 323 52 61
info@gwg.admin.ch
www.gwg.admin.ch

STEP Switzerland & Liechtenstein
P.O. Box 2521
Baarerstrasse 75
6300 Zug
Switzerland
Tel: +41 41 727 05 27
Fax: +41 41 727 05 21
www.step-switzerland.org

Swiss Insurance Association
C.F. Meyer-Strasse 14
PO Box 4288
8022 Zurich
Switzerland
Tel: +41 44 208 28 28
Fax: +41 44 208 28 00
info@svv.ch
www.svv.ch

Swiss Insurance Brokers Association
Kreuzstrasse 42
8008 Zurich
Switzerland
Tel: +41 44 254 99 70
Fax: +41 44 254 99 60
info@siba.ch
www.siba.ch

Swiss Ombudsman of Insurance
PO Box 2646
8022 Zurich
Switzerland
Tel: +41 44 211 30 90
Fax: +41 44 212 52 20
help@insuranceombudsman.ch
www.insuranceombudsman.ch

OTHER ADDRESSES

Barber Financial Advisors
355 Burrard Street
Suite 1000

Vancouver, B.C. V6C 2G8
Canada
Tel: +1 604 608 61 77
Fax: +1 604 608 2984
info@barberfinancialadvisors.com
www.barberfinancialadvisors.com

Duane Morris LLP
Stanley A. Barg
30 South 17th Street
Philadelphia, PA 19103-4196
United States
Tel: +1 215 979 1913
Fax: +1 215 979 1020
sabarg@duanemorris.com
www.duanemorris.com

Henley & Partners AG
Kirchgasse 22
8001 Zurich
Switzerland
Tel: +41 44 266 22 22
Fax: +41 44 266 22 23
zurich@henleyglobal.com
www.henleyglobal.com

Karp & Genauer, P.A.
Joel J. Karp, Esq.
2 Alhambra Plaza
Suite 1202
Coral Gables, FL 33134
United States
Tel: (305) 445-3545
Fax: (305) 461-3545
jjk@karpandgenauer.com

Millennium Trust Company, LLC
SVP—Alternative Investments
820 Jorie Boulevard, Suite 420
Oak Brook, IL 60523
United States
Tel: +1 630 368 5673
www.mtrustcompany.com

Moses & Singer LLP
Gideon Rothschild, Esq., CPA
The Chrysler Building
405 Lexington Avenue
New York, NY 10174-1299
United States
Tel: +1 212 554 7806
Fax: +1 917 206 4306
grothschild@mosessinger.com
www.mosessinger.com

STEP Worldwide
26 Grosvenor Gardens
London SW1W 0GT
United Kingdom
Tel: +44 20 7838 4890
Fax: +44 20 7838 4886
www.step.org

Swiss Annuity Consulting Group
Schifflände 26
8001 Zurich
Switzerland
Tel: +41 44 266 22 40
Fax: +41 44 266 22 41
info@sacg.ch
www.sacg.ch

Verica Trust & Capital Management AG
Bundesplatz 14
6300 Zug
Switzerland
Tel: +41 41 710 74 75
Fax: +41 41 710 74 75
invest@vericatrust.com
www.vericatrust.com

Notes

Chapter 1

1. Mercer Human Resources Consulting: www.mercer.com.
2. The Fraser Institute: www.fraserinstitute.org.
3. The Heritage Foundation: www.heritage.org.

Chapter 3

1. Schweizer Versicherung, March 2007, p. 7.
2. Schweizer Versicherung, March 2007, p. 8 ff.
3. NZZ am Sonntag, March 25, 2007.
4. Survey by SMC Schmidt Management Consulting AG, see Schweizer Versicherung, May 2007, p. 8 ff.
5. NZZ am Sonntag, June 18, 2006.

Chapter 5

1. VAG; AS 2005, p. 5269 ff.
2. AVO; AS 2005, p. 5305, SR 961.011.
3. AVO-FOPI; AS 2005, p. 5383, SR 961.001.1.
4. SR 222.229.1; AS 2005, p. 5245 ff.
5. Published in HAVE 3/2006, p. 283 ff.
6. Cf. Art. 1 Para. 1 in conjunction with Art. 2 lit. c VAG as well as Art. 1 Para. 1 and Para. 3 AVO.
7. Directive 2002 92/EWG of December 9, 2002.
8. See the section "Legal Duty to Register for Independent Insurance Broker."
9. Retrospectively calculated from the time of registration for the examination.
10. Art. 186 Para. 3 AVO.
11. 2 Art. 186 Para. 4 AVO.

Chapter 7

1. Arizona—Ariz. Rev. Stat. §33-1126A7; Florida—Fla. Stat. Ann. §22.14; Hawaii—Hawaii Rev. Stat §431-10-232; Kansas—Kan. Stat. Ann.

§§60-2313(a)(7), 40-414; Louisiana—La. Rev. Stat Ann. §22-647(B); Maryland—Md. Code Ann. Ins. §16-111; (a) Michigan—Mich. Comp. Laws Ann. §500-2207; New Mexico—N.M. Stat. Ann. §42-10-3; Oklahoma—36 Okla. St. Ann. §3631.1; Texas—Tex. Ins. Code §1108.051

2. 115 N.M. 590, 855 P.2d 1054 (1993).
3. N.M. Stat. Ann. 42-10-2 (Cumm. Supp. 1993).
4. *Thomson v. Lerner*, 25 T.2d 209, 210–11.
5. *In re Payne*, 323 B.R. 723 (9th Cir. 2005).
6. For U.S. citizens, the irrevocable designation of the annuity holder's spouse and/or dependents as beneficiaries and owners of the policy may have adverse gift tax consequences. However, such adverse tax consequences can be avoided if the annuity is owned by a foreign grantor trust that is not subject to the jurisdiction of the U.S. courts or under the control of the policy holder.
7. The U.S. generation-skipping tax is a complex topic that is beyond the scope of this chapter. In summary, in lieu of an estate tax, it is a tax that is designed to apply upon the death of subsequent generations of beneficiaries in what is typically a perpetual trust. The net effect of the GST tax is to tax each generation of beneficiaries of a trust upon their death.
8. The GST exclusion amount will remain $2 million until 2009 when it increases to $3.5 million.

Chapter 8

1. For U.S. citizens, the irrevocable designation of the annuity holder's spouse and/or dependents as beneficiaries and owners of the policy may have adverse gift tax consequences. However, such adverse tax consequences can probably be avoided if the annuity is owned by a foreign grantor trust that is not subject to the jurisdiction of the U.S. courts or under the control of the trust beneficiary.
2. This author acknowledges that not every situation involving the ownership of a Swiss annuity or Swiss life insurance policy will justify the added costs and responsibilities associated with forming and maintaining an international trust to own such Swiss insurance products. As with any planning for an individual, the need for a legal structure and the extent of the complexity of it will vary based on the overall goals of the individual, the amount of the investment, and the domicile of such individual. Ultimately, the person will have to decide the extent of the wealth preservation planning and related strategies, such as the use of a trust, appropriate for his or her particular situation.

Chapter 9

1. See also Swiss Re, sigma no. 3/2003, "Fund-linked life assurance in Western Europe: Recovery in view?" 4f (original in German).
2. Section 43 Permissible assets:

   1) ...

   2) With respect to technical provisions for life insurance policies where the investment risk is borne by the policyholder (Annex 4, section 2, E on the liability side), the following shall apply:

   a) If the benefits arising from a contract are directly linked to the value of units of an investments fund or another special fund, then the technical provisions for these benefits must, to the extent possible, be covered by the respective units or, if no units are formed, by the respective assets.

   b) If the benefits arising from a contract are directly linked to a share index or a reference value other than those enumerated in subparagraph a), then the technical provisions for these benefits must, to the extend possible, be covered either by the units that represent the reference value or, if no units are formed, by assets with appropriate security and realizability that correspond as precisely as possible to those values in which the special reference value relies.

3. See also Swiss Re, sigma no. 3/2003.
4. A detailed overview can be found in ibid.
5. As Liechtenstein insurance companies have no branches or concessions in the United States, contracts may be concluded only when the person liable to tax is resident outside the United States.
6. Directive 2003/48/EG of the Council of June 3, 2003, in the sector on taxation of interest income or the subsequently concluded agreements between Switzerland and the EU or Liechtenstein and the EU.
7. The agreement concluded on December 7, 2004, between the principality of Liechtenstein and the European Community on regulations equivalent to those of Directive 2003/48/EC of the Council concerning taxation of interest income.
8. Art. 78—Exclusion of enforcement and insolvency:

   If the spouse or the descendents of the policyholder are beneficiaries, then, subject to any liens, neither the insurance claim of the beneficiary nor of the policyholder shall be subject to enforcement on behalf of the creditors or to the bankruptcy of the policyholder or the beneficiary. A person living in cohabitation with the policyholder shall be considered equivalent to a spouse.

9. Details and application examples may be found in the next section.

10. Art. 59a Satisfaction of insurance claims:

   1) *The assets covering technical provisions shall constitute a separate insolvency estate in accordance with Article 45 of the Insolvency Code to pay insurance claims. The court shall order that the listing of assets dedicated to the separate estate be concluded immediately and submitted to the supervisory authority. The supervisory authority shall determine the separate estate for the time that insolvency is opened. Reflows and income from the assets dedicated to the separate estate and premiums for the insurance contracts included in the separate estate that are received after insolvency has been opened shall fall into this separate estate.*

   2) *The list submitted pursuant to Paragraph 1 may no longer be changed once insolvency has been opened. The estate trustee may make technical corrections to the listed assets with the approval of the insolvency court.*

   3) *If the proceeds from the conversion of the assets are lower than their valuation in the list submitted pursuant to Paragraph 1, then the estate trustee must communicate this to the insolvency court and justify the deviation.*

   4) *To the extent that insurance claims from the separate estate are not fully satisfied, they shall belong to the first category of insolvency claims.*

   5) *The insurance claims to be found in the account books of the insurance undertaking shall be deemed filed. The right of the creditor to file these claims as well shall not be affected. The filing of claims need not include an indication of ranking.*

11. Art. 45 Konkursordnung—Preferential claims

   1) *Creditors who have claims to preferential payment from specific items of the joint debtor (secured creditors) exclude, to the extent of validity of their claims, rival creditors from payments from these items (special estate).*

   2) *What remains from this special estate after the claims of the secured creditors have been settled flows into the joint bankrupt's estate. If several creditors are entitled to the claims in question, the sums released from these are used to cover the claims in relation to their amounts.*

   3) *Secured creditors who are simultaneously entitled to a personal claim against the joint debtor may concurrently assert their claims as bankrupt's creditors.*

12. See also S. D. Prince Hans-Adam II. von und zu Liechtenstein in S.D. Prinz Nikolaus von und zu Liechtenstein, *Finanzplatz Liechtenstein:*

Beiträge zu seiner Neupositionierung (Zurich: Julian I. Mahari, Publisher, 2001), 28ff.

13. Art. 44 Insurance Secrecy:

   1) The members of the organs of insurance undertakings and their employees, as well as other persons working on behalf of such companies, shall be required to maintain secrecy with respect to facts that are not publicly known and that have been entrusted to them or made accessible to them on the basis of business connections with clients. The secrecy requirement shall not be limited in time.

   2) If, in the course of their official duties, representatives of authorities gain knowledge of facts that are subject to insurance secrecy, then they must maintain insurance secrecy as official secrecy.

   3) Insurance secrecy shall be subject to the legal provisions concerning obligations to testify and to provide information vis-à-vis judicial authorities.

   4) The supervisory authority may grant an exemption to insurance secrecy if a legitimate interest exists, in particular for purposes of fulfilling the legal information requirement of identifying and reviewing insurance risks. In such an event, the supervisory authority shall consult with the Data Protection Commissioner.

14. Law of November 26, 2004, on Professional Due Diligence in financial transactions (Due Diligence Act, SPG) and the ordinance of January 11, 2005 on the Due Diligence Act (Due Diligence Ordinance, SPV).

15. As also noted by Head of Government Otmar Hasler at his press conference on June 27, 2003. on the occasion of the presentation of the positive final report of the International Monetary Fund.

16. The selection was made in June 2007 subjectively by the author and represents neither an assessment nor a recommendation.

17. CapitalLeben Versicherung AG was acquired by Swiss Life and was merged with Swiss Life (Liechtenstein) AG, so that the product range described here continues to be in place.

18. Inter alia: Hans Haumer, "Life Assurance: Wealth Structuring with a Focus on Substance," WealthNews (January 2004).

Chapter 10

1. www.Liechtenstein.li.
2. Anton Schnyder, *Die Schaffung des liechtensteinischen Versicherungsrechts nach dem Beitritt des Fürstentums zum EWR* (Liechtensteinische Juristenzeitung, 2006), p. 98.
3. www.Liechtenstein.li.
4. Bericht und Antrag der Regierung an den Landtag des Fürstentums Liechtenstein, Nr. 82/1995, p. 4.

5. Bernhard Rudisch and Klaus Feuerstein, Eckpfeiler für den "Versicherungsstandort Liechtenstein—Das neue liechtensteinische Versicherungsvertragsrecht" ["Corner Pillars for the Insurance Place Liechtenstein—The New Law on Insurance Contracts"], Versicherungsrundschau 2001/156.

6. Marco Gantenbein, "Swiss Annuities and Life Insurance Versus Asset Protection Trusts," *Trusts & Trustees 2005*, p. 13.

7. Manfred Zobl in Max Boemle et al., "Lebensversicherung als Kapitalanlage" ["Life Insurance as Capital Investment"], *Geld-, Bank- und Finanzmarkt Lexikon der Schweiz* (Zurich, 2002), p. 714.

8. Stellungnahme der Regierung an den Landtag des Fürstentums Liechtenstein zu den anlässlich der ersten Lesung des Gesetzes über den Versicherungsvertrag aufgeworfenen Fragen, Nr. 8/2001, p. 21.

9. Hefti Rudolf in Boemle et al., *Geld-, Bank- und Finanzmarkt Lexikon der Schweiz*, p. 455.

10. Thomas Geraint in John Glasson, ed., *The International Trust* (Bristol, 2003), p. 337.

11. Hans Rudolf Steiner in Francis Neate and Roger McCormick, eds. *Bank Confidentiality* (London, 1990), p. 194.

12. Johannes Gasser and Markus Schwingshackl, "Liechtenstein," in Wouter Muller, Christian Kälin, and John Goldsworth, eds., "Anti-Money Laundering," *International Law and Practice* (June 2007): 347.

13. Heinrich Honsell, Nedim Vogt, and Anton Schnyder, *Kommentar zum Bundesgesetz über den Versicherungsvertrag* (Basel/Zurich, 2001), N 1 seqq. ad Art. 76.

14. Bericht und Antrag Nr. 20/2000, p. 56.

15. Honsell, Vogt, and Schnyder, *Kommentar zum Bundesgesetz,* N 16 ad Art. 79.

16. Stellungnahme der Regierung Nr. 8/2001, p. 25.

17. Honsell, Vogt, and Schnyder, *Kommentar zum Bundesgesetz,* N 16 ad Art. 77.

18. Alexander Bove, "The Swiss Annuity—Is it as good as their chocolate? When asset protection, estate planning and tax deferral come in one box," *Trust & Estates* (March 2007): 53.

19. Maehala Nathan and Marco Gantenbein, "The Annuity Alternative," *The Step Journal* (December 2006): 42.

20. Stellungnahme der Regierung Nr. 8/2001.

21. Bericht und Antrag, Nr. 20/2000, p. 59.

22. Bericht und Antrag, Nr. 20/2000, p. 60.

23. Bundesgesetz über internationales Versicherungsvertragsrecht für den Europäischen Wirtschaftsraum, BGBl. 89/1993, EVSG.

24. Martin Schauer, *Das österreichische Versicherungsvertragsrecht [Austrian Law on Insurance Contracts]*, 3rd ed. (Vienna, 1995), p. 519.
25. The foundation is similar to a trust but is a separate legal entity. It is formed by the founder who endows the foundation with assets for a specific purpose. The founder appoints the members of the foundation council responsible for the foundation's administration and representation and designates the beneficiaries to receive the beneficial interest. After the formation, the founder generally does not hold any rights, powers, or office. He or she, however, may be a beneficiary. In addition, a family foundation can be kept completely anonymous as registration in the public register is not necessary.
26. Johannes Gasser, "Neues zum Internationalen Insolvenzrecht in Liechtenstein," *LJZ* (January 2004): 24 seqq.
27. According to Article 897 of the Liechtenstein Persons and Companies Act, a trustee within the intent of this law is a natural person, firm, or legal entity to whom another (the settlor) transfers movable or immovable property or a right (as trust property) of whatever kind with the obligation to administer or use such property in his own name as an independent legal owner for the benefit of one or several third persons (beneficiaries) with effect toward all other persons.
28. Marxer and Partner, *Companies and Taxes in Liechtenstein*, 8th ed. (Vaduz, 2003), p. 153.
29. Codice Civile, Regio Decreto 262/1942.
30. Legge Fallimentare, Bankruptcy law.
31. Giorgio Cian and Antonio Trabucchi, *Commentario breve al Codice Civile [Commentary on the Italian Civil Code]*, 6th ed. (Padova, 2002), N. 2 ad Art. 1923.
32. Corte di Cassazione, ruling 8676/2000.
33. Stephan Korinek, "Kann für inländische Versicherungsnehmer das Konkursprivileg für Ehegatten oder Nachkommen nach schweizerischem Versicherungsvertragsgesetz gelten?" *Versicherungsrundschau* 5/2000.
34. Karl Kohlegger in Herbert Batliner and Johannes Gasser, eds. *Litigation and Arbitration in Liechtenstein* (Berne, 2004), p. 77.
35. Schuldentriebverfahren or Zahlbefehlsverfahren pursuant to § 577 et seq. Civil Law Procedure Act (ZPO).

Chapter 11

1. One of the most widely accepted definitions of a trust (to be precise, of private express trusts) is the one by Sir Arthur Underhill: "A trust is an equitable obligation, binding a person (who is called a trustee) to deal with property over which he has control (which is called the trust

property), for the benefit of persons (who are called the beneficiaries . . .), of whom he may himself be one, and any one of whom may enforce the obligation." Arthur Underhill and David J. Hayton, *Law of Trusts and Trustees*, 17th ed. (2006).

Chapter 13

1. For ease of discussion throughout this chapter, the term "insurance" is used to refer to both life insurance and annuity contracts. When a reference to one or the other is intended, the terms "life insurance" or "annuity" will be specifically utilized.

2. An exception to this might apply with respect to a distribution from a life insurance contract that is characterized as a modified endowment contract. The fact that earnings held within a contract are not subject to current tax also results in what is referred to as the subsidy benefit of holding a cash value life insurance contract. That is, because the insurance company holds the cash value, it reduces the net amount at risk for the insurance company (i.e., the difference between the cash value and the face amount of the contract). To the extent that the net amount at risk gets smaller over time as a result of the growth of the cash value, it has the impact of lowering the cost of insurance for the insurance company. This process is accelerated as a result of the cash value growing on a pretax basis.

3. Recently enacted legislation, commonly referred to as the COLI Best Practices Act [part of the Pension Protection Act of 2006, Public Law No. 109-280 §863(d)], provides that death benefits received under certain life insurance contracts owned by an employer covering the lives of its employees, and in which the employer is the beneficiary, will not be fully excludable from taxable income. A significant exception to this is described in the text below. The new provisions, however, also add several requirements the employer must comply with in order to fall within the exception.

4. Unless otherwise indicated, all section references contained herein are to the Internal Revenue Code of 1986, as amended (Code).

5. This chapter is intended to provide a discussion of many of the important federal income tax considerations involved in an annuity or life insurance contract purchase or holding, and is necessarily general in nature. It is not intended to address any specific taxpayer situation. It should not be relied on as a substitute for tax advice that should be sought from a qualified advisor with knowledge of all the relevant facts of a given contemplated transaction.

6. The contracts that are the subject of this discussion are assumed to involve the purchase of coverage of U.S.-based risks—that is, U.S. insureds—from a foreign insurance company. As such, the premiums paid to the foreign insurer may be subject to an excise tax. Because this chapter deals only with income taxes, excise tax issues are not covered herein. In addition, there may be withholding taxes imposed by the foreign jurisdiction. U.S. policyholders will need to monitor those issues as well.

7. As discussed in the next section of this chapter, the rules governing the taxation of lifetime distributions and certain other transactions are contained primarily in section 72. An exception to this is contained in section 72(u) dealing with certain annuities held by nonnatural persons.

8. To the extent that payments are made under a life insurance contract due to the death of the insured, such amounts will generally never be subject to tax. See section 101(a). A major exception to this exists with respect to life insurance contracts that are the subject of certain transfers for value as well as certain employer-owned life insurance contracts that are the subject of the recently enacted COLI Best Practices Act.

9. See Tax Equity and Fiscal Responsibility Act of 1982, P.L. 97-248.

10. See Tax Reform Act of 1984, P.L. 98-369 (1984 Act).

11. See Technical and Miscellaneous Revenue Act of 1988, P.L. 100-647 (TAMRA). A contract whose premium payments exceed the maximum amounts calculated under section 7702A's "7-pay" premium test is deemed to be a MEC.

12. From the perspective of an insurance company, for each failure of an insurance contract to satisfy the product tax rules, there are several costs; these include the costs of correcting the failure as well as investigating and repairing the systems that caused the failure. In addition, failure to make the necessary repairs will lead to other costs. Finally, companies may face legal liabilities under state law as well as civil damages and lost consumer goodwill whether they correct the errors or not.

13. For example, as noted below, certain separate account products are regulated under federal securities law. As such, they are subject not just to Code requirements but are also subject to cumbersome Securities and Exchange Commission and National Association of Securities Dealers reporting requirements under the Investment Company Act of 1940 and the Securities and Exchange Acts of 1933 and 1934.

14. From a tax perspective, this terminology is not a meaningless matter of nomenclature. This is actually quite relevant for purposes of determining which contracts would be entitled to insurance tax treatment, as Congress, in enacting the rules governing variable insurance products, took great care to avoid the more common, albeit loose, terms typically

used to characterize these products, including its precise use of the term "segregated asset account" in defining the subject of the diversification requirements described in detail in the text below. Except where the context of this chapter requires more precision, loose reference is made herein to variable or separate account products.

15. The insurance companies offering these products segregate the assets supporting the products from their traditional general account investments supporting their other life insurance and annuity contracts. By segregating the assets, the insurance companies are able to separately account for each of the ledger items (e.g., income, deductions, assets, liabilities) associated with the new products and credit an investment return to the new products based on the separately accounted pool of assets—hence the reference to the term "separate account."

16. This trend began in the late 1950s to early 1960s when state insurance law changes first permitted insurance companies to establish pooled and single customer separate accounts.

17. For example, state laws typically limit the percentage of a general account that may be invested in any one type of asset. In contrast, it is not atypical for the funds in a separate account to be fully allocated to a single type of investment, such as equities, fixed maturity instruments, or real estate.

18. Moreover, most separate accounts today are divided into subaccounts that both offer policy holders a variety of investment options and reduce the administrative costs of the insurance company by not having to establish multiple separate accounts.

19. A more recent use of separate accounts involves the development of modified guaranteed contracts (MGCs). Under an MGC, the insurance company provides a guaranteed return for contracts held to maturity. Upon a surrender of the contract before maturity, however, the policy holder is entitled to a market-adjusted return. These products are not variable contracts for tax purposes. The characterization as a variable product or not does not affect the policy holder in terms of the tax treatment of the holding of a contract that qualifies as an insurance product.

20. The insurance company retains the mortality risk due to the fact that state law requires certain minimum benefit guarantees.

21. In fact, many of the early separate account insurance products were mutual funds that were sold with an insurance policy cover. One popular variation was a product referred to as an investment annuity. Under the investment annuity contract, an individual would purchase the contract from an insurance company. In turn, the insurance company would deposit the premium with an approved custodian at either a bank or

brokerage firm. As long as the assets met two tests—they could be valued and were part of an "approved" asset list—the custodial accounts were considered to be a separate account of the insurance company. Only when policy holders terminated their investment annuities were they subject to tax on the appreciation in their custodial accounts.

22. See, e.g., Revenue Ruling 77-85, 1977-1 C.B. 12 (where an investment annuity contract holder has the power to direct how the assets held by an insurance company are to be invested, then that policy holder is the owner of the separate account; accordingly, the policy holder and not the insurance company is subject to immediate tax on the separate account's current earnings).

23. See Revenue Ruling 80-274, 1980-2 C.B. 27 (here, depositors in certain savings and loan associations could transfer certificates of deposit to an insurance company in exchange for annuity contracts; the Service held that where annuity investors can select and control the certificates of deposit supporting their annuity contracts, then the investors are owners of the certificates of deposit for federal tax purposes); Revenue Ruling 81-225, 1981-2 C.B. 12 (along with describing four situations in which policy holders owned the mutual fund investments underlying their annuity contracts, the Service also identified one example where this was not the case: if (1) a mutual fund is managed by the insurer or one of its affiliates; and (2) the mutual fund shares are only available to policy holders through the purchase of the subject annuity contracts, then the Service should consider the insurance company as the owner of the mutual fund shares); and Revenue Ruling 82-54, 1982-1 C.B. 11 (the Service concluded that they will treat insurers as the owners of mutual fund shares when policy holders exercise only "general" investment control over the mutual funds supporting their annuity contracts; the ruling equated general investment control with an ability to choose among general investment strategies (e.g., between stocks, bonds, or money market instruments); the ruling involved policy holders who were free to allocate their premiums among three funds; we should view this ruling within the context of Situation 3 in Revenue Ruling 81-225). See also Revenue Ruling 82-55, 1982-1 C.B. 12 (the Service found that purchasers of annuity contracts whose funds were invested in a "closed" mutual fund [the funds were no longer offered for sale to the general public] did not own the separate account assets). (Hereinafter these rulings are collectively referred to as the investor control rulings.)

24. *Christoffersen v. United States*, 749 F.2d 513 (8th Cir. 1984), rev'g 578 F. Supp. 398 (N.D. Iowa 1984), cert. denied, 473 U.S. 905 (1985) (here, the 8th Circuit upheld the control theory articulated by the Service in Revenue Ruling 81-225).

25. Section 211(a) of the 1984 Act added section 817(h) to the Code.

26. See H.R. Rep. No. 861, 98th Cong., 2d Sess. 1053–56 (1984).

27. The debate over this issue requires that one look more broadly at the scheme of taxation of insurance products under the Code rather than just to the section 817 diversification requirements. That is, parameters now exist within the Code that make it apparent that Congress intended to occupy this field. Hence, the need for the Service to seek to impose some form of investor control doctrine appears to have waned. Moreover, for the arguably more egregious cases that the Service might be concerned about, there is sufficient body of case law involving economic substance, or substance over form, that further diminishes the need for an investor control theory.

28. Temporary regulation section 1.817-5T.

29. 51 Fed. Reg. 32,633 [T.D. 8101] (Sept. 15, 1986).

30. The final regulations incorporate the Service's positions in Revenue Ruling 81-225 and Revenue Ruling 77-85. See regulation sections 1.817-5(f)(3)(iv) and 1.817-5(i)(2). See generally LTR 9433030.

31. See Revenue Ruling 2003-91 and Revenue Ruling 2003-92.

32. Section 101(a).

33. Here, "term" insurance is loosely used as a reference to the pure insurance component of the contract. More precisely, a term insurance contract typically does not have a cash value component and, by definition, stays in effect only for a limited period of time.

34. The amount excludable is, more precisely, limited to the portion of the death benefit that exceeds the net surrender value of the contract. Since prior earnings on the contract will have already been subject to tax since the time of the contract's failure, the net surrender value would have already been subject to tax. A limited amount may still be subject to tax with respect to increases in the net surrender value that occurred during the tax year in which the death occurs.

35. The practical effect of this is that the future benefits under the contract may not be considered in determining the premium or cash value limits, resulting in lower limits, or greater restrictions on the cash value.

36. Section 7702(b)(1).

37. A higher interest rate is less favorable than a lower rate from a policy holder's perspective, as the higher the interest rate that is utilized, the lower the net single premium, and hence, less opportunity for cash value growth.

38. The Code provides for reliance on either regulations or standard, state prescribed mortality tables for purposes of determining reasonable mortality charges. Since final regulations have never been provided under

section 7702, it is necessary to rely on the state prescribed mortality tables.

39. Including items in future benefits is a positive from a taxpayer perspective, as doing so will have the effect of increasing the cash value limits.

40. The rules setting forth the guideline premium portion of this test are generally found in section 7702(c).

41. The rules setting forth the cash value corridor portion of this test are generally contained in section 7702(d).

42. Section 72(v).

43. Section 72(e)(12).

44. For purposes of the illustration, it is assumed that there are no policy expenses.

45. As provided in section 817(h):

> *For purposes of subchapter L, section 72 (relating to annuities), and section 7702(a) (relating to definition of life insurance contract), a variable contract (other than a pension plan contract) which is otherwise described in this section and which is based on a segregated asset account shall not be treated as an annuity, endowment, or life insurance contract for any period (and any subsequent period) for which the investments made by such account are not, in accordance with regulations prescribed by the Secretary, adequately diversified.*

The rules setting forth the diversification requirements, including those discussed below, are contained in section 817(h) and regulation section 1.817-5.

46. Section 851(b)(3).

47. Unlike the proposed regulations, the final regulations do not require members of an affiliated group to be treated as a single issuer.

48. The legislative history behind the 1984 act similarly does not provide any guidance.

49. From the insurance company's perspective, failure to meet the diversification tests means that the company must determine, and report to the Service, the amount of income earned on the separate account contracts that have now become taxable to the contract holders. In addition, the company may also be faced with severe nontax costs of failure. These might include legal exposure under state or federal insurance or securities law.

50. Section 7702(g).

51. Revenue Ruling 91-17, 1991-1 C.B. 190.
52. A private letter ruling is issued to a single taxpayer with respect to a specific set of facts. Such rulings do not have precedental value for any taxpayer except for the specific taxpayer that sought the guidance provided.
53. Regulation section 1.72-2(a)(1).
54. See, e.g., *Samuel v. Commissioner*, 306 F.2d 682 (1st Cir., 1962); and *Bodine v. Commissioner*, 103 F.2d 982 (3d Cir., 1939).
55. *Igleheart v. Commissioner*, 174 F.2d 605 (7th Cir., 1949); and *Commissioner v. Meyer*, 139 F.2d 256 (6th Cir., 1943).
56. *Igleheart* and Revenue Ruling 75-255. See also section 72(j); and regulation section 1.72-14(a).
57. The discussion above regarding investor control and the diversification applies to annuities as well. As such, those topics are not repeated in this description of the annuity definitional rules.
58. The designated beneficiary is an individual named by the holder of the contract as the designated beneficiary.
59. The rules do not apply to annuity contracts provided under certain qualified and other retirement plans. The rules dealing with those plans, however, contain provisions similar to section 72(s). The rules also do not apply to certain structured settlements.
60. The term "net premiums" for purposes of this calculation refers to the amount of premiums paid under the contract less any policy holder dividends.
61. Regulation section 1.1275-1(j)(2).
62. Regulation section 1.1275-1(j)(6)(iii).
63. Regulation section 1.1275-1(j)(7)(ii).
64. Section 264(a)(1). Personal expenses are not deductible. Life insurance contracts are generally considered to be personal expenses, though some might disagree as it relates to a life insurance contract purchased by a business entity.
65. Section 264. The use of debt to purchase life insurance has been the subject of a great deal of IRS scrutiny and litigation beginning in the 1990s, in particular with respect to certain corporate life insurance transactions involving coverage on large groups of employees. In the mid-1990s, Congress took steps to almost completely eliminate the ability of non-individual taxpayers to deduct interest associated with the purchase or carrying of life insurance policies. This was the most recent of a series of limitations on the ability to deduct such interest that have been added to the Code over the years. The ability of individuals to deduct such interest was terminated in 1986, with the restrictions included in the 1986 Tax Reform Act with respect to personal interest expense.

66. Section 264(e). With respect to these situations, there is a limit on the amount of interest that may be deducted based on rates set forth in the Code.

67. Section 264(a)(2) and (3). Despite the reference to "borrowing of cash value," typically, a policy holder borrows on the security of the cash value rather than borrowing the cash value itself. Technically, "cash value" is an accounting concept that reflects the amount that an insurer has credited to the account of the policy holder and for which it would be liable to pay the policy holder upon the surrender of the contract.

68. Section 264(c).

69. Section 264(d).

70. It should be noted, however, that increases to the cash surrender value of a life insurance contract held by a corporation are included in the calculation of alternative minimum taxable income.

71. Regulation section 1.72-6(a). The concept of investment in the contract is often analogized to the general tax concept of basis. The Service has articulated a position that the two terms might not be analogous. This is based on a position that a taxpayer's basis in its life insurance contract should be reduced by cost of insurance charges incurred during the time the contract is held.

72. An exception to the investment first distribution rule will apply in the event of certain section 7702 "force-out" transactions that occur as the result of certain changes, or reductions in policy benefits. In such case, income on the contract will be deemed to be received first, up to certain limits depending on when in the life of the contract the force-out occurs.

73. Regulation section 1.72-11(d).

74. Section 72(e)(4)(B).

75. Section 101(c).

76. Note that a life insurance contract may be involved in a 1035 exchange for another life insurance contract, an annuity contract, or an endowment contract. It is not possible for a holder of an annuity or endowment contract to exchange such contract for a life insurance contract. Presumably this is because of the more favorable tax treatment accorded life insurance contracts.

77. As opposed to an initial purchase of a policy from an insurance company.

78. Section 101(a)(2).

79. Section 101(g).

80. Section 72(e)(10).

81. A minor exception to the rule relating to pledges and assignments applies if the transaction is undertaken solely to pay certain burial and funeral

expenses and the maximum face amount of the contract is $25,000 or less. Section 72(e)(10)(B).

82. Section 72(v).

83. See generally section 7702A for detail regarding circumstances in which such increases will not be treated as a material change.

84. The rules governing the tax treatment of distributions from and other transactions involving annuity contracts are generally found in section 72 and the regulations thereunder. As noted above, many of these rules are also applicable to certain lifetime distributions from life insurance contracts.

85. As previously discussed, the investment in the contract as of any date is the aggregate amount of premiums or other consideration paid for the contract before such date, minus the aggregate amount received under the contract before such date, to the extent that amount was excluded from gross income.

86. In the case of a divorce, the transfer must occur within one year after the date the marriage ceases or the transfer must be related to the cessation of the marriage. Section 1041(c).

87. The concept of exclusion ratio is discussed below with respect to amounts received as an annuity.

88. The rules governing the tax treatment received upon the death of the insured under a life insurance contract are generally found in section 101. But see the discussion below with respect to the employer-owned life insurance.

89. National Association of Insurance Commissioners.

90. Public Law No. 109-280 section 863(d). These rules are primarily found in section 101(j), brought into the Code as part of this act.

91. Exceptions also exist with respect to contracts under which the death benefits are payable to the insured's beneficiaries or are used to purchase an equity interest in the business from the insured's heirs.

92. For exclusion ratio components, see section 72(b) and (c).

93. Regulation section 1.72-2(b)(3).

94. Regulation section 1.72-4(b)(1)

95. Section 72(b)(3).

96. Regulation section 1.72-11(e).

Chapter 14

1. A "QTIP trust" is a trust for the benefit of a surviving U.S.-citizen spouse that allows the trust assets to qualify for the unlimited estate-tax marital deduction even though the trust assets do not pass outright to that spouse.

2. See, e.g., *N.Y. Ins. Law* § 3212(b)(1).
3. See Georgiana J. Slade, 807 T.M., *Personal Life Insurance Trusts,* at A-3.
4. See, e.g., *Rockwell Est. v. Comm'r,* T.C.M. 1984-654 (holding that an individual's incapacity at death will not negate incidents of ownership otherwise possessed by such individual), *rev'd on other grounds,* 779 F.2d 931 (3d Cir. 1985).
5. Revenue Ruling 75-70, 1975-1 C.B. 301.
6. Revenue Ruling 84-179, 1984-2 C.B. 195.
7. Private Letter Ruling 91-11-028. Under IRC § 6110(k)(3), Private Letter Rulings may not be used as precedent.
8. See the discussion above of issues regarding IRC § 2042.
9. Revenue Ruling 71-497, 1971-2 C.B. 329.
10. See the discussion above of issues regarding IRC § 2042.
11. Even so, the insured could exercise some control over the irrevocable life insurance trust by funding it serially with term policies. Should at some point the trust no longer suit the needs of the insured, he or she simply could (i) let the current policy lapse and (ii) decline to contribute a new policy to the trust. Even if the trust remained intact until the insured's demise, it would have no corpus to distribute.
12. The values given are for 2008 and will be adjusted for inflation in future years pursuant to IRC § 2503(b)(2).
13. See the examples at Treasury Regulation 25.2503-3(c). Even if the ILIT provides for fixed income payments to trust beneficiaries, transfer of a life insurance policy to the ILIT will constitute a gift of a future interest, since the payments will not begin until the death of the insured. See Treasury Regulation 25.2503-3(c), Ex. 2.
14. See Slade, 807 T.M., *Personal Life Insurance Trusts,* at A-12.
15. See, e.g., Revenue Ruling 80-261, 1980-2 C.B. 279.
16. *Crummey v. Comm'r,* 397 F.2d 82 (9th Cir. 1968).
17. Revenue Ruling 81-7, 1981-1 C.B. 474.
18. Treasury Regulation § 20.2036-1(a)(ii) includes in a decedent's taxable estate any property transferred by the decedent in trust over which he or she retained the right "to designate the person or persons who shall possess or enjoy the transferred property or its income...."
19. See Technical Advice Memorandum 96-28-004. It is possible, however, to include in the ILIT a provision granting to the trustee or the grantor the power—*before a contribution is made*—to exclude a beneficiary from having withdrawal power over that contribution. In this way a worrisome beneficiary can be prevented from upsetting the estate plan by exercising his or her withdrawal right. *See* Slade, 807 T.M., *Personal Life Insurance Trusts,* at A-13.

20. The "hanging" or unlapsed portion of the withdrawal power will carry over into future calendar years until its lapse is no longer treated as a taxable gift under IRC § 2514(e).
21. See the discussion above of issues regarding IRC § 2042(2).
22. See the discussion above of issues regarding IRC § 2035(a).
23. See Treasury Regulation § 20.2042.1(c)(4).
24. See the discussion above of issues regarding Private Letter Ruling 91-11-028.
25. See, e.g., *N.Y. Est. Powers & Trusts Law* § 10-10.1 (prohibiting a trustee from exercising a discretionary power to pay income or principal to him- or herself except where limited by an ascertainable standard).
26. See IRC § 2041(b)(1)(A) and Treasury Regulation § 25.2511-1(g)(2) for this and other examples of "ascertainable standard" language.
27. See Treasury Regulation § 26.2612-1(d)(2).
28. The values given are for 2008 and will be adjusted for inflation in future years pursuant to IRC § 2642(c), which piggybacks on IRC § 2503(b)(2). Although IRC § 2642(c) refers to the GST annual exclusion as a "nontaxable gift," we prefer here the term "GST tax annual exclusion" so as to underscore the differences between it and the gift tax annual exclusion.
29. See the discussion above of issues regarding IRC § 2503(b) and Treasury Regulation 25.2503-3.
30. IRC § 2612(a).
31. IRC § 2612(b).
32. The amount shown is for 2008. In 2009, the exemption amount will increase to $3,500,000.
33. See IRC § 671.
34. See the discussion above of issues regarding IRC § 2514.
35. Stephan R. Leimberg et al., "Life Settlements: Risk Management Guidance for Advisors and Fiduciaries," *Estate Planning Journal* (August 2006): 4.
36. See Stephan R. Leimberg et al., "Life Settlements: Tax, Accounting, and Securities Law Issues," *Estate Planning Journal* (September 2006): 3.
37. See, e.g., Re: Life Insurance Transactions (State of N.Y. Ins. Dep't, Dec. 19, 2005).
38. Note that the definition of "terminally ill" for these purposes differs from that (discussed above) employed in the context of viatical and life settlements.
39. Revenue Ruling 69-74, 1969-1 C.B. 43. Although this Revenue Ruling pertains ostensibly to private annuities, its guidelines as outlined here can apply equally to commercial annuities.

40. Under IRC § 72(c)(2), the investment in the contract must be adjusted downward where the annuity contract contains a "refund feature." An annuity contract contains a refund feature if (i) the expected return under the contract depends in whole or in part on the life expectancy of one or more individuals, (ii) the contract provides for payments to be made to a beneficiary (or to the estate of an annuitant) on or after the death of the annuitant or annuitants, and (iii) such payments are in the nature of a refund on the consideration paid. Specific rules for making this adjustment are found in Treasury Regulation § 1.72-7(b), (c), (d), (e), and (f).

41. See Proposed Treasury Regulation §§ 1.72-6(e), 71 Fed. Reg. 61441 (Oct. 18, 2006), and 1.1001-1(j), 71 Fed. Reg. 61441 (Oct. 18, 2006), which, when final, will be effective for transactions initiated on or after October 18, 2006 (for commercial annuities), and April 18, 2007 (for private annuities).

42. Of course, if the surviving annuitant is the deceased annuitant's U.S.-citizen spouse, the value of the annuity passing to the survivor will be eligible for the unlimited estate-tax marital deduction under IRC § 2056(a).

Glossary

Age at entry   The age at entry is a deciding factor in the calculation of a premium when a life insurance contract is being drawn up. It corresponds to the difference between the commencement date of the insurance and the date of birth of the prospective insured person. Age at entry is expressed in whole years with fractions over six months being rounded up to the greater whole year.

Age at term   Age of the insured person at the expiry of the insurance contract.

Annualize   To convert a rate of any length into a rate that reflects the rate on an annual (yearly) basis. This is most often done on rates of less than one year, and usually does not take into account the effects of compounding. The annualized rate is not a guarantee but only an estimate, and its accuracy depends on the variance of the rate. This rate is also known as annualized return and is similar to "run rate."

To convert a taxation period of less than one year to an annual (yearly) basis. This helps income earners to set out an effective tax plan and manage any tax implications.

Accumulated Value   Total of the number of Accumulation Units times the Accumulation Unit Value for a Variable Annuity. Similar procedure is followed in the calculation of the current market value of a mutual fund found by multiplying the number of accumulation units times its net asset value.

Annuitant

1. A person who receives the benefits of an annuity or pension.
2. The person upon whom a life insurance contract is based, in other words, the annuitant is the beneficiary of an annuity or pension.

An annuitant can be the policy holder or someone else to whom the title was designated. Proceeds of the contract are given to the beneficiary upon the annuitant's death in order to protect the beneficiary from a loss of income.

Annuity　A financial product sold by financial institutions (mainly insurance companies) that is designed to accept and grow funds from an individual and then, upon annuitization, pay out a stream of payments to the individual at a later point in time. Annuities are primarily used as a means of securing a steady cash flow for an individual during their retirement years.

Annuities can be structured according to a wide array of details and factors, such as the duration of time that payments from the annuity can be guaranteed to continue. Annuities can be created so that, upon annuitization, payments will continue so long as either the annuitant or their spouse is alive. Alternatively, annuities can be structured to pay out funds for a fixed amount of time, such as 20 years, regardless of how long the annuitant lives.

Annuities can be structured to provide fixed periodic payments to the annuitant or variable payments. The intent of variable annuities is to allow the annuitant to receive greater payments if investments of the annuity fund do well and smaller payments if its investments do poorly. This provides for a less stable cash flow than a fixed annuity, but allows the annuitant to reap the benefits of strong returns from their fund's investments.

The different ways in which annuities can be structured provide individuals seeking annuities the flexibility to construct an annuity contract that will best meet their needs.

Annuitization　The process of converting an annuity investment into a series of periodic income payments. Annuities may be annuitized regularly, over a long or short time period, or, in some cases, in one single payment.

After an annuity has been through the process of annuitization, the investment is said to have been annuitized. Annuitized investments are not necessarily paid out completely to the beneficiaries.

Application　The expression of intention by which the applicant expresses his/her will to conclude a contract in binding fashion, such that a positive counterdeclaration (acceptance) by the recipient is all that is required for the establishment of the contract. The application for concluding an insurance contract is normally initiated by the person interested in obtaining insurance (the potential policy holder). It must contain all objectively significant contractual points (insured perils, insured objects, insured benefits, premiums, inception and duration of the insurance) and any other points that either party considers to be significant. Normally an application form is used to make an application. The General Conditions of Insurance (GCI) are either included in this or are referred to therein. In the latter case, the GCI must be issued to the applicant before submission of the application, as otherwise the application is not binding.

Asset class A group of securities or other investments that exhibit similar characteristics, behave similarly in the marketplace, and are subject to the same laws and regulations. The three main asset classes are equities (stocks), fixed income (bonds), and cash equivalents (money market instruments).

In addition to the three main asset classes, some investment professionals would add real estate and commodities, and possibly other types of investments, to the asset class mix. Whatever the asset class lineup, each one is expected to reflect different risk and return investment characteristics, and will perform differently in any given market environment.

Asset classes and asset class categories are often mixed together. In other words, describing large-cap stocks or short-term bonds asset classes is incorrect. These investment vehicles are asset class categories, and are used for diversification purposes.

Average return The simple mathematical average of a series of returns generated over a period of time. An average return is calculated the same way a simple average is calculated for any set of numbers; the numbers are added together into a single sum, and then the sum is divided by the count of the numbers in the set.

Banking secrecy See *secrecy*.

Bankruptcy A proceeding in a court in which an insolvent debtor's assets are liquidated and the debtor is relieved of further liability.

Beginning value The market value of a portfolio at the inception of the period being measured by the customer statement.

Benchmark A standard against which the performance of a security, mutual fund, or investment manager can be measured. Generally, broad market and market-segment stock and bond indexes are used for this purpose.

Beneficiary The beneficiary, who may be either a natural person or a legal entity, has an expected entitlement to the insured benefits. The beneficiary is specified by the policy holder and may be named as the beneficiary of the entire sum insured or of a proportion thereof.

Broker An individual or firm that acts as an intermediary between a buyer and seller. Insurance brokers are usually remunerated by commissions from the insurance companies. By arranging an insurance through a broker, the clients pay no more in premiums than going directly to the insurance company. Rather, the clients save time and money because they benefit from the broker's comprehensive advisory and support services.

Capital sum insurance This form of insurance provides for the payment of the insured benefit in the form of a capital sum (a single payment), the amount of which is stipulated in the insurance contract.

Commission Insurance brokers are remunerated by commissions from the insurance companies. Such commissions as well as other administrative costs/fees are included in the calculations of the insurance company. There are no extra fees and, in case of Swiss annuity and life insurance, there are practically no penalties for cancellation of the policy even after a short period of time.

Conclusion Establishment of the insurance contract subsequent to acceptance of the application by the insurer.

Contingent beneficiary The person or persons designated to receive the death benefit if the primary beneficiary dies prior to the death of the insured.

Contract A binding agreement between two or more parties for performing, or refraining from performing, some specified act(s) in exchange for lawful consideration.

Contract date The date of issue of the contract.

Creditor protection The legal safeguards that prohibit any person or governmental authority from seizing a life insurance or annuity policy that is governed by insurance laws.

Currency risk (exchange rate risk) The risk that a business's operations or an investment's value will be affected by changes in currency exchange rates. For example, if money must be converted into a different currency to make a certain investment, changes in the value of the currency relative to the home currency will affect the total loss or gain on the investment when the money is converted back. This risk usually affects businesses, but it can also affect individual investors who make international investments.

Death benefit The amount on a life insurance policy or pension that is payable to the beneficiary when the annuitant dies.

Deferred annuity A type of annuity contract that delays payments of income, installments or a lump sum, until the investor elects to receive them. This type of annuity has two main phases, the savings phase in which you invest money into the account, and the income phase in which the plan is converted into an annuity and payments are received.

A deferred annuity can be either variable or fixed.

This type of annuity also provides a death benefit, so that the beneficiary of the annuity is guaranteed the principal and the investment earnings.

Deferred fixed-term annuity Annuity payments begin after a deferral period predefined by the owner if the insured person is alive at that date. Payments end with the death of the insured person or, at the latest, at the time fixed by the owner.

Deferred life annuity Annuity payments start after the end of a deferral period, predefined by the owner (provided the insured person is alive at that date), and continue throughout the lifetime of the insured person.

Diversification A risk-management technique that mixes a wide variety of investments within a portfolio. The rationale behind this technique contends that a portfolio of different kinds of investments will, on average, yield higher returns and pose a lower risk than any individual investment found within the portfolio.

Diversification strives to smooth out unsystematic risk events in a portfolio so that the positive performance of some investments will neutralize the negative performance of others. Therefore, the benefits of diversification will hold only if the securities in the portfolio are not perfectly correlated.

Studies and mathematical models have shown that maintaining a well-diversified portfolio of 25 to 30 stocks will yield the most cost-effective amount of risk reduction. Investing in more securities will still yield further diversification benefits, albeit at a drastically smaller rate.

Further diversification benefits can be gained by investing in foreign securities because they tend to be less closely correlated to domestic investments. For example, an economic downturn in the U.S. economy may not affect Switzerland's economy in the same way. Therefore, having Swiss investments would allow an investor to have a small cushion of protection against losses due to an American economic downturn.

Most noninstitutional investors have a limited investment budget, and may find it difficult to create an adequately diversified portfolio. This fact alone can explain why mutual funds have been increasing in popularity. Buying shares in a mutual fund can provide investors with an inexpensive way of diversification.

Duration of a contract The period of time from conclusion of the contract until expiry of the contract.

Endowment life insurance Endowment insurance is one type of life insurance. It not only guarantees benefits in the event of premature death, but also when the insured person is still alive at the term of the contract. It combines insurance protection with a savings plan for the policy owner. Endowment policies usually have a fixed maturity date. Typical maturities are 10, 15, and 20 years up to a certain age limit.

Exchange rate risk See *currency risk.*

Exempt assets Property that a debtor is allowed to retain, free from the claims of creditors who do not have liens on the property. All the property of a debtor that is not attachable under bankruptcy law.

Expense

1. The economic costs that a business incurs through its operations to earn revenue. In order to maximize profits, businesses must attempt to reduce expenses without also cutting into revenues. Since expenses are such an important indicator of a business' operations, there are specific accounting rules on expense recognition. Expenses are the opposite of revenues. Examples of expense include payments to suppliers, employee wages, factory leases, and depreciation.
2. Money spent or costs incurred that are tax deductible and reduce your taxable income.

Face amount   The amount stated on the face of a life insurance policy that will be paid in case of death or at the maturity of the contract. The face amount does not include dividends.

Financial center   See *international financial center.*

Fixed annuity   A contract that allows you to accumulate earnings at a fixed rate during a build-up period.

You pay the required premium, either in a lump sum or in installments. The insurance company invests its assets, including your premium, so it will be able to pay the rate of return that it has promised to pay.

Among the alternatives is receiving a fixed amount of income in regular payments for your lifetime or the lifetimes of yourself and a joint annuitant. That is called annuitization. Or you may select some other payout method.

The insurance company assumes the risk that you could outlive your life expectancy and therefore collect income over a longer period than it anticipated.

Fixed-term annuity   Annuity payments are made for a fixed number of years determined by the owner (five years minimum).

Fraudulent conveyance (fraudulent transfer)   A fraudulent conveyance is a civil cause of action. It arises in debtor/creditor relations, particularly with reference to insolvent debtors. The cause of action is typically brought by creditors or by bankruptcy trustees. The usual fact situation involves a debtor who donates his or her assets, normally to an "insider," and leaves him- or herself nothing to pay creditors as part of an asset protection scheme. However, it is not uncommon to see fraudulent conveyance applications in relation to bona fides transfers, where the bankrupt parties have simply been more generous than they should have or, in business transactions, the business should have ceased trading earlier to avoid giving certain business creditors an unfair preference (see generally *wrongful trading*). If prosecuted successfully, the plaintiff is entitled to recover the property transferred or its value from the transferee who has received a gift of the debtor's assets.

Fraudulent transfer   See *fraudulent conveyance.*

Going naked   Professionals in high-liability professions (such as lawyers, medical doctors, etc.) who go without malpractice insurance are sometimes described as "going naked."

Guaranteed interest amount   The minimum interest rate under Swiss insurance law that an insurance company can pay on an annuity contract.

Immediate annuity   Immediate annuities convert a sum of money to a source of regular income. One way they are frequently used is as a source of retirement income.

You buy an immediate annuity contract with a lump-sum purchase. You begin receiving income from the annuity either right away or within a specific period of time.

A fixed immediate annuity guarantees the amount of income you will receive in each payment, based on the claims paying ability of the insurance company selling the contract.

A variable immediate annuity pays income based on the performance of the annuity funds, or subaccounts, you select from those available through the contract.

Immediate fixed-term annuity   Annuity payments begin immediately and end after a specified period, but not later than the death of the insured person.

Immediate income life annuity   Annuity payments start immediately and continue throughout the lifetime of the insured person.

Immediate payment annuity   An annuity contract that is purchased with one payment and has a specified payment plan which starts immediately.

Insurance company   See *insurer.*

Insurance secrecy   See *secrecy.*

Insured person   The person whose life is covered by an insurance policy.

Insurer (insurance company)   A financial institution that is in the business of selling contracts to indemnify losses for a premium.

Inflation   In the mainstream economics, the word "inflation" refers to a general rise in prices measured against a standard level of purchasing power. Previously the term was used to refer to an increase in the money supply, which is now referred to as expansionary monetary policy or monetary inflation. Inflation is measured by comparing two sets of goods at two points in time and computing the increase in cost not reflected by an increase in quality.

International financial center A term used to refer to a jurisdiction or particular city where major providers of cross-border fiduciary services, banking, and insurance as well as securities exchanges are located. Besides the large international financial centers (IFCs) such as, for example, New York, London, Switzerland, Hong Kong, and Tokyo, many smaller jurisdictions or "offshore" jurisdictions are often also referred to as IFCs.

Investment Investment or investing is a term with several closely related meanings in business management, finance, and economics related to saving or deferring consumption. An asset in usually purchased, or equivalently a deposit is made in a bank, in hopes of getting a future return or interest from it. Literally, the word means the "action of putting something in to somewhere else" (perhaps originally related to a person's garment, or "vestment").

Investment portfolio See *portfolio.*

Irrevocable beneficiary A beneficiary designation that can be changed only with the permission of the beneficiary.

Irrevocable trust A legal arrangement used by people in high-liability professions to thwart malpractice claims.

IRS Form 720 The tax form used to report the purchase of any foreign annuity to the Internal Revenue Service. A 1 percent excise tax is due on the initial purchase price of the annuity. However, Swiss annuities are exempt from the 1 percent U.S. excise tax.

Joint life annuity An annuity issued on two individuals under which payments continue in whole or in part until both individuals die.

Life annuity, "X" years certain Annuity payments are made as long as the insured person is alive. Annuity payments are made for a guaranteed minimum number of years, determined by the owner. If the insured person dies during this period, payments continue to the beneficiary for the rest of the period. If the insured person survives this period, payments continue for life.

Life expectancy The time span of how long a particular person is expected to live. Life expectancy is the average number of years a human has before death, conventionally calculated from the time of birth, but also can be calculated from any specified age.

Life insurance A contract you sign with an insurance company, obligating it to pay a benefit of a certain value in case of death or disability. Life insurance can also be used just for saving reasons.

You may select either term or permanent (whole life) insurance. With a term policy, you are insured for a specific period of time. When the term ends, you must renew the policy for another term or change your coverage. Otherwise, you are no longer insured. With a permanent or whole life policy, you can buy coverage for your lifetime.

You pay an annual premium, typically billed monthly or quarterly, for the coverage. The insurer sets the cost, based on your age, health, lifestyle, and other factors. With a permanent policy, your premium is fixed, but with a term policy it typically increases when you renew your coverage to reflect the fact that you are older.

Lifetime payments   An annuitization option that provides fixed monthly payments guaranteed to last for the life of the annuitant.

Liquidity   The ability of an asset to be converted into cash quickly and without any price discount. All capital, plus all accumulated interest and dividends, is freely accessible. Depending on the type of annuity, a minimal penalty in case of withdrawal applies only to an initial period of up to one year. So if funds are needed quickly, they are available and not tied down for a fixed period of time. Furthermore, all Swiss banks will accept Swiss life insurance policies as collateral. Swiss annuities offer instant liquidity.

Loan provision   A provision in Swiss insurance and annuity contracts that allows the owner to borrow up to 90 percent of the cash surrender value of the policy.

Lump sum   A sum of money settled in a single payment.

Market   A social arrangement that allows buyers and sellers to discover information and carry out a voluntary exchange of goods or services. It is one of the two key institutions that organize trade, along with the right to own property. In everyday usage, the word "market" may refer to the location where goods are traded, sometimes known as a marketplace, or to a street market.

Maturity   Date at which an insurance policy is due for payment.

Mortality tables   An actuarial table indicating life expectancy and probability of death.

Mutual fund   A form of collective investment that pools money from many investors and invests their money in stocks, bonds, short-term money market instruments, and/or other securities.

In a mutual fund, the fund manager trades the fund's underlying securities, realizing capital gains or losses, and collects the dividend or interest income. The investment proceeds are then passed along to the individual investors. The value of a share of the mutual fund, known as the net asset value per share (NAV), is calculated daily based on the total value of the fund divided by the number of shares currently issued and outstanding.

Offshore Generally means a jurisdiction/country other than one's home jurisdiction. The term often is used, however, to refer to jurisdictions that specialize in certain international financial services, in particular fiduciary services, administration of investment funds, banking. and insurance.

Offshore private placement variable universal life insurance (OPPVULI or more commonly offshore PPLI) A variable universal life insurance policy that is offered by a foreign insurance company on a private placement basis, and which is highly customized for the specific needs of the policy holder. See also *private placement life insurance.*

Pension annuity Benefit paid out periodically. Payment may be limited in time as in a temporary pension. Alternatively, it may be payable up to the death of the insured person as in the case of old-age pensions.

Policy A private document setting out the rights and obligations of the parties, issued by the insurer to the policy holder. The policy serves as proof that an insurance contract has been concluded and of its contents.

Policy holder The contractual partner (individual or group) of the insurer.

Portfolio A collection of investments held by an institution or a private individual. In building up an investment portfolio, a financial institution typically conducts its own investment analysis, while a private individual may make use of the services of a financial advisor or a financial institution that offers portfolio management services. Holding a portfolio is part of an investment and risk-limiting strategy called diversification. By owning several assets, certain types of risk (in particular specific risk) can be reduced. The assets in the portfolio could include stocks, bonds, options, warrants, gold certificates, real estate, futures contracts, production facilities, or any other item that is expected to retain its value.

Portfolio bond Another term for a variable annuity/life insurance product that functions as a holding vehicle through which an investor can structure a tailor-made portfolio of investments.

Preferred claim under bankruptcy Pursuant to the Swiss federal law on insurance contracts, beneficiary entitlements shall cease if the insurance benefits are pledged or if bankruptcy proceedings are instigated against the policy holder. The entitlements shall be reinstated if the pledge lapses or bankruptcy is revoked. An important exception to this rule is the case of a preferred claim under bankruptcy. In this situation, the life insurance policy is not considered part of the estate during bankruptcy proceedings if the primary beneficiaries are the spouse or the children. Thus insurance coverage may be maintained for the family.

Premium The price that the policy holder pays to the insurer in return for which the agreed benefits are provided in the event of a claim. The premium is generally calculated for a period of insurance, a year unless otherwise specified, even if other payment methods are agreed (e.g. monthly installments, single premium).

Premium payer Any individual or business that pays premiums to the insurer.

Premium refund Used mostly in connection with old-age pensions. It implies that, in the event of the insured person's death, the premiums paid or the single life insurance premium (without interest) are paid out—after deduction of any pension payments already made—to the person designated as beneficiary in the contract's beneficiary clause. Premium refund also exists in life insurance. On the death of the insured person, the premiums already paid are refunded, also without interest.

Primary beneficiary The individual first designated to receive the proceeds of an insurance policy. There can be more than one primary beneficiary.

Private letter ruling A written statement issued to a taxpayer by the U.S. Internal Revenue Service that interprets and applies the tax laws to a specific set of facts described in the letter ruling request. Under U.S. Internal Revenue Code Section 6110(k)(3), private letter rulings may not be used as precedent.

Private placement life insurance (PPLI) A very effective wealth-building and tax management strategy for high-net-worth, accredited investors. It is best utilized as an income tax management tool and investment tool that fits into an integrated estate plan.

PPLI utilizes a highly specialized insurance policy customized exactly to the needs of the insured and his/her estate.

Private placement deferred variable annuity (PPDVA) A variable annuity with annuity payments initially deferred that is offered by a foreign insurance company on a private placement basis, and that is typically customized to the specific needs of the policy holder. From the asset protection viewpoint, the hoped-for advantage is that the creditor will not be able to garnish payments until the deferral period ceases and the annuity payments begin.

Rating In general, the evaluation or assessment of something, in terms of quality (as with a critic rating a novel), quantity (as with an athlete being rated by his or her statistics), or some combination of both.

In insurance/financial services, a credit rating assesses the creditworthiness of an individual, corporation, or even a country. Credit ratings are calculated from financial history and current assets and liabilities. Typically, a credit rating tells a lender or investor the probability of the subject being able to pay back a loan. Credit ratings are also used to adjust insurance premiums, determine employment eligibility, and establish the amount of a utility or leasing deposit.

Rate of return   The gain or loss of an investment over a specified period, expressed as a percentage increase over the initial investment cost. Gains on investments are considered to be any income received from the security, plus realized capital gains.

A rate of return measurement can be used to measure virtually any investment performance, from real estate to bonds and stocks to even things such as fine art, provided the asset is purchased at one point in time and then produces cash flow at some time in the future. Financial securities are commonly judged based on their past rates of return, which can be compared against assets of the same type to determine which investments are the most attractive.

Revenue Ruling   Revenue Rulings represent the U.S. Internal Revenue Service's official interpretation of the U.S. Internal Revenue Code as it applies to a particular set of facts.

Revocable beneficiary   A beneficiary designation that may be changed by the policy holder without the consent of the existing beneficiary.

Risk   The uncertainty of future rates of return, which includes the possibility of loss. This variability or uncertainty causes "rational" investors to expect higher returns on investments where the actual timing or amount of payoffs is not guaranteed.

Risk evaluation   Determination of the declared risks and any additional investigations such as medical examinations, in order to decide whether an application for insurance may be accepted and, if so, whether it should be accepted under normal conditions or with restrictions imposed. The applicant's acceptance period gives the insurer time to carry out this evaluation.

Risk insurance   In risk (or term life) insurance, the insurer does not pay benefits if the insured risk (death or disability) does not occur during the duration of the contract. In contrast to whole life insurance, risk insurance contains no savings element.

Risk premium   The difference between a rate of return and the risk free rate of return is a risk premium. Risk premiums may be calculated for a particular security, a class of securities, or a market.

ROI   Return on investment.

Secrecy—banking secrecy, insurance secrecy   "Banking secrecy" refers to the professional discretion of the banks, their representatives and employees in the business matters of their clients, or third parties, of whom they have gained knowledge in the performance of their duties. The same criminal and civil penalties for violation of a client's privacy imposed on all Swiss bank employees also apply to insurance company employees and brokers for life.

Security   An investment instrument, other than an insurance policy or fixed annuity, issued by a corporation, government, or other organization that offers evidence of debt or equity.

Single life annuity   An annuity that provides income benefits for one person only.

Single-premium life insurance   Whole life insurance requiring one initial lump-sum payment.

Surplus participation of insured persons   Within the context of a life insurance contract, the benefits and premiums are guaranteed for the whole duration of the contract. Care is therefore necessary when calculating the amount of the premiums, and factors such as mortality, disability risk, changes in interest rates, and costs all have to be considered. As a general rule, the risk trend and interest income performance turn out better than forecast. This is why life insurance companies offer policy holders a share (participation) in the company's surplus as a kind of compensation for an overcontribution. The right to surplus participation is given after one to three years of insurance, and the policy holder's participation in the company's surplus may be arranged on the basis of different systems. The shares of surplus may be used as:

- Accrual with interest
- Increase in insurance benefits
- Reduction in premiums

Surrender   The early termination of an insurance product by the policy holder.

Surrender charge   A penalty for liquidating an insurance or annuity contract early in the deferral period.

Technical Advice Memorandum   Written statements furnishing advice prepared by particular U.S. Internal Revenue Service divisions in response to requests from and primarily for the use of U.S. Internal Revenue Service field personnel during the examination stage of a tax controversy. Under U.S. Internal Revenue Code Section 6110(k)(3), Technical Advice Memoranda may not be used as precedent.

Technical interest   The guaranteed minimum interest rate over the total duration of the contract applied to the savings component of the premium for cash value insurance policies. If more than the technical interest is earned, this is often credited to the policy holder in the form of a participation in surplus.

Temporary life annuity   This form of insurance guarantees the payment of a number of prearranged periodical installments on the condition, however, that the insured person is still alive. Payment of the annuities ends on the death of the insured person or when the number of agreed installments has been paid. This kind of insurance can be financed either by periodical premiums or by a single premium. Temporary life annuity insurance is of interest to those who are only looking for benefits paid during their lifetime and income paid over a given period.

Term   In term life (or risk) insurance, the insurer does not pay benefits if the insured risk (death or disability) does not occur during the duration of the contract. In contrast to whole life insurance, risk insurance contains no savings element.

A term is also the length of time between when a fixed-income security, such as a bond or note, is offered for sale and its maturity date.

Variable annuity   An insurance product designed to allow you to accumulate retirement savings.

When you purchase a variable annuity, either with a lump sum or with periodic payments, you allocate the premiums you pay among the various separate account funds offered in your annuity contract.

The (possibly tax-deferred) return on your variable annuity fluctuates with the performance of the underlying investments in your separate account funds, sometimes called investment portfolios or subaccounts.

Withdrawal   The removal of part of the cash value from a life insurance policy or annuity contract.

Whole life insurance   Life insurance that provides coverage for an individual's whole life, rather than a specified term.

1035 exchange   An IRS-approved, tax-free transfer of funds from one insurance policy to another insurance policy, from an insurance policy to an annuity, or from one annuity to another annuity.

Bibliography

Adkisson, Jay D., and Christopher M. Riser. *Asset Protection—Concepts & Strategies for Protecting Your Wealth* (2004).

Aviss, Darell. *Strategies for Protecting Wealth* (2006).

Barber, Hoyt. *Secrets of Swiss Banking: An Owner's Manual to Quietly Building a Fortune* (2008).

Barber, Hoyt. *Tax Havens: How to Bank, Invest, and Do Business—Offshore and Tax Free* (1992).

Barber, Hoyt. *Tax Havens Today: The Benefits and Pitfalls of Banking and Investing Offshore* (2007).

Beattie, David. *Liechtenstein—History & the Present* (2005).

Bove, Alexander. "The Swiss Annuity: Is it as good as their chocolate? When asset protection, estate planning and tax deferral come in one box," *Trusts & Estates* (2007).

Brody, Lawrence, et al. "Compensating Employees with Insurance," *Tax Management Portfolio* 386-3rd (2007).

Budin, Beverly R. "Life Insurance," *Tax Management Portfolio* 826-2nd (2006).

Choate, Natalie. *Life and Death Planning for Retirement Benefits*, 6th ed. (Ataxplan Publications, 2006).

Gaugler, Hans. *Die paulianische Anfechtung unter besonderer Berücksichtigung der Lebensversicherung*, Band 2 (1945).

Icon Group International, Inc./Services Industries Research Group. *Insurance Services in Switzerland: A Strategic Entry Report* (2000).

Jungo, Daniel, and Wolfgang Maute. *Lebensversicherungen und Steuern* (2003).

Kälin, Christian H. *Switzerland Business and Investment Handbook* (2006).

Korinek, Stephan: "Kann für inländische Versicherungsnehmer das Konkursprivileg für Ehegatten oder Nachkommen nach schweizerischem Versicherungsvertragsgesetz gelten?" *Versicherungsrundschau* (2000).

Küng, Rudolf, in Heinrich Honsell, Nedim Peter Vogt, and Anton K. Schnyder (Hrsg.), *Kommentar zum schweizerischen Privatrecht, Bundesgesetz über den Versicherungsvertrag* (2001).

Lee, Gary R., *et al.*, *Life Insurance—A Practical Guide for Evaluating Policies, Tax Management Portfolio* 827 (2004).

Liechtenstein Bank Association. *Finanzplatz Liechtenstein—eine Dokumentation*, Publication series of the Liechtenstein Bank Association no. 2, 2003

Loury, Kirk. *The PPLI Solution: Delivering Wealth Accumulation, Tax Efficiency, and Asset Protection through Private Placement Life Insurance* (2005).

Mackenzie, George A. (Sandy). *Annuity Markets and Pension Reform* (2006).

Marxer, Wilfried. *Liechtensteins Wohlstand—wie er entstanden ist: eine Literatur-analyse [Swiss Private Insurance Law]* (2002).

Maurer, Alfred. *Schweizerisches Privatversicherungsrecht*, 3. Auflage, 1995

McCord, William T., and Donald J. Moine. *Better Than Gold: An Investor's Guide to Swiss Annuities* (1998).

Muller, Wouter, Christian H. Kälin, and John Goldsworth. *Anti-Money Laundering: International Law and Practice* (2007).

Nathan, Maehala, and Marco Gantenbein. "The Annuity Alternative," *STEP Journal* (2007).

Pehrson, Gordon O., *et al*. Annuities, Life Insurance, and Long-Term Care Insurance Products, *Tax Management Portfolio 546* (2007).

Pfleiderer, Andrea. *Die Überschussbeteiligung in der Lebensversicherung* (2005).

Roelli, Hans, and Carl Jaeger. *Kommentar zum Schweizerischen Bundesgesetz über den Versicherungsvertrag [Commentary on the Swiss Law on Insurance Contracts]*, 3. Band, 1933

Rudisch, Bernhard, and Klaus Feurstein. "Eckpfeiler für den 'Versicherungsstandort Liechtenstein—Das neue liechtensteinische Versicherungsvertragsrecht [Corner Pillars for the Insurance Place Liechtenstein—The New Law on Insurance Contracts]," *Versicherungsrundschau* (2001).

Schnyder, Anton. "Die Schaffung des liechtensteinischen Versicherungsrechts nach dem Beitritt des Fürstentums zum EWR [The Creation of the Liechtenstein Insurance Law after Joining the EEA]," *Liechtensteinische Juristenzeitung (LJZ)* (2006).

Simon, Silvia. "Der Kleinstaat Liechtenstein im Zeitalter der Globalisierung," Papers from the Liechtenstein Institute no. 34 (Vaduz 2006).

Slade, Georgiana J. *Personal Life Insurance Trusts, Tax Management, Portfolio 807* (2006).

Swiss Re, sigma No. 3/2003: "Unit-linked life insurance in Western Europe: Regaining momentum?" (Zurich 2003).

Viret, Bernhard. *Privatversicherungsrecht*, 3. Auflage, 1991.

Von und zu Liechtenstein, S.D. Prinz Nikolaus, and Julian I. Mahari (Hrsg.), *Finanzplatz Liechtenstein: Beiträge zu seiner Neupositionierung [Finance Center Liechtenstein: Contributions to Repositioning]* (Zurich 2001).

About the Authors

MARCO GANTENBEIN, TEP

Marco Gantenbein is an international insurance specialist and a partner with the Swiss Annuity Consulting Group, Zürich/Switzerland, a leading niche insurance consultancy. After completing Zürich Business School and training at a leading Swiss insurance company, he lived and studied abroad. Upon returning to Switzerland, he worked for many years as an insurance consultant in both the private and business sectors. During this time he received his Swiss Federal Insurance Diploma and acquired, in addition to managerial experience, considerable expertise in complex insurance solutions for private and business clients. He is a member of the Society of Trust and Estate Practitioners (STEP) and holds an unrestricted license from the Swiss Government to act as an independent insurance broker. As one of the co-authors of the *Switzerland Business & Investment Handbook*, he contributed the chapter on Swiss Annuities and Life Insurance. He is also the author of many articles on Swiss annuities, which have been published in the Swiss and international media.

MARIO A. MATA, TEP

Mario A. Mata, a business and estate planning partner, joined Cantey & Hanger, LLP, in 2001 after having established himself as a nationally recognized authority on international trusts and related wealth preservation planning. Mr. Mata is a graduate of the University of Texas School of Law in Austin, where he received his law degree in 1978. Prior to that, Mr. Mata graduated from the University of Texas School of Business, where he received his BBA in Accounting with Honors in 1976.

Mr. Mata has experience in all aspects of business, estate, and tax planning for high-net-worth individuals and families, including strategies to efficiently transfer family and personal wealth, both during life and at death, to existing and future generations. However, Mr. Mata is best known for his use of offshore wealth preservation structures for high-net-worth individuals to protect assets and family wealth against potential legal claims and other threats. All structures are specifically designed to be fully compliant with U.S. tax laws.

He is a member of the International Tax Planning Association and is vice-chair of the Asset Protection Planning Committee of the American Bar Association. Mr. Mata was licensed as a Certified Public Accountant (1981–1985) and was board certified in Commercial Real Estate by the Texas Board of Legal Specialization (1991–1999).

Mr. Mata is a frequent speaker on international trust and related wealth preservation topics. He is also a contributing author to the American Bar Association's book *Asset Protection Strategies: Planning with Domestic and Offshore Entities* and has also contributed articles published in *Texas Lawyer* and *The Practical Tax Lawyer*.

CHRISTIAN H. KÄLIN, MLAW, TEP

Christian H. Kälin is an international real estate, tax, and estate planning specialist and a partner at Henley & Partners, Zürich, as well as one of the founding partners of Verica Trust & Capital Management, Zug, an investment advisory firm. He is also a member of the board of the International Financial and Legal Network (IFLN), a member of the Society of Trust and Estate Practitioners (STEP), as well as of numerous other professional associations. After completing Zürich Business School and training at a Swiss private bank, he lived and studied for many years in France, the United States, New Zealand, and Switzerland. A holder of a cum laude master's degree in law from the University of Zürich, he is a frequent writer and speaker on international legal issues and is regularly quoted in the international media. He is the editor and a coauthor of the *International Real Estate Handbook* and the *Switzerland Business & Investment Handbook*, both standard works in their fields. He holds unrestricted licenses from the Swiss government as an independent insurance broker and as a financial intermediary.

PROFESSOR CLIVE H. CHURCH, PHD

Clive Church is Emeritus Jean Monnet Professor of European Studies at the University of Kent, in Canterbury. Educated at the universities of Exeter and London, he taught in London, Dublin, and Lancaster before moving to Kent in 1982. He has published widely on European and Swiss history and current affairs. He retired in 2003 but remains active academically as a member of the University's Centre for Swiss Politics. His research focuses on the evolution of constitutional projects for Europe, including those currently under discussion, and on Swiss politics, history, and foreign relations.

His most recent books are *Understanding the European Constitution,* with David Phinnemore, published by Routledge 2005 and an edited volume titled *Switzerland and the European Union: A Close, Contradictory And Misunderstood Relationship,* also published by Routledge, in 2006.

PETER LÜSSI

Peter Lüssi has been with PricewaterhouseCoopers for about 20 years, and provides assurance and advisory services to both insurance companies and banks. In 1996, he became a partner for international and national mandates as well as for special assignments for life, nonlife, and reinsurance companies. In 2006, he took on the role of PricewaterhouseCoopers' insurance industry leader for Switzerland. He has spent over 10 years targeting clients in the insurance industry. Due to his audit activities, he has been deeply involved in the European network of PricewaterhouseCoopers and has thus had access to all areas of insurance. Captives and companies located in the principality of Liechtenstein also are part of his client portfolio. The Financial Market Authority of Liechtenstein licensed him to audit insurance companies based in Liechtenstein.

DR. PETER FIERZ

Peter Fierz is PricewaterhouseCoopers' knowledge manager for the financial services industry and the auditing line of service. He holds a doctorate in general history from the University of Zürich, where he studied history, business administration, and media science. After his studies, he started working for the former Coopers & Lybrand as an auditor and acquired the degree of a fiduciary in Switzerland. Various special projects in the banking industry led him into the field of knowledge management, in which he is currently responsible for the flow of information and knowledge within and between the financial services industries and the firm. He is also the editor of PricewaterhouseCoopers' *Flash* magazines and an author of some of the firm's publications.

DR. MONICA MÄCHLER

Monica Mächler has served as director of the Federal Office of Private Insurance since January 1, 2007.

She graduated in 1980 from the Faculty of Law and Political Economics at the University of Zürich. She received her doctorate in 1984 and obtained admission to the bar in Zürich the following year. From 1985 to 1990, she worked in a Zürich law office with a focus on banking and business law. In 1990, she joined the Zürich Insurance Company as a corporate legal advisor. She assumed the function of Group General Counsel of Zürich Group and Head of the Secretariat of the Board of Directors in 1999. Monica Mächler became a member of the extended group management in 2001.

Ms. Mächler was a member of several expert commissions of the Confederation, such as the Zimmerli Commission on implementation of integrated financial supervision legislation, the Zufferey Commission on financial market supervision, and the Schnyder Commission on revision of the Insurance Supervision Act. She is a lecturer for postgraduate studies in International Business Law at the University of Zürich and has published numerous articles on current issues of insurance and financial market law and international private law.

On September 13, 2006, the Federal Council appointed Monica Mächler director of the Federal Office of Private Insurance.

PROFESSOR DR. MORITZ W. KUHN

Professor Dr. Moritz W. Kuhn, attorney-at-law and partner with MME—Meyer Müller Eckert Partners, is a recognized expert in international and national insurance law. He qualified as a professor for private and insurance law at the University of Zürich. He worked for many years as general counsel and head of the legal and tax department of the largest Swiss life insurance company. In addition to his functions at MME Partners, he acts as professor for private law and insurance law at the University of Zürich. He is the current president of the Supreme Court of the Canton Zürich, lecturer on insurance law and economic law at the LL.M-postgraduate courses at the University of Zürich, chairs the Swiss Insurance Brokers Association, and is a member of the board of the Swiss Employers Association.

PD DR. JOACHIM FRICK, LLM

Joachim Frick, PD Dr. Iur, LLM, is a practicing lawyer and partner with Baker McKenzie in Zürich, where he advises Swiss and international clients in litigous and nonlitigous insurance and corporate matters, including mergers and acquisitions, arbitrations, and regulatory insurance matters. He graduated from Zürich law school (lic. Iur. 1989, Dr. iur. 1992, PD 2002) and obtained an LL.M. and JSD degree from Yale Law School. In 2002, he was appointed associate professor of law by Fribourg Law School. After practicing with Baker & McKenzie in Zürich, Taipei, and Chicago, he returned to

Zürich in 1997 and now heads the insurance practice group of the Zürich office; in addition, he co-heads the European Insurance Practice Group of Baker McKenzie. He has published various articles and is a frequent speaker in insurance and corporate matters. He is a lecturer in law at Zürich Law School.

DR. ALEXANDER T. SKREINER

Dr. Alexander T. Skreiner was managing director of CapitalLeben Versicherung AG in Liechtenstein, where he was responsible for all sales, legal, and compliance activities. He started his career with the Allianz group (sales, marketing, and controlling) in Vienna and London, worked at the Institute for Civil Law at the University of Vienna, and joined CapitalLeben shortly after founding it in 1997, building up the company to the market leader of the life insurance industry in Liechtenstein. In addition to his managerial experience, he acquired considerable expertise in complex cross-border insurance solutions especially for wealthy private clients. His main focus is on tax and legal consulting in connection with product engineering and product structuring for international clients. As tax specialist, he develops tax-optimized insurance products integrating financial instruments and individualized legal solutions.

Dr. Skreiner graduated with a doctor's degree in law summa cum laude from the University of Vienna.

DR. JOHANNES GASSER, LLM

Johannes Gasser is an attorney at law and partner in the law firm Dr. Dr. Batliner and Dr. Gasser, Vaduz/Liechtenstein. After studies at the University of Innsbruck/Austria (Dr.iur. 1995), he worked for Austrian and Liechtenstein law firms. After his admittance to the Liechtenstein and the Austrian bars, he earned a degree as Academic Expert on European law and the diploma for Trustees in Liechtenstein. His areas of practice are corporate law, litigation, real estates, tax law, and white-collar crime. He speakes German, English, French, and Spanish.

MAG. MARKUS SCHWINGSHACKL

Markus Schwingshackl is an attorney at law admitted to the Liechtenstein bar. He is an Italian citizen and studied law at the universities of Bologna/Italy and Innsbruck/Austria (Mag.iur. 2001). After a judicial clerkship in Austria and Liechtenstein, he also passed the Austrian bar exam. Mr. Schwingshackl specializes in the areas of litigation, civil law, corporate law, international taxation, and white-collar crime. Since 2006, he has been a student at the University St. Gallen and will graduate as a master of European and International Business Law. He speaks German, Italian, English, and Spanish.

MAEHALA R. NATHAN, BSC

Maehala R. Nathan is one of the directors of Swiss Annuity Consulting Group, Zürich/Switzerland, a leading niche insurance consultancy. Born and raised in Kuala Lumpur/Malaysia, she went to New Zealand to complete her secondary education. She then studied science at the University of Auckland and completed her studies there with a BSc. After taking her degree, she traveled extensively in Asia and Europe and later on settled in Switzerland. She started working for Henley & Partners in Zürich. Since 1998, she has been with the Henley & Partners group and for the last eight years has specialized in international insurance solutions for private clients.

FREDERIC J. GELFOND, JD, LLM, MBA

Mr. Gelfond is a principal located in the Deloitte Tax LLP, Washington, DC, national tax office. Since he joined the firm over 15 years ago, he has provided tax consulting services to clients in all sectors of the insurance industry, including the life, property and casualty, and reinsurance arenas. Over the past several years, he has been primarily involved in leading the firm's insurance product tax practice that provides consulting services both to large corporate and high-net-worth policy holders as well as to insurance companies seeking to better manage the design and tax compliance of their products. Mr. Gelfond has spent much of this time representing clients regarding matters involving broad-based life insurance, including situations involving major litigation support and various administrative processes. Recently Mr. Gelfond has been heavily involved in developing innovative risk transfer vehicles and various unique product structures. Prior to joining Deloitte, Mr. Gelfond served as an associate at a large Manhattan law firm.

Mr. Gelfond has had numerous articles published in leading tax journals. He is also an editorial board member and contributing author to the Society of Actuaries *Taxing Times* journal. He is also a frequently requested speaker at insurance tax conferences and seminars and serves on the Advisory Board for the Federal Bar Association Insurance Tax Seminar.

Mr. Gelfond holds an LL.M. in Taxation from the New York University School of Law. He earned his JD at the Boston University School of Law and his master's degree in business administration from the Boston University Graduate School of Management. He received a Bachelor of Science degree in accounting from the State University of New York at Albany.

GLENN G. FOX, JD, LLM, TEP

Glenn G. Fox is a partner in the law firm of Alston & Bird LLP in New York and focuses his practice on domestic and international estate planning, estate and trust administration, taxation and exempt organizations. He is a member of the American College of Trusts and Estates Counsel, co-chair of the International Estate and Trust Law Committee and a member of the Executive Committee of the International Section of the New York State Bar Association, a member of the Society of Trust and Estate Practitioners, and a member of the Estate and Gift Tax Committee of the Association of the Bar of the City of New York. He is a frequent writer for periodicals such as *Estate Planning Magazine*, *Taxation of Exempts Magazine*, and the *Bureau of National Affairs Estate Planning Journal* and a frequent lecturer for various bar and accounting associations as well as for international organizations. Mr. Fox received his LL.M. in taxation from New York University School of Law, his JD from Albany Law School of Union University, and his BA from Cornell University.

PAUL A. FERRARA, JD, LLM, PHD

Paul A. Ferrara, PhD, is an associate at the law firm of Alston & Bird LLP. He focuses his practice on domestic and international tax and estate planning and has lectured on estate planning for nontraditional families, a special interest of his. In addition, he has handled a wide range of planning and compliance matters for tax-exempt organizations. Admitted to practice in both New York and Connecticut, he is currently serving on the Trusts, Estates and Surrogate's Courts Committee of the Association of the Bar of the City of New York. Dr. Ferrara is a member of the New York State Bar Association International Law and Practice Section and serves as an editor of its *International Law Practicum*. He also is a member of the Section of Real Property, Probate and Trust Law of the American Bar Association and the Trusts and Estates Law Section of the New York State Bar Association. Dr. Ferrara earned his LL.M. in taxation and his JD from New York University School of Law, where he was editor in chief of the *New York University Journal of International Law and Politics*. He received his PhD in Italian from the University of California at Berkeley and his BA from Tulane University.

Index